with MediaStudio Pro 8

the essential, no-nonsense guide to video editing with Ulead's software

by Charlie Hills

Getting Results with MediaStudio Pro 8

Copyright © 2006 by Charlie Hills. All Rights Reserved.

No part of this book shall be reproduced, stored in a retrieval system, or transmitted by any means, electronic, mechanical, photo-copying, recording, or otherwise, without written permission from Getting Results Publishing.

Disclaimer
Every effort has been made to make this book as complete and as accurate as possible, but no warranty or fitness is implied. The information provided is on an "as is" basis. Although every precaution has been taken in the preparation of this book, the author and the publisher shall have neither liability nor responsibility to any person or entity with respect to any loss or damages arising from the information contained in this book or from the use of the CD accompanying it.

Trademarks
All terms mentioned in this book that are known to be trademarks or service marks have been appropriately capitalized. Getting Results Publishing cannot attest to the accuracy of this information. Use of a term in this book should not be regarded as affecting the validity of any trademark or service mark.

Use of Materials
All accompanying material (including, but not limited to: projects, video clips, music and audio files, image files, etc.) has been supplied for the sole purpose of completing the exercises and tutorials found in the book. Any use of the materials outside this context is prohibited, unless otherwise explicitly stated. The materials, in whole or in part, may not be redistributed in any form.

Music licensed from Shockwave Sound, Production Trax, and Chameleon Music.
NASA footage provided by VideoUniversity.com.
Stock photography licensed from Photos.com and from stock.xchg.
All other video, images, and audio by Charlie Hills.

Acknowledgements
While I did ninety percent of the work to get this book done, I would be remiss if I didn't acknowledge those who helped with the other ninety percent.

Technical Review: Brian Ellis and Dustin McCartney
Proofreading: Angela Swift
Margin Icons: Jeff Stephens
Support Crew: Laura, Sarah, and Rachel

On the Web
Please visit our web site for new product information, updates, downloads, and support at: http://www.getting-results.com. Please report errors to errata@getting-results.com.

Fifth Edition
ISBN 0-9749732-5-4

Printed in the United States of America

5 4 3 2 1

Preface

Welcome to *Getting Results with MediaStudio Pro 8*: The essential, no-nonsense guide to video editing with Ulead's software. This book has been designed to be your guide to learning and using MediaStudio Pro effectively. Whether you're just starting out or you're an old veteran, the goal is for you to discover everything you need to improve your video editing skills with MediaStudio Pro.

Why Getting Results?

Because getting results is the whole point. Software is a means to an end, not an end in and of itself. I'm sure very few of us started using Media-Studio Pro just for the sake of pushing clips around a timeline. No, we all wanted to produce videos. We all wanted to use the software to achieve a specific goal. We all wanted results.

While software documentation generally does a good job of describing the functionality of an application, it rarely ventures much past the basics. *Getting Results* goes far beyond that. Your standard documentation typically succeeds at explaining *how* to do something, but it rarely tells you *why* to do something. As you've probably already guessed, there is much more to video production than "this is how you create a title clip; this is how you change the volume of an audio clip." Mastery of the mechanics is only the beginning. There's an art to video editing which you will never be able to get out of the standard documentation. This isn't to say that documentation is worthless—quite the contrary. The documentation is an important first step. But it's just that: a first step.

The Goal of this Book

Don't believe the marketing people. Flip through any video magazine and you'll see countless ads of how "easy" video editing has become. (I am not singling out Ulead; it's the entire industry. Nor can I blame the perpetrators anyway. I mean, how many products would ever be sold if advertising actually told the truth?) "Simply capture your clips, place them on the timeline, click 'Make My Video' and you're done!" How easy! While they may not be telling outright lies, they're certainly guilty of leaving out a thing or two. They might as well say, "Just get some paper and a pen, start writing, and before you know it you'll have your very first novel!" We all know there's more to it than that.

The goal of *Getting Results* is to get past all that. The goal is to present the material in the most useful manner possible. It's not written by the company, or their marketing department, or the magazines dependent on advertising revenue. I wrote it and I don't have to answer to anyone except you. There will be no careful picking and choosing of words. I will tell it like it is, because I won't help anyone by doing it any other way. When you're done with the book, you'll possess the knowledge necessary to accomplish whatever you set out to do with this product. And if MediaStudio Pro isn't capable of what you want to do, you'll be able to recognize this too. True mastery means knowing everything the product can't do as well as everything it can.

Intended Audience

Video Experience. While the knowledgeable video editor can certainly get helpful information from this book, it's really aimed towards beginning and intermediate MediaStudio Pro users. Knowledge of other video editing tools is helpful, but not required.

It is also a fact that MediaStudio Pro is only one part of a three-part process: 1) you start with your source footage; 2) you process this footage with MediaStudio Pro; and 3) you deliver your finished product. While I can assume that everyone reading this book is using MediaStudio Pro for the second part, I cannot assume that everyone will be using the same formats for the first and last parts. Your source footage may be old 8mm home movies or Hi8 camcorder tapes. You may wish to deliver your final video on VHS or upload it to your web site. Most of the time, this won't matter. However, from time to time, it *will* matter, and I'll try to make a point of that as we go.

Computer Experience. A basic working knowledge of Microsoft Windows is assumed. You should already be familiar with and comfortable using the computer's operating system and performing common tasks. Launching programs, using the mouse, accessing menus, and dragging and dropping are just a few of the key skills needed.

You should also feel comfortable handling hardware. For example, if you haven't already installed some sort of video interface, you probably will soon. You shouldn't be afraid of plugging in cables and moving devices around from time to time—it's all part of the desktop video game. Be ready to get those fingers dirty once in a while!

Conventions

There are a few conventions used throughout this book that you might want to make note of. Doing so now will give you a "heads up" and might help avoid a puzzle later on.

Menu Commands

When the text refers to a specific menu *command* it will be written like this: Menu | Item | Subitem. The vertical bars ("|") separate the menu items. For example, File | Create | Video File means to click the "File" menu on the main menu bar, followed by the "Create" menu item, and then finally the "Video File" menu item.

Exercises

Most exercises list both an Objective and one or more Reference Projects. The *Objective* is just that. It answers the question, "What in the world would I get out of doing this exercise?" The *Reference Project(s)* name the corresponding project files on the CD. These are provided so you can check your work or examine techniques more closely. Typically, you'll do the exercises on your own first, and then cross-check your results afterwards.

The original location of these files is in the top-level projects folder on the CD. Projects are divided by chapter, and the chapter folders project files, media clips, and everything needed to complete the exercises. It's recommended you move these files from the CD to your PC, following the directions on page 112.

Use of Color

Certain illustrations or diagrams may require color to be properly viewed. If you are reading the book and something doesn't look quite right, please refer to the PDF for a full color view. The entire book in PDF format can be found on the accompanying CD.

Margin Icons

Throughout the book, you will find small pictures in the margins of the pages. I use these to draw attention to a certain subject being covered at that point, which might not normally stand out on its own.

This icon means an important piece of information is being given, and you should make special note of it. It is typically information that is critical to the given task. Skipping over this would likely mean not being able to correctly finish the task.

 Like the hand icon, this "thumbs up" represents an important piece of information. However, it is not critical for continued processing. It is simply something to take note of—something that might be helpful. But you'll live if you happen to miss it.

 This icon is used to visually identify the beginning of an exercise or project. Scanning through pages is easier with a visual indicator at the beginning of each exercise. Make sure you don't skip over these. They're the whole point of the book!

 This icon identifies an online link or resource. For example, if someone else has written a good tutorial on the given topic, then a link will be placed in the document and noted with this icon.

 While this book is more or less aimed at beginners, I have to admit sometimes I go off the deep end. Some readers may eat this stuff up. Others might not care at all and just want to get on with the task at hand. For this reason, we have the *Geek Alert*. If you see this symbol, you can safely skip to the next section. If you're like me, however, and love the nitty-gritty details, read on!

Table of Contents

Preface iii
PART I ▪ GROUND SCHOOL 13
1. The Obligatory Boring Intro Chapter 15
    So What Can I Do With MediaStudio Pro? 16
    And What Can't I Do? 18
    A Brief History of Video Editing 18
    A Few Common Terms 20
    Key Concepts 21
    Online Resources 30
    Moving Right Along… 32
2. A No-Nonsense Overview of Video Editor 33
    Background 33
    The Timeline 36
    Preview Window 50
    Source Window 52
    Effects Manager 54
    The Production Library 58
    The Project Tray 60
    Audio Mixing Panel 62
    Quick Command Panel 64
    Trim Window 64
    Window Shortcut Keys 65
    So Is That Everything? 66
3. An Overview of Everything Else 67
    Video Capture 67

Audio Editor 80

DVD MovieFactory 84

DVD DiskRecorder 86

4. Failure to Plan is Planning for Failure 87

The Planning Process 87

Storyboarding 96

Reusability 97

File Management 98

Project Management 103

That's a Wrap! 106

PART II • FLIGHT TRAINING 109

5. First Things First: Essential Editing Skills 111

Getting off the Ground 111

Getting Results Installation 112

Timeline and Clip Basics 114

Transitions 116

Basic Trimming 121

Trim the Middle of a Clip 123

Trim Multiple Parts of a Clip 125

Split by Scene 128

Saving Trimmed Files 129

Timeline Trim Options 131

Adjusting Audio Volume 133

Ripple Editing 135

Adding to the Middle of a Project 138

Previewing 139

Additional Timelines & Virtual Clips 142

6. The Standard Bag of Tricks 147

We're Still Just Editing 147

Slow & Fast Motion 147

Going Backwards 149

Freeze Frame 150

Adding Text to Your Video 152
Audio Mixing 154
J-Cut & L-Cut.. 156
Fade to Black Transition.. 160
Fade to Black Transition Again... 162
Make Your Own: a Fade to White Transition 163
Camera Flash Effect.. 164
Camera Flash with Freeze Frame 167

7. Beyond Just Editing..169

Ready? 169
Video Filters.. 169
Effects Manager.. 171
Keyframing Filter Settings.. 174
Multiple Keyframes 176
Picture in Picture.. 177
Split Screen 180
Mirror Image 181
Matchmoving 182
Moving Path Mania 186
Keying 187
A Brief Keying Exercise.. 192
A Longer Keying Exercise 193
Creating a Garbage Matte... 196
Dealing with Common Keying Problems.................................... 200
Matchmoving Revisited 204
Fade to Black, One Last Time 207
Soft Edge Split Screen.. 208
Smart Compositor.. 209

8. Text and Titling...215

Why Titling? 215
Title Animation 216
Animating Two Titles at Once 219

Simple Scrolling Text..221

Two Column End Credits..224

Text That Isn't...226

Applying Filters to Title Clips...228

Applying Filters to Graphical Text...232

Typing Text...233

9. Slightly More Advanced Tricks 235

Color Correction...235

Fading from Black & White to Color...239

Old Film 240

The Lens Flare 240

A Stitch in Time...241

Freeze Frame with a Frame 243

The Next Level Freeze Frame...245

Apply Video Filters to Keyed Clips 247

One Clip Transitions...250

Three Clip Transitions..251

Roll Your Own Smart Compositor Clips..252

PART III • INSTRUMENT RATING 259

10. Our First Projects: Tackling the Montage 261

Definition & Purpose...261

The Photo Montage..261

The Video Montage 278

Formats Demystified 300

Getting Video Out..303

11. Two Real Life Editing Situations..307

Pulling It All Together..307

The Scripted Project...307

Multi-Camera Editing 321

12. Examining Longer Projects 335

Where Do We Go From Here?..335

A Music Video..335

Table of Contents

 The Promotional Video 352

13. DVD MovieFactory **361**

 Background 361

 The Project 363

 The End 373

PART IV • APPENDICES **375**

A. Getting Reoriented with MediaStudio Pro **377**

 What Happened Here!? 377

 Track Order 377

 Transitions 378

 Multiple Timelines 382

 Virtual Clips 383

 Importing Old Projects 384

 What Happened to CG Infinity & Video Paint? 385

 So What Else Is New? 385

B. Better Shooting and Composition **387**

C. Text and Typography **409**

 Terminology 409

 Quick Typographical & Titling Tips 411

 Elements of Design 415

 Character Tables 422

D. Tips and Things **427**

 General Tips 427

 System Tips 428

 Editing Tips 429

 Navigation & Keyboard Tips 431

 Selection Tips 433

 Miscellaneous Tips 434

E. Troubleshooting **437**

Glossary **447**

Index **461**

Part I

GROUND SCHOOL

As much as the budding pilot wants to jump right in the plane and take off, that probably isn't the best approach. Before the pilot-to-be ever climbs into the cockpit, a solid understanding of the basics is essential.

Chapter 1 The Obligatory Boring Intro Chapter

Chapter 2 A No-Nonsense Overview of Video Editor

Chapter 3 An Overview of Everything Else

Chapter 4 Failure to Plan is Planning for Failure

1
The Obligatory Boring Intro Chapter

If you're new to video, this chapter will get you up to speed by giving you a firm grasp of key concepts.

Admit it. You really don't want to read this book. You just want to create videos. And to be perfectly honest, I don't blame you. I mean, that's all I wanted to do when I got started. But unlike those who've recklessly chosen to jump in the airplane first just to "see what happens," you've made the decision to learn a little bit up front. (Either that, or you've already crashed and burned once, and this is now your second time around.)

Either way, I'm just glad you're here. I believe that even the smallest amount of guidance can make an enormous difference. And I even promise to try and make it interesting along the way.

Part I of this book is for the beginner. If you've never used MediaStudio Pro before (or any video editing tool for that matter) then this is for you. This first chapter covers the basics, explains the jargon, and sets you on your way to becoming the editor you want to be. The remaining chapters ease you into the MediaStudio Pro video production tools.

Part II covers MediaStudio Pro's essential editing skills. Starting with fundamental tasks such as transitions and trimming, you'll progress into more interesting topics such as video filters and virtual clips.

Part III puts it all together. All the skills learned up to this point are applied within the context of larger projects. You'll see how photo and video montages are put together. You'll create a music video and try your hand at multi-camera editing—and more.

Part IV contains helpful reference material: appendices, glossary, and the index. The appendices cover everything from getting reoriented with the Version 8 changes to troubleshooting common problems.

So What Can I Do With MediaStudio Pro?

You most likely purchased MediaStudio Pro with an initial project in mind. It's often difficult to tell merely from the box (or the web) exactly what a program is (or isn't) capable of. Sure, you get the basics. Sure, they say you can "make movies." But what does that mean? What can you *really* expect out of the product? Let's take a look.

- Bring video from the outside world into your computer. You can grab video from almost any source. In particular, if you're using DV as a source, you have the additional benefit of being able to watch your tape first and mark the segments you want. After that, MediaStudio Pro will do all the work for you unattended.

- Remove unwanted portions of your video. You can trim the beginning, lop off the end, or chop out a whole section in the middle.

- Add titles to your video. Use any font, any color, any size you want. You can add movement to your text for some pizzazz, or apply a slow fade for emotion.

- Mix multiple video sources. This can be anything from a simple picture-in-picture effect, to a complex, organic mixture using masks, mattes, and keying. A full range of sizing, shaping, and motion options are available.

- Create transitions between video clips—everything from shattering glass to an elegant crossfade. Over one hundred and twenty different effects are right at your fingertips.

- Add some spice to your clips with video filters. You can blur or brighten your video. You can crop or kaleidoscope it. Even add lens flare or lightning effects.

- Grab songs from CDs. Place any audio CD into your CD drive and MediaStudio Pro's Audio Editor will let you pick which track to add to your project.

- Generate musical accompaniment of any length with SmartSound™ technology. The supplied sources come in many different styles. Trust me, this is seriously cool.

- Record audio from a microphone or other external source. Use this to add narration or for capturing audio from analog sources.

- Edit in Dolby® Digital 5.1 Surround Sound audio.

- Get your final edited video ready for publishing on the web. Create ready-to-stream videos in Windows Media or Real formats.

- Author and burn your own DVDs. If the web isn't your thing, produce your own DVDs, playable in home DVD players. Share your masterpiece with friends and family.

- Edit in High Definition. There's no doubt that HDV is going to be the next big thing. It's good to see Ulead at the forefront of this technology. MediaStudio Pro allows you to edit in native HDV formats or use proxy mode, allowing you to work on low-resolution equivalents of high-resolution sources efficiently.

- Add Smart Compositor clips to your projects. Think of these as slick, multi-layered, stock clips that you can use as-is or freely edit to fit your particular project.

- Lastly, you can have fun. Video editing shouldn't be all work and no play, even if you *are* doing it strictly for business. Don't ever forget what got you into video in the first place. It's a lot of fun.

MediaStudio Pro provides all these tools allowing you to tackle almost any kind of project you can think of:

- Transfer old home movies to DVD.

- Put those shoeboxes of family photos on VHS for an anniversary.

- Make your vacation videos actually enjoyable to watch.

- Create a video yearbook for your school.

- Do a family history project.

- Turn in a school report to rival an *A&E* documentary.

- Shoot an infomercial for your company's web site.

- Produce impressive business presentations.

- Edit and mix multi-camera events.

- Make your own music videos.

- Just show off!

And What Can't I Do?

Ah yes, the part no one wants to tell you about. While the last section sounds impressive, I'm not going to hide the fact that MediaStudio Pro is not the be-all, end-all of video editing tools. It's simply not capable of doing *everything*. (But then again, no tool is.) A few random examples:

- Moving paths (used, among other things, for Picture in Picture effects) don't support curved paths or "easing."

- Alpha channels are a key ingredient in compositing, yet MediaStudio Pro does not provide a facility for creating your own.

- Many video filters cannot generate smooth transitions between keyframes. Additionally, many of them do not have an "off" setting—useful for keyframing a non-effect during the filter.

- Although the Video Editor module has a Title Clip tool for placing text on your video, it has its limitations. For example, you may find it somewhat of a chore to create traditional two-column end credits, if that's your thing.

- While you do have the ability to create video composites through track layering, keying and moving paths, you're still using a video editor and not a full-blown compositing tool.

Of course, no single video editing tool will give you every tool you'd ever need. Most (well, actually *all*) serious editors have many different tools in their video production studio. However, it's still nice to explicitly know what is or isn't possible, to save you hours of frustration trying to search for a non-existent feature.

A Brief History of Video Editing

You're about to embark on what possibly may be your very first attempt at editing. While you may run into difficulties capturing video, editing your work, or burning your DVD, it's good to put these problems into perspective. With a little knowledge of how things used to be, you'll appreciate how easy things are today.

In the very earliest days of movie making, editing was simply the process used to discard unwanted footage and assemble multiple reels of film into one long piece. Editing was purely a mechanical function mainly to overcome the limitations of short source reels. It didn't take long, however, for early filmmakers to realize that there was a wee bit more potential for editing than simply making long films out of short segments. Instead of simply splicing footage together, end-to-end, a small amount of creativity applied to cuts would result in something worth more than the sum of its parts. The first two decades of the twentieth century saw rapid growth in this area. The job of editing shifted from mechanical to artistic.

Fast-forward to the late 1950s and early 60s when videotape entered into common use in television. The early cut-and-splice film editing techniques were directly translated to the new magnetic tape medium. Video editors took razor blades, cut the actual videotape, and taped it back together. Think of *that* the next time you grumble about the steps needed to remove a scene from a captured video clip.

The next couple of decades saw various advances in videotape and editing techniques. Reel-to-reel video was gradually replaced with the videocassette. Non-destructive editing came into overwhelming widespread use. Special effects hardware grew increasingly sophisticated. Technology moved forward, slow but sure.

That is, until the late 1980s when the inevitable collision between movie making and computers occurred at an affordable level. At first, it was just convenient to have the computer control the editing bay. But gradually each piece of external equipment was replaced by computer hardware or software. You no longer needed standalone special effects hardware. Soon you no longer even needed video players and recorders, once it became possible to digitize sound and pictures and store it on disk. At that point, the possibilities were endless. As the popularity of these systems grew, the prices inevitably dropped. Systems that were hundreds of thousands of dollars were soon just tens of thousands. And it didn't stop.

> **How Times Change**
> Back in 1981, Apple introduced its first hard disk: a gigantic five-megabyte unit that would set you back about $3,500. You were a bit more fortunate on the PC platform, as Seagate released its 5 MB disk the same year for only $1,700.

Now we live in a world where for just a few hundred dollars you can build complete, end-to-end video production suites hundreds of times more powerful than the half-million dollar systems of thirty years ago. It boggles the mind to think of what could be coming next. Thirty years from now you'll hover into your corner grocery store, buy a massively powerful video production system for just $19.95, then go home and create the video you waited more than a century for, "The 2036 World Series: How the Chicago Cubs Finally Pulled It Off."

A Few Common Terms

Not knowing the meaning of common terms can be the largest stumbling block for anyone entering any new field. It can be exasperating learning a new subject when you can't even speak the language. For that reason, I suggest you take a quick look through the Glossary starting on page 447 before doing anything else. Go ahead. I'll wait.

Back already? You didn't do it, did you? That's okay, no one does. So we'll just go over the most important terms here.

Project. For the purposes of this book, a *project* is the Video Editor file. This file is essentially a list of instructions for creating your final video. It does not contain any video data itself. You can open only one project at a time in Video Editor.

Timeline. The primary work area for editing and assembling your video productions. Each project can have multiple timelines.

Video Clip. Any digitized video file on your computer. These can come from many sources and in many formats. The format can be roughly identified by the file extension. For example, myvideo.avi is a Microsoft AVI formatted file (AVI stands for Audio/Video Interleave). The file myvideo.mpg is an MPEG formatted file. The file myvideo.mov is a QuickTime movie. However, even within these broad file formats are formats that are more specific. We will address that when the time comes.

Audio Clip. Similar to the video clip, but it only contains sound. And, like the video clip, audio can be digitized in a variety of formats. The two most common formats in PC-based video editing are WAV and MP3.

Virtual Clip. A virtual clip is a "package" of other clips treated as if it were a normal video clip. When a virtual clip is opened, a new timeline is created allowing you to edit the component clips that make up the virtual clip. Virtual clips themselves can be made up of other virtual clips. This is known as "nesting."

Titling. The art and practice of creating text or titles for video.

Overlaying. The process of mixing two or more video sources into one. There are a number of different methods of combining videos, and we'll touch on them all.

Capture. This is the process of bringing video, audio, or other data from the outside world into your computer.

Key Concepts

If you're completely new to MediaStudio Pro and non-linear editing, be sure to have a good handle on the following concepts. It will definitely make life easier later on.

Linear versus Non-Linear Editing

In video editing, the term *linear* originates with tape-based systems. This is because the video is laid out in a straight *line* from one end of the tape to the other. In order to view footage at the end of the tape, you were required to physically go past every inch of tape in between.

Non-linear editing does away with that. Like a wormhole in a science fiction movie, it means having the ability to jump from one point to another without traveling the space between. This made for a quantum leap in editing efficiency. Suddenly the wedding processional was no longer ninety minutes distant from the cake-cutting. Both were now the exact same distance away, and that distance was astonishingly short.

But whether linear or non-linear, all video streams are described as having various attributes. Many of these attributes will be discussed regularly, so you should have a good working knowledge of them.

Video Attributes

Video is made up of a sequence of **frames**. You can think of each frame as you would a photograph. Take enough photos and play them back quickly enough, and you have motion. But just to make life complicated, the frame isn't always the smallest unit of a video clip. That distinction goes to the **field**. There are two fields for every frame, each field containing exactly half the image—but it isn't a nice clean half. It's more like taking your frame and putting it through a paper shredder. All the odd strips make up one field and all the even strips make up the other.

So what's the point of *that* mess? Well, it wasn't everyone's first choice. While it's true that painting 24 to 30 frames per second is enough to produce fluid motion, displaying it on a cathode ray tube presented two problems. First, the frame image faded quickly, producing a headache-inducing flickering. Second, the difference between the video rate and the power rate created visible hum bars. These were eliminated by increasing the video frequency to match the power frequency. Unfortunately, this then exceeded broadcast bandwidth limits. The only viable solution was to send each frame through in halves, which solved both problems. Not a bad solution, considering it's still in use 75 years later.

When we speak of **field order** we're referring to which of the two fields displays first. This wouldn't be such an issue if we didn't have so many names for the fields: A/B, 1/2, upper/lower, odd/even. These last two name pairs are the most common. Here's a helpful trick to keep them straight: 1 is odd, 2 is even. 1 is *above* 2, so odd is above even: 1 is *upper*!

Now for **color**. Each frame is made up of rows and columns of pixels, and each pixel is a single color. The amount of data used to describe this color is called the **color depth**. If you only have 1 bit, you can only have two values: on or off. This picture shows a "blue" sky and clouds in 2 colors.

Compare that to the next picture where we use eight bits to store each color. Eight bits means we have 256 colors to play with. This picture is an example of the same sky using 256 colors. It's a big improvement, but still leaves a lot to be desired. Higher quality means more numbers.

When you move up to using 24 bits to describe each color, you're now at the level we call *true color*. Instead of 2 colors, or 256 colors, we now have 16,777,216 colors in our palette. This is enough to produce a photorealistic image. This should now give you a good idea of how data and picture quality are inextricably related.

The next attribute we'll look at is **frame size**. This is the width and height of the image data measured in pixels. When a video stream is 720 pixels wide by 480 pixels high, we call it "720 by 480" or just "720x480" for short.

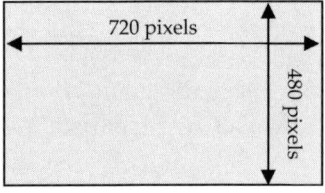

Next up is **frame rate**. When we play our pictures back to create motion, the frame rate describes how many are being played back every second. In North America, Japan, and a few other parts of the world, a TV standard called NTSC is used. It has a frame rate of 29.97 frames per second. (If you're having trouble picturing 97% of a frame, it's easier to think of it as 2997 frames every 100 seconds.) Most of the rest of the world uses a TV standard called PAL, which plays back 25 frames every second. Movies you see in the theater play 24 frames every second.

The last attribute is **data rate**. Like frame rate, the data rate (also sometimes called *bit rate*) is measured in seconds. When you multiply the frame size by the frame rate by the color depth (and take compression into consideration—see below) you end up with your total data rate. This number is important for performance. If it's higher than what your computer can handle, you will not be able to get smooth playback.

What Do We Mean By "Digital?"

We hear this term all the time. In fact, a lot of the time it sounds like just a buzzword. But what does it really mean? And why do the marketing people make this term synonymous with "better?" In its most basic sense, a *digital* something is a *numeric representation* of something. Why is this better? Well, once in numeric format, it's easier to manipulate. And that leads to all sorts of possibilities.

To be honest, an in-depth understanding of how digitizing works isn't necessary to successfully use MediaStudio Pro, but having an appreciation of what's going on under the hood can never hurt. For the technically curious, here's a little bit of detail on how it all works. We'll digitize some audio, since it's easier to understand than video.

Sound travels through the air in waves. What we perceive as sound is simply the inner ear sending neural impulses to the brain. These impulses begin at the point where sound waves vibrate the eardrum. Just as the brain receives sound as encoded electronic input, so too is it with your computer. Sound can be recorded using one of two basic methods: analog or digital. Analog audio recording works by directly translating sound waves into a continuous or *non-discrete* electronic signal. Digital audio recording works through something called *sampling*.

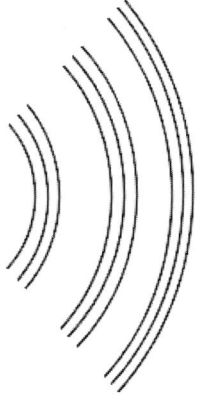

Sampling

What is sampling? Well, it's basically just what the word says: a *sample* of an analog signal is taken at regular intervals. The amplitude of the signal is measured at each interval and this measurement is stored somewhere. For example, let's say we have this sine wave that we want to digitize.

The analog waveform can be represented on a graph, as shown here. The vertical value is *amplitude*, which the human ear perceives as volume. The horizontal value is *time*. The distance between crests is the *wavelength*. The shorter the wavelength, the higher the pitch.

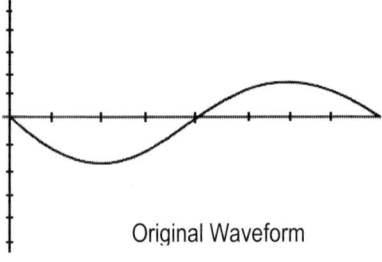

Original Waveform

Digitizing is the process of taking measurements of the amplitude at regular intervals and storing them as numbers.

Let's say we sample this waveform at each horizontal tick mark. We would then have a series of points as seen here at the right. Each point has a value representing the amplitude at that point in time. This

Digital Samples

value is essentially arbitrary, except that it has meaning in relation to the other points. For example, these nine points might translate to the following values: 0, -10, -12, -10, 0, 10, 12, 10, and 0. See what we've just done? We've just *digitized* some audio: our analog waveform has been turned into a stream of digits.

In order to hear digital audio, we have to go the other way: take the numbers and turn them back into a waveform. As you can tell from these pictures, our digital represen-

Reconstructed Waveform

tation of the audio isn't as smooth as the original waveform. The original signal contains far more information than what we've collected. When we play back our digital sequence of audio data, what we're actually going to hear is something *close to* but not *exactly* the same as the original waveform. To get better reproduction, you need more samples, until the human ear can't tell the difference. This means one thing: more data.

That's a **fundamental aspect** of the digital world. To increase quality, you need more numbers to describe your original. The fewer numbers you have, the worse the approximation is going to be. High quality means big files.

And speaking of numbers: digitizing creates a *lot* of them. Too many, to be honest! It didn't take long to realize that we'd have to figure out a way to cut down on the number of numbers to make it all feasible.

Compression

Think of a typical video stream. If you grab 30 frames every second, and each frame is 640 pixels wide by 480 pixels high, and the color information is represented by 3 bytes of data, then one second of video will take up 27,000 kilobytes of data. Over 26 MB of data for each and every second of video! And that's just for (what we used to call) "full-screen" video. To really blow your mind, think of a high definition frame 1920 pixels wide by 1080 wide. A single uncompressed second of video would be nearly 178 MB!

Your gigantic, new 200 GB disk would barely hold eighteen minutes of uncompressed, high-definition video. The hardware required to store and play back this amount of data is way outside the realm of possibility.

> **How Times Change**
> I bought a 4 GB SCSI disk drive in 1996 for $1,400. I clearly remember being impressed by how cheap it was since only about a year earlier the 3 GB disk was $3,000. I dreamt of the day I could justify buying a huge nine gigabyte disk drive!

The only way to make digital video work, and to be commonplace, was to get these numbers down. That's where compression comes in. The basic job of compression is to throw away data in a manner that it doesn't render the resulting picture unusable. It's rather unbelievable that you can discard up to 90% of the image data and still have a reasonable-looking picture. How is this even possible? Here's one good way to think about it. It's not a completely accurate explanation, but it does get you thinking in the right direction. Let's say you have a completely blue frame: 640 by 480 pixels of nothing but pure blue. Uncompressed, you would store this data a pixel at a time: it would be 640 times 480 times 3 bytes, or 900 kilobytes total. Now consider a compression algorithm where you only store a *description* of the frame. In this case you would store three pieces of information: width=640, height=480, color=blue. Look at that! We can now store a description of the very same frame in just a few bytes. Granted, this is overly simplistic but it does illustrate the basic concept and how compression can dramatically reduce file size.

Codec

The exact method used to determine what data stays, what data goes, and how to arrange what's left is called a *compression algorithm*. Suffice it to say that compressing data is rather pointless unless you also intend to decompress it at some later time. Therefore *decompression algorithms* also exist. Bundle them up together and you have a **codec**, a portmanteau of the words **co**mpressor/**dec**ompressor. In general practice, the codec also includes information on how the video data interacts with your hardware and how your software interacts with the video data.

When you create a video file from MediaStudio Pro, the codec is chosen from the "Compression" tab of the video options dialog box, which we'll discuss in detail later on in the book.

> **Did He Say Portmanteau?**
> Yes. A portmanteau is a word made up from two other words. Another one is modem, which stands for **mo**dulator / **dem**odulator. Another one is pixel, which is short for **pic**ture **el**ement. They changed the pronunciation from "pic" to "pix" because—let's face it—who would buy a three megapickle digital camera?

For many video capture devices, the captured video is stored using a codec specific to that piece of hardware. If that hardware is not present, then all you'll see is "unable to access codec driver" when trying to play back the video. There are software-only codecs that free you from requiring a specific piece of hardware, such as Indeo® or DivX®. And, of course, there's DV, which is supported by many different manufacturers.

So why are there so many different ways of encoding video? It's primarily because there are so many different delivery and storage requirements for video. Some provide better quality, while some have smaller storage requirements. Some try to be both. And like a lot of things, not all the old ones go away when new ones come along. They tend to collect like old magazines.

Digital Video and DV

While all video on your computer is technically "digital video," when you call it "DV" you're referring to a very specific encoding format. It has a fixed frame size, frame rate, bit rate, and so on. DV is just one of many formats of digital video, but it's the only one that calls itself "DV."

DV was introduced in 1996 and refers to both the compression algorithm and the tape format used to store the data. Most consumer and semi-professional videographers today are using MiniDV, which is DV in a smaller, more compact cassette.

Thanks to the proliferation of digital camcorders, DV is now a very common format. Not only because it's popular with consumers, but also because so many hardware and software vendors support the format. Back in the olden days of digital video editing (early to mid 1990s) each manufacturer had its own encoding format. So if you owned a video capture card from Brand A, and your friend had Brand B, you could not play each other's video files. Standardizing on a common format has advanced the field tremendously.

High Definition and HDV

Simply put, high definition means packing more data into each frame, thus increasing video quality. High definition is *definitely* on the way. You're probably already inundated with ads for upgrading your television service to high definition. (And many of you have probably done so already.) Tens of millions of HDTV displays are expected to ship within the next four years. Ready or not, here it comes.

You can think of HDV as "HD plus DV." That is, high definition video on DV media. The astute reader will realize this conflicts with the previous section, which stated DV was *both* a compression scheme and a tape format. HDV adopted the tape format and uses its own compression for the video data.

One of the biggest differences between DV and HDV (aside from the quality and compression, of course) is that DV compresses each frame without respect to any other frames. HDV (being at heart an MPEG format) leaves out frame data if hasn't changed (much) from the previous frame. Therefore a "talking head" would compress very highly, since most of the image changes very little from frame to frame.

File Types

It's common for the first-time user to get confused among the various file types encountered during video editing. To make things easy, you can logically divide them into two categories:

- Project Files
- Everything Else

This may seem simplistic but it does make an important point. You work on projects and the projects refer to other files. Several times over the years, I've seen newcomers complain in frustration, "I can't put a video on the timeline! This stupid thing doesn't work!" Once they've calmed down, I discover that they were trying to use the File | Open command to open a video file. This isn't dumb. This is what we've been conditioned to do in software applications. It's just that Video Editor takes a different approach. File | Open opens a project.

Project Files

From a conceptual point of view, the project file is said to contain video clips, images, and audio. In reality, however, the project file is only a set of instructions and not the files themselves. This is what allows for *non-destructive* editing, since your sources are never touched during the editing process.

Translated into English, your project file might look something like this: *"play 001.avi starting at 2 seconds for 3 seconds, then fade to 012.avi for 1 second; after 012.avi is done, cut to 014.avi ..."* The project file grows with respect to the number of instructions in it and not the amount of video. Therefore a project file 1-hour long may be just a few kilobytes while a project only 1-minute long could be several megabytes.

Everything Else

This set of files includes the actual video, audio, image data. Video files come in many, many, many flavors. Some may be familiar and obvious (like *avi*) and some may be otherwise (like *ogg*). Audio and image files are no different: formats abound. But what they all have in common is Video Editor's ability to deal with them at an abstract level. Once they're "in" the project, you rarely have to worry about the raw, underlying data.

A Note on Containers

It's important to realize that the file extension does not embody a specific data encoding. For example, just because you have an AVI file doesn't mean you really know anything about the audio and video streams within that file. The file extension simply tells you the type of container.

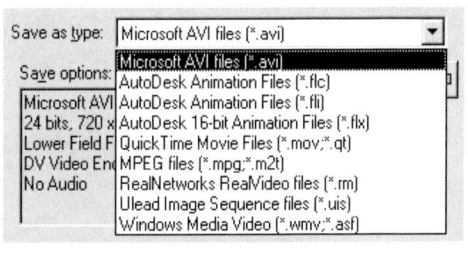

You can think of a container as a bucket. The bucket itself has properties (aluminum or plastic) and rules for how to use it (grab it by the handle, hold it upright to avoid spilling). But it tells you nothing of what it holds (could be water, could be liquid nitrogen).

So it is with an AVI file. The container has strict specifications for how to store chunks of data within the file. But other than that, it's wide open. The data itself may be uncompressed. It may be encoded with old Cinepak or Indeo codecs. It may be DV or HDV. It may be DivX or even MPEG-4. The important thing is: you can't tell just by the file extension.

Rendering

Without diving into another deep technical discussion, you can think of rendering as the process by which your project file is converted to a video file. Using the currently loaded project, Video Editor walks down the timeline, frame-by-frame, and *renders* each frame to an output file.

Why is this necessary? Let's say you have two video clips, with a transition between them. You already have digital representations of the clips. They are, after all, your source files. What you don't have is the digital representation of the time where they overlap. This is brand new: something you've created. In order to achieve perfectly fluid playback, the software needs to create a final file containing copies of the two original clips plus the transition between them.

So let's say we have a flying 3D cube transition between our clips. At the first frame of the transition, we see all of one clip and none of the other, as shown here. On the second frame of the transition, we start to see a 3D cube appear. Each of the six faces of the cube is painted with the contents of this frame. As the cube begins to roll away from our point of view, the background image is taken from the second clip.

Here on the right, we see the image as we're five frames into the transition. The cube is clearly visible. We can see our first clip on the three visible faces of the cube. We can see the background showing through. We can see the software doing a *lot* of math as it attempts to create this image. As it calculates what each frame of the transition should look like, it writes each finished frame out to disk. When it's all done, we can say we've *rendered* our project.

Real Time

This has arguably been the biggest buzzword in the industry in recent memory. And it has probably caused more confusion than anything else, with the possible exception of the eighty-seven different DVD formats out there.

So what is "real time"? In its most basic sense, it's a one-to-one relationship between the length of an event and actual clock time. Let's say you have two five-second video clips in your project that overlap for a one-second transition. This means your total project is nine seconds long. If playing this project takes exactly nine seconds, then you've seen your project play in real time. So why would it take any more time than that? Well, this takes us back to our last topic: rendering. Remember, the computational power needed to send those frames to your output display and to calculate all the new frames created by the transition takes time. Depending on the complexity of the project, it can take a *lot* of time. Your computer has to grind through millions of calculations. That nine-second project could take 90 seconds to calculate. Or 900. Or worse.

So you can see why real time has generated such buzz in the industry. For years we had to deal with 90- or 900-second waits for those 9-second results. When we suddenly got the ability to see that project *in real time*, everything changed. No more waiting for results. Instant gratification! What could be better than that?

Interesting question: what *could* be better than that? Well, what about *faster than real time*? Depending on your project attributes and processor, you may be there already. For example, I've been able to render a two and a half minute project in less than two minutes.

For our purposes, the term "real time" specifically refers to the ability of the software to preview output at the rate of one second per second. But it can be a gray area. It's not something that you either have or don't have, but depends on many factors.

Online Resources

That pretty much wraps up our introduction. I've talked about a number of topics from a high level, but serious, in-depth discussions are outside the scope of this chapter.

For more information, be check out the following sources.

- ***The MediaStudio Pro Users Group***. If you're not already a member of MUG, you should be! This is a large online group of users and it's probably the fastest and easiest way to get in touch with other people exactly like you. To my knowledge, it's also the oldest such group, founded back in 1996.

    I may be a wee bit biased towards it since I started it and still run the day-to-day administrative duties. MUG today has over 6,000 members with everyone participating via email. You send a mail message to the list, and the mail message is automatically distributed to all other members.

    http://www.mugcentral.org

Chapter 1 • The Boring Chapter   31

- **Ulead User to User Board.** Some people prefer a web interface to an email interface. While you can send and read MUG messages from Yahoo! Group's web site, it's still an email list at heart. A good web-based alternative is Ulead's own boards. They have many set up, including, of course, one for MediaStudio Pro.

  http://phpbb.ulead.com.tw/EN/viewforum.php?f=5

- **DMN Forums.** Another popular web-based forum is the one sponsored by Digital Media Net Communications.

  http://www.dmnforums.com/cgi-bin/displaywwugindex.fcgi?forum=uleadmediastudio

- **Creative Cow.** This is yet another popular web based forum. For me, personally, I spend most of my time with the first two groups listed above. It gets really hard to visit all of them, all of the time.

  http://www.creativecow.net/index.php?forumid=10

- **Ulead Tech Support.** You can find information on updates, patches, and other technical support related issues at:

  http://www.ulead.com/tech/msp/msp.htm

  http://www.ulead.co.uk/tech/msp/msp.htm (United Kingdom)

  http://www.ulead.de/tech/msp/msp.htm (Germany)

  http://www.ulead.fr/tech/msp/msp.htm (France)

  http://www.ulead.com.cn/tech/msp/msp.asp (China)

  Ulead has links for all international sites on the home page of each main site. Click on the "Ulead Worldwide" drop-down list at the top-right of their home pages.

- **Usenet.** There are also two usenet groups you can use to browse or post questions: rec.video.desktop and comp.graphics.apps.ulead. If you do not have a dedicated newsreader client, I highly recommend using Google Groups, the most comprehensive usenet archive in existence. You can jump directly to a group, like so:

  http://groups.google.com/group/rec.video.desktop

  http://groups.google.com/group/comp.graphics.apps.ulead

- Stefan Burger has free transitions at http://www.burgers-transition-site.de. These are very much worth your while.

- When all else fails, head to Google!

- And if Google fails, head to Wikipedia!

Moving Right Along...

I hope you feel a bit more at ease after going through this introductory material. All of these concepts will come up again at one point or another throughout the rest of the book.

If you still feel confused in spots, go ahead and re-read the sections you might have had trouble with. Don't be afraid to check the above resources and user groups. Remember, the only stupid question is the one you don't ask. (Well, that's not entirely true. In history class I once asked the teacher what year the War of 1812 started.)

Anyway, if you're ready, then let's turn the page and continue our journey with a no-nonsense overview of Video Editor.

2

A No-Nonsense Overview of Video Editor

Take a down-to-earth tour of the suite's central tool. We'll look at the good, the bad, and everything else.

Background

Because the purpose of MediaStudio Pro is to edit videos, it should come as little surprise that *Video Editor* is all but synonymous with *MediaStudio Pro*. While the suite is indeed made up of three (or four, or more—depending how you count) programs, there is little argument that Video Editor towers above the rest. In fact, it's entirely possible you may spend all of your time here and never even realize other modules exist.

With Video Editor you can:

- Trim and order media clips into a final production.
- Mix video and audio sources with virtually no limits.
- Overlay and blend multiple video sources.
- Move, resize, rotate, or reshape video.
- Apply a wide range of special effects to video and audio clips.
- Create titles with a large assortment of text effects.
- Mix audio data in real time.
- Manage your media files.

This list just scratches the surface and doesn't really convey the full breadth and depth of its capabilities. Still, it's important to note that Video Editor is a *video editor*. Its primary job is to mix existing media sources into a final result. It is not intended to be an imagery or special effects generator itself. True, you can do some of that. (*Lots* of that, actually.) But it's not the *main* function—an important yet subtle distinction, which we'll discuss more later. For now, let's take a look at the Video Editor interface.

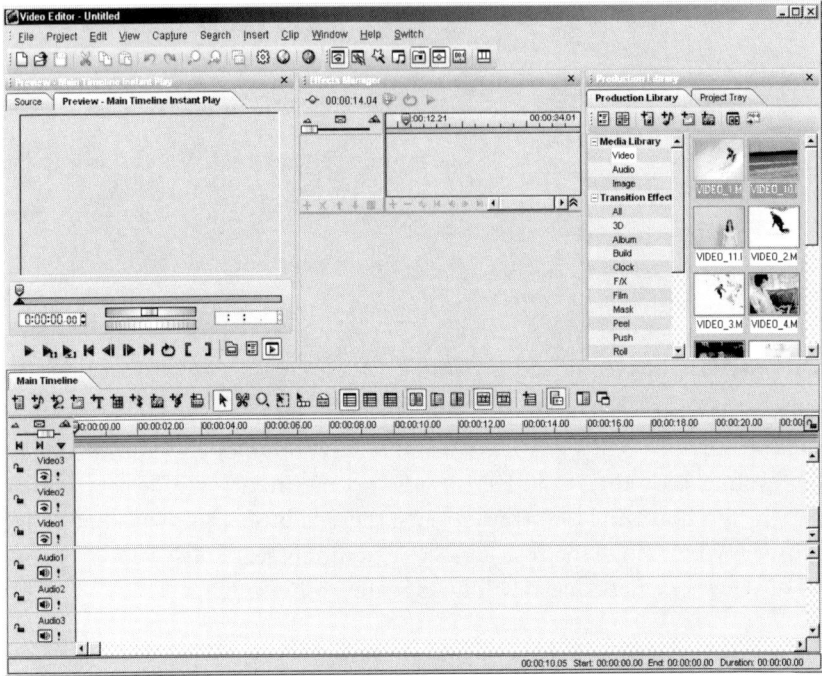

That's the default window layout. There sure are a lot of things to click on, aren't there!? While it may look daunting at first glance, you'll quickly find the interface is built up from several distinct components. You might be surprised how quickly it all comes together for you. Most people find it very easy and intuitive, once you get over that first hump. The primary pieces are:

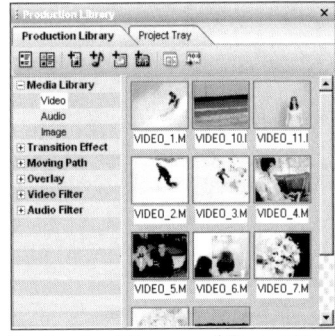

The Timeline   Production Library and Project Tray

Chapter 2 • Video Editor Overview   35

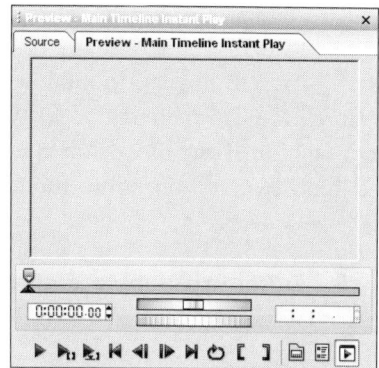
Source and Preview Windows

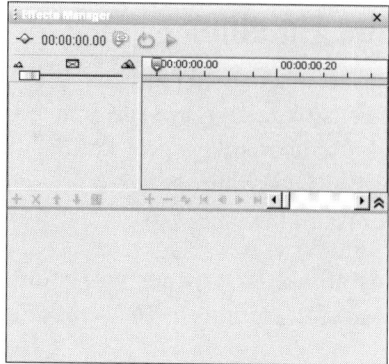
Effects Manager

The size, position, and location of every object, be it a toolbar, tool panel, or other window, is **completely customizable**. Move them, resize them, shuffle them to your heart's content. When they're docked, as shown above, they automatically fill the available screen space when moved or resized. This makes keeping a tidy and efficient workspace a snap.

Upon finding an arrangement you like, you can save it using the Window | Layout Manager command. You can save as many layouts as you like, although you'll probably stick to just one or two for your day-to-day work. You can recall previously saved layouts using any one of these methods:

- The Window | Layout Manager command.

- A previously assigned keyboard shortcut.

- The ⊞ button on the toolbar.

You'll find several layouts already defined, any one of which may already suit your needs perfectly.

> *Note.* The menu bar, standard toolbar, and panel layouts are not affected when recalling saved layouts. Their positions remain no matter which layout you choose. And although the track size and cue bar visibility is stored with the layout, the track colors are not.

But what good is loading and saving layouts if you don't know what the heck anything is? Well, I'm glad you asked. Because if you didn't, the book would probably end right here.

Let's take a closer look at each component, starting with your editing canvas: the timeline.

The Timeline

This is where it all happens. It's your canvas. Everything else in the interface is there to serve the timeline. The timeline is so named due to the fact that it displays project time in a linear fashion. Time moves from left to right, beginning at zero and ending a good twelve hours into the future.

Just think! That means you could use Video Editor to assemble all three extended editions of *The Lord of the Rings* into a single video[1].

The timeline can be subdivided into five distinct sections: the toolbar, the ruler, the track buttons, the tracks, and the status bar. We'll look at each in turn, starting with...

The Timeline Toolbar

This toolbar runs nearly the entire width of the timeline and comes with a wide array of buttons. They're logically grouped, which helps to understand their functions.

> While the toolbar is certainly convenient, I'm the kind of person who prefers to use keyboard shortcuts wherever possible. In many cases, it's just hands-down faster to hit a couple keys on the keyboard than to hunt them down with your mouse.
>
> Many toolbar button functions have keyboard shortcuts (for example, "Z" for zoom). For the ones that do not have explicit shortcuts, you can still use the keyboard because they'll have menu equivalents (for example, Alt+I+V to execute the Insert | Video File... command). Each section below will list the keyboard equivalents in the "Mouse-Free Operation" guide.

Let's take a close look at each button grouping on the toolbar:

Insert Group:

The little plus signs on each button are your visual cue that each of these is meant to insert something into the timeline. From left to right, insert: video file, audio file, voice file, image clip, title clip, color clip, silence clip, project file, auto music clip, and Smart Compositor. The clip types are discussed starting on page 48.

---

[1] Hmmm, that gives me an idea...

Mouse-Free Operation. Although there are no true keyboard shortcuts for this group, you can still use their menu equivalents by typing Alt+I+V, Alt+I+A, Alt+I+O, Alt+I+I, Alt+I+T, Alt+I+C, Alt+I+S, Alt+I+M, Alt+I+P, and Alt+I+R respectively. *Tip.* If you have a programmable keyboard or software program that allows you to reassign keystrokes you may be able to define your own shortcuts.

Select Group: ▶ ✄ ⚲ ▣ ⬚ 🎞

This group contains buttons for altering the way you select and edit clips on the timeline. You can group clips, slice clips, select across time, and even apply audio cross-fades. Here are the details.

The first button activates the **clip selection tool**. This is the default mode while working in Video Editor. While the clip selection tool is active you can grab clips, move them, change their lengths, and perform other editing functions. If you hold down the **shift key** while this tool is selected, you can multi-select contiguous clips. If you hold down the **control key** you can select non-contiguous clips, or add clips to an existing selection.

The second button activates the **scissors tool**. This tool allows you to slice a clip in two or to join two clips back into one. However, you can only join clips if the following conditions are met: 1) both clips are the same type; and 2) the join point is where the two clips would otherwise naturally meet. In other words, you cannot join two random clips, or join two halves of the same clip if they've been trimmed.

The third button in this tool group activates the **zoom tool**. It's just another interface to the ruler unit button. However, it has one added benefit, you can specify where you want the zoom to "center." For example, if you change the timeline resolution using the ruler unit button, the leftmost side of the screen stays constant. When going from a larger resolution to a smaller, this almost always means what used to be in the center of your screen has now flown way off to the right. Using the zoom tool, you can specify what you want centered. You'll find yourself using both, depending on what you need to do at any given time. Holding the Shift key while zooming will zoom out of the timeline.

The fourth button activates the **time selection tool**. This allows you to select blocks of time, and manipulate them as a unit. It cuts your timeline straight down through every track. This unit then can be deleted or moved as needed. Click on the clip selection tool to deselect any current time selection.

The fifth button activates the **track selection tool**. With this tool selected, clicking on a clip causes every clip on that track to be automatically selected, from that point on. For example, if you have four clips on track Video1, one right after the other, and you click on the second clip with this tool, all but the first clip will be selected. You can add to the selection by clicking on another clip in another track. If the **shift** key is held down, this works across all tracks. That is, every clip on the timeline, to the right of the selected-clip, in any track, will be selected. To get a true feel for this tool, you really have to try it out for yourself!

The sixth and last button activates the **time stretch tool**. With this tool selected, dragging the end of the clip will adjust the speed of the clip to match the new duration. If you have a two second clip and drag this out to four seconds, the new speed will be 50%.

Mouse-Free Operation. If you need to change tools quickly and temporarily, you can press S, Z, Shift+Z, T, E, or I to temporarily change the tool to scissors, zoom-in, zoom-out, time-selection, track-selection or time stretch. More than other keyboard equivalents, these can significantly increase the efficiency of your workflow. I would highly recommend getting used to these shortcuts.

And if that weren't enough, the U key also acts as a scissors tool. It has the added benefit of requiring no mouse clicks at all. Instead it cuts all selected clips at the current playhead position. If no clips are selected then *all* clips are cut. You really should try this out when you get a chance. It's an indescribable timesaver.

Ripple Group:	🗐 🗐 🗐

Video Editor has three basic **editing modes** that determine how a change to one clip affects all the other clips on the timeline. They are: normal, single-track ripple, and multi-track ripple.

By default, when you add, change, or delete a clip on the timeline, this action does not affect any other clips. But what happens when your project is all finished, and then you decide to add a new clip near the beginning of the project? Moving everything down to accommodate the change can be tedious at best. This is where ripple editing helps out. Ripple editing forces Video Editor to adjust clips on one or more tracks in your timeline to fit the change.

Chapter 2 • Video Editor Overview

"No ripple" is the default mode, meaning: when you add, change, or delete clips on the timeline, no other clips are affected. Single-track ripple will only adjust clips on the current track. For example, placing a new clip in track Video2 will push all clips on track Video2 to the right of your insert point to accommodate the new clip. Multi-track ripple adjusts clips on all tracks, both video and audio. The only clips not affected are clips in tracks that have been locked.

Mouse-Free Operation. Pressing the "R" key will toggle through the ripple options.

Trim Group:

The Trim Group allows you to specify trim options. Trim options are explained in detail beginning on page 131, so I won't go over them at this point. For now, just be aware that you can change trim options from Normal, to Stitch, to Overwrite using the toolbar.

Mouse-Free Operation. Pressing the "M" key will toggle through the trim options.

View Group:

The View Group gives you two different ways to view the timeline. The default is called "General Timeline." This displays clips on the timeline with lengths proportional to their durations. In other words, a one-second clip is half as wide as a two second clip.

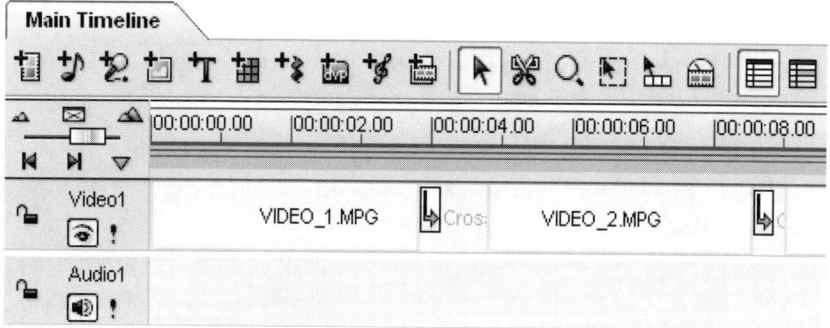

While this is both natural and intuitive, it can also be difficult to work with when you have clips with greatly differing durations. Fortunately, you can use the "Summary Timeline" mode to help cope with this. This displays clips on the timeline with equal lengths regardless of duration.

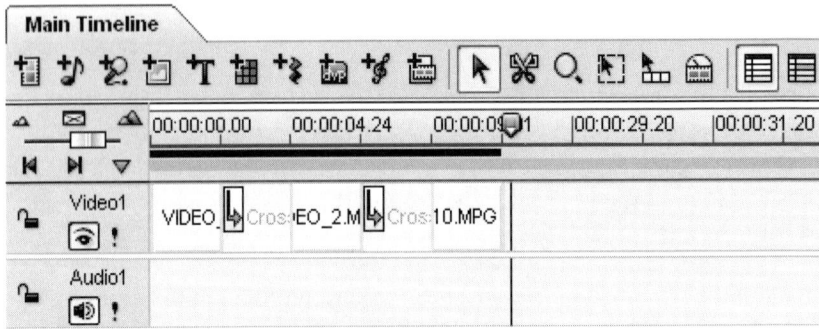

Now the three video clips and two transitions are all the same length. You can quickly spot-check transitions to make sure they're all going the right direction or visually scan for any other editing anomalies.

Mouse-Free Operation. Alt+W+G for General and Alt+W+R for Summary.

The first button allows you to **add or remove tracks** from the timeline. Click it and you'll see this dialog box. I really like the fact that you can add more than one track at a time. Even better, you can add tracks *before* track Video1. This is a great feature!

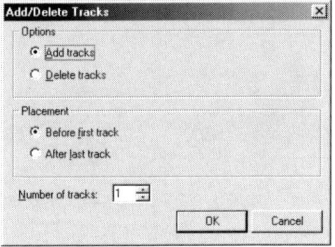

The second button **enables or disables Video Proxy mode**. When "on" the button appears blue and proxy mode has been enabled. The tool tip doesn't come right out and tell you this.

The third button displays the **timeline display mode** dialog box. Use this to set lots of display options such as track and clip colors, clip sizes, and cue bars. (Details below.)

The last button allows you to **save the current project settings** as a template for future projects. Once saved, they will appear as template options on the New project dialog box. If you click on an existing template, the template name and description will default to those values: handy for when doing minor tweaks to existing templates.

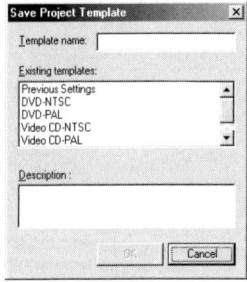

The Ruler

This picture shows a close-up of the ruler. This feature holds a lot of information, and since you'll be using it all the time, it's best to get familiar with it right away. Let's look at the ruler components from top to bottom.

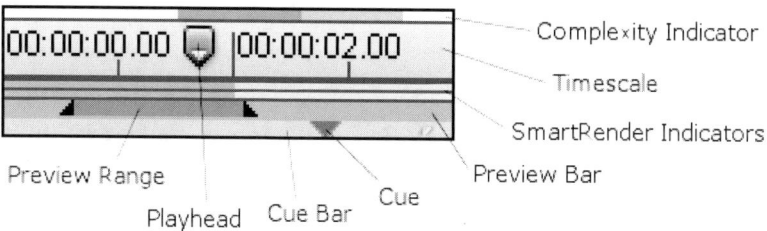

Complexity Indicator

When doing real-time previewing (or *Instant Play*) this will indicate how complex a given part of the timeline is using various shades of red. No color means no problem. Red tells you, "Go buy a more powerful computer." Seriously, though, red only means that the sequence is too complicated for *instant* playback. A normal, time-consuming render will handle edits of any complexity on any speed computer.

Timescale

The first frame of every project is 00:00:00:00. This number, also called "time code," represents the four basic units of video time: hours, minutes, seconds, and frames. The *hours* field begins at 0 and goes up to 23. The *minutes* and *seconds* fields can be from 00 through 59, as you'd expect. The maximum value for *frame* field will be the maximum for the video standard you're working under. For example, if you are working with PAL, your frame counter can be any integer between 0 and 24. If you are using the US standard NTSC, the range is between 0 and 29.

The bar with the frame numbers is called the timescale. The actual numbers you see will depend on the ruler-unit setting. But in all cases, it represents where you are in the timeline at any given time. If you move your mouse cursor into the timescale, the mouse pointer will change to a small star-shape, like this: ※.

When you click the left mouse button with this star-shaped cursor visible, Video Editor will render the current frame and display it in the preview window. If you move the mouse to the right and left while the left mouse button is held down, Video Editor will continually update the preview window.

This "on the fly previewing" using the mouse is known as *scrubbing*. It's an industry standard term used for both video and audio tools.

SmartRender Indicators
To be honest, I have no idea what these are called. I've never actually seen them documented anywhere. So, for lack of an official term, I'm calling them "SmartRender Indicators."

Their origin hearkens back to the introduction of SmartRender. Creating (or *rendering*) a video file means Video Editor must read each input frame in the timeline and calculate the corresponding output frame. This is done when you add transitions, filters, moving paths, or other effects that alter the original source. But if the original source has not been altered, why re-calculate everything? If the attribute of your clip exactly matches the attribute of the project, then Video Editor can copy the data from the input file to the output file without any time-consuming math. *Much* faster! This is called SmartRender.

If the top indicator bar in your ruler turns orange, it means the video clip attributes match the project attributes. If the bottom bar turns green, it means the audio clip attributes match the project attributes. In both cases, that portion of the timeline is marked for SmartRendering, making that part of the video file creation quite speedy.

Preview Bar
The next bar is your preview range indicator. When your mouse cursor is over the preview bar, you'll see 〖 〗 attached to the cursor. Dragging the mouse along the preview bar creates a new preview range. The previous preview range is automatically deleted. (If you wish to delete a preview range without creating a new range, right-click the preview bar.)

So what is the preview range for? It simply allows you to define a subset of your project, so that when previewing or rendering, you work with only the portion you want, and not the entire project. It's extremely handy: you will use it all the time.

Cue Bar
If you move your mouse over the cue bar, the cursor changes to ⌘. Clicking with this cursor creates a cue, and a small triangle appears. There are two types of cues: Project and Chapter point.

A **project cue** acts as a "bookmark" in your timeline, and can be used for anything you need them for. For example, let's say you know that at 45 seconds and 10 frames into your project, you need to have a certain clip start. You can place a cue there to remind you of this. Another good use is to break your project down into sections. Let's say you have an introduction, a series of clips, and then some credits. You can use cues to mark the start-points of each location, and quickly find your way back to these points. Cues can be named (by default, they are named after their location in the timeline, e.g., "00:00:45:10"). You can manage them with the View | Cue Manager command. If you want to delete one, click on it, and drag downwards, effectively pulling it off the timeline.

A **chapter point cue** is used for DVD authoring. When you place chapter point cues on the timeline and render a video, these points are accessible to the authoring application via the automatic scene detection tool. An example from DVD MovieFactory is shown here. Click OK and your project will have chapters corre-

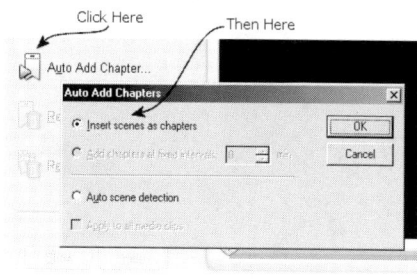

sponding to the cues you placed on the timeline. This can be a real time-saver when authoring!

Tracks

Below the ruler are the tracks. This is where all the action happens. On the far left you'll see the track buttons. Each track button itself contains four buttons. On the far left is the **track lock** button. When a track is locked, you cannot make changes to it. The **track name** is also a button. Click it and you'll automatically select each clip on that track. The eye button is not part of an Illuminati plot. It's a **mute button**, or in MSP parlance, "Show/Hide." If the eye is open, clips on this track will appear when rendering. A closed eye means video editor won't see them. The last button is the **solo button**. (I'm still not sure what the little exclamation point means.) Soloing a track is the logical opposite of muting.

       Mute: play **all** tracks except this one.
       Solo: play **no** tracks except this one.

It is possible to solo more than one track. If two tracks are soloed, you get a duet: both will play, all others will be suppressed. Soloing all tracks is therefore the same as soloing no tracks: all will play at once.

There are two types of tracks on the timeline: video and audio. Video tracks can contain any type of visual media: video files, image files, title clips, color clips, and so on. Audio tracks can accept a number of audio file formats as well as video files which contain audio. Place a video file on an audio track and you'll just get the audio.

For video files that contain both video and audio, the clip will display in both areas, like this:

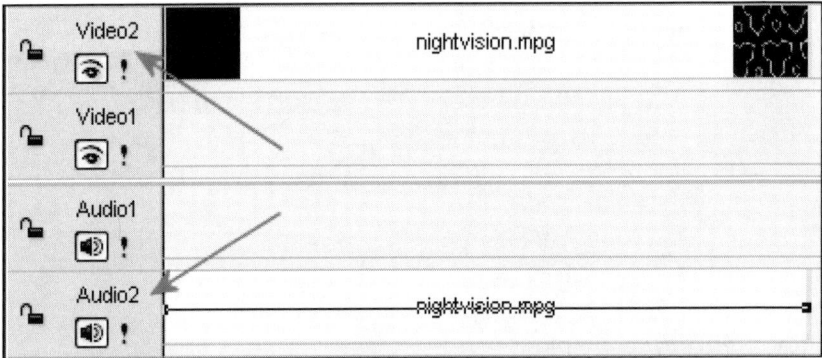

The clips will stay joined unless you split them. Once split you can move them independently, or completely remove one or the other.

Extra Buttons at No Extra Charge

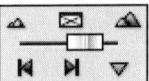 This appears in the upper left hand corner of the timeline. The slider control lets you zoom in or out of the timeline by changing the timeline ruler unit. The little mountain buttons do the same thing: just a different interface. You can also right-click this area to bring up the ruler unit menu. This lets you see the exact scale. Pressing F9 toggles between the two most recent ruler settings.

Zooming in on the timeline is like a using a microscope to look at something: it gets bigger, but you can see less of the surroundings at the same time. Here is a 5-second color clip viewed at two different ruler units:

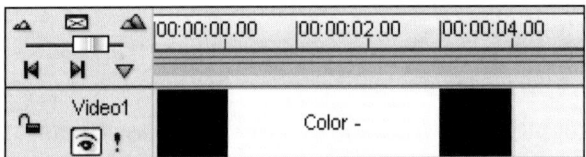

At 1-second resolution, you can see the clip in its entirety. Note the ruler units: 00:00:00.00, 00:00:02.00, 00:00:04.00. Compare this to:

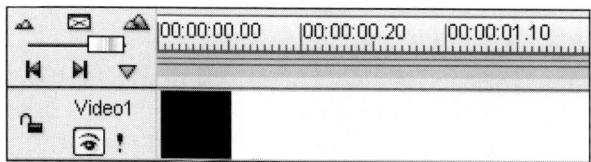

The zoom slider has moved to the right, now representing 1/3-second resolution. You can no longer see the entire clip, and the visible part of our timeline which spanned six seconds now shows a lot less. But look! There are now tick marks for individual frames. One method of getting down to frame-accurate editing is to zoom into the point where you can actually see individual frames.

And the Other Buttons?

Well, these two ◄ ► move the playhead between edit points. An edit point is essentially defined as, "anything that isn't just clip." Here are some common edit points: start and end of a clip, clip overlaps, cues, scissor cuts, and so on.

This button ▽ toggles the timeline between displaying project cue points and DVD chapter cue points. If you have neither kind, then it might seem like this button is broken. (Kind of like one of those light switches that doesn't do anything.)

There's one last button. Can you see it? It's waaaaay over on the right. Another lock button! This is the scroll lock button. It synchronizes scrolling between the video and audio tracks, ensuring like-numbered tracks are always visible together.

Status Bar

In the lower right corner of the timeline is the status bar:

`00:00:03.12  Start: 00:00:00.00  End: 00:00:00.00  Duration: 00:00:00.00`

Keep an eye on it. It can really help you to nail your edits. Instead of just guessing how long a clip looks (or even just finding out where on the timeline you are) you'll know for sure by looking at this.

The first number, the unlabeled one, is the current timeline position under the mouse. It updates as the mouse moves. The labeled Start and End numbers apply to the currently selected clip, showing where it begins and ends with respect to the entire timeline. The Duration also applies to the current clip. Like I said, keep an eye on it. It really does help with frame-accurate editing.

Fundamental Timeline Concepts

If your eyes have glazed over at this point, then it's time to wake up. It's one thing to know what all the little buttons do. It's another to understand how everything behaves.

Let's take a look at these fundamental timeline concepts, in order of importance. Some of this may seem rudimentary, but I'd rather play it safe and make sure we're all starting from the same point.

1. Clips to the left appear earlier in the video than clips on the right.

    As you can see, time flows from left to right. Placing a clip at time 00:00:01.00 will appear before a clip at time 00:00:05.00. Can't get more basic than that. If for some reason you intuitively feel that the clip on the right should appear first, I would look for a new hobby.

2. Clips on higher tracks appear in front of clips on lower tracks.

    A clip on track Video2 is above (numerically and visually) Video1. Therefore the clip on Video2 will obscure the clip on Video1. (We'll learn about *not* obscuring overlaid clips later.)

3. Clips that overlap on the same track create a transition.

    If the end of Clip #1 occurs after the start of Clip #2 on the same track, you get a transition. By default, this will be a soft "Crossfade". You can change the default for all future overlaps under Preferences. You can change each individual transition by dragging and dropping from the Production Library, which we'll learn about in a bit.

4. Clips can be placed anywhere.

    Video Editor does not enforce contiguous placements of clips. They can be dropped anywhere.

5. Audio clips have no precedence. They are mixed together.

    It's not as if audio in track Audio2 will be louder than audio in track Audio1. So rule #2 above really just applies to video tracks. This isn't to say you have no control over how they are mixed. You can change the relative volume and panning of clips for stereo mixes and change the spatial positioning of audio for 5.1 Surround Sound mixes.

Customizing the Timeline

Select View | Timeline Display Mode or click the Display Mode toolbar button to show this dialog box. This is where you customize the timeline to suit your preferences.

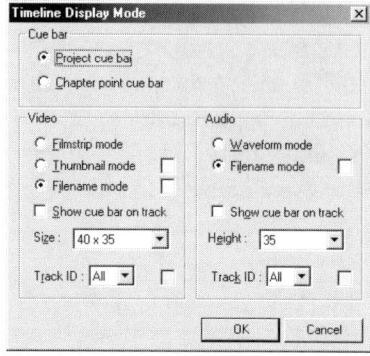

The top radio buttons are obvious: select which cue bar you want to display. The default setting is as shown here.

The Video and Audio groups have a variety of settings. First up, the clip display modes: Filmstrip, Thumbnail, and Filename. **Filmstrip** displays a constant stream of images from the clip along the length of the clip:

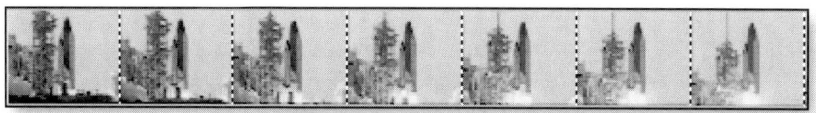

Thumbnail mode displays the first frame of the clip on the left, the last frame of the clip on the right, and the filename in the middle, like this:

Finally, the **Filename** mode displays only the name of the file. No image information is displayed on the clip anywhere. It is the most efficient form of display because Video Editor has the least amount of work to do as you move around the timeline.

Thumbnail mode takes more work. Filmstrip mode takes the most work. I spend most of my time in either thumbnail or filename mode. Once you get familiar with a project and your files, you can get along very well without the visual references.

There are similar settings for audio files. Here you have just two choices: waveform or filename mode. With waveform mode, you actually see a rough estimate of the underlying waveform data on the audio file:

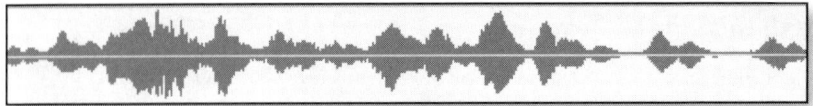

This is useful for picking out music beats, audio pops (for example, a member of the audience coughing during taping), quiet spots, or other "visible" audio data. Filename mode, like the video equivalent, simply shows the name of the file in the clip:

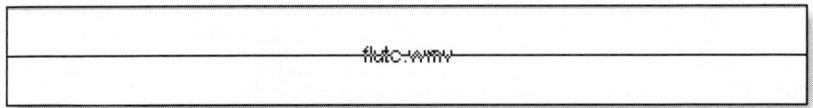

And just like the video equivalent, filename mode is far more efficient. You'll see why after you leave waveform mode on for more than a few minutes.

Checking this box (available for both audio and video tracks) adds a cue bar along the bottom of each track. I use clip cues quite often (as you'll see when we get to the longer projects) so I always leave both of these checked.

This allows you to change the size of your clips. You might find larger clips easier to work with, but they also take up more screen real estate.

Lastly, you can change the background color of the tracks. This doesn't have any effect on the background color of the *video*. It's simply an interface setting. You can set all tracks to be the same color, set them individually, or have different color tracks for video and audio.

Types of Clips

It's all well and good to understand the timeline but the timeline is not very interesting in and of itself. The timeline is just a container and it's very *raison d'être* is to build a project out of clips.

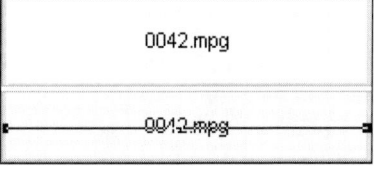

But what exactly is a clip? Here's the quick definition: a clip is a clip. I know that sounds stupid, but it's one of those words you come to inherently know the definition of—like trying to define the word "word."

For those of you who just won't accept that poor excuse for a definition, try this instead. A clip is the basic unit of information in your project. It represents a block of visual or aural information, beginning at a certain point in time, lasting for a certain duration, and existing in a certain layer. Clips are to your video project what words are to a book. They're your basic building blocks.

Since video clips contain video frames, you might be tempted to think of the frame as the basic unit of information. But you cannot work with a frame as a distinct object on the timeline (especially since not all clip types use frames). If clips are the words that make up the book, then frames are the letters that make up the words.

There are ten clip types in Video Editor.

File Based Clips

- **Video** clips represent moving picture files.

- **Audio** clips represent sound files.

- **Voice** clips are also audio files, but you can record them in real-time during timeline playback.

- **Image** clips represent graphic files.

Video Editor Objects

- **Title** clips are used to place text in your video.

- **Color** clips are used for backgrounds and rudimentary shapes.

- **Silence** clips are "blank" audio clips. They can be used as placeholders or as filler.

- **AutoMusic** clips are pre-packaged SmartSound music files which can be stretched to any duration.

- **Virtual** clips represent an entire timeline of clips in a single clip. We'll *definitely* be using this a lot later on.

- **Transition** clips are used to tell Video Editor how to treat the overlap between two clips on a single timeline. Unlike other clip types, these cannot stand alone on the timeline.

Preview Window

As clips are dropped and arranged on the timeline, all eyes turn towards the Preview Window. This is your visual feedback device, showing you what the frame looks like at any point in the project.

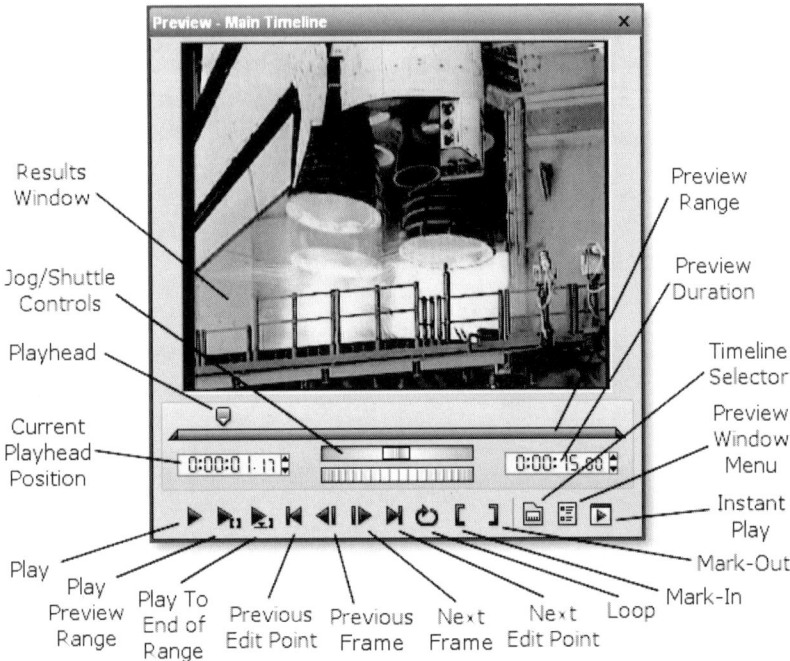

As you scrub the timeline, the output appears here[2]. You will see the *playhead* move as your cursor moves across the timeline. The thick blue bar shows your preview range with respect to the project length. In the picture above, these lengths are equal. The playhead position and preview ranges are displayed numerically for precise editing. You can click on these boxes to change their values directly.

The array of VCR-like controls behave as expected. The three play buttons may seem redundant at first, but they have their purposes. While editing, you'll often want to change how much gets played and where play starts. These buttons give you those options.

---

[2] You do have the option of sending the output to other places—both in addition to and instead of the Preview Window. It's not uncommon to send the preview output to an external video monitor for true WYSIWYG editing.

Keyboard **shortcuts** are quite helpful. Press the Enter key to begin play at the current playhead and continue playing until you press Enter or Esc. This mode ignores any selected preview range. Press Shift+Space to play the full preview range, regardless of the playhead's current position. Press Space to play to the end of the preview range, starting from the current playhead position.

The **Instant Play** button turns real-time previewing on and off. When off, Video Editor will render the video to an intermediate file first before playing it back. When Instant Play is turned on, the results are played back almost immediately in the preview window.

You might ask yourself, if you can see instant results like that, why would you ever turn it off? Simply because it won't always work. As the complexity of your video increases, the likelihood that instant play can handle it decreases. When Video Editor renders your file first, it takes longer, but it's worth the wait if you need to see every frame, in full, fluid motion.

The **Preview Window menu** has lots of options. I won't go over every single one here because: 1) the manual should do a good job of that; and 2) when the time comes to learn about these commands more in-depth, we'll hit them as we go.

That said, I do want to bring your attention to the Save Image to menu. A frequently asked question is, "How can I create a still image from the timeline?" Here's your answer. Whatever you see in the Preview Window can be sent to a file, to the Production Library, or straight to the clipboard.

Even better, the image's frame size will match that of the project, not the current Preview Window setting. So even if your Preview Window is half-sized, you'll get a full-sized image.

Source Window

The Source window is where you can view, trim, cue, and otherwise edit clips. Clips can come from the timeline, the Production Library, or directly from the file system.

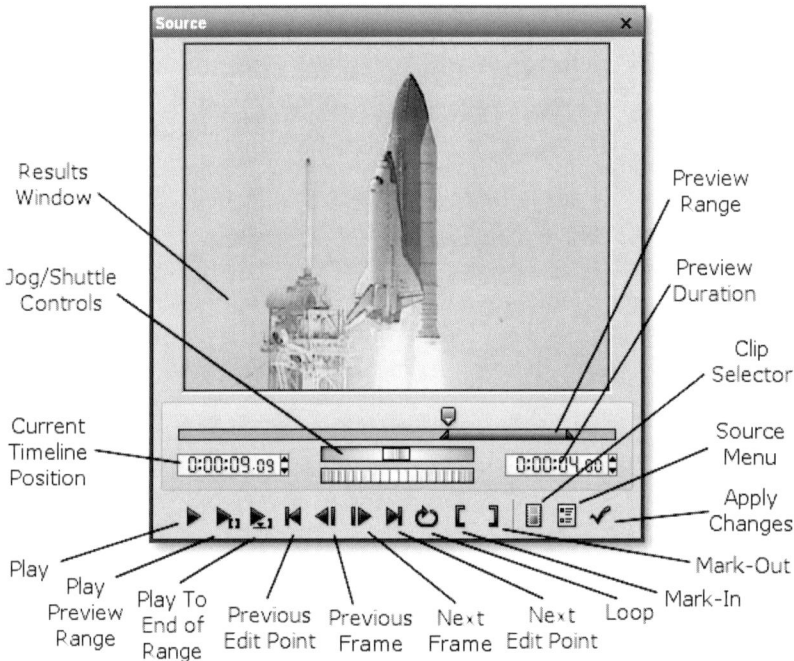

You might have noticed this looks a *lot* like the Preview window. In fact, most of the time they share screen space by being docked in the same window, and it's hard to tell them apart at a glance. There are two main differences:

1. The Preview Window shows all clips, the Source Window just one.

2. The Source Window has editing capabilities.

Other than that, the way they look and behave is remarkably similar, so you don't have to learn two different sets of skills.

You can quickly load a timeline clip into the source window by double-clicking it. Clips from the Production Library or files from the file system can be dragged directly to the Source Window. More than one clip can be loaded at a time. You switch between them by using the Clip Selector button.

Keyboard **shortcuts** help here too. You can change the mark-in point of a clip by pressing F3. Change the mark-out with F4. The nice thing about this is you can even do it while the clip is playing. My most-used keyboard shortcut is probably F5, which creates a cue. I use cues a lot. The PageUp and PageDown keys are helpful for moving between edit points (and cues count as edit points).

The **Source Window menu** shows where the Source and Preview windows diverge. While they do share a number of same menu items[3], there are important differences.

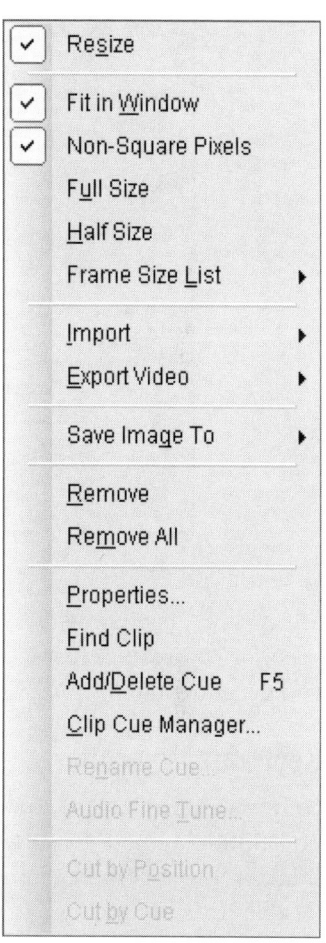

Since the Source Window works with files rather than project contents, there are Import and Export menu items. The Export menu is a duplicate of the main File | Export menu. This allows you to launch DVD MovieFactory directly from the Source Window.

The Remove commands simply remove clips from the Source Window. They do not remove files from permanent storage.

Preview & Source Conflicts
When these windows are docked together you might notice some mutually exclusive settings. For example, what if the Preview window is full-sized and the Source window is half-sized? Or what if one is resizable and the other isn't? At the time of this writing, these are real issues. If this hasn't been fixed by the time you read this, be aware of these potential conflicts.

To fix any weirdness, I suggest undocking them (by double-clicking the window title bar), synching the settings, and trying it again.

---

[3] Although, much to my own annoyance, the same items are not in the same locations. Right when I think I remember where the Resize menu command is, I switch to the *other* menu, and it's in a different place.

Effects Manager

For those times you're not staring at the Timeline or the Preview Window, odds are you'll be looking at the Effects Manager. This is one-stop shopping for all sorts of clip work.

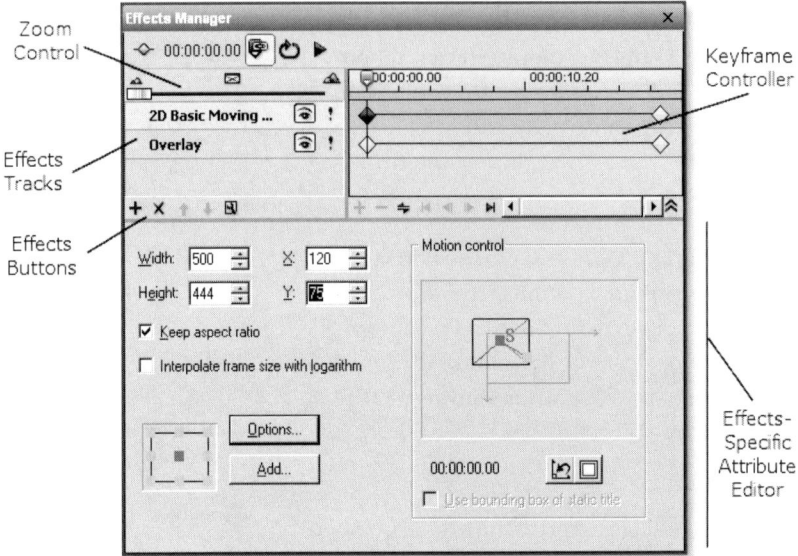

Mercifully, I have not labeled every single control on this thing. This has been for clarity. Not just to make the diagram easier to read, but to help you get a mental grasp on what this thing is doing. Let's take it in pieces.

Keyframe Controller

Before we learn how to control these keyframe things, it would probably be helpful to know exactly what one is. In its simplest terms, you can think of it as an object containing a set of related attributes necessary for describing the effect.

Yeah, I didn't understand that either. Let's start with a history lesson.

The term comes from the world of traditional animation. As artists painted the individual frames for a cartoon movie, the work was divided into parts. Senior artists would be responsible for drawing major changes in the action. Let's say, a cat holding a sledgehammer over his head, followed by the cat hitting the sledgehammer on the ground.

Chapter 2 • Video Editor Overview

The senior animators were the most talented (and presumably) the most expensive, so it didn't make sense for them to draw all sixteen frames every second. They would draw the *key* frames and junior artists were responsible for drawing everything in between. With key frames to guide them, drawing the "in between" work became mechanical. This job became known as "tweening."

It's the same thing with video editing. Let's say you want to create a picture in picture effect where the inset image moves from the top left to the bottom right for a 300-frame period. Which do you think would be easier: manually placing the picture at its exact position 300 times in a row **or** setting the start and end positions and letting the computer do the rest?

Obviously this second approach would be a lot less work and produce far better results. Your job, as senior animator, is to create two keyframes. Your junior animator, Video Editor, is stuck with the grunt work.

Here is the Effects Manager's keyframe controller:

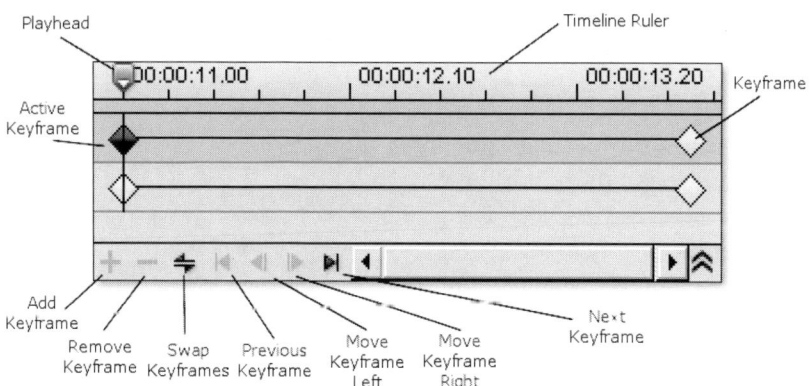

The timeline ruler here corresponds to the big timeline. As you can see in this picture, the keyframe timeline starts at time 00:00:11.00 because that's the position of this particular clip.

Each track represents an effect applied to the clip. I've created a moving path and an overlay, hence the two tracks. The diamonds are keyframes and the red diamond is the current, or active keyframe.

The other buttons should be self-explanatory. The add and remove buttons become active when those functions make sense. In this picture you can't add a keyframe because you're on a keyframe. But you can't remove it either, because it's the first keyframe. There will never be fewer than two keyframes: start and end. (Audio filters are an exception: they have no keyframes since the effect applies evenly to the entire clip.)

Right-click a keyframe and you get this popup menu. The top group gives you access to basic copy/paste/etc. functions. The bottom group lists each keyframe. Selecting it will make that keyframe active. The middle group is the *really* useful one and of these, I use Copy and Paste to All constantly. I've probably selected that menu item several thousand times over 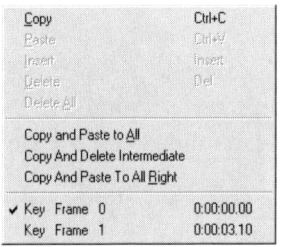 the last several months. It means, "Make every keyframe match this one." It's a great way to re-sync all keyframes or start from scratch.

Effects Tracks

Each effect applied to the clip appears in this track list. The effects themselves, just like tracks on the timeline, also have mute and solo buttons. The buttons along the bottom allow you to add, remove, or change the order of effects.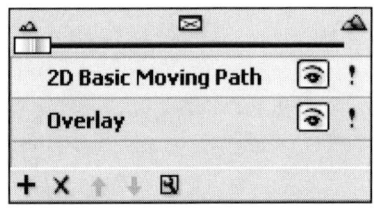

Note: you can only change the order *within* an effects group, not the order of the groups themselves. Therefore the order of the Moving Path and Overlay cannot be changed but the order of the video filters (within the Video Filter group) can be changed. This order matters, as we'll see later.

The last button looks like a little wrench. Click it and you'll display the corresponding dialog box for editing this effect. At first, this might be confusing. Take a look. For the DiffuseGlow filter, the Effects Manager displays these keyframable settings:

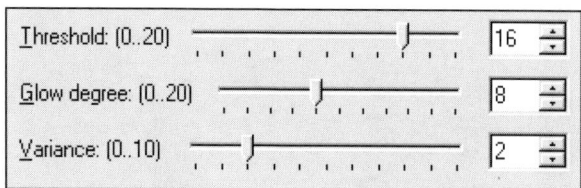

If you click the little wrench you get access to these settings:

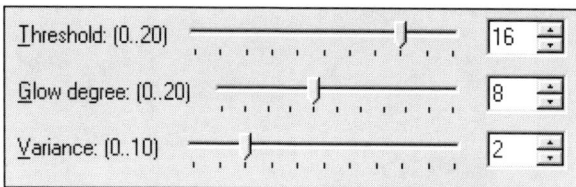

Hmmm... *what the heck's the difference?* Well, in this example, nothing, which is why this might all seem confusing on the surface.

The wrench brings up what we call a *legacy* dialog box. This is how all effects were handled in prior versions (before the Effects Manager) and they are retained for backward compatibility. While these two are identical, not all of them are, and you may find yourself in a situation where you have to use a legacy dialog.

I would hazard to guess that in the future we'll just have a single interface for editing effects. But these kinds of inconsistencies are found everywhere. I mean, take the keyframe controller for example. The Effects Manager isn't the only place where you can edit keyframes. Here are other keyframe controllers:

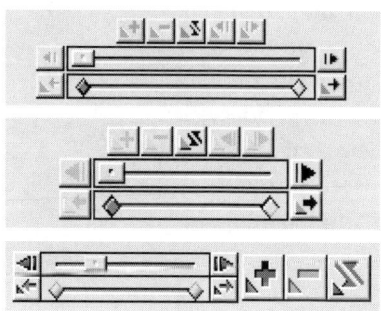

Sure, they all *basically* look the same, but each has its own personality.

Not only that, but these other keyframe controllers have very tiny controls: the very thing the Effects Manager was meant to do away with. They seem to be a relic of the 800x600 displays of days gone by.

The Production Library

Here you have one-stop shopping for pretty much everything. The objects found in the library can be divided into two broad groups: *things Video Editor puts there* and *things you put there*.

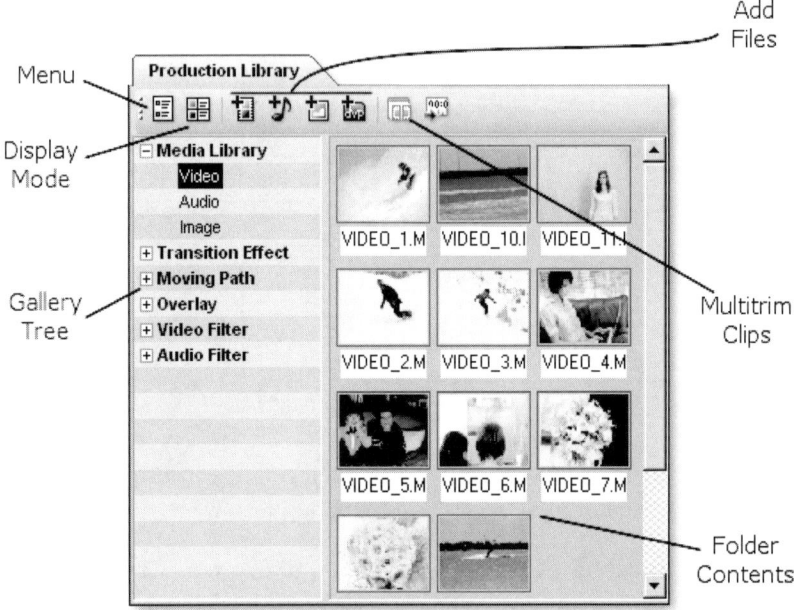

As you can tell from the left-hand tree, this is where Video Editor stores all its effects, paths, and filters. It also ships with a few default video, audio, and image clips that you can use in projects or to try out editing techniques without needing your own clips. (For example, the clip VIDEO_11.MPG is useful for trying out green screens without needing to go through the hassle of setting up your own.)

Your own media clips may be stored in these existing Video, Audio, and Image folders, or you may create your own. Right click an existing folder and this popup menu displays. Select Create to add your own folders. There's **nothing magical** about the Video, Audio, and Image folders that restrict their contents to files of those types. In other words, you can put anything in any folder. If you find this division meaningless, feel free to do your own thing.

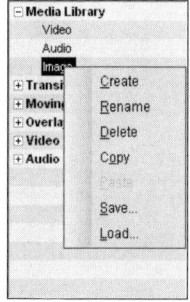

You're not limited to saving media clips to the library. Even though transitions, moving paths, etc. are all built-in objects, Video Editor lets you customize almost all of them and save them in the Production Library for later use.

For example, if you've taken a standard transition and customized it, click the Add button. You'll get this dialog box where you can give it a name and description. Click OK and it will appear in the Custom folder under the Transition gallery.

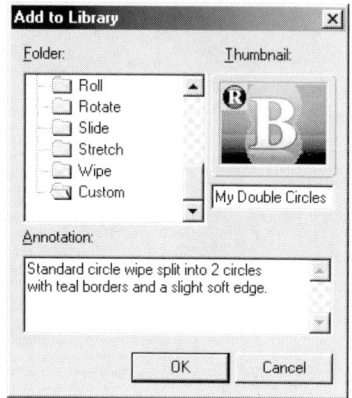

You can also export your customizations. Right-click a folder and select the Save command. This will export the settings to a file. Doing so allows you to share them with other MediaStudio Pro users, or to back them up if you have to reinstall your system or migrate to a different PC.

Do I Have to Use It?
Good question. Like any good politician, I'll reply, "yes and no." Yes, you'll have to use it when it comes time to add a transition, moving path, or filter to your project. As far as storing customizations or your own media clips, that's totally your call. I've created hundreds of projects without ever dropping a clip in the Production Library. If you're wondering why I would pass up this wonderful tool, I have a simple answer: *overhead*. Let me explain.

Let's say I have a couple dozen clips for a project. I can drag and drop them into the timeline directly from Windows or I can double-click a track to open an Insert dialog box to place them in my project. Theoretically it would be easier to drag them from the Production Library to the timeline because then I would never have to leave the interface. But how do my clips get to the Library in the first place? Well, I can drag and drop them directly from Windows or I can open an Insert dialog box to place them in the Library. Sound familiar? All I've really done is added an extra step. Worse, I'll just have to go and delete them when I'm done with my project, since I rarely re-use clips between projects and the Library would get too cluttered. But this is completely a personal call. You may find it indispensable. Further, you may have *lots* of files which you use in multiple projects.

The Project Tray

This is very similar to the Production Library, but whereas objects in the Production Library apply to all projects, the Project Tray is only for the current project.

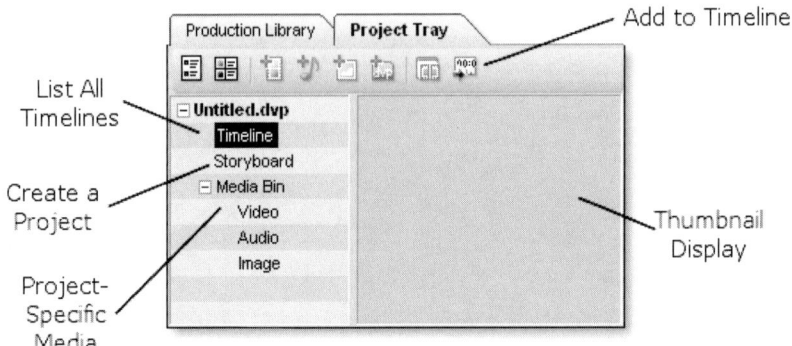

Note the project name at the top of the gallery tree ("Untitled.dvp"). This is somewhat misleading since everything in this tray is stored in a file with a veproj extension. Therefore, if I were to save this project, two files would be created: Untitled.dvp and Untitled.veproj. If you delete the veproj file, your project will still open, however the Project Tray comes up empty.

There are only three galleries in the Project Tray: Timeline, Storyboard, and Media Bin.

Timeline
When the Timeline gallery is selected one thumbnail will appear for each timeline *other than* the main timeline. Clicking on the thumbnail will automatically jump to that timeline.

Media Bin
This is identical to its Media Library counterpart in the Production Library with one very important distinction: it only applies to the current project. Remember my complaint about thirty seconds ago over Production Library overhead? Problem solved! I rarely bothered with it before because I never wanted to clear out the Library after every project. But now, with unlimited *project-specific* libraries, that's suddenly a non-issue.

To think, after all these years, I finally have a really good reason to use in-program media storage.

Storyboard

I've saved this one for last because this is such a nice feature. If you populate the storyboard folder with clips and click the Add to Timeline button then Video Editor will automatically create a project for you, complete with transitions and synchronization.

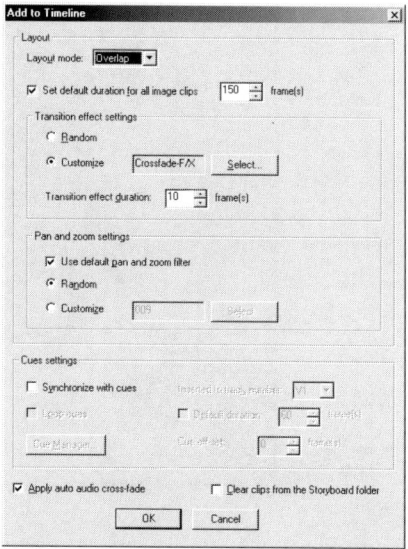

Check out these options! Your very first choice is to select Sequential or Overlap mode, which effectively asks, "Do you want transitions or not?" Nine out of ten times, this is probably "Yes" so select Overlap. When Overlap mode is selected, the Transition effect settings box becomes active. I don't recommend "Random" since this will leave your production with little aesthetic value. Best to leave the default at Crossfade, and then individually override transitions only where it makes sense.

I would also recommend *not* using the Pan and Zoom filter willy-nilly. It's the same problem with random transitions: drifting all over each frame in a haphazard fashion might make your audience reach for airsickness bags. I'll go out on a limb and guess this isn't what you want.

The last major setting is cue synchronization. If you've placed cues on the timeline, the Add to Timeline function will make attempts to synchronize transitions with these points. And if you don't have any timeline cues, you can add some with the Cue Manager button found here.

To get the best feel for how this feature works, I suggest loading up a few clips and give it a shot. Try the different options (even the ones I don't recommend) and see how they turn out.

Audio Mixing Panel

You can do plenty of mixing, overlapping, and volume control on your audio tracks directly from the timeline without ever having to use the Audio Mixing Panel.

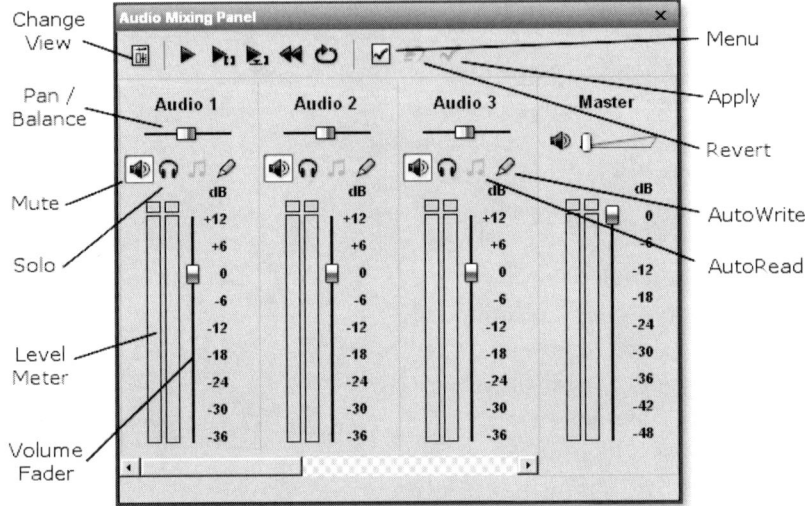

So in many ways, this can be considered an advanced tool. You may create a year's worth of projects and never do any advanced audio mixing. Others may use this all the time. It allows you do real time panning and volume control on single tracks or groups of tracks all at once. Additionally, if your project is changed from stereo to multi-channel surround sound, the mixer looks like this:

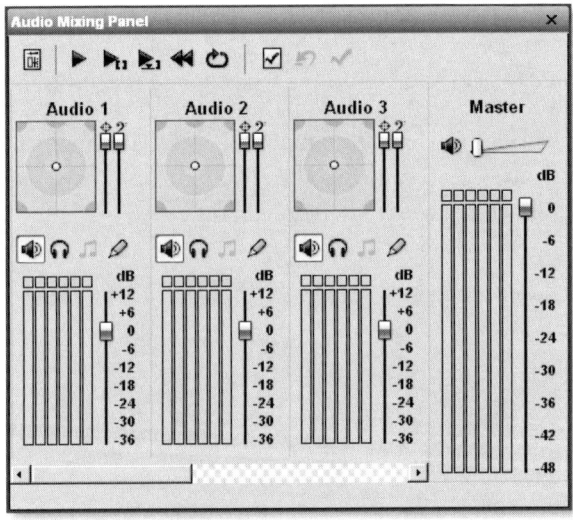

Chapter 2 • Video Editor Overview   63

The simple pan control has now been replaced with a virtual room. Move the yellow dot around the room to change the spatial positioning of that track.

In order to record changes, click the Options Menu button on the toolbar and make sure "Apply Audio Filter While Playing" is selected, as shown here. On the main window, click the little pencil to switch to Auto Write mode. When you press Play, the timeline begins to move and any volume or panning adjustments you make are re- 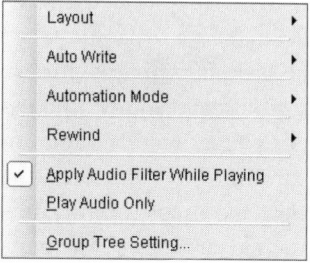 corded. When done, click the Apply button and your audio clip will look something like this:

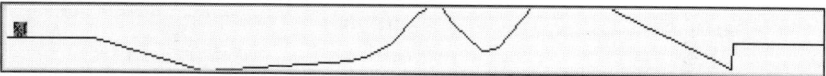

The small icon on the left shows you've recorded a mix for this clip. If you made any volume adjustments, then the volume line will reflect that. (Aren't mine wonderful?)

In order to apply changes to multiple tracks at once, use the Group Tree Setting dialog box from the Options Menu. In this case, I've grouped tracks Audio1 through Audio3 and Audio4 through Audio7. You can group by multi-selecting tracks and clicking the Group button, or just dragging and dropping the tracks right within the tree view. I prefer the latter, since it feels more intuitive.

Once grouped, the panning and volume controls for the grouped tracks will move in unison. When you click Apply, the changes will be applied to all grouped tracks at once.

Quick Command Panel

The Quick Command panel allows easy access to commonly used functions. It is divided into two parts: a custom area and a cached area.

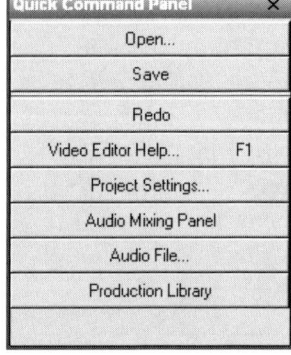

The custom area allows you to specify up to sixteen commands for quick access. Video Editor continually updates the cached area. As you execute various menu and tool button functions, the cached area changes to reflect the most recently used commands. The cached area can also be configured to store up to sixteen commands. To configure the Quick Command panel, right-click anywhere, and select Layout Options or Modify. Note, you can also save and load Quick Command panel custom settings. Saving these options is a good way to store your customized settings outside of Video Editor. This is useful if you ever need to reinstall the product, or if you have customized settings that you'd like to share with other users. You can display this window using the Window | Quick Command Panel command, or by clicking the ⚝ toolbar button.

Trim Window

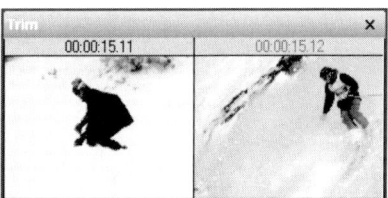

With stitch trim enabled, this window displays frames from two clips side-by-side. As shown here, you see the last frame of one clip and the first frame of the adjacent clip, at the frame where they touch. It's very useful for tweaking trim points, especially so if you are zoomed out of the timeline. To use this feature, set your trim option to "Stitch." (Use the Edit | Trim Options command. See also page 131 for complete information on Trimming and Trim Options.) Now you can drag the touch-point between the two clips and see how your editing affects the last frame of one clip and the first frame of the next. You can display this window using the Window | Trim Window command.

To be honest, you'll probably never display this window by itself. Screen real estate is often at a premium and all of the Trim Window functionality has now been incorporated directly into the Preview Window.

I know I never use it any more.

Chapter 2 • Video Editor Overview

Window Shortcut Keys

Keyboard shortcuts can be quite handy. In a busy work environment, you may lose track of a window that's already open. It may even be completely hidden behind other windows. If you remember the keyboard shortcuts, you can bring a window to the top instantly.

Preview Window
Ctrl+2

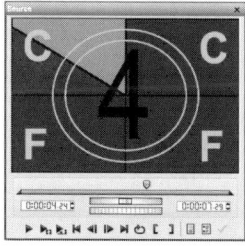
Source Window
Ctrl+3

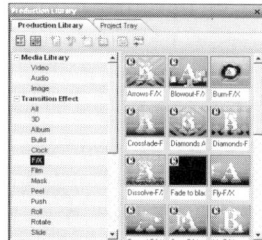
Production Library
Ctrl+4

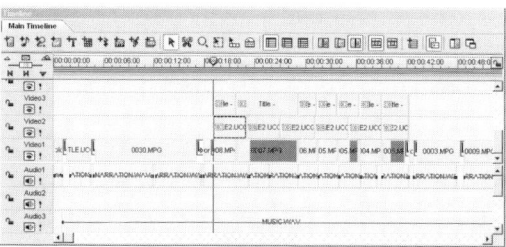
The Timeline
Ctrl+1

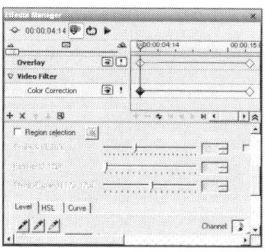
Effects Manager
Ctrl+8

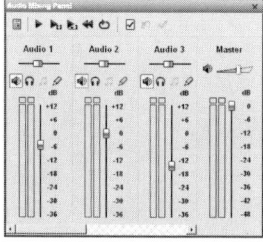
Audio Mixing Panel
Ctrl+7

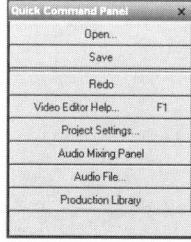
Quick Command
Ctrl+5

Trim Window
Ctrl+6

So Is That Everything?

Hardly! This is, of course, just an overview. The point isn't to hit on every single possible Video Editor feature, but instead to touch on the most important (or—at the very least—the most obvious) points. For example, we've barely mentioned the integrated DVD authoring tool. We haven't discussed a tenth of the things you can do to a video clip, including freeze frames, reverse play, speed changes, and so on. I mean, just look at the context-sensitive menu displayed when you right click on a video clip.

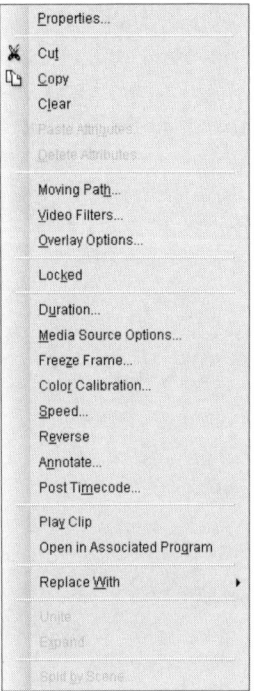

At this point you should have a solid concept of what Video Editor is, what it's for, and what it can do. The rest of the book is all about learning new concepts by building on previous concepts. If there's anything you're unsure of at this point, go back and read it again. It's important to feel comfortable with each topic before moving on.

3

An Overview of Everything Else

The remaining tools are Video Capture, Audio Editor, and DVD Movie-Factory. It's time to meet them.

Video Capture

To be perfectly honest, this is an optional component. Not that capturing video is optional in and of itself, but that there are other ways of getting raw footage from the outside world onto your computer.

Certainly some hardware packages come with their own capture software, and you may find a preference for the native tools. But first and foremost is Video Editor itself. Although we didn't discuss it last chapter, Video Editor includes an integrated video capture component, allowing you to bring in video from the outside world without having to leave the editing workbench.

For this reason the Video Capture tour we're about to embark upon is going to be a bit odd. There's a tremendous amount of overlap between the stand-alone Video Capture program and the integrated video capture tools in Video Editor. Even some of the parts that look different only *look* different but otherwise behave exactly the same.

Therefore as we discuss the topic of "video capture" I will be talking about both of these tools, only noting differences where appropriate.

So let's start with the basic feature list. You can:

- Capture from many different video sources and formats.
- Import data from a DVD.
- Control digital video devices.

- Perform seamless video capture, allowing capture of an unlimited amount of video, in 4 GB chunks for FAT32 file systems.

- Capture DV directly to MPEG or WMV formats.

- Batch capturing, DV tape scanning, and scene detection.

- Color calibration with a Waveform Monitor and Vectorscope.

Let's start by comparing the interfaces. Video Editor's integrated capture module is accessed via the Capture | Video Capture command.

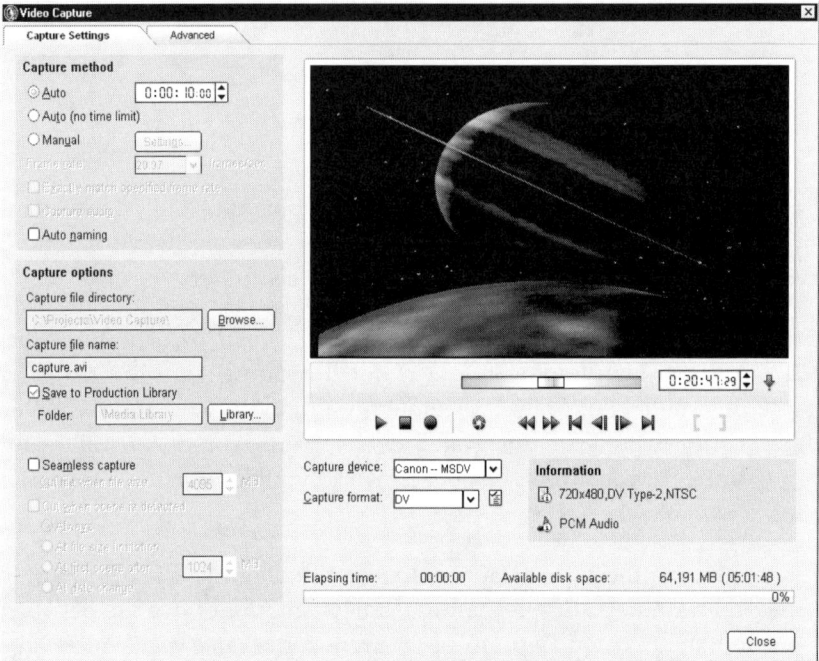

Most visible is the capture window. It doesn't look a whole lot different from the Source Window in Video Editor. You have an output display, a shuttle control, a timecode box and basic VCR controls. Below that you'll find various input and output controls regarding the capture device, formats, and available disk space.

On the left are capture settings and options. The **Auto** setting lets you specify a capture time limit. Below that is an option with no time limit. The **Manual** setting lets you capture odd sequences, like one frame every second for 30 seconds.

Beyond that you can specify the capture directory, file name, and whether or not to save it in the Production Library.

Chapter 3 • An Overview of Everything Else   69

Now take a look at the stand-alone Video Capture program:

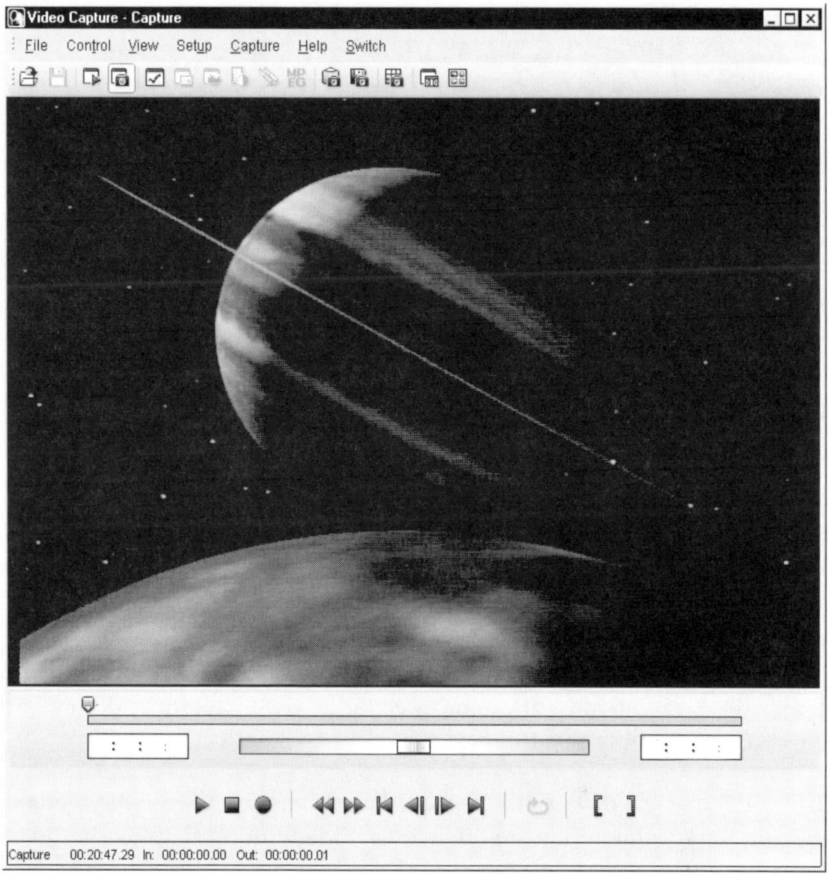

[Screenshot: Video Capture - Capture window showing planet/moon image with playback controls. Status bar reads: Capture 00:20:47.29 In: 00:00:00.00 Out: 00:00:00.01]

It looks quite similar to the capture window area on the last page, except larger. Pressing F5 initiates the capture process by displaying this op-

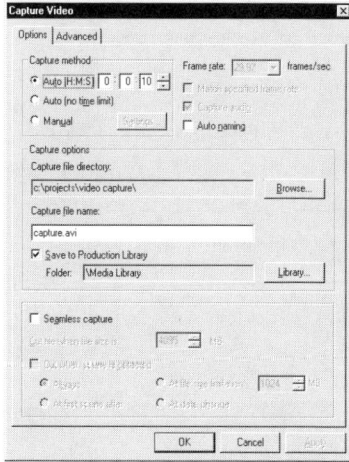

tions dialog box. This also looks remarkably similar to the capture options on the left hand side of the integrated video capture module shown on the last page.

The only difference is look and feel. Functionally, they're identical. I prefer the integrated version primarily because having them both displayed at the same time is a benefit. The fewer modal dialog boxes, the better.

There is an advanced tab for both, once again with remarkably similar buttons and functions:

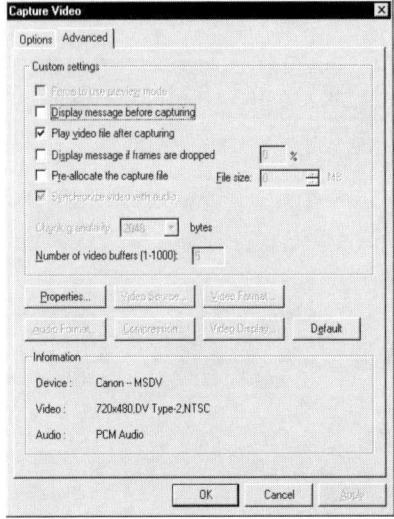 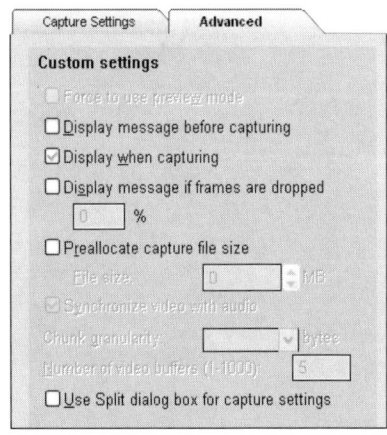

You may be thinking to yourself at this point, "If the two capture programs are so similar, why do both exist? Is there any reason to use one over the other?" Well, if you actually *are* thinking that right now, then I must be some kind of mind reader. Please let me know at mind.reader@getting-results.com.

The only answer I have right now is, "I don't know." To my knowledge, the only thing Video Capture offers over Video Editor's capture is Color Calibration. But this works only for analog sources and even then is useful only when you have color bars. Analog sources with color bars are a rarity for the vast majority of MediaStudio Pro users. We're largely a group of serious hobbyists and semi-pros. Most of us are shooting DV with one eye open for HDV. Video capture in these formats is a file transfer. There's nothing to calibrate.

If you want my educated guess, standalone Video Capture won't exist in the next major version of MediaStudio Pro. I think we'll have just this one "overlap" version, where most (but not all) of VC's features made it into VE, and it was kept around for that very reason.

But enough of that. Let's get down to the business of actually capturing video, no matter which way we choose to get it!

Capturing

Before you can begin capturing, your hardware must be ready to go. The most important thing to establish is: *what are you capturing*? Do you have a DV camcorder? An S-VHS camera? A VCR or TV source? Maybe a webcam? *What* you're capturing will dictate *how* you capture it. There are three main transports for importing video: FireWire, analog, and USB.

FireWire

Digital Video (DV/HDV) sources travel down a pipe called *FireWire*[4]. If you're not sure if your source device supports this, check the documentation. Odds are it will, though. This is easily the most common transport for video editing today.

What Do I Need? You'll need a DV or FireWire cable, as shown here. You will also need a special hardware card in your computer. If you don't have one, looking for one can be a bewildering experience. You'll find complete "solutions" costing hundreds or even thousands of dollars. Save your money. All you need is a simple PCI FireWire interface card. I've seen them for as low as $10. This allows your DV camera to interface with the computer, and the software does the rest.

Analog

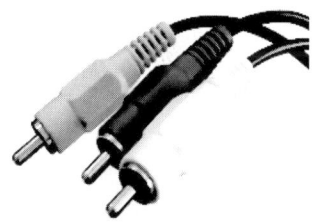

This category includes virtually all video equipment produced between 1821 and 1995. This includes, but is not limited to, VHS, S-VHS, 8mm, Hi8, and BetaSP. These devices will output video using the RCA jacks (shown here) or via an S-video cable.

What Do I Need? The theoretical answer is simple: some sort of hardware/software combination to read analog video signals and create video files on your computer. Exactly *how* you do this is dependent upon a large number of variables. A whole section is devoted to this starting on the next page.

---

[4] FireWire is Apple Computer's trademarked name for their IEEE-1394 implementation. (Sony calls theirs I.Link.) While IEEE-1394 is the proper term, the fact is, it wouldn't be what it is today without Apple's efforts. Therefore, I use the name with the biggest mindshare: FireWire.

USB

Video via USB, or *universal serial bus*, comes in a couple different flavors. Web cams commonly use USB interfaces, so you can go directly from a live source into your computer. There are also video capture devices that can read analog signals, convert, and send them down the USB wire.

What Do I Need? The nice thing about USB is that it's the epitome of "plug and play." If you have a USB device, then all you need is a cable to go between the device and your computer. If all your USB ports are taken, you will also need a hub, allowing you to plug in additional devices. But after that, it pretty much takes care of itself.

The downside to USB is speed. Full-frame video is a *lot* of work for this pipe, especially if you have other USB devices plugged in as well.

Capture Setup

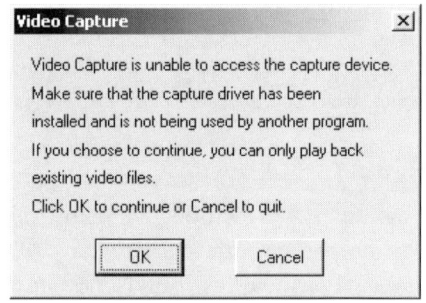

When you first launch Video Capture it attempts to access your capture device. If it can't find one, it will let you know about it in no uncertain terms.

If you're pretty sure you do have a capture device connected and working, then check all connections. I don't know how many times I've scratched my head over this one, only to find the FireWire cable ever so slightly pulled out of the jack on the camcorder. Another tip: make sure your camcorder is on. It's common for cameras to have "power saver" features and they'll shut off after a period of inactivity.

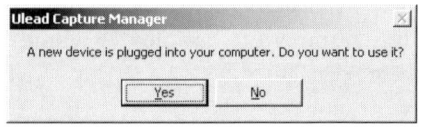

If your problem was just a bad connection, upon fixing it you'll get this message. Most definitely click "Yes" and you'll now be able to successfully move on and start capturing.

DV Capture

DV is about as easy as it gets. Because of the strict specifications of the format (fixed frame size, color depth, and data rate) you don't really have any say in the matter. This is a good thing. For this reason, Video Format, Audio Format, Color Calibration and other setup menu items are unavailable.

Well, I shouldn't say you don't have *any* say in the matter. You do get to pick the DV type. If all the other video file formats weren't confusing enough, you now also have *two* subtypes within DV. Without going into the ugly details, DV Type-1 is the exact same format that your camera uses. All DV Type-2 does is change the way it internally stores the video and audio data. Because not all software understands the Type-1 format, this choice allows for greater compatibility.

DV also gives you built-in device control. This means you can play, stop, rewind, and fast-forward your camcorder directly from the Video Capture interface. Device control also opens the door to another benefit: **batch capture**.

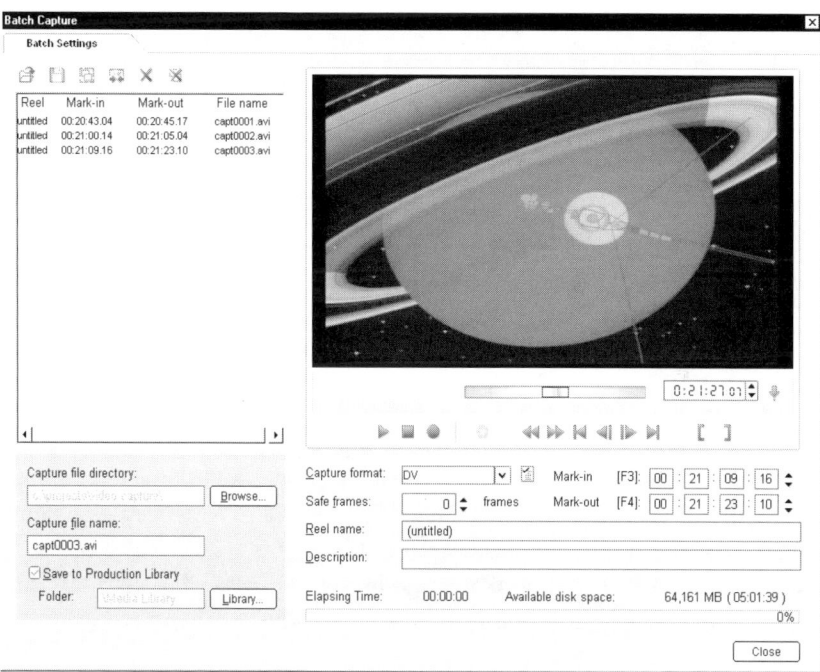

Batch capturing allows you to specify a list of scenes you want to capture from tape. By playing the source video and marking in and out points while it plays, you create a batch capture list. Once you've finished your list, press Record. Video Capture will find all your listed scenes on tape, and transfer them to your PC completely hands free. This is a real time saver. It allows you to make one quick pass through your tape, then leave all the mechanics to the software.

The compliment to batch capture is **DV tape scan**. This lets you forget details like exact in and out points and instead allows scene changes to drive the capturing.

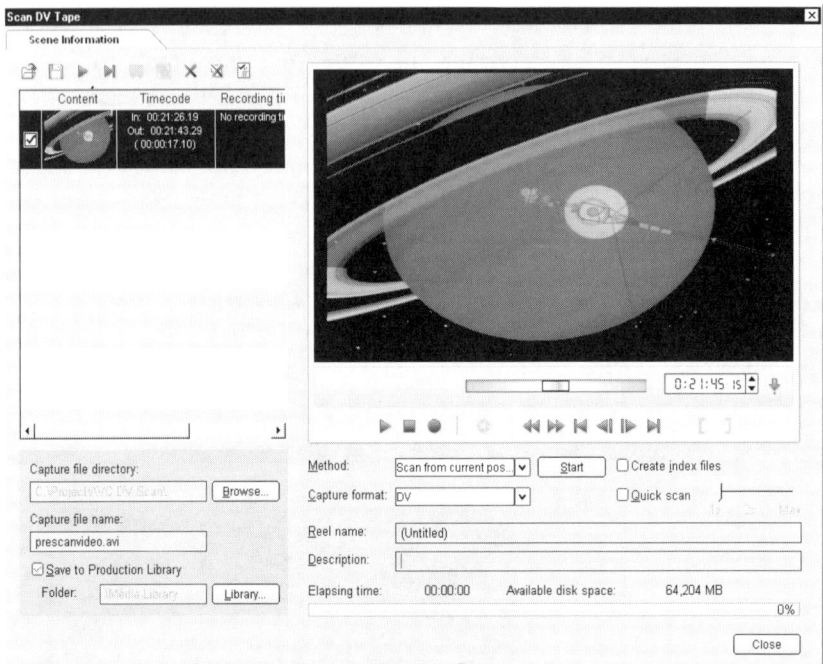

After scanning some or all of your DV tape, it will present you with a list of scenes. It shows a thumbnail of the scene's mark-in point. It shows the timecode for the exact in and out points. It may even show you the date/time of the recording, depending on your hardware.

Oh what I wouldn't have given for this kind of technology ten years ago. The pains I went through analog capturing from S-VHS tapes via a vintage MJPEG capture card. I'm sure many of you experienced the same things I did (or worse). It's easy to forget how far we've really come in such a short amount of time. The only thing that could be easier than this will be when the cameras themselves write to non-linear storage.

That isn't to say analog capture is *completely* a thing of the past...

Analog Capture

It gets more interesting in the analog realm. Because there are more variables, there are more settings, and consequently more manual control over the digitization process. These features start at the Video Format menu command and continue down to Color Calibration. This area, however, is *very* dependent upon specific hardware.

For example, this is the Video Format dialog box for my old Bravado 2000 capture card. Everything on here is specific to that hardware: the image dimensions, field order, and compression settings. If you're using different analog capture hardware, then you'll see different settings.

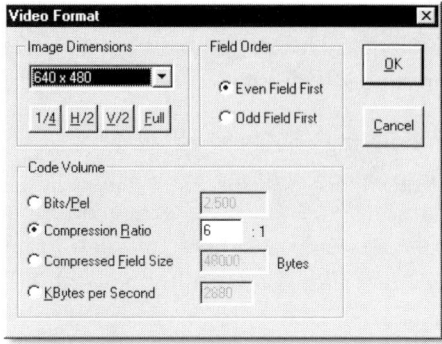

Analog Capture via DV

It's common for modern DV camcorders to accept analog input. If your camcorder can do this: great! You've just made analog capture almost as easy as DV capture. If your camcorder can't, external A/D converters are available. What makes this such a great approach is that the camera hardware takes care of all the conversion headaches for you. By the time it hands the video over to the FireWire port, you're back to a simple file transfer. The only thing you don't have is device control, but that's a small price to pay for getting old analog video into a DV world.

I remember when I first moved from analog video to DV, I primarily worried about two things:

- Am I going to have to buy an expensive video capture card?

- How am I going to capture miles of old Hi8 footage?

I was thrilled, of course, to find out that my "video capture card" was nothing more than a ten dollar FireWire PCI card. This made the days of the $1,000 analog card seem like a lifetime ago. I was even more thrilled to find out the camera could do the A/D conversion for me. With my worries erased, I never looked back.

Compression and File Size

On page 25, we first discussed the concept of compression. Setting the compression ratio is where you decide exactly how much data is thrown out. The higher the ratio, the more data is thrown out. The more data you throw out, the smaller your file will be. The smaller the file, the worse it looks. A lower compression ratio preserves more of your image, but creates larger files.

A common statement made by newcomers to video is, "My video files are huge!" When you're used to dealing with files in kilobytes and megabytes, it can be alarming to suddenly have single files measured in gigabytes. The next most alarming discovery, of course, is that a one minute video file can be ten times as large as a two minute video file.

So how big should files be? Well, it all depends on the file format and compression settings. Files with an AVI extension generally run larger than files with an MPG extension. (It should also be noted that the file extension only describes the file format, and not the video data format: e.g., AVI files can certainly hold MPEG video. Refer back to page 28 on *containers*.)

Here's a video file size guideline. All clips are assumed to be one minute long and thirty frames per second and without audio. For certain formats, audio will increase the file size to some degree:

Compression	Extension	Frame Size	File Size
None (Uncompressed)	AVI	720x480	1,800 MB
HDV	AVI	1440x1080	210 MB
DV	AVI	720x480	210 MB
DVD (MPEG2)	MPG	720x480	28 MB
VCD (MPEG1)	MPG	352x240	10 MB
Indeo 5 (85% quality)	AVI	720x480	3 MB
Windows Media Video V8	WMV	320x240	1 MB

When capturing in an analog format, your job is to find that "sweet spot" where image quality and file size come into balance. Your overall goal is to get the best quality you can, based on what your hardware can support. So there are no hard and fast rules. The best thing you can do is to try out some test captures at various compression levels. And try it out on different kinds of footage too. Compression effectiveness is dependent on the images being compressed.

Compression and Image Quality

Now let's explore how compression affects the image quality. Consider the uncompressed image on the right. Starting on the next page, we will zoom in on three different versions of this image. The first is at a 15:1 compression ratio, the next is at 30:1, and the last is at 90:1.

Chapter 3 • An Overview of Everything Else

Here's the above area enlarged and shown at a 15:1 compression ratio. MJPEG compression shows the most artifacts with high-contrast areas. If you look at the edges between the tower and the background sky, you see how it becomes mottled and blocky. "Blocky" is the key: because blocks are the basis for this compression algorithm. It subdivides the picture into smaller areas and calculates what single color best represents that entire area.

On the right is that same area, but shown at a 30:1 compression ratio. Here the blocks are far more evident: details become lost, and the picture looks "noisy" when played back to your television. The noise is due to the fact that each frame is compressed independently. Slight variations from one frame to the next will result in a "shimmering"

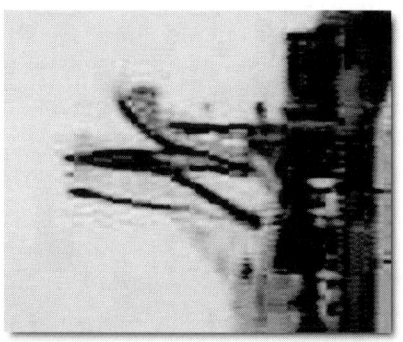

effect when the video is played back at normal speed. While this video will take up less space than the previous, you must decide if it's worth it.

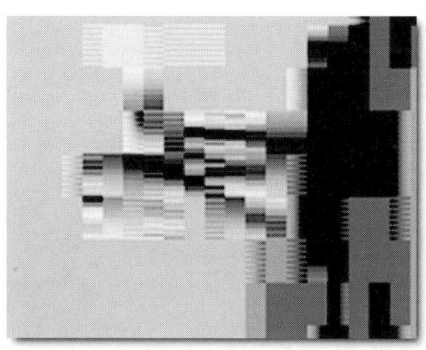

At 90:1 compression, the image becomes unrecognizable. Here the artifacts of the compression algorithm are plain to see.

In real life you will probably use compression ratios in the 5:1 to 10:1 range. S-VHS still looks good at 6:1 or 7:1. VHS looks good up to 10:1. You may find for your own needs that 12:1 or even higher is acceptable. Different source images are treated differently, so you have to find your own sweet spot.

You can easily see why Digital Video is so popular. Among its many benefits is *not* having to worry about compression ratios. It's all built into the spec. Doesn't matter how good or bad it is—it's out of your hands!

A Word on MPEG

When setting up video capture, you have the option to specify the captured file format. I recommend setting the capture format to match your video *source*—not your video *destination*. And since I'm making the assumption that most readers will be using DV as a source, that means rarely, if ever, capturing directly to formats in the MPEG family (which include VCD and DVD). You might ask why, given that this is such a big marketing point. After all, the typical MPEG benefits are:

1. No conversion later on

2. Smaller file sizes.

Why would you want the opposite? Why would you want lengthy conversions later on and larger file sizes? Well, I'll tell you. First up, point number 1: "no conversion later on." This is *only* true if you don't do anything to the video in between. If you capture to MPEG, then put a title on top of it within Video Editor, it's not MPEG anymore. It's now a *project* and a new video file must be created—one that combines the original video with the new overlay text. So you're not really saving anything. More importantly, let's also say that you'd like to burn a DVD for yourself, and give VCDs to your friends, and then post a small version on your web site. Which one of these formats should you have captured in?

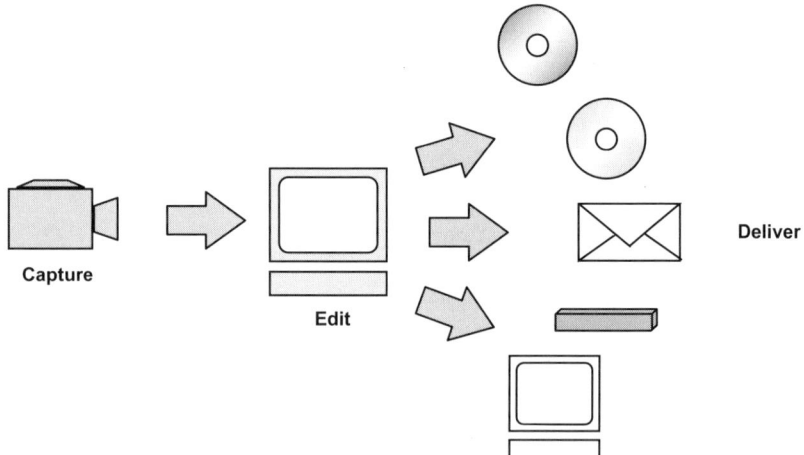

MPEG isn't really the best format for this, as you'll find out in the next paragraph. But hopefully the diagram gives you a good enough idea of why keeping the source and edit formats in top-quality is a good thing. It allows you to always work in the most optimal format and generate any output format you want later on. And if that takes a little extra time to "convert" later on, it's more than worth it.

Next up, point number 2: "smaller file sizes." The reason MPEG has such small file sizes is that it's pretty smart about what image data it stores with every frame. Let's illustrate this using the traditional "talking head" example. If you film someone speaking, about the only thing moving is his or her mouth. If the speaker is behind a podium, or sitting in a chair, or in front of a wall, those are all static things that don't change much between frames. So if most of a frame is the same as the previous frame, it doesn't bother to store this data. This, combined with other mathematical tricks, does make for some nice file sizes. Here's the catch: this is optimized for storage and playback, not for editing. If you edit a "frame" of an MPEG video, you may have to go back one, two, or more frames to find all the data that makes up that image. Editing MPEG directly can be problematic. It works, certainly, but it isn't optimal. The same goes for using compressed audio formats on the timeline. Use WAV files over MP3s for all the same reasons you'd use a DV file over MPEG.

Further, have you ever noticed how long it takes to encode video data into an MPEG format bound for VCD or DVD? Ever wonder how video capture can seemingly do the same thing *on the fly?* Why the gigantic difference? Again, it comes down to quality. You will get much better results if you let the encoding engine take its time.

So, given all that, when *would* you want to capture straight to MPEG? Well, as I said, if your captured file **is** your finished file. If I want to put a home video on DVD without any editing (perhaps because you have 472 hours of home movies, and you simply don't have time to edit) then this is a perfect time to capture directly to MPEG. Then all the benefits are benefits again. Using DVD MovieFactory (explained later) you'll just add the video, tell it to not bother converting compliant files, and bam: no time spent re-encoding the video. Same with Windows Media. It's a good format for the web, in spite of portability issues. If you know whatever you capture is going straight to your web site, then it's in your best interest to capture directly to that format.

Audio Editor

To be honest, Audio Editor has the fewest unique features of the suite. It's always felt to me like it gets the least amount of attention. Not that this is necessarily bad, because it takes care of the basics quite well. Nonetheless, I can't help but get the feeling that Audio Editor was left on Ulead's doorstep as a baby and they've kept it in the cupboard under the stairs ever since.

The primary Audio Editor features are:

- Capture audio through your system's sound hardware.

- Copy (or *rip*) tracks from CDs.

- Convert audio files between different formats and sampling rates.

- Allow you to view and edit waveform data with a large canvas.

- Save cues in the audio file to be read by Video Editor later.

- Split stereo tracks into two mono tracks, combine two mono tracks into stereo, or even convert a mono track to stereo.

- Choose from built-in effects or DirectX Audio and DMO Audio Effect plug-in effects, including noise reduction.

- Change volume, pitch, speed, and direction.

Audio Format Settings

You have two ways to create a new file. The first is to select the File | New... command. The second is to simply begin recording with no documents open. Audio Editor will automatically create a new document for you before it begins recording. Two quick ways to begin recording: pressing Ctrl+R or clicking the big red dot at the bottom of the window.

Using File | New command displays the dialog box you see on the right. It defaults to CD-quality audio, although in this DV age it would be nice to see preset support for 12-bit 32 kHz and 16-bit 48 kHz audio.

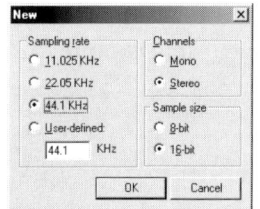

If you change these attributes, the program won't remember them. So you'll have to set them each time you start Audio Editor.

If you instead use the Record command, you will see the Sound Selection dialog box. Oddly enough, this dialog box does have settings for 32 kHz and 48 kHz rates, but only choices for 8 or 16 bit samples, and only mono or stereo channels.

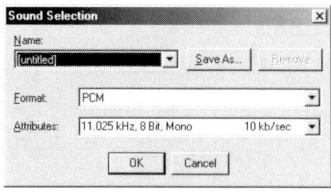

Once you've set up your audio format, you can begin recording. You'll have to make sure your input levels are correctly set. I can't go over the details here, since these settings are primarily hardware-dependent. Each audio card will typically come with its own calibration software. Check your hardware documentation for more information.

Audio Editor Features

Once you've loaded or recorded audio, the main window looks something like this.

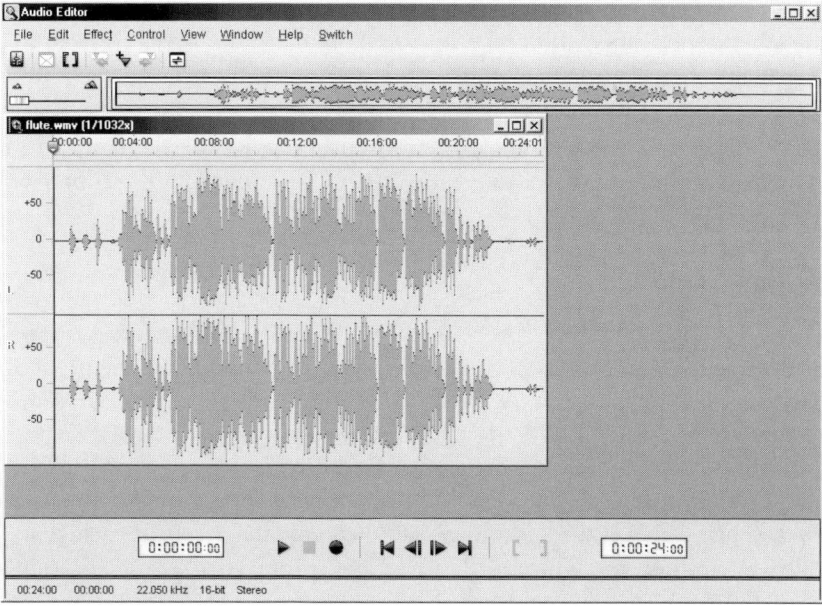

For every open file you have, you will see a window split into one or more channels. This example shows a stereo file: two channels, one for left and one for right. The area right under the toolbar shows the entire waveform at all times and the gray box tells you which portion of the wave file is currently displayed in the document window below. The vertical line shows the current position within the file. The standard "VCR" controls are along the bottom.

Cues

Once an audio file has been recorded, the first thing I like to do—particularly if it's a music file—is mark it with cues. Unless your audio is simply going to be a backdrop to your video, and the ins and outs don't matter, you'll want cues.

Why not just use Video Editor to cue it? Well, you can, but you're already here, so why not get it out of the way? If you need a better argument than that, if you mark your cues here, the audio file itself contains the cues. If you mark the cues within Video Editor, only that project will contain the cues. If you use the same audio in a different project, you'll have to re-cue it. For these reasons, I always cue the file within Audio Editor.

Editing Functions

You have the basic cut, copy, and paste editing features within Audio Editor. You can move data around within a file or between files, using the Windows clipboard to store information along the way. You can insert blank space into files, split stereo files into two mono files, and merge mono files into stereo. There are several paste options: you can insert the clipboard data into a file, or you can replace (or even mix with) the existing material. You can create a brand-new file from the clipboard data as well.

Audio Effects

There are several audio effects, such as Amplify, Normalize, Reverse, Pitch, Fade, Pan, and Echo/reverb effects. As previously mentioned, they're functional, but don't look for anything overly fancy. If you're unfamiliar with any of these terms, check the glossary.

I will mention one of my personal peeves here. The panning function doesn't *pan*. What it does is allow you to change the levels of each channel over time. If you run your left channel from 0 to 100, and the right from 100 to 0 what you'll get is a pseudo-panning effect, meaning the audio will appear to move from one channel to the other. However, this isn't actual panning, this is *balance*.

True panning allows you to take any mono track and position it anywhere within the stereo image. In other words, data in the left channel can be moved over to the right channel. I worked with audio and music for years before moving into video, so this always seemed strange to me.

One last note: audio effects are always applied to the current selection. If there is no selection, they are applied to the entire file. This is important to keep in mind, since "the current selection" and "the entire file" can be two very different things!

Viewing Audio Files

When you first open or record an audio file, you will see the entire file, as shown above. You'll often find that you need to view only certain parts of the file. There are a few ways to vary your audio "viewport."

You can zoom in or zoom out of the file using the corresponding View | Zoom commands. The keyboard shortcuts are the + and – keys *on the numeric keypad*. Pressing these keys on the main keyboard won't do anything. As you zoom in and out, you'll see the title bar of the document window change. The picture above shows a zoom level of (1/1032). The smaller the denominator the more you're zoomed into the file. If you're zoomed in as far as you can go, you'll see a value of 1x. This means there's a 1 to 1 relationship between the displayed samples (or, pixels) and the actual samples. The original 1/1032x means every pixel represents 1032 samples.

I use the Zoom commands only occasionally. Invariably, I zoom in and out of a file by selecting an area and pressing Ctrl+F. You select an area by clicking with the mouse and then dragging. The Ctrl+F command tells Audio Editor to fit the current selection to the window. If you press Ctrl+1, you'll automatically zoom back out to see the entire file.

One very handy feature is the ability to toggle between the current and previous zoom levels. Do this by pressing Ctrl+T. The arrow keys and the PageUp and PageDown keys move your viewport over the file (but not the PgUp and PgDn keys marked on the numeric keypad).

A more obvious zoom control should be familiar to your from our Video Editor timeline walkthrough. Slide that back and forth, or click anywhere along the slider line to change the zoom.

The last way to change the zoom size is by directly changing the size of the gray viewport box below the toolbar. The best way to get a feel for these things is to load up (or create) a file and play with them.

DVD MovieFactory

This program lets you complete your digital video journey by delivering on DVD, VCD, and SVCD formats. Its wizard-style interface guides you through the authoring process, from adding clips to creating menus, to burning the final disc. Additionally, it offers a large number of menu and layout customization options too, which might be more than enough to meet your immediate needs.

By default, you send one video clip to DVD MovieFactory and it appears on the timeline like so. Each clip you send to the storyboard becomes a Title in the final disk. If you check that little box above the storyboard, the first video clip will automatically play when the disk is inserted into the player. This will typically be your logo or something frightening like:

By default, you get one menu in your project. Each title added to the project can have its own sub-menu if you add chapters to it. This is the nesting limit for DVD MovieFactory. It's also important to note you cannot create "standalone" menus. Each menu is either attached to the overall project or to a clip within the project. That's it.

Menu Example

Let's say you have the following four final, rendered videos, MyLogo.mpg, MyMovie.mpg, TheMakingOfMyMovie.mpg, and BloopersFromMyMovie.mpg.

Drop all four on the storyboard, check "First Play," and you have:

The MyLogo.mpg file obviously has no chapters. The blooper reel is short and isn't going to get any. The middle two files are significantly long to warrant chapters. Therefore, our project might be organized something like what's pictured here.

Each title can be divided into an arbitrary number of chapters. Chapters can be created in four ways: from cues stored in the file, at fixed intervals, by scanning for scene changes, or set manually.

This disc will have three menus. The first (or *top*) menu displays thumbnails for each of the three titles. The second menu displays thumbnails for the six chapters under MyMovie. The third and last menu has thumbnails for the three chapters of TheMakingOfMyMovie.

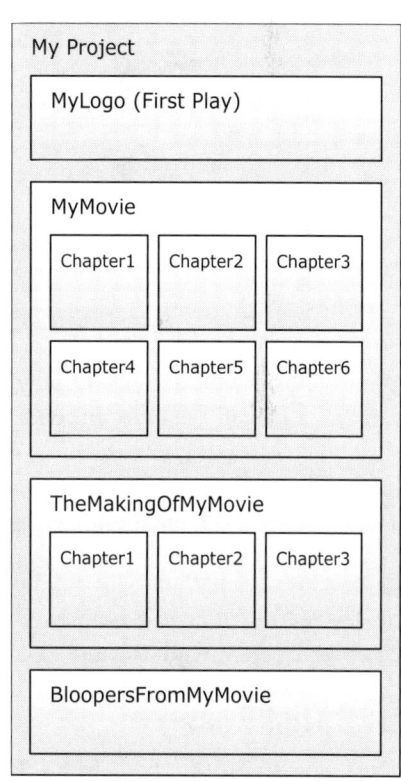

Each menu can be customized to a high degree. The menu backgrounds can be either still images or video files. Any font can be used for menu or thumbnail text. A wide variety of layouts are available for displaying thumbnails on the page. And if you don't like the default thumbnail positions, you can click and drag them around—even resize them.

And if you happen to, um ... "over customize" a menu, you can right-click and reset it back to the default at any time.

Previewing

Once your clips have been chosen, your chapter points set, and menus customized, you can preview your work.

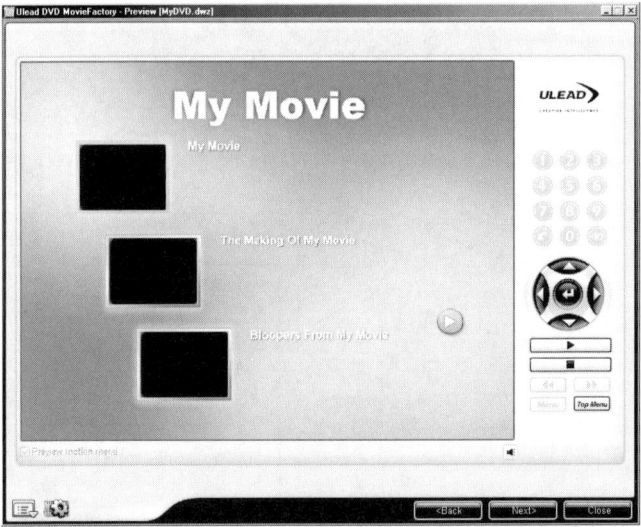

What you get here is a DVD player simulator. The control panel on the right side has all the basic functions of a DVD remote. The main window serves as your television screen. While it responds to mouse movements, if you *really* want to test it, try to restrict yourself to the remote controls. That gives you the most realistic experience.

Once you're satisfied with your work, you can burn your disc on the next screen. We won't bother with that now. This is just an intro. In Chapter 13 we'll walk through a complete authoring project.

DVD DiskRecorder

This allows you to record in the DVD-VR format. With traditional DVD burning, you burn the disk once and you're done. DVD-VR allows to you create a disk which can be edited later. You can add contents, edit menus, and even remove video. The format was developed to help replace the recording capabilities of videotape and is used primarily by set-top boxes and direct-to-DVD camcorders.

4
Failure to Plan is Planning for Failure

> Basic project planning and management skills because there's more to getting it right than just editing.

While it's entirely possible to produce great videos just by winging it, you'll increase the odds greatly with just a little bit of planning. And beyond just planning you'll find there are management tips and techniques to help you make the most of your resources: time, money, ... and disk space. By the end of the chapter, you'll be thinking about things you probably never thought to think about, and I think those thoughts will make you think the same thing I'm thinking.

The Planning Process

Over the years, we produced a fair number of dance school recitals. We shot with two, three, or even four cameras for the events. We've done both post-production editing and live switching right at the show. And over the years we've hauled a lot of gear from the parking lot to the auditorium (which, for some cruel architectural reason, is always at least a quarter mile hike). Given all that's involved for such a production, the only way to make sure you're ready for it is by having a checklist. There are more things to remember than our feeble memories can handle. Writing it down is the time-tested method for not forgetting stuff.

One would think that the last thing you would forget for an important event would be the videotape. I mean, it's *videotape* after all. Who could ever forget that? "Bring enough videotape" wasn't on the checklist for the same reason "put your pants on" wasn't on the checklist: it's just one of those things one does without requiring a reminder. You've probably already guessed by now. Yes, it happened to me. As you can expect, from that point on "bring enough videotape" was in the #2 spot on the checklist. Right after "put your pants on." I wasn't going to take any more chances.

The Idea

What do you want to do? Maybe you've always wanted to make a short film. Maybe your kids want to make their own music video. No matter what you want to do, it starts with an idea: a picture in your mind's eye of the end result. Once that's set, you can start your plan. The size and complexity of your plan will vary greatly with what you're trying to accomplish. Your plan may take you all of a minute, "put this stack of pictures on a video." If you've volunteered to videotape and distribute copies of your school's video yearbook then you've got a pretty big task ahead of you. In order to begin your plan, ponder your answers to the following five questions:

- *Is there a deadline?* This, more than anything else, will determine what you can and cannot do with your **project**. And while having a deadline can be stressful, it's also extremely helpful. As they say, "If it wasn't for the last minute, nothing would ever get done." A deadline is the great motivator.

- *Can you do it alone?* Involving other people always adds to the complexity of a project. If your project requires other people, they can be divided into two categories: in front of the camera or not. If they're in front of the camera, will they be following a script or just winging it? If they're not in front of the camera, what will they be doing? Is it just Aunt Tilly mailing you some family photos or will you require a small army of camera people to shoot lots of footage? Think about the people involved as you form your plan.

- *Is the footage new or old?* Are you editing footage you already have or does this project require acquiring new footage?

- *How fancy do you want it?* If your editing is going to be simple cuts from clip to clip, then editing won't be that big a deal. If you want to really spice it up, or synchronize it with music, or add 3D sequences, then you've obviously just upped the amount of work by quite a bit.

- *Can you spend any money on it?* If it's a simple home movie, then you probably don't want to spend any more than you already have. If you're doing something for-profit, you might have a small budget to work with—spending justified by the anticipated sales. Or if you're a serious hobbyist, you might not mind spending money on a production, even if it is just for your own personal gratification.

Chapter 4 • Failure to Plan is Planning for Failure   89

By genuinely thinking through these questions and your answers, you will mentally prep yourself for the task at hand. Not knowing the answers to these questions might land you in a tight spot later on.

When you're ready, *write down your plan.* Like the checklist, it's too easy to forget an important item without a written record. How you write it down is completely up to you. It's a combination of what you're comfortable with and the complexity of the project. A couple quick sentences on a post-it note might be all you need for a formal plan. If you're like me, you'll want to write an unnecessary, verbose ten-page essay. Everyone is different. Find what works best for you.

> *"Good plans shape good decisions. That's why good planning helps to make elusive dreams come true"*
> —Lester R. Bittel

Pre-production

In the film industry, pre-production refers to all the work done on a project before a single frame of film is exposed. This can include (but is no way limited to): finding locations, building sets, creating props and costumes, and casting. Basically, everything that *has* to be done before filming can begin. You certainly do not want to take time out of your filming schedule to build a set. Not that we, users of MediaStudio Pro, are going to build elaborate sets or hire actors. Regardless of scale, this phase still exists: getting as prepared as possible before you start shooting video.

In order to help grasp the planning process, we need to speak less of abstract theory and more about practical, real-life applications. A bit of reality will make all our tasks and concepts easier to understand.

For people like us, the home video enthusiast, there are three broad categories of video projects.

- *Events*. This is the standard "point and shoot" video project. The basic idea is that someone else is doing all the "stage" work and your role is that of recorder. Keep in mind, because you are indeed shooting someone else's work, make sure you **have permission** to record the event. This is very important!

- *Montages*. The montage is a set of sequenced, related clips, generally without words or narrative and with added musical accompaniment.

- *Productions*. By far the most complex of the three, this typically involves writing a script, finding locations, lighting, acquiring new footage, possible interviews, and ultimately combining video, stills, and audio to form a polished package.

These are rather loose definitions. And like many things in life, you'll come across hybrid projects that have attributes from more than one category.

Here are sample projects for each category. The list is by no means exhaustive.

Events	Montages	Productions
Weddings	Recent Vacations	Video Yearbooks
Dance Recitals	Holidays/Family Events	Family Histories
Instrumental Recitals	Class Reunions	School Reports
Choir Performances	Sporting Events	Biographies
Stagework or Plays	Parties or Gatherings	Documentaries
Keynote Speakers		Product Profiles
Meetings		Business Presentations
Classes or Seminars		How-To Videos
Demonstrations		Music Videos

In order to give you an idea of some of the possible pre-production work ahead, the next section lists some typical "to do" items for each project category. The list isn't meant to be exhaustive, nor is it hard-and-fast. Think of it more as a guideline, or—even better—a spark to help you develop your own work list. Every new project will always have some new aspect about it; something you've never done before.

Events

Pick Your Topic. This involves scouting out an event that interests you, or just showing up for the play your spouse volunteered you for without asking first. Yes, it's a sad fact of event videography: sometimes the event picks you.

Write Your Script. Even though you're shooting another production, you still need some sort of script. This helps you decide where to set up, what to shoot, when to pan, zoom, or otherwise change framing.

Pick Locations. I highly recommend studying the event's location beforehand.

Get Your Props. You're generally not responsible for props. But a nice, comfy chair *is* a good thing to have if you're anticipating a long, boring event.

Rehearse. If you can attend a dress rehearsal, **do**! If you're familiar with the event, you'll end up with **much** better camerawork than if it's your first time through. If it's a play or other scripted performance, get a script. If it's a recital, get a copy of the program. In short: **be prepared**!

Chapter 4 • Failure to Plan is Planning for Failure   91

Montages

Pick Your Topic. The topic for a montage often picks itself. For the ones I've done, they've either been spur-of-the-moment, one part of a larger project, or at the request of a friend or family member.

Write Your Script. A script is not generally necessary for a montage, other than having a general idea of what you're trying to accomplish. The order of video and image clips is normally dictated by topic, chronology, or both.

Pick Locations. n/a.

Get Your Props. n/a.

Rehearse. n/a.

Productions

Pick Your Topic. If you know the project will involve others, get commitments to your chosen topic from all involved parties up front. If you're on your own, make sure *you're* committed to yourself!

Write Your Script. The formats for production scripts will vary, but all will need to be fairly involved and well-thought out if you want to minimize problems.

Pick Locations. For a yearbook, you will have to plan for many locations for the whole year. A documentary might involve travel to a specific historic location.

Get Your Props. Find, build or buy anything you need to support the scenes in your project. Family histories might have family heirlooms. A product presentation will have various product samples. A school report might go better with period costumes.

Rehearse. You won't rehearse the entire project, but you will rehearse specific scenes. For example, do a warm up with the subject of an interview. Always tape the rehearsals. You might get an unexpected gem. Don't let it go by.

Production

In movie making, this is the primary phase of filming, known as *principal photography*. This involves shooting all scenes with all the actors. It's quite similar for us. This is the phase when we gather all our footage: everything after prep is complete and before the editing task begins.

> **That's a Lot of Film**
> In major film productions, principal photography lasts anywhere from six weeks to a few months. Both *Apocalypse Now* and *The Lord of the Rings* reportedly had 274 days of shooting spread out for more than a year, according to The Internet Movie Database.

Our production to do lists will, as expected, vary by project category. And, like the pre-production to do lists, these are just guidelines. Be sure to think through your *own* project, and make adjustments accordingly.

Events

Set Up. If you're lucky, you can set up during rehearsal and leave the cameras where they are. Otherwise, set up the day of the shoot. Leave plenty of time for finding the best position and angles. If more than one camera is involved, get a good spread. Duct tape plugs to outlets. If you can, always bring one more camera than you need. Events don't stop for you.

Sound. Test your audio, whether it's using the camera's mic or an external mic. In an auditorium, watch for speakers and avoid setting up in a loud "speaker zone."

Lighting. You won't have control over the lighting, but you will be able to adjust the camera for whatever lighting you encounter. All the rules for aperture and shutter speed still apply. For staged events, be prepared for spotlights and uneven lighting situations.

Filming. Begin rolling before you have to and stop rolling at least 10-15 seconds after you think you're done. Remember, you can always cut out stuff later, but you can't add it back in. Keep in mind all the rules and guidelines of composition. Don't forget to use an external monitor if at all possible.

Clean Up. The "camping rule" applies here: leave the site better than you found it. If you unwrapped cassettes, or used duct tape, or had any twist-ties, clean it all up. Pack up your gear carefully.

Montages

Set Up. Montages sure are easy! Here's yet another "n/a."

Sound. n/a.

Lighting. n/a.

Filming. Although you're going to be working with footage you've already shot, that doesn't mean you can't shoot better footage for the next time. Remember everything we discussed about lighting and composition to get the best source footage possible. Evaluate the footage you've just worked with and make notes about how to improve next time.

Clean Up. n/a.

> **Productions**
>
> **Set Up**. If coordinating with actors (even if it's grandma) make sure you're set up and ready to go when they are. Don't make them wait for you to unpack your camera and set up your tripod. Also, consider and adjust for natural light sources. Use test subjects where possible to make sure you're ready.
>
> **Sound**. Check your audio levels using headphones. Watch balance between subject(s) and background noise. Listen for interference, such as traffic outside or planes overhead.
>
> **Lighting**. During a production, you'll have more control over the lighting, both natural and artificial. If you have the means, look into lighting kits. Otherwise, work with what you have to the best of your ability.
>
> **Filming**. See boxes above. It all applies here. The only thing extra is that you might want to use a "clapper" to record shot information before each take. That can help you sort out footage during capture and editing.
>
> **Clean Up**. As with events, leave a site better than you found it. This goes whether you're shooting on public or private property, indoors or outdoors. Pack gear carefully for transportation.

Post-production

This is the filming industry term for, "everything that happens after filming is complete." This is where it's all done: editing, special effects, titles, credits, audio mixing, and so on. This is the reason you bought MediaStudio Pro. This is where you turn unwatchable source footage into your masterpiece.

> **Events**
>
> **Capture Video**. Due to the nature of most events, you will likely be capturing very long video clips. I recommend not batch capturing and instead do it manually. This gives you a chance to review the footage you took, and to take notes along the way that will help you edit later on. If you mark your ins and outs without watching everything in between, it's too easy to miss something.
>
> **Capture Audio**. There isn't usually any extra audio to be captured for events. If you shot with multiple cameras, you may have to take this step to decide which audio source to use for the production. That is, if you're not mixing multiple audio sources into one.
>
> **Edit**. Editing an event is minimal; generally limited to cutting out dead air, false starts, or just plain bad or unusable footage. Mixing footage from more than one camera, though, takes extra work. Multi-camera editing begins on page 321.

Montages

Capture Video. You can capture one scene at a time or capture many scenes in batch mode. Both involve marking the start and end points of the footage you want and capturing it. Capture more than you think you'll use, but not too much more. At this point it's taking up space on your computer. Additionally, as many montages employ still photos, you might also have scanning to do at this point.

Capture Audio. As montages are typically synchronized to music, there will be a distinctly separate audio capture step. If you're using music from commercial CDs, watch for copyright restrictions, especially if you're charging money for your product and/or distributing it.

Edit. Montage editing is relatively easy, and mainly involves properly trimming clips and getting them in the right order. How you do this can have a big impact on the emotional level of your production, but there's an exercise later on to discuss this very topic.

Productions

Capture Video. The rules for both events and montages still apply. You may find your productions have elements common to both. As with events, only use batch capture if you're sure you've thoroughly reviewed all your footage. The goal is to know your material as well as you can before editing. It will make editing decisions go much faster. Trust me!

Capture Audio. Again, same as the other two categories. You will use a mixture of audio from your cameras, any external recording device you might have used, and probably music for portions of the production.

Edit. Due to the potential interrelationship of video, stills, and audio, this could be a complex editing task. However, with the right script and footage, a simple cuts-only edit can have just as much impact.

Delivery

When everything is ready, it's time to deliver. You need to pick your final format or formats, and then do what you need to do to get it in that format. You may be uploading work to a web site, or burning a DVD, or distributing good ol' VHS tapes. That's all part of this step, which we'll look at in detail later on in the book.

For now, just decide on what that format's going to be. Knowing this ahead of time can significantly affect your editing decisions

Isn't That a Lot of Work?

I know what you're thinking. You just read all that and are now asking yourself, "All I wanted to do was edit some footage of my daughter's last birthday party. Does it have to be *this* complicated?" The answer is, "Of course not." If the last few sections seem overwhelming, it's only because we've crammed a *lot* of information about a *lot* of different project categories into a short space. The best way to digest all this is to pick your project, re-read the planning sections, and ignore everything that doesn't apply to you.

Your daughter's birthday party is an event, but what you really want to make out of it is a montage. So if we keep this in mind, let's take a second look at all those planning steps:

Montage: Daughter's Birthday Party

Pick Your Topic. Daughter's birthday party. Time to complete: 1 minute.

Write Your Script. "Take 37 minutes of video and make a 2-minute montage." Time to complete: 1 minute.

Pick Locations, Get Your Props, Rehearse, Set Up, Sound, Lighting. n/a.

Filming. Footage all shot yesterday. Nothing more to do.

Clean Up. It will take a while to get all the cake off the ceiling. This applies to 3-year old daughters as well as the 16-year olds too.

Capture Video. Run through footage and pick the best parts. Rule of thumb for montages: budget about 2½ times the amount of raw footage. Time to complete: 1.5 hours.

Capture Audio. Find a song; get it on your PC. Time spent depends if you know what music you want. Choosing the right song can take longer than anything. Let's assume you already have it. Time to complete: 10 minutes.

Edit. Trim clips, drag and drop them in order, drop in music. Fade in and out. Add a title. Rule of thumb here is about 2½ times the length of the footage you captured. If you had 37 minutes of raw footage, and captured about 20 minutes of it, expect to spend 50 minutes assembling it on the timeline.

Deliver. Let's burn a quick DVD. You can drag and drop a pre-existing menu to the authoring tool, then grab a cup of coffee while it encodes and burns. Depends greatly on your hardware, we'll budget twenty minutes for this short project.

Total Project Time: Less than three hours, from tape to DVD. Not too bad!

Storyboarding

If your project is of the "production" category as discussed in the preceding sections, then you might want to give a serious look at storyboarding. Otherwise, you can skip ahead to the next section on Reusability.

Storyboarding is an age-old method of project planning. The idea is to take a series of scenes, typically as drawings, and string them together in sequence to get an idea of the flow of your project. The storyboard does not have to be in an electronic format. You can make sketches on napkins and lay them out on the floor if that's what helps you think through your project. Later on, we will look at using MediaStudio Pro itself for storyboarding, but that's not a requirement.

Creating the storyboard forces you think through everything before you start any production work, saving you much time and energy down the road. For example, let's say you're going to create a "how to" video on baking chocolate chip cookies. Using the recipe itself as a guideline, you can create a set of drawings depicting each scene in the process. You might want to have a short introduction and wrap-up on either end of your project too. The storyboard will cover all this. You can mentally "play" your video looking at the parts. This helps you get a firm grasp on your project concept. It also helps you convey this information to others, without going through the time and expense of an actual production, even a rough one.

> "I may not have gone where I intended to go, but I think I have ended up where I intended to be."
> —Douglas Adams

The next step up from a storyboard is an *animatic*. Unlike the storyboard, this *is* in an electronic format. This is a pre-production cut of your video, using a combination of rough audio, image, and video clips. Strictly speaking, of course, an animatic *is* an animation. Animatics are an indispensable tool in both traditional and 3D animation allowing everyone involved to truly visualize the content and (most importantly) the pacing of the production. They're useful for non-animation productions as well.

The audio may contain music, narration, or any other pre-recordings you might need for your production. The image clips may be scans of your storyboards, drawings, or other artwork representing certain scenes. The video clips may be rough shots, or even image sequences from 2D or 3D animation tools, if you're so inclined—whatever it takes to get a better idea for the project content, timing, and flow. Using motion and sound helps in ways that you could never get from just a storyboard, and MediaStudio Pro is more than capable of helping you with this step.

Reusability

This is all about not reinventing the wheel. As you get more and more projects under your belt, you'll find that many of the same elements might occur from project to project. One good category of examples is the title page. I did a good many weddings early in my career and each one basically began the same way: with a title page. After a while, I settled into a pattern, and they all had the same basic look. The background was a soft washed-out still of the bride's bouquet. The foreground text was simply, "The Wedding Of," followed by two names, and lastly a date. The various parts would fade in, in sequence, and the whole thing turned out rather pleasant.

To speed up the editing process with each project, I kept a generic graphic file handy. All I had to do was switch the names, date, and background image, and presto: I had a complete ready-to-go title page in about a tenth of the time it would have taken me to create from scratch.

Templates & Templates
Another good reusability tool is the use of project templates. Video Editor lets you create a set of project attributes and then save them with a name and a description. Now, every time you create a new project, you can use a saved template, and you don't have to reset every project setting with every new project. But here's a riddle for you: when is a template not a template? Answer: when it's not a template! Let me explain:

The project templates that Video Editor lets you create are only one small piece of reusability. Sure, using these can get you started quickly, but there's far more to reusability than just basic project settings. If you produce many projects of the same format, and if these projects contain the same tricks and effects, it's best to create a generic version of the project, and save the DVP file as your "template." This isn't a Video Editor feature. It's simply reusing a common project file for multiple projects. The exercise starting on page 252 in Chapter 9 demonstrates this technique.

Another standard feature of my wedding videos was presented at the end of each "pre-ceremony" segment. I would grab a still of the bride's face, a still of the groom's face, and locate a nice background shot. The face images were set in moving paths: bride first followed by the groom. Lastly, they would both appear together, and then everything would fade to black. In order to save time, I created a project file containing *just* this part of the project. I had annotated color clips substituted for the image clips. The project was called flyingfaces.dvp. The next time I was editing a video and got to this part, I would use the Insert | Project File command, grab the flyingfaces, and drop it on the timeline at that point. Right-clicking each placeholder clip, I would select Replace With | Image Clip and drop in the stills I had prepared for this particular thing. I would tweak the ins and outs to fit the music, but for the most part, these would work nearly as-is.

Smart Compositor

Ulead's ultimate answer to reusability is Smart Compositor. You can customize the out-of-the-box templates and save them within Smart Compositor. You can also save the result as a DVP file and edit it just as described in the last section. You can also use Smart Compositor Designer, a free tool from Ulead for creating your own templates from scratch. As of this writing it can be found at http://www.ulead.com/msp/free.htm.

File Management

In almost any project, it doesn't take a vast number of source files before you can become quickly overwhelmed. If you have twenty video files, two dozen image files, three audio files, and these are all mixed up with color clips and transitions on your timeline, it can be all too easy to lose track of what's what. This section will help you tackle this problem.

Naming Source Files

While naming a file seems like a simple thing, it can lead to problems if not done carefully. If you're capturing individual clips, it might be tempting to name them sandy beach.avi, big waves.avi, dolphins.avi, and so on. After all, aren't descriptive names helpful? They are at first, but you'll soon find that video editing isn't about worrying what names your files are. It is about *managing* them. And if you can't keep track of them, it doesn't matter what you originally named them.

Way back years ago, when I first started using MediaStudio Pro, I quickly learned that giving files meaningless numeric names was actually a pretty good way to work. When Version 5 came out, and the Video Capture module could automatically generate these file names for me, I was ecstatic. What a great feature: auto-incrementing file names.

So why do I think this is such a great way to work? It comes down to manageability. If I've captured fifty clips and I've only used thirty-four of them in my project, I might want to know, at any given time, exactly which clips I have and haven't used. There are two quick ways to see which clips you've used. 1. Press Alt+Enter and look at the "Files Used" section. 2. Open the Find Clip dialog box and sort the list box by clip name. If I sort a list and see thirty-four clips with names like:

> big waves.avi
> dolphins.avi
> sandy beach.avi

how would I know which sixteen *weren't* in the project? You can use the Smart Package function, which will take your project and move it (and all its files) to one location. But that seems rather resource-intensive just to find a list of files used. If, on the other hand, your files are named numerically, a list of thirty-four clips might begin like this:

> 0001.avi
> 0002.avi
> 0005.avi

Now it's extremely clear which clips are (or aren't) in your project. If I'm done with my project, and want to get rid of the clips I haven't used to save disk space, I can bring up a Windows Explorer folder window, list all the clips, and simply Ctrl+Click on all the missing files (e.g., 0003.avi, 0004.avi). When I'm done, I have a clean folder with only the files I'm using in my project.

File Archiving

So what happens when you have five gigabytes of clips at the end of your project, and it's time to start the next project? If you have a 300 GB hard drive, maybe this isn't a big deal. Drives become larger and cheaper with each passing day. But at some point, you will run out of disk space and will want to archive your projects and files. And even if you're not out of disk space, you're going to want to keep your disks in top-notch performance by clearing out files that aren't needed any more.

You don't want to outright delete everything. Not after you spent all that time getting it just right. You're going to need a backup solution someday. But with so many choices, which is the right one for you?

There are many storage formats out there, but we can break them down into three main categories: magnetic tape, magnetic disk, and optical disc. (There are other formats, of course, but for all practical and commercial purposes, these cover it.) Each has its advantages and disadvantages, regarding cost, speed, and capacity. Some examples of each:

- Magnetic Tape: DAT, DV, DDS, DLT
- Magnetic Disk: Floppy, Zip, SuperDisk, HD
- Optical Disc: CD, DVD

DV Considerations
Although I said you don't want to delete everything, if you're using DV sources you may be able to delete most of it. With DV you can do a batch capture of your sources and save the batch capture list for future reference. Once your project is complete, save everything but the DV sources. If you ever need to go back and make any changes, you can re-capture the footage. I would only recommend this approach for projects where there's a low probability of ever going back and editing it. If you know you have a "living" project, by all means, keep the sources close by.

Long Term Storage
If you really can't part with the files (or you simply aren't sure when that client will come back looking for "just one more change") then there's no better backup system than hard disk drives. While it may seem strange to use a HDD as a backup device—something traditionally better suited to tape—there's little arguing that byte-for-byte, hard disks make for pretty cheap and convenient storage.

Back in the mid '90s, I backed up about 100 GB worth of projects to DDS tape. (Keep in mind, this was off a giant 4 GB editing drive.) The price of the internal SCSI tape drive plus fifty 2 GB tapes was, all told, probably about US$2,000. This was remarkably inexpensive, considering 100 gigabytes of disk space could have run about $10,000 or more, at the time.

Today is different. For 100 GB of tape media (plus the drive) you can expect to spend about $500. A few days ago I just bought a 200 GB disk drive for $60. So unless you're backing up terabytes of video, the hard disk wins on two levels: cost and convenience.

Sliding IDE disks into disk caddies makes them nearly as easy to use as a floppy disk.

Do I Need Special Hard Disks?

When it comes time to stream video off your computer there are two types of disks: those that are fast enough and those that aren't. Unfortunately, the only way to find out which kind of disks you have is by anecdotal evidence, manufacturer's promises, and good old trial and error.

As a beginner, it's easy to make the mistake of thinking you need all the highest performance disks in the world, and as much disk space as money can buy. But the truth of the matter is there are three phases of video storage: capture, editing, and playback. Each of these requires a different level of performance from your disks. Playback requires the highest performance, capture is just below that, and editing can be done anywhere, since editing is a slow, user-centered, time-consuming process. Buying top-of-the-line storage media for this phase doesn't make sense. This is the perfect time to buy those cheap, huge IDE drives you see advertised everywhere. And, as we just mentioned, they're also the perfect backup solution.

Just make sure it's running at 7200 RPM or faster, and you keep it clean. You do this by removing unnecessary files and most importantly, defragmenting.

Folder Locations

By default, MediaStudio Pro, like nearly all modern Windows applications, likes to save files in various folders under your "My Documents" folder. This folder is normally found on your **c:** drive. If you're comfortable with this and see no need to change, you can continue doing so. However, I would highly suggest doing otherwise. It's always a good idea to have a separate disk set aside just for video.

Why do this? The main reason is for performance. You see, if your c: drive is anything like the average c: drive, it has thousands of folders and tens of thousands of files. Worse, file sizes range anywhere from 0 bytes to hundreds of megabytes. While you can't see it with the naked eye, trust me: your disk is a mess.

Without getting too technical, here's how it works. Windows writes files to disk starting at a chunk of empty space. If that space fills up before it's done writing the file, it finds another chunk— perhaps miles and miles away—and continues writing the file over there. This continues until the

Actual unretouched photo of your hard disk.

entire file is saved. So you can see why things get pretty messy after a while. The system always reads the files in order, but the more scattered they are, the longer it takes, and everything slows down. Including video.

With a separate disk just for video you'll have far fewer folders and files on it at any given time. It will be easier to maintain and to keep it running optimally. Remember, video files are quite large: they'll need all the optimization they can get.

So! If at all possible, install a second disk (which will likely end up being your **d:** drive). Once that's set up, create top-level folders for each project you work on.

Charlie's Pet Peeve #173

I can't stand the way Microsoft decided to name their standard folders. While I can see how giving folders long and descriptive names might be helpful for novice users, when it gets right down to it, they're very difficult to work with on a day-to-day basis. If you combine that with MediaStudio Pro's out of the box default file location, you end up with something like this:

C:\Documents and Settings\Administrator\My Documents\Video Editor\8.0

Sure, if you point and click you don't have to type all that out, but come on! That's even too much pointing and clicking. To make matters worse, many applications don't seem to expect file names will ever be that long. They either stretch menus and dialog boxes to great widths, or worse, names are truncated so you can't tell exactly where it is.

If you like the "My Documents" default and only need the performance benefit, you can move it to a better location. Right-click the My Documents icon on the desktop and select Properties from the popup menu.

At this point, click the "Move" button and you can specify your new **d:** drive as the new location for your documents. After that, it will ask you if you want to physically move all existing documents from c:\Ridiculously Long Path Name to the new location. How you answer that depends. If this computer is used primarily for video editing, and you don't have a lot of documents, go ahead and move stuff. But remember, this affects all programs for this computer. If, after changing it, you

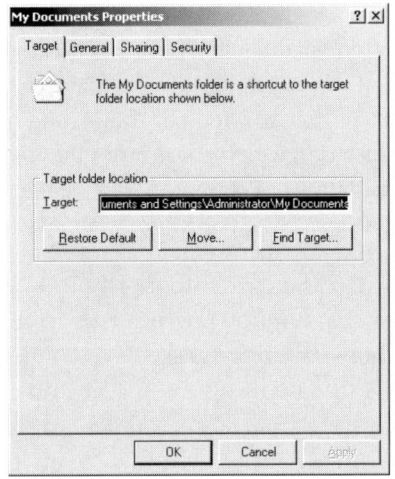

decide you don't like the new behavior, use that "Restore Default" button, and you'll be able to move things back to the way they were.

Ulead Folders

This is one area I would really like to see improved. The various programs in the suite don't seem to want to share folders. Each is an island to itself, not very concerned with its brethren.

I don't think I'm in the minority, preferring to work in a project-oriented fashion. That is, I like to create a folder (c:\projects\NextBigThing) and keep everything related to that project in that folder (with subfolders, of course). This doesn't seem crazy. It seems like the whole point of a hierarchical file system.

I would love to say, "Hey, MediaStudio Pro. I'm working on the NextBigThing at the moment." Then, every program suddenly uses this as the default working directory. I find it extraordinarily unhelpful to have:

C:\Documents and Settings\Administrator\My Documents\Ulead DVD DiskRecorder
C:\Documents and Settings\Administrator\My Documents\Ulead DVD MovieFactory 4.2
C:\Documents and Settings\Administrator\My Documents\VC DV Scan
C:\Documents and Settings\Administrator\My Documents\Video Capture

I find it counter-productive when I'm constantly forced to switch the defaults as I move from program to program.

Project Management

In general, this term refers to the planning and control of a project throughout the course of its lifespan. But in this case, I'm limiting the term to the Video Editor *project*—specifically, the DVP file.

Preview Files Manager

As you preview parts of the timeline, Video Editor saves these already-rendered scenes to disk. SmartRender uses these files to help speed up the final render (or timeline playback) of your final project. If you begin to run out of disk space, or if things seem to be slowing down rather than speeding up, you may want to take a look at this dialog box. See how many preview files are out there, and clean them up if you need to.

Project Packaging

I often wonder how many people even know about this little gem. If you're anything like me, you probably accumulate a large number of extra files during bigger projects. There will be multiple copies of the project file as I make my way through revisions. There are extra image files, test renders, scraps, and who knows what. When the final project ends up containing seventy clips across twelve timelines, it's hard to know what's in use and what isn't.

That's where Smart Package comes in. Video Editor will copy (or move) all the files for a given project into a single destination. It even has provisions for physically trimming off the parts of clips you don't need. This can be a real space saver if you frequently capture minutes of video but only end up using seconds.

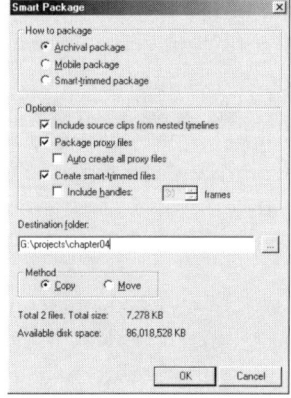

I definitely recommend looking into this great little tool.

Project File Backups

There are two reasons to frequently backup your project files. The first is to protect you against the Forces of Evil: program crashes, lockups, power outages, system freezes, and very small children. The second is to protect you against yourself ("Dang! I wish I'd saved a copy of this project from yesterday before I went and screwed it up today!")

For these and many reasons, you're going to want to have backups. Plenty of backups. They'll help you recover from crashes as well as providing for "undo" points that last between Video Editor sessions.

Auto Backup
In the middle of the program Preferences dialog box is this section:

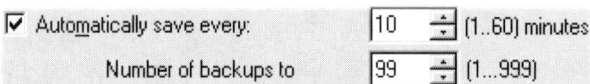

This does just what you think it does. And trust me, you'll want to keep this on. Not necessarily every 10 minutes—find an interval that matches your working style. But definitely something other than, "Nah, don't save anything, thanks."

The backups are saved in a subfolder next to your project file. Therefore, if your project is d:\projects\wedding.dvp then the backups will be stored starting with d:\projects\wedding\wedding001.dvp. When the maximum number of backups is reached (1…999) then the numbering starts over, overwriting any existing backups.

If Video Editor crashes for whatever reason, when it restarts, you'll be asked if you want to open the most recent backup. Most of the time you'll want to say yes.

Note. Video Editor creates a backup project in this subfolder every time you save the project. So even if you don't use the Auto Save feature, you will still find the subdirectory there with backups.

Manual Backup

This isn't so much a "backup" technique as it is an undo technique. As I craft longer, more involved projects, I frequently change the name of the project as I work. For example, I may begin with dev1.dvp (for the first development stage). When I get to a point where I think I'm about to do something significant, I save it as dev2.dvp and continue working. This process keeps me comforted that I can always go back to an earlier checkpoint if I need to. Granted, I could do this with a single file name and automatic backups. But physically saving the project to a different file name gives me a psychological advantage.

You'll end up with files and folders like this:

d:\projects\wedding\dev1.dvp
d:\projects\wedding\dev1\dev1001.dvp
d:\projects\wedding\dev1\dev1002.dvp
d:\projects\wedding\dev1\dev1003.dvp
d:\projects\wedding\dev2.dvp
d:\projects\wedding\dev2\dev2001.dvp
d:\projects\wedding\dev2\dev2002.dvp
d:\projects\wedding\dev3.dvp

This may seem a bit like overkill. But trust me, having more projects saved than you need is *far* better than having fewer. No one ever said after a crash, "Gee, I wish I hadn't backed up so much."

Caveats

Some people have reported—at least with the initial release of the program—corrupt project files. I hope this never happens to you (and it doesn't for the vast majority of people).

One of the more insidious effects of the corrupt project is the fact that the Auto Save feature starts saving them that way. Believe me, there's nothing worse than having the program crash, and none of your backups are any good. There's no point in auto-saving every ten minutes if they're corrupt.

Therefore I recommend closing and reopening your projects periodically. Don't do an intense twelve hour editing run without checking to see if any of your saved projects can be re-opened. About once or twice an hour, save the project, press Ctrl+W to close it, then Ctrl+O to reopen it. The sooner you catch a corrupt DVP file, the better.

Hopefully I haven't made you too paranoid!

That's a Wrap!

For those of you who've read this whole chapter, congratulations! I know these aren't the most glamorous topics, and when you're anxious to learn some cool editing techniques, it's easy to skip over "the boring stuff." But giving due diligence to these planning suggestions can make each project go just a little more smoothly. And when time is working against you, as it almost always is, good planning can make all the difference in the world.

Part II

FLIGHT TRAINING

With all the bookwork and theory now behind you, it's time to put it all into practice. It's one thing to just read about climbing in the cockpit and taking off. It's quite another to get up there and actually do it.

Chapter 5 Essential Editing Skills

Chapter 6 The Standard Bag of Tricks

Chapter 7 Beyond Just Editing

Chapter 8 Text and Titling

Chapter 9 Slightly More Advanced Tricks

5

First Things First: Essential Editing Skills

This chapter covers the most basic video editing concepts: the timeline, clips, transitions and trimming.

Getting off the Ground

Sometimes you just can't get going. It's tough to admit sometimes—especially when all the marketing materials tell you what a piece of cake this is all supposed to be—but it happens. If, on the other hand, you're already comfortable with the interface, along with basic concepts like dragging and dropping and overlapping clips, you can skip ahead to the next chapter. If you're just not getting it, stay here.

Okay. You probably have a bunch of video you want to edit and put on DVD or tape. But this is your first time with all of this. It's all brand new and you just don't know where to start first. There are three basic steps:

- Get video into your computer.
- Make any modifications you'd like.
- Get the video back out of your computer.

To help you with this, you have four resources. The first is Part I of this book. It might have been tempting to skip past the boring stuff and jump right in. You don't have to read all of it, but I would suggest Chapter 2 if nothing else. The next resource is the manual. While it's not all encompassing, it does explain some of the most basic tasks. The third resource is Ulead's web site. They have some tutorials for common tasks that may prove helpful.

Lastly, the various user groups mentioned on page 30. They're a veritable treasure chest of valuable information. No matter your skill level, ask away.

Getting Results Installation

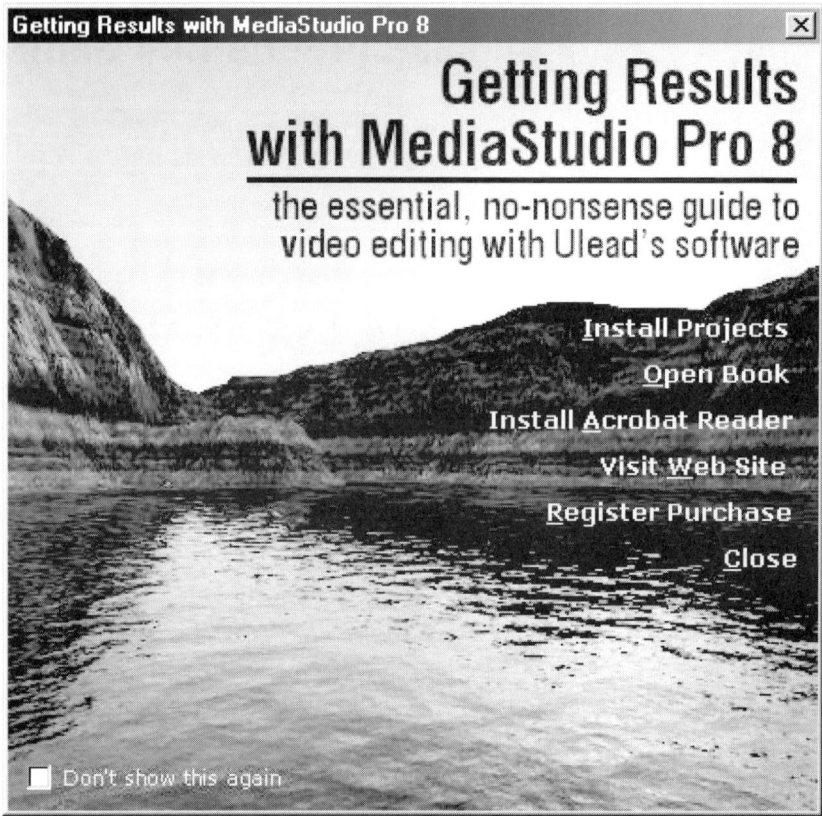

Insert the accompanying *Getting Results* CD and you should see this window. If not, open the My Computer icon on your desktop and locate your CD drive. Once you've found it, launch the autorun.exe program.

The Install Projects button copies all the material from the CD to a location on your PC, preferably a dedicated video editing disk drive. Working from a local disk rather than the CD is recommended for two reasons: 1) it's faster, and 2) it's writeable.

You can open the PDF version of the book from this window. If you don't have Acrobat Reader installed (Version 6 or above is highly recommended) click Install Acrobat Reader.

If you think you've done everything you're ever going to do here, check Don't show this again and you won't be bothered with this little window ever again.

We're almost ready to begin, just a few more bits of housekeeping...

Chapter 5 • Essential Editing Skills   113

How the Exercises Are Set Up

▸ **Opening Paragraph**: Background, setup, or anecdotal information.

▸ **Objective**: The purpose or goal of the exercise.

▸ **Reference Projects**: Most exercises are accompanied by two reference projects. The first one represents the state of the exercise before you start. The second one shows you what the project should look like at the end of the exercise. You don't have to use either one. However, the "start" project is a good way to make sure we're getting off on the right foot. The "end" project allows you to check your work.

▸ **Steps**: The exercise! If it's lengthy, Steps will be broken into groups.

Standard Project Settings

For optimal editing performance, your project settings should match the clip properties. All the clips on the CD are in NTSC VCD format.

When starting a new project, set the "Edit file format" to MPEG Files, then look for "Video CD-NTSC" on the list. If you're a PAL user, **don't panic**. These clips aren't intended for broadcast and therefore the major NTSC vs. PAL distinctions are meaningless.

Where Are the Clips?

Where Are the Clips? If you completed the installation instructions on the previous page, the clips will be wherever you installed them. If you did not complete the installation, then the clips are on the CD and split up into the various project folders. Installation is recommended for performance reasons.

When you open the reference projects, you will also find clip thumbnails in the Project Tray's Media Bin folders.

Relinking

Timeline. Since these projects were created on a computer other than yours, Video Editor will not be able to find the clips. The first time you open a project, it will complain about this and ask you to relink the clips. Fortunately, you only need to relink one clip. Once it finds one, it can find the rest by itself. Save the project to save the new links.

Project Tray. Thumbnails in the Project Tray act differently. It won't prompt you to relink. The first time you click on a thumbnail, it will attempt to relink without asking. Once relinked, you can then use the clip. In short, before using a thumbnail in the Project Tray, click it twice!

Image Sequences. Relinking an image sequence involves rebuilding the image sequence. Video Editor will prompt you through the steps when the time comes.

Timeline and Clip Basics

If you've never used MediaStudio Pro before, then getting familiar with the timeline might actually be easier for you. Video Editor 8 brought with it more than a few radical changes. These changes are more likely to throw off the long-time user than the uninitiated. If you're a long-time user, I would recommend reading Appendix A first. Then come on back.

Objective
To introduce you to the timeline and basic clip manipulation.

Reference Projects
projects\chapter05\start.dvp
projects\chapter05\clip-basics.dvp

Steps

1. Open the starter reference project, start.dvp. This project has one single clip, which serves as a placeholder.

2. Without actually selecting the clip, right-click it. This is the standard method for displaying a quick property sheet for the clip:

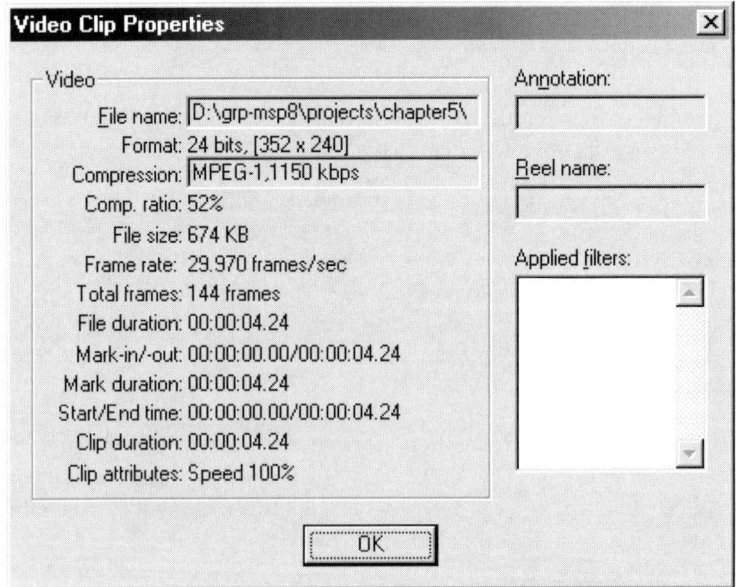

Chapter 5 • Essential Editing Skills 115

If you don't see this box (but see a menu instead) then the clip was selected before you right-clicked on it. Deselect clips by clicking any blank area in the timeline.

3. Move your cursor over the ruler until it turns into a star, as shown here.

4. While the ✻ cursor is displayed, press the mouse and move it right and left along the timeline. You should see the Preview Window change as you move. This is called **scrubbing** and is a common technique for previewing your work.

If both the Effects Manager and Preview Window are displayed, you will see both of their playheads ▽ moving too.

5. From the Project Tray, open the Media Bin and click on the Video folder.

6. Drag clip 0002.mpg to the timeline and place it on top of clip 0001.mpg in track Video2.

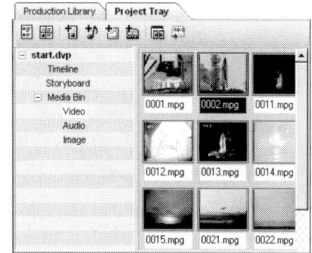

7. Scrub the timeline again. This time you will see 0002.mpg play in the Preview Window instead of 0001.mpg. Clips on higher numbered tracks appear in front of clips on lower numbered tracks. By default, the lower clips are completely obscured by the higher clips. As you might expect, there are ways of altering this behavior! More on that later.

8. Now drag 0002.mpg down to track Video1 and move it to the left so that the two clips overlap, like so:

The little yellow area (shown here with the partial name "Crossfa") is a transition. This is a set of instructions that tell Video Editor how to get from one clip to another. The next exercise will go into more detail about transitions.

Note that if you move either clip away from the other, the transition will vanish. This is because unlike other clips on the timeline, transitions cannot exist all by themselves. They require an overlap.

9. Transitions can exist on any track. Drag clip 0011.mpg to track Video2 and clip 0012.mpg next to it, so they overlap as well. The exact overlap doesn't matter. We're just illustrating a point.

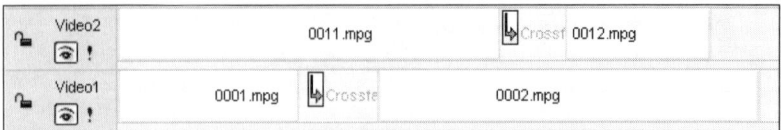

If you scrub the timeline you'll see 0011.mpg fade to 0012.mpg. The two clips on Video1 remain obscured.

10. Double-click any video track. This displays the Insert Video File dialog box.

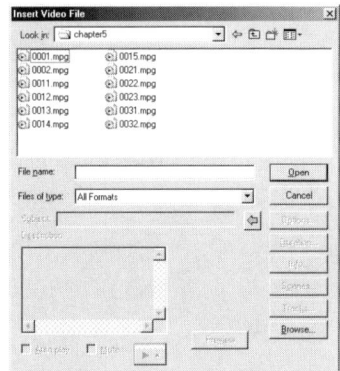

As you can see, dragging from the Project Tray isn't the only way to get clips into your project.

You can also right-click on any empty track or use the Insert | Video File menu command.

In a product like MediaStudio Pro, you'll often find many ways of accomplishing the same goals. While this might make the program seem overly complicated, you'll soon find this is also what makes it so powerful.

Now let's take that closer look at...

Transitions

How you get from one clip to another is extraordinarily important. If not done right, the entire production—no matter how good—will be all for naught.

Objective
To learn what transitions are, how to choose them, how to use them, and how *not* to abuse them.

Reference Projects
projects\chapter05\start.dvp
projects\chapter05\transitions.dvp

Chapter 5 • Essential Editing Skills

Steps

1. Once again, open the starter reference project, **start.dvp**.

2. Drag 0002.mpg next to, but not overlapping, 0001.mpg.

Tada! There's your very first transition. "But wait a minute!" you exclaim. "That isn't a transition. Nothing happened. It's just one clip butted up right against another clip."

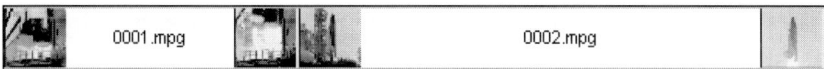

Yes, yes. That is true. But that doesn't mean it isn't a transition. All we've done is decided that our transition will be to jump instantaneously from the last frame of 0001.mpg to the first frame of 0002.mpg.

Welcome to the **cut**. It is the most common "transition" in the history of editing. Its simplicity and utter unobtrusiveness gives it the title it most certainly deserves: the king of all transitions.

3. Now drag 0002.mpg to the left so the two clips overlap. By default, a Crossfade transition appears out of nowhere.

Of all the transitions to appear out of nowhere, this is definitely the one you want. If the **cut** is the reigning King of Transitions, then the **crossfade** has certainly earned the rank of Queen. Just as simple and elegant as the cut, it too is unnoticeable when used correctly.

> And that, my friends, is the single most important word you'll come across when talking transitions: **unnoticeable**. Because as soon as your attention is drawn to the transition itself, you've lost sight of the purpose of the transition. The transition is there only to support, never to dominate.

So why does MediaStudio Pro come with over one hundred different transitions? Why do other companies provide hundreds and hundreds more as plug-ins? Why are we always looking for more, more, more? Bigger! Better! Flashier!

Because more isn't a bad thing. Using something other than a cut or crossfade can actually be really good. As long as you uphold the law: keep it **unnoticeable**.

"But Charlie, you moron. If I have a really cool plug in transition that looks like fireworks exploding: how on earth will the audience not notice *that*?" Easy. It becomes unnoticeable when it blends in perfectly with your subject matter. A transition all by itself isn't inherently "noticeable" or "unnoticeable." It only becomes one or the other due to context. Take, for example, the aforementioned cool firework transition. If you're editing a wedding video and you use this to cut between segments of the wedding ceremony, tell me if you think the audience will notice? Contrast that with a video actually about fireworks. Now it is absolutely appropriate. Because your audience is already in that "flashy" mindset, the transition becomes thoroughly acceptable. While this may sound like "the bleeding obvious," let's take a look at something more subtle.

Consider this innocent circle wipe. We have two different views of a Shuttle landing. The circle wipe is unobtrusive. It isn't particularly showy and enjoys a spot as a standard transition in every video toolbox out there. So what's wrong with it?

Well, if the "noticeable" test is too esoteric for you, try this instead. Imagine yourself at a podium in front of a couple hundred fellow editors and you have to explain to them why you chose this transition. If you cannot come up with an answer other than, "Uhh... I don't know," then you've made the wrong choice.

So How Do You Choose?

One of the biggest mistakes the beginner can make is "going overboard." If you've never done any video editing at all, it can be very tempting to drop in every transition into every video project. The result is very similar to the output of word processing novices:

<u>This Weekend Only</u>
*** 𝓝𝓔𝓘𝓖𝓗𝓑𝓞𝓡𝓗𝓞𝓞𝓓 𝓖𝓐𝓡𝓐𝓖𝓔 𝓢𝓐𝓛𝓔 ***
Friday, Saturday, Sunday
8 am to 4 pm
Lots of Stuff

If *less is more* then, by symmetry, *more is less.* You've demonstrated nothing except your knowledge of how to change fonts, without regard to content, presentation, or emotion. Similarly, a video fraught with dissimilar transitions, only shouts out, *I know how to drag and drop! And not much else!* Your family and neighbors may be impressed with the new tools at your disposal, but it won't go much beyond that.

Chapter 5 • Essential Editing Skills   119

When it comes time to choose, ask yourself, "Does this transition have *anything* to do with the two scenes?" How does it help the viewer get from point A to point B? Is there anything going on in either clip that would be enhanced by this transition? Avoid ending up with something random and pointless. You may find yourself at a podium one day explaining your actions.

Now, where were we... Holy cow! We were in the middle of an exercise! Don't let me get off on tangents like that. Otherwise we'll never get anywhere.

4. Let's see ... oh, that's right. We just created a Crossfade transition between our two clips. Now press F6 to display Video Editor preferences. Then click the Edit tab. In the middle of that dialog box is this option:

If you click the Select button, you can change the transition that gets created when two clips overlap. You already know what I'm going to say: resist the temptation to change this for the sake of changing it. Think it through.

5. Click Cancel to leave the Preferences dialog.

6. Back on the timeline, double click the transition. This opens the transition options dialog box, shown here.

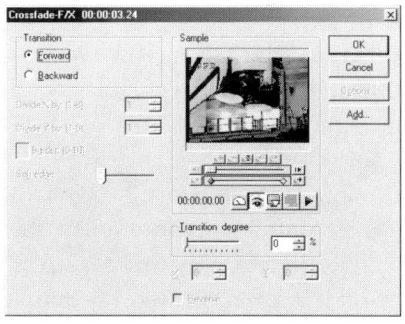

I won't go into the details right at this moment. We have other things to learn first. What I *do* want you to do now is take a look at things. Although the exact look of this dialog changes depending on which transition is being edited, a few things stay the same: transition direction, the keyframe controller, preview options, and so on.

7. Click OK to close the dialog. Scrub the timeline to see how it looks. You should have a nice, smooth fade between them.

Before wrapping this up, here are a few more things to know about transitions.

Replacing. Swapping one transition for another is easy. Simply drag a new transition from the Production Library and drop it on the existing transition. Try it out. Drag the Wipe | Barn Door transition and drop it between our two clips.

Saving. If you've customized your transition and would like to reuse it later, just click the "Add" button, typically at the lower right of the Effects Manager window. This will display the pictured "Add to Library" dialog box. The transition goes into a Custom folder. You can name the thumbnail and give it a description.

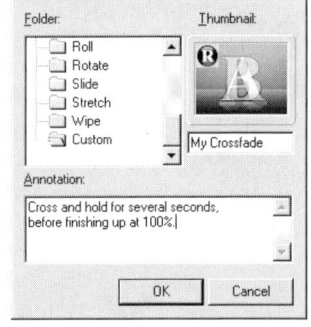

If you want to port this setting to another Video Editor installation, you can right-click the Custom folder in the Production Library and save the transitions as a .TEG file. This file can then be loaded into another instance of Video Editor.

Adding. Transitions aren't hard-wired into Video Editor. They're in the form of plug-ins and can be added (or removed) outside of the program. Transitions are files stored in the vfx_plug folder under your MediaStudio Pro installation. If you download or buy additional transitions, this is where they'll go.

Creating Your Own. And by this I mean, *really* creating your own: completely from scratch. It's possible, of course, but don't expect to find a nice graphical "Transition Workshop" out there. Ulead provides an SDK ("software development kit") which is a set of technical specifications for the interfaces between software modules. But unless you're a professional computer programmer, this probably isn't an area you want to wander in to. I only bring it up at all because people have been curious about it in the past. Here's a sample:

```
nWidth=(int)pEffData->nProcessW;
nHeight=(int)pEffData->nProcessH;
nBytesPerPixel = 3;
dwBytes=4*(((int)((PBIH)pEffData->pBIHSrcA)->biWidth*nBytesPerPixel+3)/4);
nStartPosition = pEffData->nBeginY*dwBytes + pEffData->nBeginX*nBytesPerPixel;
lpDest  = (PBYTE)pEffData->pDest + nStartPosition;
lpSrc1  = (PBYTE)pEffData->pSrcA + nStartPosition;
lpSrc2  = (PBYTE)pEffData->pSrcB + nStartPosition;
```

Basic Trimming

Easily the most important part of editing (in fact, the entire *reason* for editing) is trimming away unwanted portions of clips. Get rid of the front, back, or stuff in between. Video Editor has lots of ways for doing this. The next several exercises cover them all.

Objective
To learn basic front and back clip trimming using several methods.

Reference Project
projects\chapter05\start.dvp

Steps
1. Open the starter reference project.

2. Move the mouse to the rightmost edge of the clip until the cursor changes to double arrows: ⇨⇦

3. Press the mouse button, and one of the arrows will disappear. The remaining arrow (in this case the left-pointing arrow) tells you which direction to drag.

4. With the mouse button held, drag to the left. As you drag, you'll see the Preview Window update with a split screen. This shows you two adjacent frames, helping you zero in on your trim point. The red number is the current frame. If you release the mouse button, *this* frame will be the last frame of the newly trimmed clip. This can be better observed when the frames are visibly different, as shown with this count-down clip. Note too that the time code shown is with respect to the timeline, not the clip.

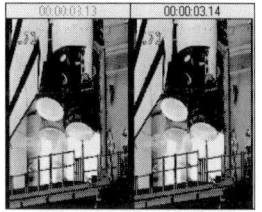
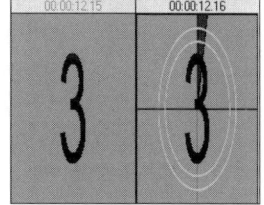

5. This time, move the mouse to the leftmost edge of the clip. The double arrows appear again, only this time you can trim material from the beginning of the clip.

Congrats! You've just trimmed a clip. Twice no less! Here's a little certificate for you. You can hang it on your wall.

Trimming with the Source Window

This has the advantage of letting you see the video properly as you're selecting your in/out points as well as giving you access to normal playback controls.

To open a clip in the Source Window, double-click any clip on the timeline. The two bracket buttons are used for setting the in/out points on the clip. Additionally, the F3 and F4 keys will set mark in and out points respectively. You can move through your clip using the VCR-like buttons or by dragging the slider control. Double click the clip and try it out now.

Here's a good Source Window hint: Let's say you've set your in and out marks so that the duration of the clip is perfect, yet now you want to change the in and out marks *without changing the overall duration*. The best way to do this is by moving the blue bar, as marked in the picture here.

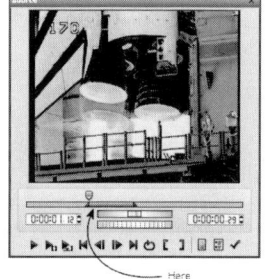

By sliding this to the right or the left, you can change the in and out points of your trim, without affecting the overall duration. This is nice when you've locked a clip into the middle of a complex timeline, but then realize the in and out points are wrong. You can tweak these without affecting the timeline.

Scissors. While the scissors technically slice one clip into two separate clips, this is still a trim. Just discard the unwanted portions. What you will be left with is a clip with a mark-in and mark-out point exactly at the point you cut. There are three ways to use the scissors 1) Click the scissors tool on the timeline toolbar; 2) Press "S" to temporarily switch to the scissors tool; 3) Press "U" which will slice the selected clip(s) at the current *playhead* position (not mouse position). If no clips are selected, pressing U will cut all clips at once.

By the Numbers. Right-click a selected clip and select Duration from the pop-up menu. This displays the Duration dialog box. If you want exact placement of your in and out points without relying on any graphical controls, this is the place to do it. Often this is a quick way to adjust an in or out point by a frame or two, when this would otherwise be difficult to do graphically.

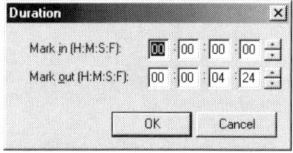

Trim the Middle of a Clip

Trimming the front or back of a clip gets you a long way. But what if the ends are fine and you want the middle of the clip trimmed? As you might expect, you have several options.

Objective
To learn how to remove the middle of a clip.

Reference Project
projects\chapter05\start.dvp

Steps
1. Open the starter reference project.

2. Delete the clip.

3. Open the Project Tray and drag 0031.mpg to the timeline.

    As you can see, this is a long clip. The start and end are fine, so this is a perfect choice for good old-fashioned middle-trimmin'.

4. First, bring the entire clip into view. On the left hand side of the ruler is this collection of buttons. Click the top-middle button. It looks like an envelope. This rescales the timeline so the entire project, whatever its length, fits in the window.

5. Switch to the scissors tool (or press "S") and click once near the left side of the clip, once near the right. Like so:

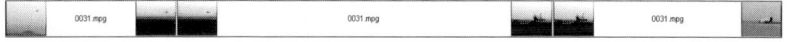

6. Click the middle piece once, and press Delete.

7. That's it! You took the middle out of a clip.

8. What?

9. That was a lame way of doing it, you say?

Yes, you're right. That wasn't the least bit elegant. Primarily because you had no idea *what* you were cutting. It was random. But I don't do things like this for no reason at all. This is just mental prep for what we're about to do next. The fact is, you *did* cut out the middle.

Steps, Part 2

1. Press Ctrl+Z three times to restore clip 0031.mpg to a single unit.

2. Make sure cues are visible. Click View | Timeline Display Mode and click the "Show cue bar on track" checkbox. Make sure it's checked for both video and audio tracks.

3. Double-click the clip to load it into the Source Window.

4. Drag the playhead over to about 6 seconds or so.

5. Press F5. This creates a cue.

   The cue name, which defaults to the cue's position, is displayed in the Source Window tab. The cue has **not** however taken effect.

   That's a very important feature of the Source Window: none of the editing you do here takes effect until you press the Apply button on the lower right:

6. Now move to the playhead to the right, to the 27 second mark.

7. Press F5 to create a second cue.

8. Click the Apply button.

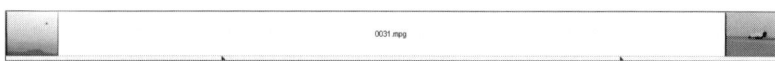

The timeline now shows two little black triangles under the clip. This is your visual reference that the clip has cues (and why Step 2 above was important).

Cues are also snap points, which makes for quick alignment while editing. Drag other things close to them, and they'll snap.

9. It's now time to split the clip. Click the Source Window Menu. It's the button right next to the apply button.

10. At the bottom of this menu are two cut commands. The one we want is the second one, Cut by Cue. Select it.

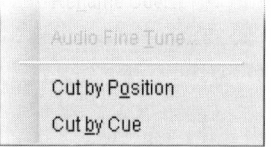

11. Examine the timeline.

    At this point you have three clips where there used to be one clip. The results are very similar to the first set of steps, but as you can see, we had a lot more control over where the cuts happened.

    You're now free to discard the middle portion and do whatever you want with the remaining pieces. And in case you're wondering, Cut by Position will slice the clip at the current playhead position.

Trim Multiple Parts of a Clip

If you want to make multiple trims you can certainly use the Cut by Cue method we just learned. But it does leave both the wanted and unwanted portions on the clip. There is a way to get only the parts you want.

Objective
To learn how to remove the middle of a clip.

Reference Project
projects\chapter05\start.dvp

Steps
1. Open the reference project.

2. Go to the Project Tray.

3. Click once on the last clip, 0041.mpg, to select it.

4. Click the Multi-Trim clip button to display the trim tool, shown here.

    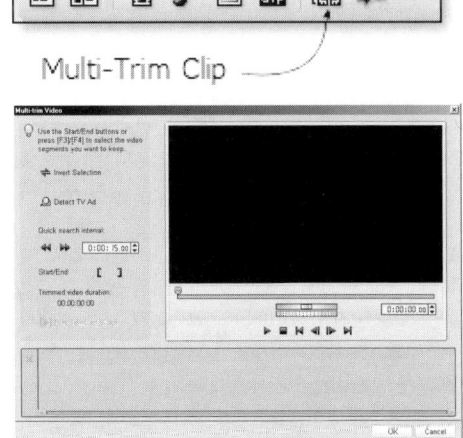

    This tool allows you to mark multiple trim points within a single clip *and* discard the parts you don't want, all at the same time.

    The clip we've loaded has four parts. There's some unwanted black at the beginning and end, then two different shuttle scenes in the middle. We'll discard the outer parts and keep the remaining two. We have several ways to approach this.

Steps for Way #1

1. Click the play button.

2. When a scene comes that you want to include, press F3 or hit the left bracket button: [.

3. When the end of that scene comes, press F4 or hit the right bracket button:].

   Analysis. This approach is recommended for longer segments where you don't really need frame-accurate results. The benefit is that you can get through the clip in real time. The drawback is the accuracy issue. This won't work for us. Delete any thumbnails you might have created and let's try again.

Steps for Way #2

1. Drag the playhead, as if you were scrubbing the timeline.

2. Release the mouse to see where you are.

3. If you're at a desired in or out point, press F3 or F4 respectively.

4. Repeat until the end of the clip.

   Analysis. This approach is recommended for short segments or if you know beforehand exactly where you want your cuts to be. The benefit is you get to take time to make frame-accurate cuts. The drawback is that the window does not update while scrubbing, and therefore this can be an annoying way to go about this. Like last time, delete any thumbnails you may have created and we'll start over.

Steps for Way #3

1. Click and drag the shuttle controls to move.

2. Use the left and right arrow buttons to fine-tune the mark in and out point.

3. Use F3 and F4 to mark in and out.

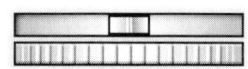

   Analysis. This approach is recommended for varying length segments. Since the two controls let you move at variable speeds, you can make both short and long hops with a single control. That's the primary benefit. The drawback is the controls themselves can be difficult to deal with. You may find zeroing in on a frame requires a lot of trial and error scrolling.

Further, using the graphical buttons for navigation presents one problem: clicking them too fast results in *clicks* turning into *double-clicks*. These controls do not respond to double-clicking. Therefore, the faster you click, the less responsive they become.

Anyway! Delete any thumbnails from the Project Tray, and let's try again. You can Ctrl+Click to multi-select them and press the Delete key to send them to the Great Bit Bucket in the Sky.

Steps for Way #4
1. With your left thumb, hover over the space bar.

2. With your right hand, keep two fingers hovered over the right and left arrow keys.

3. Press the spacebar to begin playing the clip.

4. When you get to an in or out point, press the spacebar again.

5. Use the arrow keys to move back and forth a frame at a time. This is a *great* way to position. You don't need extraordinary mouse skills and the display updates with each key press.

6. Press F3 or F4 to mark your ins and outs.

7. Repeat until done.

   Analysis. This is the hands-on approach (literally). As far as workflow efficiency goes, being freed from the mouse makes for a huge leap in productivity. If you're the type who simply cannot tear themselves away from "point and click" I *really* recommend trying. I realize it can be difficult at first, but quite often you'll find clicking keys to be amazingly faster than dragging a mouse around the desk.

Final Steps
1. Compare your mark-in and mark-out points with mine:

	Mark In	Mark Out
Trim 1	00:00:01.00	00:00:05.23
Trim 2	00:00:05.26	00:00:14.10

2. Click OK.

You might be wondering at this point, "Where'd my clips go?" Clicking OK does not place them on the timeline. Instead, it creates new thumbnails in whatever gallery you were in at the time. In our case, that's the

Project Tray | Media Bin | Video folder. This isn't immediately apparent. *Especially* if the folder fills the entire window, and new contents (added at the end) are completely invisible. I have to admit, this had me scratching my head the first time I tried it. That being said, this is a good way to work. Now they're in the clip bin and all ready to be dragged (pre-trimmed!) to the timeline.

Split by Scene

If you know your clip is mostly made up of usable scenes, it can be a real time saver to have Video Editor do all the work for you. A built-in scene analyzer can easily handle all the grunt work.

Objective
To learn how to split a clip into multiple clips using scene detection to create trim boundaries.

Reference Projects
projects\chapter05\start.dvp
projects\chapter05\split-by-scene.dvp

Steps

1. Open the start reference project.

2. Delete the clip.

3. Drag the *original* 0041.mpg clip from the Project Tray to the timeline. Recall: if you completed the previous exercise, you now have three clips named 0041.mpg in the Media Bin.

4. With the clip on the timeline selected, right-click on it.

5. Near the bottom of the menu, select **Split by Scene**.

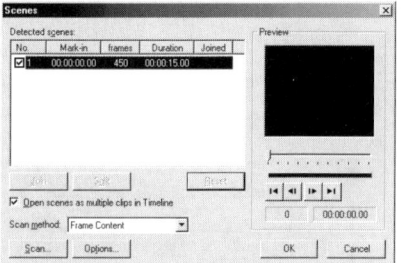

So far, I've never had the need to change any of the defaults. Under the **Options** button is a slider where you can adjust the scanner sensitivity. This tells Video Editor how much difference between frames constitutes a *scene change*.

If it's too sensitive, you'll end up with more scenes than you thought you had: especially during fast camera pans or zooms.

If it unwittingly breaks up a single scene into multiple scenes, you can select them and re-join them with the Join button.

6. Click Scan.

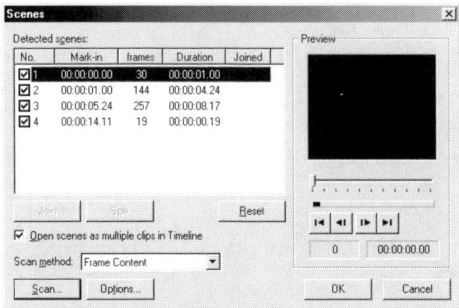

7. Click OK. The original timeline clip will now appear as four clips, one per scene. Now you can do whatever you want with them.

Saving Trimmed Files

All the trimming we have done up until now has been *non-destructive*. This means edits are applied to the *clip* but not the underlying *file*. There are times, however, when you really do want to change the physical disk files. Here's how.

Objective
To learn how to save trimmed clips to physical files.

Reference Project
projects\chapter05\split-by-scene.dvp

Steps
1. Open the reference project. This time the reference project is where we left off in the last exercise.

2. Select Project | Smart | Smart Trim from the menu. You'll see this tool.

   If you're wondering what to do now, I don't blame you. This actually had me stumped for a short while. It turns out there's a slight bug in

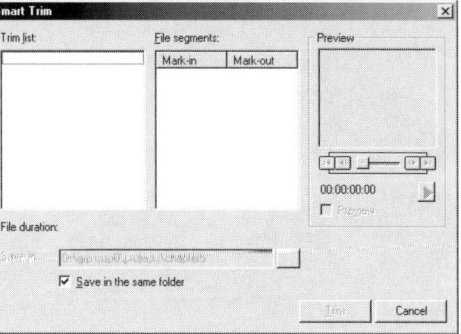

Video Editor. If you trim a clip and all the trimmed parts add up to the length of the original clip, it doesn't think anything's been trimmed. Which is odd. Because we've *obviously* trimmed this clip!

To continue, press Cancel.

3. Delete the first clip: the "1-second of black" clip. We don't really want that one anyway.

4. While you're at it, delete the last clip. You should now have just the two good clips left.

5. Select Project | Smart | Smart Trim from the menu again. This time, you'll see this:

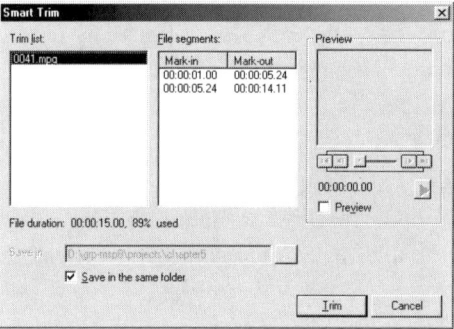

The fact that we've now fixed the contiguousness of the clips (contiguousness?) means Video Editor now recognizes that some trimming has been done.

6. Click Trim. Before trimming starts, Video Editor asks you:

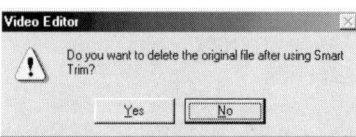

7. For our purposes, select No. However, it's not uncommon to use Smart Trim just to save disk space. In those cases, select Yes.

Either way, it creates the files and presents you with a report which tells you, among other things, the exact names and location of the files it just created.

Timeline Trim Options

In our first trimming exercise we trimmed clips by dragging the ends of the clips directly on the timeline. However, we didn't discuss the various trim behaviors. That's what we'll look at now.

Objective
To learn how Video Editor treats clips under the various trim modes.

Reference Project
projects\chapter05\trim-options.dvp

Steps, Normal Trim
1. Open the reference project.

2. Look in the timeline toolbar for the trim group.

3. Make sure the first one ("Normal Trim") is selected.

4. Move the mouse to the rightmost edge of the first clip.

5. Click and drag to the right.

6. Since clip 0002.mpg was adjacent, you've created an overlap, and consequently added a transition between them.

Had we dragged to the left, we would have created a gap between the two clips. Normal trim mode means trimming one clip has no effect on the trim of other clips.

Steps, Overwrite Trim
1. Press Ctrl+Z or select File | Restore to undo your changes.

2. Select the second button ("Overwrite Trim").

3. Move the mouse to the rightmost edge of the first clip.

4. Again, move it to the right.

5. Examine the difference:

The most obvious difference is the lack of a transition. The astute reader will realize: no transition means no overlap. Instead, clip 0001.mpg, on its journey to the right, has *overwritten* the corresponding frames of clip 0002.mpg and consequently trimming it in the process. Clip 0002.mpg now has a new mark-in point.

Clip 0002 Before:

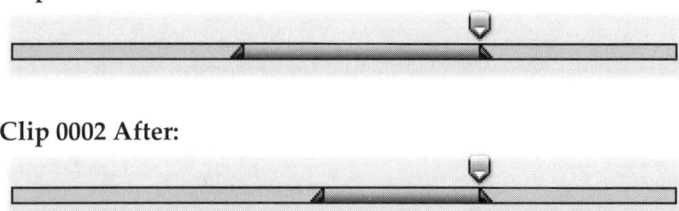

Clip 0002 After:

6. Now drag the end of 0001.mpg back to the left, and take a look:

It left a big hole. That's the key to overwrite trimming. It only goes one way. If you want it to snap back both ways, that's where stitch trimming comes in.

Steps, Stitch Trim

1. Press **Ctrl+Z** twice or select **File | Restore** to undo your changes.

2. Select the third button ("Stitch Trim").

3. Move the mouse to the rightmost edge of the first clip.

4. Drag to the right, as with the Overwrite exercise.

5. Release the mouse.

6. Now drag to the left.

This time you can see how the edges of each clip stay in contact, no matter which way you drag them. Also, when in Stitch

mode, you'll notice that the Preview Window turns into a split screen, as shown here. This lets you know simultaneously which frames are showing in each clip.

One final note on the trim modes. These exercises worked because the two clips I gave you had extra video to spare. To put it another way, if these two clips were fully trimmed out, we wouldn't have been able to drag their edges at all. (Can't normally drag past the end of a clip.)

Adjusting Audio Volume

Video Editor provides several mechanisms for changing the volume of audio tracks. One prominent method is to use the audio mixer. However, for many quick and easy adjustments, the audio mixer is overkill. In this exercise we'll learn a much easier way to change the volume.

Objective
To learn what rubber bands are and how they affect volume.

Reference Project
none

Steps
1. Start a new Video Editor project.

2. Place countdown-cued.wav on track Audio1.

3. Make sure cues are visible. Click View | Timeline Display Mode and under the Audio section make sure Show cue bar on track is checked.

4. Note the line running lengthwise down the center of the audio clip:

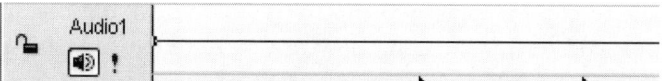

This line represents the volume level. It is also known as a rubber band. By default it's set to 100% (or +0.00 dB). And although it might not be obvious from looking at it, you can edit this line.

5. Move your cursor anywhere over this center line and the pointer changes to a hand:

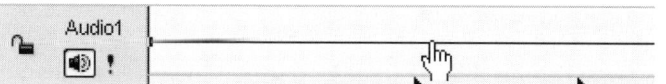

6. With the hand pointer showing, click once. This creates a control point:

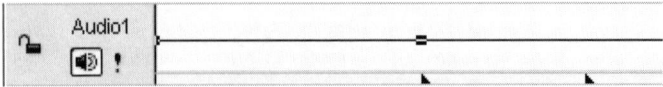

Moving this control point up increases volume. Moving it down decreases volume. If you press and hold the Shift key before doing this, a numeric representation of the level change is displayed, like so:

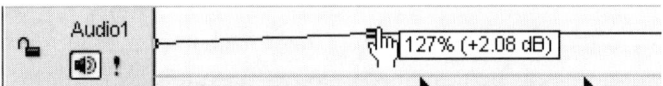

There's no limit (that I've found) on the number of control points you can have on a clip:

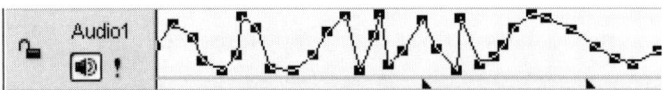

You **delete** a control point by clicking and dragging it down off the bottom of the clip. You can delete *all* control points by selecting the audio clip, right-clicking, and selecting Reset Volume.

Okay, now back to the exercise!

7. If you've made any edits, get back to this point:

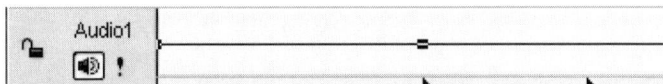

Every audio clip contains two control points by default: one at the beginning and one at the end. They are no different from the user-created control points and therefore can be adjusted up and down.

8. Let's fade in the clip. Click the starting control point and drag down:

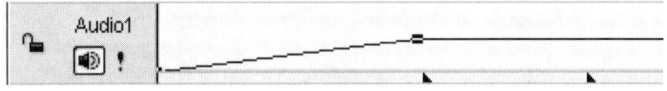

Tip. If you end up creating a control point instead of selecting the first, zoom into the timeline closer.

Fading Out. Fading audio should now be obvious. Try it on your own at the end of this clip. Scrub the timeline or render to preview.

Other Ways to Change Audio Volume

When two audio clips on the same track overlap, by default, a **cross-fade** is applied. This behavior can be changed on the Edit tab of the Preferences dialog box. When enabled you can also select the type of fade: Linear or Logarithmic. I've found in many cases the difference is negligible.

Volume can also be changed using **Audio Filters**, such as Normalize and Amplification. These are useful when you want to change the entire clip.

Ripple Editing

Once you've laid all your clips out on the timeline, you may actually find the need to go back and make changes. I know! It sounds crazy, doesn't it? As common as this is, it can be easier said than done. What happens if you change your mind and want to insert a new clip near the beginning of the project? Is there a tool to help with this? You bet: it's ripple editing.

Objective
To learn how ripple editing automatically adjusts your project in response to duration-changing timeline events.

Reference Project
projects\chapter05\ripple.dvp

Steps
1. Open the reference project.

2. First, make sure ripple editing hasn't already been turned on. Use the Edit | Ripple Editing | No Ripple command.

3. Play the project, just to get familiar with it.

4. Let's say we want to shorten the opening clip, 0011.mpg. Double click it to open it in the Source Window.

5. Move the source playhead to 0:00:03.00.

6. Click the mark-out button or press F4 to change the trim duration.

7. Click Apply to push the changes to the timeline.

We indeed changed the duration, but at the expense of messing up our project. If we want to keep the edit intact, we'll have to close the gap. Without ripple editing, this would mean moving everything from 0012.MPG on down over to the right by an amount equal to the trim duration. Ugh.

Steps, Single Track Ripple

1. Press Ctrl+Z to undo the trim.

2. Switch to single-track ripple mode. You can use the menu command, the toolbar button, or simply press the R key once. The toolbar reflects the current mode.

3. Return to the Source Window, move the playhead back to 3-seconds, and trim again. This time, everything from 0012.MPG on down moved to the left automagically filling the gap:

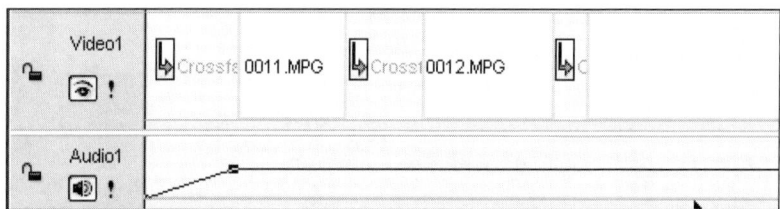

4. Play the project again. While we fixed the gap problem, there are other issues. The audio is off and the title clip in Video2 is no longer aligned at the right point.

Steps, Multi-track Ripple

1. Press Ctrl+Z again to undo the last edit.

2. Press R to advance from single to multi-track ripple mode.

3. Repeat the trim on 0011.mpg for a third time.

4. Now look at the timeline again:

Chapter 5 • Essential Editing Skills

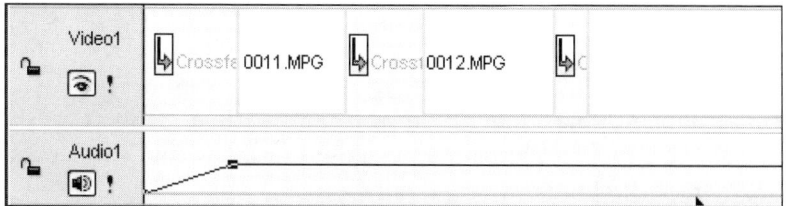

Ummm... Wait a minute. Isn't that the exact same thing as before? Yes, it is. The gap closed up but the title clip stayed put.

You see, ripple editing is a most mystical and magical thing. There are certain rules it follows and every now and then it will do something unexpected. To me, I see no reason why this duration change should not have adjusted the clip on Video2 as well.

Now let's do something that will *for sure* make it move.

5. From the Project Tray's video folder, drag 0001.mpg to track Video2 at time zero.

This time everything moved down to make room for the new clip. To help understand how and when ripple editing works, you can follow these rules of thumb. This should begin to dispel their mystical aura:

- Inserting new clips on the timeline always makes ripple editing work as expected. This is ripple editing's primary purpose.

- Moving existing clips around the timeline will not cause rippling.

- As near as I've been able to tell, changing existing clip durations only causes single-track rippling, even if multi-track rippling is on.

- Rippling won't happen if it would cause clips to move left of zero.

    As an example of this, try deleting 0011.mpg in multi-track ripple mode. No clips move. Press Ctrl+Z to restore the clip. This time move the audio clip right so it aligns with the title clip. Delete 0011.mpg again. It worked because the audio clip had a place to move.

- Deleting clips triggers ripple editing in single-track mode. In multi-track mode, nothing happens.

It's hard to tell what's designed behavior and what's a bug. The best thing to do is to just get used to it on your own. Try inserting, deleting, and trimming clips in all three ripple modes. The more you internalize the behavior, the better off you'll be in a pinch.

Tip #1. When ripple editing is off, you can still do a "push away" insert by holding down the Shift key when inserting a new clip. This works like single-track ripple editing. Try it out.

Tip #2. When ripple editing is on, and you hold down Shift when inserting a new clip, you can split an existing clip in two. I've never actually used this in real life, but I'm kind of looking forward to it.

Adding to the Middle of a Project

Let's put our new ripple editing expertise to good use. On the surface, it would seem like inserting a clip into the middle of a product is a no-brainer, with ripple editing doing all the work. The reality is you still have some work to do yourself to get it just right.

Objective
To learn how ripple editing can help when inserting a clip into the middle of a project.

Reference Project
projects\chapter05\ripple.dvp

Steps
1. Open the reference project.

2. Turn on multi-track ripple editing.

    Our goal is to place a new clip on Video1 between the existing clips 0012 and 0014.

3. From the Project Tray, drag clip 0001.mpg to the timeline right at the point where the title clip starts. Drop it on 0014.mpg.

    You can't do it, can you? This is another one of those times where ripple editing can't quite figure out what it should do, so it disallows the operation completely. Hit the Escape key to cancel the drop. Instead, we're going to have to drop it to an empty track first.

4. Repeat Step 3, but this time drop 0001.mpg on the timeline on track Video3 directly above the title clip.

    Take a look at the result:

Chapter 5 • Essential Editing Skills   139

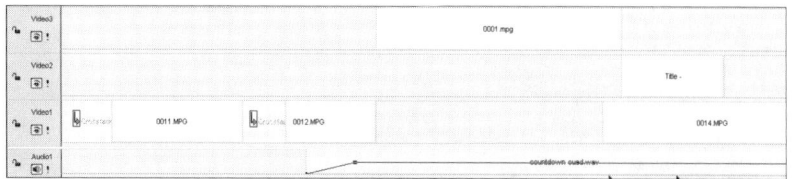

Well, that mostly helped. The primary unintended side effect is that the audio track moved too. Rippling helped, but we still have work.

5. Slide the audio clip back to where it was.

6. Drag 0001.mpg down to Video1.

7. Make further adjustments as necessary, to suit your project.

Previewing

Everything we've done so far has been pretty small, so we haven't been overly concerned about setting preview ranges or sending preview results to an external device. But as projects grow in complexity, you'll definitely want to vary your preview settings to fit your editing needs.

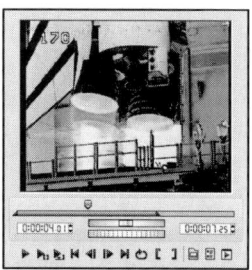

Objectives
To learn how to set a preview range and redirect output to an external display device.

Reference Project
projects\chapter05\preview1.dvp

Steps, Preview Range
1. Open the reference project.

2. Move the mouse to the timeline until it changes to this: ▿.

3. Around the 1-second point, click and drag to the right for a couple seconds, then release. A blue line will appear like this:

This is a preview range. It is very helpful when working on a very specific part of the timeline, and you want to focus only on the task at hand, and not the entire project.

4. On the preview window there are three play buttons:

	Description	Shortcut
▶	Play from current point to end of project	Enter
▶₁	Play entire preview range	Shift+Space
▶₁	Play from current point to end of range	Space

Get used to the shortcut keys because they help out a lot. Get used to me repeating that a lot too.

5. Click the middle button to play the preview range.

Additional Methods
As you might expect, there's more than one way to skin this cat. You can also set or change your preview range by directly dragging the end-markers in the preview window. You can also change the location of the preview area (preserving its duration) by dragging the blue bar itself. This works both from the Preview window and from the timeline itself.

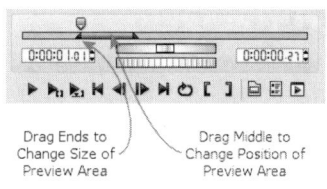
Drag Ends to Change Size of Preview Area
Drag Middle to Change Position of Preview Area

You can also use the Edit | Preview Range command to tweak your preview range by the numbers. Use this if you know exactly what your preview range is supposed to be beforehand, as there's no visual reference with this method. If you know your range is a frame or two too long, this can be an easier way to adjust, than trying to click and drag.

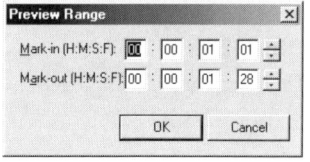

Redirecting Preview Output
Watching the output on the Preview Window is good, but if you know your video isn't destined for a computer monitor, it isn't optimal to preview it that way. You don't get true WYSIWYG editing that way.

Video Editor gives you the option of sending the Preview output to an external device. The most common approach is to send the output back down your FireWire line to a DV camera or A/D converter.

In doing so, you can take the tiny on-screen Preview Window and send it to a full-sized external TV monitor. But the larger size is only half the benefit: seeing your work "as is" is the big advantage, especially when it comes to television overscanning (see page 215).

Chapter 5 • Essential Editing Skills   141

To continue this particular exercise, I will assume you have a DV camcorder (or equivalent) hooked to your PC via FireWire. Further, you have an external monitor hooked to the analog A/V output of the camcorder. I realize this doesn't cover every single situation, but it's definitely representative of the concept.

Also note that this setup is optimal for DV sources. We, on the other hand, are working with small VCD clips, so the results may not be quite as stunning! If possible, try this out on your own, using real DV clips.

Steps, External Device

1. Go to the Preview Window.

2. From the Preview Window Menu, click Playback Options...

3. In the middle of the dialog box, under "Playback in" you'll see several selections. In this case select DV Camcorder.

   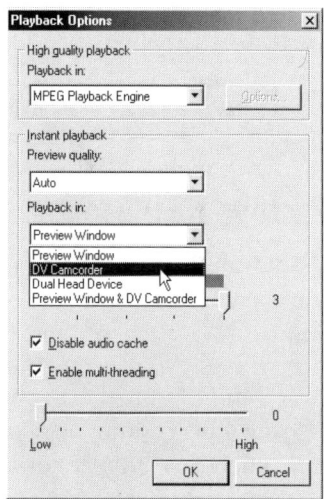

   Note there's an option for sending it to both places at the same time, but this may be problematic depending on your particular hardware setup.

4. Make sure your camcorder is in VCR or playback mode (not camera or record mode.)

5. Double check all cable connections. Turn everything on.

6. Now press Shift+Space to play the preview range. The output should be visible on the external monitor.

Additional Timelines & Virtual Clips

Everything we've done up until now has been on a single timeline. Video Editor actually supports an *unlimited* number of timelines. For the beginning editor, the benefits of multiple timelines may seem elusive. Heck, even the seasoned editor might not see the advantages at first. I know more than a few people who just said, "Huh?"

So before we advance to the next set of editing topics, let's make sure we're fully aware of what multiple timelines are and how they can help us. I hope you're not tired of learning yet. We're only on page 142!

Reference Projects
projects\chapter05\start.dvp
projects\chapter05\timelines.dvp

Steps
1.   Open the starter project.

2.   Move the cursor to the Main Timeline tab and right-click.

3.   Select Create New Timeline. You should now have a second timeline called Timeline1:

The timeline itself will be blank. If you want, click back and forth between the two to see the difference.

Avoiding Misunderstandings
As soon as you see this new, blank timeline in your project, you might jump to a few conclusions. Let's make sure they're not the wrong ones.

- "Multiple timelines" does not mean "multiple open projects." You are still working on a single project—a single DVP file. To put it another way, this is not like having two word processing documents open at the same time.

- Individual timelines cannot be saved as projects. But this sure would be nice sometimes.

- Individual timelines *can* however be rendered to their own video files. This sort of makes them feel like individual projects. But they're not. See the first bullet.

Chapter 5 • Essential Editing Skills   143

- Multiple timelines, additional timelines, secondary timelines, and nested timelines are terms generally used interchangeably.

- Individual timelines may or may not be linked to clips in other timelines. (More on this in just a couple of pages.)

For now, let's continue with the exercise.

Steps, Part 2
1. Right-click on the Timeline1 tab.

2. Select "Rename Timeline"

3. Rename it to: Through the Clouds and click OK.

4. Click on clip 0014.mpg in the Project Tray.

5. Hold the Ctrl key down and click on 0015.mpg.

6. Drag both to the timeline.

7. Admire your work.

   Amazing, isn't it! No? Hmmm... well, you do have a point. We really haven't done anything special at all—nothing we haven't already done up to this point. And since we can't save this as a separate project, you might be wondering what all the hoopla's about. Don't worry. We're almost there.

8. Right-click on the timeline tab again. Follow this path:

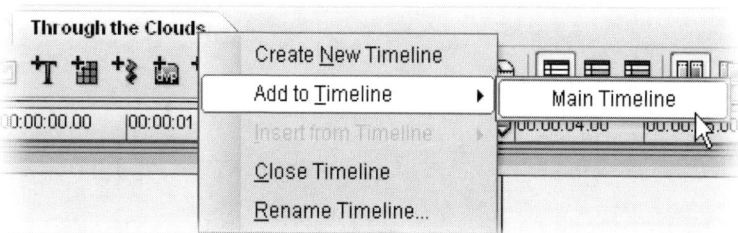

9. When Video Editor switches back to the main timeline, drop the clip to the right of the existing clip.

You just created a Virtual Clip. At the moment, you may not realize how cool this is, but think about what just happened here. An entire timeline is now a single clip. And now that it is a clip, you can do anything to it that you can do to any other clip. *That* is just what's so cool about this.

We've barely scratched the surface, so I don't expect the full impact of this to hit you for a while. For now, just trust me.

Steps, Part 3
1. Right-click anywhere in the timeline tab row.

2. Select Create New Timeline again.

3. Drag clips 0021.mpg and 0022.mpg to the new timeline.

4. Trim 0022.mpg to around 3 seconds (doesn't have to be exact).

5. Make them overlap for about 1 second.

6. Switch from the Project Tray to the Production Library.

7. Open the Transitions gallery. Open the Clock folder.

8. Drag Sweep to the existing Crossfade transition and click to overwrite it. It will look like this if you scrub it.

9. Rename the timeline to "Landing."

10. Now add it to the Clouds timeline:

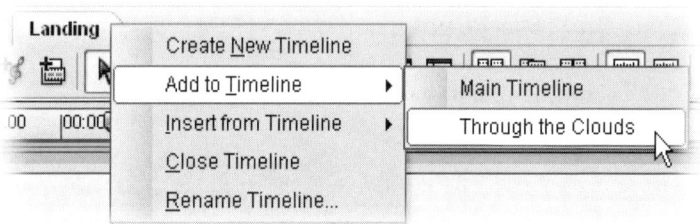

11. Drop it anywhere on track Video2 for now. We'll get back to it soon.

12. Trim the two cloud clips to each be about 3 seconds in duration. Again, specifics don't matter. We're just demonstrating.

13. Make them overlap about 1-second too:

14. Now, take the Landing virtual clip and make it overlap clip 0015.mpg, again, for about 1-second.

15. Drag two random transitions between 0014.mpg & 0015.mpg and between 0015.mpg & Landing. I used a Page Peel and a Barn Door Slide. You can choose your own transitions or use my selections.

    (This is one time when I *do* advocate pulling meaningless, random transitions out of the air—to make a point.)

16. Now, without doing anything else, switch to the Main Timeline.

You should notice something interesting. Changes made to the secondary timeline are now available in the corresponding virtual clip on the main timeline.

When we added the secondary timeline to the main timeline, we created a *link* between these two objects. This link stays there forever. This means adding a clip to the end of a secondary timeline allows you to extend the virtual clip to include this new content. There's no need to delete the virtual clip and re-add it due to a change.

Link Demonstration

1. Change your timeline display mode to either filmstrip or thumbnail mode, if it isn't already.

2. Make note of the rightmost thumbnail on the main timeline.

3. Switch to the Through the Clouds timeline. Make note of its rightmost thumbnail too. (It should be identical!)

4. Switch to the Landing timeline.

5. Drag clip 0001.mpg to the end and overlap it with 0022.mpg.

6. Switch back to Through the Clouds. The rightmost thumbnail is different.

7. Switch back to the main timeline. Ditto.

You've now witnessed this "live link" property between virtual clips and timelines first hand. At this point, play the main timeline and you'll see all our clips and all our transitions all in one project.

Virtual Clip Durations

You might have noticed that the end clip appears to have a freeze frame. This is because we shortened the clips on the secondary timeline, yet did not change the duration of the virtual clip. While its true that content-wise the virtual clips and their corresponding timelines are linked, this is not true about their durations.

While at first glance this might seem like a bug, it's probably more of a blessing. Consider the case where you have two virtual clips on the main timeline overlapped with a transition. You then edit the first virtual clip by adding another clip to its end. Now, what should happen when you return to the main timeline? Should it adjust? Auto-fit? Ripple? I think the (wise) decision was made to leave that up to *you*, the editor. This "bug" is actually a tight lid on a can of worms.

Closing Timelines

1. Click on the Landing timeline.

2. Right-click on the Landing tab, select Close Timeline, and you'll see this frightening message.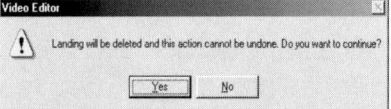

   Makes you think all your hard efforts are about to go down the drain, doesn't it? The fact is there are *two* kinds of timelines: those that are linked to a virtual clip on another timeline and those that aren't. If your timeline is linked to a virtual clip on another timeline, then clicking Yes does **not** mean it's all gone for good. Clicking Yes simply carries out the action you started, namely: Close Timeline.

   If, on the other hand, you have not inserted this timeline into another timeline, then the timeline will indeed be deleted and the action cannot be undone. I wish there were different messages for each situation. It would help us understand the underlying links better.

3. Click Yes.

4. Go to the Through the Clouds timeline.

5. Double-click the Landing virtual clip.

6. See? It's back! Nothing was lost.

This brings us to the end of the first *real* chapter of the book. As always, make sure you're comfortable with these basic editing techniques before moving on. They are all used in one way or another throughout the remainder of the book.

6

The Standard Bag of Tricks

Like the previous chapter, you will learn standard editing techniques guaranteed to pop up in your editing.

We're Still Just Editing

I know, I know. Things have been rather dry up to this point. We spent the entire last chapter on mundane things like trimming. And while there's no arguing that trimming is a very important aspect of video editing, learning about it is about as exciting as watching a three hour MPEG file encode.

In this chapter, we still stick to "just editing" but don't worry. It should be a bit more interesting than just randomly changing the length of clips on the timeline.

Slow & Fast Motion

Changing the speed of a clip changes everything. Slow motion can add emotional intensity. Fast motion can grab your audience's attention.

Objective
To see how videos can be sped up or slowed down.

Reference Projects
projects\chapter06\start.dvp
projects\chapter06\speed.dvp

Steps, Part 1
1. Open the starter project.

2. Click the Time Stretch tool on the toolbar—the far right button in the selection group.

3. Move the mouse cursor the rightmost edge of the clip. When it's in place, the cursor will change to this: ⇥⇤.

4. At this point, drag just as if you were trimming. But *unlike* trimming you can actually extend past the end of the clip.

This is because you're not trimming, you're stretching. If you stretch the clip out to twice its length, it will play at half speed. If you squish it to half its length, it will play at double speed. Video Editor will drop or duplicate frames in order to compensate.

Press the play button on the Preview Window to observe the effects of various speed changes.

Steps, Part 2

1. Revert your edits with File | Restore and return to Clip Selection mode.

2. Click once on clip 0001.mpg to select it.

3. Right-click and from the popup menu, select Speed...

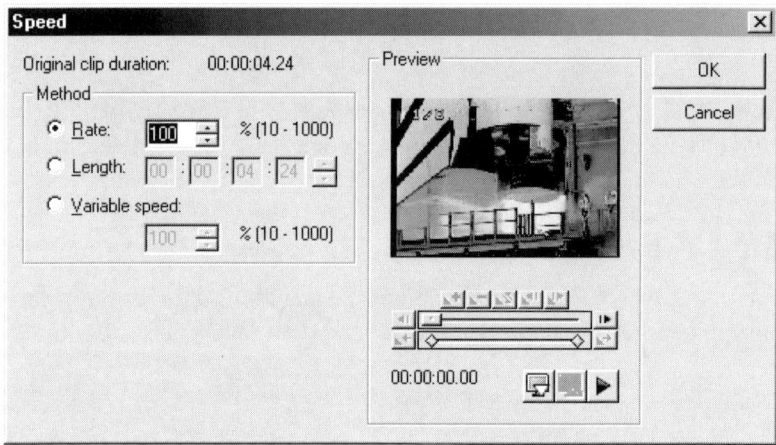

There are two basic methods for altering the speed of a clip. The first is by setting a **fixed rate** (50% is half speed, 200% is double speed, and so on). The second is by **setting the length** of the clip, and allowing Video Editor calculate the necessary rate to fit that length.

4. Manually change the rate to 50% and play the clip.

5. Go back and change the rate to 500% and watch it fly.

6. Now take a look at the Variable speed setting.

6. Now take a look at the Variable speed setting.

The Variable speed option is similar to the fixed Rate setting, but allows you to set multiple rates per clip. Video Editor interpolates the in-between rates. The variable rates are set with the keyframe controller on the right. We'll study keyframes in the next chapter. For now, though, look at the speed settings of clip 0031.mpg in the project. Each diamond is a keyframe, so I have six different speed settings in this one clip. Play the project to see how variable speed works.

A Note on Slow Motion

Any speed setting less than 100% will appear to be in slow motion, however this isn't *true* slow motion. By doubling the length of time a clip plays, Video Editor simply copies frames to fill the spaces. You get a reasonable approximation of slow motion, but it ain't the real thing. The slower the speed, the more visible the "fill frames" become. The result: jerky playback.

True slow motion requires the use of high speed cameras. A camera shooting at 60 frames per second, when played back at 30 frames per second, will provide true slow motion.

That said, software does exist to give smooth slow motion based on normal speed sources. Instead of simply copying frames to fill the gaps, the software interpolates what it *thinks* the missing frame should look like, and uses that in place of the duplicated frame. DynaPel's MotionPerfect software is just one example.

Going Backwards

For hours and hours of family fun, get out your video camera, tape yourself running around, eating, drinking, etc. Then load it up in Video Editor and play it all backwards.

Objective
To learn how to play video clips in reverse.

Reference Projects
projects\chapter06\start.dvp
projects\chapter06\reverse.dvp

Steps
1. Open the starter project.

2. Drag clip 0002.mpg from the Project Tray to the timeline.

3. Right-click the clip.

4. Select Reverse from the popup menu.

5. That's it.

Preview your work. You'll see the Space Shuttle making an odd return home. (I can hear the commander now, "I told you to go *before* we left.")

Freeze Frame

The freeze frame is one of my all-time favorite effects. It can be used for many different emotional responses, and can add a classy touch to your video when used appropriately. There are two methods for creating a freeze frame. I call them *the old way* and *the new way*.

Freeze frames were not directly supported before Version 5, so you had to create them by hand. That's the old way. From Version 5 on, a built-in freeze frame function was introduced. This is the new way.

Using the built-in freeze frame, you can specify either an in-point (freeze before), an out-point (freeze after), or both. Each freeze can have its own duration. There is also a "Deinterlace freeze frame" checkbox, which is helpful if you are working with interlaced video and are getting interlacing artifacts, such as "striped" or jittery video. If not, just leave it unchecked.

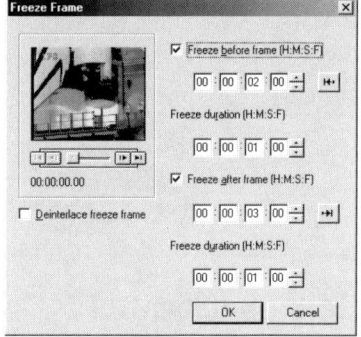

Once you've set your freeze points and returned to the timeline, you will notice that your clip now looks different. That's because Video Editor color-codes the freeze area. This is a *great* improvement from earlier implementations of this feature. Let's take a closer look at the color coding:

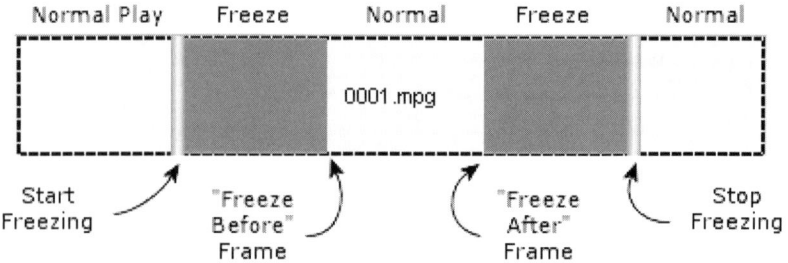

Chapter 6 • The Standard Bag of Tricks 151

The shaded areas represent the periods where the clip is frozen. The exact frame being duplicated is indicated by the "freeze before frame" and "freeze after frame" points. The gold bars mark the opposite end of the freeze. (If you don't see the gold bars, select the clip first. They do not appear when the clip isn't selected.) You can change the duration of the freeze without displaying the Freeze Frame dialog box. If you hold down the shift key and click one of the gold bars, you can drag the end of the freeze accordingly. The gold bars will snap to normal edit points.

> The reference project freeze-frame1.dvp contains the above pictured clip for you to examine. Try changing the freeze points and durations on your own.

Now that you've seen how the new way works, let's try doing one the old way. It's a good exercise for some other Video Editor features.

Objective
To learn how to create your own freeze frame effect by hand.

Reference Projects
projects\chapter06\start.dvp
projects\chapter06\freeze-frame2.dvp

Steps

1. Open the starter project.

2. Double click the clip to bring it into the Source Window.

3. Go to the end of the clip by clicking the "Last Edit" button or by pressing the Page Down key.

4. Click the "Previous Frame" button three times and press F4. This should have created a mark-out point at 00:00:04.21.

5. Click the Apply button.

6. Now, from the Source Window menu, select the Save Image To | Production Library command. (Introduced on page 51.)

7. Now try and find it. ☺

    The thumbnail is placed under the main Images folder in the Media Library. The physical file has been saved to an Images directory under your My Documents folder. I wish there was a way to change this, but there isn't.

8. Drag the image file 0001-1.bmp to the timeline and drop it immediately to the right of the video clip, like so:

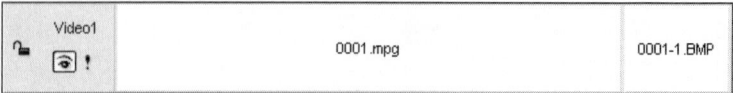

9. Preview your work and you'll have a freeze-frame much in the same way the built-in freeze frame function works.

You're probably asking yourself, "Well, if this does the same thing as the built-in function, why not just use the built-in function? Sheesh!" And to that I say, "Please hold all questions until the end of the tour." Otherwise we'll never get through this.

Actually, you have a very good question. There are two reasons you might want to do it this way:

- A separate image clip means just that: *a separate clip*. You have the advantage of being able to move it to another track, if you need the space immediately to the right of the clip.

- Freeze frame settings and speed settings are mutually exclusive. If you decide to halve the speed of your freeze-frame clip, Video Editor will delete the freeze information. Using the two-clip method describe here means you can have your cake and freeze it too.

Adding Text to Your Video

Video Editor has a special built-in clip for adding text. It's called the Title Clip. It's rather versatile, allowing you to do all sorts of funky things with text. Some of it, frankly, is a bit *too* funky. I don't think I have ever used (or will ever use) ninety-seven percent of the effects in here. But, different strokes for different folks. Let's take a look.

Objectives
To learn how to add a simple Title Clip to your project.

Reference Projects
projects\chapter06\start.dvp
projects\chapter06\title-clip.dvp

Steps
1. Open the starter project and select the placeholder clip.

2. Click the Insert Title Clip button (**T**) and stand back.

Chapter 6 • The Standard Bag of Tricks

Wow. There's a lot going on here, in just one little title clip. It takes a little while to get used to the buttons and where everything is and what everything does. It takes a little longer to discover all the quirks. In some ways, I think it's trying to do *too* much at once.

3. Continuing the exercise, double-click there to add a title.

   At this point, the window goes into full WYSIWYG mode. The background shows a complete rendering of the timeline at the current playhead position. You get pixel-accurate positioning of your titles in the frame. No guesswork involved.

4. Enter "Lift Off" for the title text.

5. Click on 001 for the Title Style.

6. Drag the lower left hand handle on the clip to change the size.

7. This style has a drop shadow. Using the blue handle to the right of the title, move the shadow out a bit. This is a nice and quick way of placing shadows.

8. Or if you like making precise shadow settings, click the shadow properties button. It's the right-most button on the shadow group.

9. Set the shadow properties to match these values.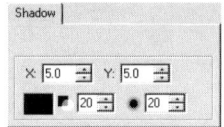

   Note that the main display changes in response to changes made on this dialog box.

10. Lastly, center the title in the frame. You can do this visually by dragging it into position. An easier (and more accurate) way is to simply click one of the nine standard alignment buttons.

11. Click OK to close the Title Clip dialog box.

12. Drop the clip in track Video2 over the video clip in track Video1.

13. Align the right edges of the clips, like so:

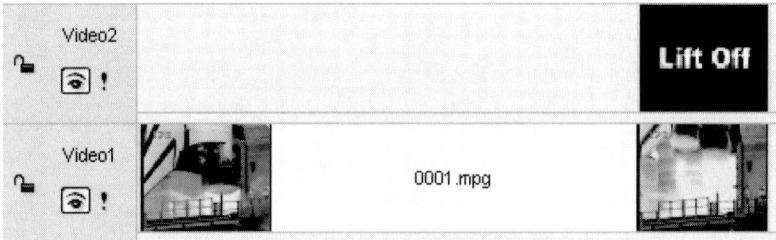

14. Preview your work.

There is, of course, *lots* more that can be done with the Title Clip than just this. This was just a basic introduction, suitable in the context of this chapter. We'll do quite a bit more titling in Chapter 8.

Audio Mixing

Video without audio is like a pizza without toppings. Of course, there's audio, and then there's *audio*. If you're throwing some camera clips on the timeline or adding a simple music track, most of your audio mixing can be done directly from the timeline. But if you need total over control volume and pan settings (including creating 5.1 Surround Sound) you need the Audio Mixer.

Objectives
To learn how to mix audio tracks in real time.

Caveat
This exercise is a fine example of dealing with "the way it should work" versus "the way it really works." As of this writing, the audio mixer has

more than a few problems. This leaves me in a dilemma: do I just pretend there is no audio mixer? Do I note the problems and discuss the workarounds? Do I write it as if it works and hope a patch is on the way?

Well, in the "no nonsense" spirit, here's what I decided on. First, I acknowledge that the audio mixer exists. Second, I have provided a short exercise to help you get familiar with it. Third, I have abruptly ended the exercise in frustration. I can't lie to you. This mixer drives me nuts.

For this reason I would read through this first before trying anything out on your own. Please use the *Getting Results* feedback page and let me know about your personal audio mixing experiences.

Reference Projects

projects\chapter06\audio-start.dvp

Steps

1. Open the audio starter project.

   I didn't want to spend time with more editing steps, so you'll find a pre-edited project with three clips in the video tracks: two video and one color, with transitions. We're going to focus on the audio portion, of course: one music track and one audio file with voice.

2. Open the Audio Mixing Panel by pressing **Ctrl+7**. If it appears in a docked state, float it for now by double clicking the title bar.

   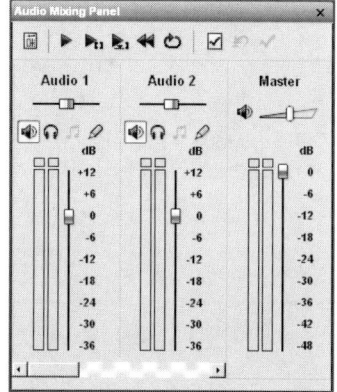

   I've sized mine to display the first two audio tracks. (Unless you have two computer monitors, conserving screen real estate is always an issue.)

3. For now, just click the play button on the panel and watch it light up.

4. Click play again, but this time move the volume and pan sliders around. Try it on both audio tracks. Try it out on the master track. For now, just get a feel for them.

5. And click play one more time. Did you hear your changes play back this time? No? Well, that's because you didn't record them, silly.

This mixer comes up in "read only" mode by default. This allows you to mess with the sliders and practice your takes before messing up your actual project. Once you have an idea of what you want to do, click the little "pencil" button above the track's dB setting. This puts you in write mode.

6. Click the pencil for track Audio 2. I want to fade the volume of the voiceover as the project fades out *and* I want to pan it to the far left. This requires two passes:

- First pass: gradually decrease volume on fade out starting at just after the "Lift off" phrase. When done, click the Apply button.

- Second pass: give up.

I had some luck doing one audio mix at a time. But as soon as I tried to do multiple mixes, things just went out the window. It very well may be that this does work and I'm just not holding my mouth right. If that's the case, then there are bigger issues than bugs.

J-Cut & L-Cut

If you even recognize these terms, then odds are you already know how to do them, and you're free to move on. There's nothing magical about the way Video Editor handles them.

The J-cut and L-cut are two sides of the same editing technique (known as a "split edit") where the audio portion of the clip is a different length than the video portion. As you can see below, these look *just* like the letters J and L. (Don't they!?)

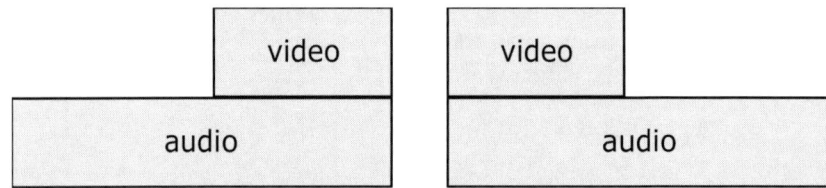

Keep in mind the audio and video are part of the exact same clip and where they overlap they are in sync together. It's a technique I happen to like quite a lot. There are times I've done it just for the sake of the effect, and there are other times I've used it to cover up a mistake.

One mistake in particular happened during a wedding reception. My camera operator was off shooting some family shots when the best man unexpectedly began the toast. She turned on the camera and began recording, just to start capturing the all-important audio, while at the same time running to the table where the toast was being given. Once there, she filmed the remainder of the toast with a steady shot. When it came to post-production, I had a good five seconds or more of the camera pointed at the floor running, with the audio from the toast. This was a perfect opportunity to use the audio for a J-cut.

I replaced the unusable footage with a montage of good footage. I used the audio from the toast under the montage. The result: perfect.

Unusable	Best Man's Toast (video)	Original Footage
	Best Man's Toast (audio)	

Montage	Best Man's Toast (video)	Final Cut
Music	Best Man's Toast (audio)	

Objectives

This exercise has multiple objectives:

- To learn how to create a project from scratch (it's about time!)

- To learn how to populate the Project Tray.

- To learn how to split the audio from the video in a clip.

Reference Project

projects\chapter06\j-cut.dvp

Steps, Create a New Project

1. Start Video Editor.

2. Press **Ctrl+N** or select **File | New...** to start a new project.

3. Change the Edit file format from AVI to MPEG.

4. At the bottom of the list of existing templates, select **Video CD-NTSC**.

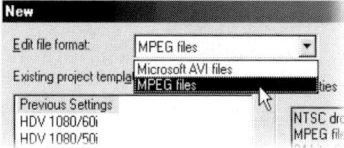

The next time you start a new project, Video Editor will default to this value (under the name "Previous Settings"). The downside to starting a new project is you don't have a pre-loaded Project Tray. So let's do that.

Steps, Load Your Own Project Tray

1. Click on the Project Tray tab, if it isn't already in view.

2. Open the Media Bin and click on the Video folder.

3. In the open area on the right, right-click and select Import Video File.

4. Select all video clips. There are several ways to do this:

    - Press Ctrl+A. If there are any folders, they will be selected too, but ignored during the import. *Or...*

    - Click 0001.mpg. Scroll (if necessary) to bring 0042.mpg into view. While holding the Shift key, click on 0042.mpg. *Or...*

    - Hold down the Ctrl key and select each clip individually. This is recommended for non-contiguous selections.

5. Click Open. You will see a sorting dialog box.

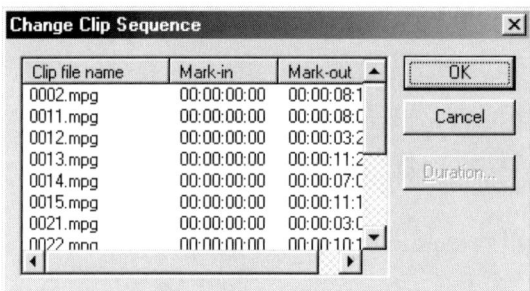

Odds are, no matter which order you selected the clips, they'll come up in a different order here. That's just a peculiarity of Windows. Click the "Clip file name" heading to sort by name. Then press OK.

6. Wait a few moments, and the Project Tray will now be populated with thumbnails of each clip.

Steps, Performing the J-Cut

1. Drag clip 0042.mpg from the Project Tray to the timeline.

2. Double-click it to load it in the Source Window.

3. Click play and listen. After the announcer says, "3... 2... 1..." stop playback and hit F5 to create a cue. This should be around 00:00:05.20.

4. Click Apply. If the cue doesn't appear on the timeline, make sure the timeline cues are displayed, as discussed on page 124.

5. With the clip selected, right-click on it and select Split from the popup menu. This will divide the audio and video portions into two distinct clips.

6. Holding the "S" key (for scissors) position the cursor on the video clip right at the cue. Click to slice, and you'll have this:

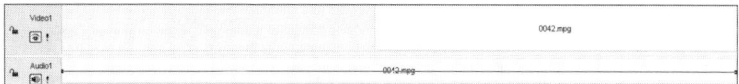

7. Click on the left-hand portion of 0042.mpg and press delete:

You now have a perfect J shape!

Important: Now that the video and audio have been split, they can be moved independently, which is bad, because you really want the parts that overlap to stay in sync. You have two choices to fix this.

A. Lock The Clips

- Click on either clip.

- Right-click and select Locked from the popup menu. At this point the clip is locked to that timeline position and cannot be moved. A small indicator icon appears on the clip as well.

- Repeat for the other clip.

This works well if you know the clips are going to stay where they are and never move. If instead you think you will need to move them, then it's better to…

B. Group The Clips

- Unlock the clips if you already locked them. (Right-click and uncheck Locked from the popup.)

- Click on what's left of the video half of 0042.mpg

- Holding the Ctrl key, click on the audio.

- Right-click and select Group from the popup menu.

Now the clips will move as a unit, thus giving you the best of both worlds: maintaining synchronization without inhibiting mobility.

Now back to the exercise! To properly complete our J-cut, we need to fill in the blank space.

8. Drag 0011.mpg to the timeline. Drop in track Video1 at time 0. It will extend into the 0042 clip.

9. Slice the clip right at 3 seconds. I've done this and changed my display mode to "thumbnail" for reference:

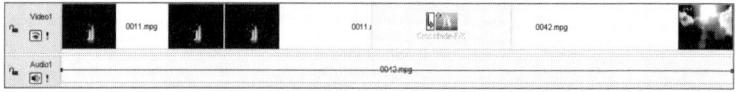

10. Discard the right-side portion of 0011. This will also automatically delete the Crossfade transition.

11. Drag clip 0001.mpg to the timeline and drop it in the newly created gap. A new Crossfade transition will appear.

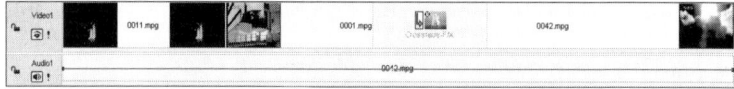

12. Now preview your work.

We've replaced nearly 8 seconds of the original clip with two other video clips, yet left the synchronized audio intact. If you watch television news shows, you'll find this technique used incessantly. And with good reason: it's a great cut.

Fade to Black Transition

This is an extremely common effect used to bring an elegant ending to a production. Fading up from black at the beginning is also very nice. If you look through the transition effects, you'll find one called "Fade to Black" in the F/X gallery. However, that isn't want we want for this effect.

Objectives
- To learn how to fade out video clips to a specific color.
- To learn how to deal with transitions that completely obscure the clip(s) being transitioned.

Reference Projects

projects\chapter06\start.dvp
projects\chapter06\fade-to-black.dvp

Steps

1. Open the starter project.

2. Insert a color clip on the timeline. You can right-click on the timeline and select "Color Clip" from the pop up menu. You can also use the Insert | Color Clip command. Lastly, there's a toolbar button:

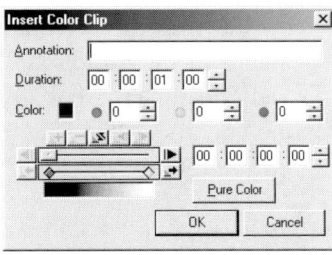

   The default duration is going to correspond to the Default inserted clip duration on the Preferences dialog box. You will also see Default background color on the Preferences dialog that will be used as the default starting color for your clip. The end color, as shown here, is white.

   Any time you see a small color square, like the little black Color box shown above, you can change the color by clicking on the square. This will display the "Ulead Color Picker" dialog box. However, if you are changing colors frequently, you might find it rather tedious having to open that dialog, select your color, and close the dialog repeatedly. It can interrupt the workflow, and get annoying after a while. If you find yourself in this situation, **right-click** the color square instead. You'll now get a neat little popup window that has thirty-two pre-defined colors for you to quickly choose. You also get the choice of bringing up the Ulead Color Picker dialog box, or the built-in Windows Color Picker dialog box. If the Ulead dialog seems overwhelming, you might feel more comfortable with the traditional Windows dialog.

3. On the Insert Color Clip dialog, click "Pure Color." Click OK.

4. Drop it on the timeline right next to 0001.mpg.

5. Now drag it to the left until complete overlapping 0001.mpg:

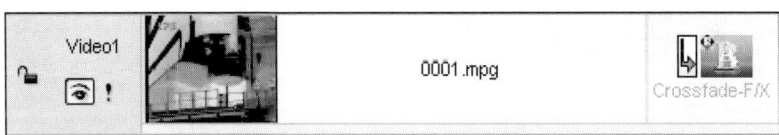

What you've just witnessed is the first casualty of single-track editing. If the transition length and the clip length are identical, you can no longer see your clip from the timeline. It's there—but completely obscured.

The way to work with this "invisible" clip is to select it. And the only way to select it is to right-click on the transition. Doing so displays this popup menu. In the middle are two options: Select Clip A and Select Clip B. That's what you want. "A" is on the left, and "B" on the right. (Not sure why they just didn't say "left" and "right.")

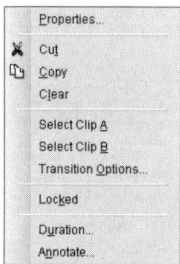

6. Preview your work.

You should now see a nice fade to black at the end of the project. If you want to fade in from black at the beginning, do the exact same thing, but place the color clip at the beginning.

Fade to Black Transition Again

In the last exercise the "Fade to Black" transition was mentioned. We couldn't use it for that situation because, being a transition, it requires two clips to overlap. We only had one clip. Let's try with two.

Objective
Mental setup for the next two exercises. That's all.

Reference Projects
projects\chapter06\start.dvp
projects\chapter06\fade-to-black2.dvp

Steps
1. Open the starter project.

2. Drag 0002.mpg from the Project Tray to the timeline.

3. Make sure the two clips overlap.

4. Drag the "Fade to Black" transition between them. You'll find it in the "F/X" folder.

5. Now preview your work.

You can easily see how this works. It's very similar to a crossfade, but halfway through the transition it fades to black for the first clip. It then fades up from black during the second half for the second clip.

Yes. I know this isn't *that* interesting in and of itself, but it's a mental springboard for the next exercise. Because—and this is the big question—what if you wanted the same effect but have it fade to white instead? If you notice, this is one of those transitions where you cannot customize anything except the duration and degree.

One of the things about being a good editor is the ability to take two different techniques and combine them to achieve something else.

Make Your Own: a Fade to White Transition

In our analysis of the last exercise, we discovered the "Fade to Black" transition is just like two crossfade-to-color transitions pushed right up against each other. So essentially that's all we have to do manually in order to construct a Fade to White transition. But once we do that, not only will we have our fade-to-white transition, we'll have all the parts and skills needed to do all sorts of other things.

Objectives
- Use multiple transitions to create a single transition.
- To learn how to trim clips you can't see.

Reference Projects
projects\chapter06\start.dvp
projects\chapter06\fade-to-white.dvp

Steps
1. With the starter project open, drag 0002.mpg to the timeline.

2. Drop it directly next to, but not overlapping, 0001.mpg.

3. Place a white color clip on track Video2 so its end aligns with the end of 0001.mpg.

4. Place a second white color clip to the right of the first color clip. Make sure they're touching, like this:

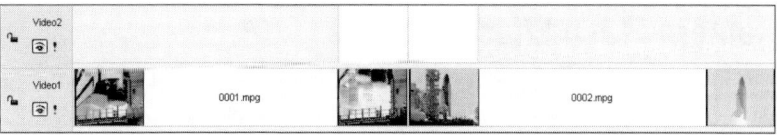

5. Lastly, just pull the two color clips straight down to the Video1 track. This will create Crossfade transitions for each:

Now preview the project. A perfect fade-to-white, isn't it? You may wonder why I had you drop the color clips to Video2 before moving them to Video1. Seems like an extra step, doesn't it? It is, but we did it that way to better illustrate what's going on. Otherwise, the color clips would have disappeared before you could see what was going on. You can (and should) drop directly to the target clips in the future.

If you want to change the duration of this effect, you'll need to change the color clips. It's not a problem that we can't see them.

Steps, Shorten Clips
1. Move the mouse until it's over the left hand edge of the first crossfade clip. You'll see the double arrow cursor again.

2. Drag to the right or the left.

That's it. You've now changed the length of the color clip. It's just another oddity about single track editing. But keep in mind: the transition itself doesn't technically exist. It's only the by-product of two clips overlapping. So any trimming you do to the transition is really a trim done to the underlying clips, whether you can see them completely or not.

Final Note. You may or may not have noticed that this effect could have been achieved with a single color clip. In this case, clip #1 would fade to the color clip, then the color clip would fade to clip #2. There are two reasons for the double-clip approach.

The first is simply because I believe using two clips is a better way for beginner's to grasp the concept. It makes tweaking and editing the effect easier. The second is that there may be times where you will require two color clips for a given effect and you'll have this experience already behind you.

Camera Flash Effect

I've always liked this effect. It simulates a camera flash going off. If you're wondering why it's here in the midst of crossfades and color clips, there's a very simple answer to that. The project is nearly identical to the previous project.

Objectives
- Use crossfades and color clips to simulate a camera flash.
- To demonstrate how the timing of an effect can completely change the effect.

Reference Projects
projects\chapter06\fade-to-white.dvp
projects\chapter06\camera-flash.dvp

Steps
1. Open the fade-to-white.dvp project from the last exercise.

2. Click the first transition to select it.

3. Right-click to display the popup menu and select Duration...

4. Change its duration to 15 **frames**: 00:00:00:15.

5. Click OK.

6. Examine what's happened.

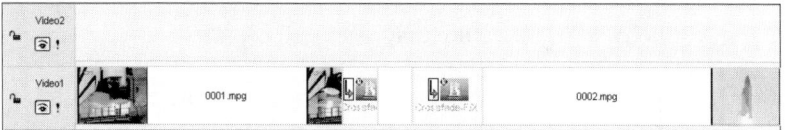

You know what? This doesn't look right. It changed the duration of the transition itself to 15 frames, and left our color clip at a full one-second length. We want the color clip changed.

Oops—Try Again
1. Press Ctrl+Z to undo this.

2. With the Crossfade still selected, right click on it.

3. Click on Select Clip B, since that's the color clip.

4. Right-click again (different menu this time).

5. Select Duration again. This time it's the color clip's duration and not the transition duration.

6. Change it to 15 frames again: 00:00:00:15.

7. Click OK.

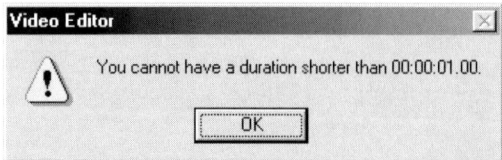

Hmmm... now what's going on? This isn't right either. Well, as it turns out, you're getting this error because Video Editor doesn't want the underlying clip shorter than the transition.

This flies in the face a bit with my earlier statement, "The transition itself doesn't technically exist. It's only the by-product of two clips overlapping."

Unfortunately, we aren't going to be able to change the length of this thing numerically. We're going to have to do it by dragging.

One Last Try

1. Zoom into the timeline to 1/6-second resolution. You can zoom to a specific resolution quickly by right-clicking anywhere on this thing.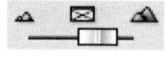

2. Click the ruler to move the playhead to 00:00:04.20.

3. Drag the left-hand edge of the transition until it snaps to the playhead position at 00:00:04.20. At this point the transition will be 4 frames in duration (as opposed to fifteen, which I only used for illustrative purposes above).

4. Scroll to the right, so the rightmost edge of 0002.mpg is visible.

5. Drag the edge to the left until the clip is 10 frames in duration. Use the status bar as a guide:

   00:00:05.02 Start: 00:00:04.24 End: 00:00:05.04 Duration: 00:00:00.10

6. Preview your work.

Functionally speaking, this is no different from the last project, yet the impression is quite different. Instead of a nice slow fade from one clip to another, we get a quick flash followed by a slow fade, as if an old fashioned flash bulb were being used. Change the duration of the second color clip to change the flash decay rate. The best part is we didn't even have to learn any new techniques to generate the new effect.

Camera Flash with Freeze Frame

To really make the camera flash effect suggest the use of a *camera*, applying a freeze frame immediately following the flash is important.

Objective
Combine different editing techniques into a single, overall effect.

Reference Projects
projects\chapter06\camera-flash.dvp
projects\chapter06\camera-flash-frozen.dvp

Steps
1. Open the camera-flash.dvp project from the last exercise.

2. Delete clip 0002.mpg. (The associated transition will also go.)

3. Move the color clips up to Video2 for now.

4. Select 0001.mpg.

5. Right click and select Freeze Frame.

6. Check "Freeze after frame."

7. Change that frame to 00:00:04:21.

8. Change Freeze duration to 00:00:00:08.

9. Zoom into 1/6-second resolution again.

10. Press "S". We're going to cut this clip.

11. Cut 0001.mpg at the freeze mark. If the cursor says you can't, it's because you're in the frozen zone. Move left until it turns back into scissors, and click.

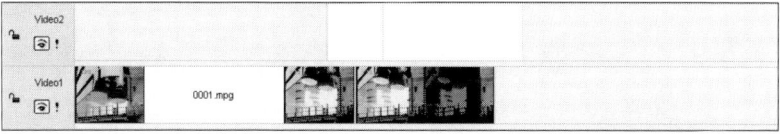

At this point, due to our scissor cut (restricted by the freeze frame) the color clips are off by two frames.

12. Drag the smaller color clip down until its right side aligns with 0001.mpg's right side.

13. Drag the larger color clip down until its left side aligns with the frozen portion of 0001.mpg's left side. This will cause the two color clips (and consequently, the two transitions) to butt up against each other:

14. Preview your work.

Freezing the image really helps suggest a photograph being taken. You not only get the flash, but a still image to go along with it. If you really want to go the full cliché, add the camera sound effect. I've already done that for you in the reference project. Check it out before moving on.

7

Beyond Just Editing

With the editing essentials now mastered, it's time to look at the key tools used for creating special effects.

Ready?

Before proceeding, let's make sure you're comfortable with everything covered in Chapters 5 and 6, because we're about to pick up the pace. The last two chapters, aimed squarely at beginners, took their own sweet time explaining the ins and outs of the core skills. But from this point out we will assume you're at ease with the Video Editor environment. Basic instructions will sound more like, "Freeze the clip at 5 seconds," rather than, "Click the clip once. Now right-click it. Select Freeze Frame from the popup menu, etc."

The exercises in this chapter will cover these Video Editor features:

- Video Filters
- Keyframes
- Moving Paths
- Overlays and Keying
- Smart Compositor

Video Filters

This is where a lot of the fun is. You can do plenty of visual effects without the use of filters, but to really spice up your clips, this is the way to go. Some filters are simple and elegant, but many are rather wild, and you must take care to use them appropriately. Just like transitions (see page 118) video filters can also have a very negative effect on your video if misused.

I won't go through dozens and dozens of video filters. However, I will pick a couple just to get you started. This is definitely one place where you really have to explore things on your own.

Objective
To familiarize yourself with applying and configuring video filters.

Reference Projects
projects\chapter07\start.dvp
projects\chapter07\filter1.dvp

Steps
1. Open the starter project.

2. In the Production Library, open the Video Filter gallery.

3. Locate the folder called 2D Mapping.

4. On the right, find the Water Flow thumbnail.

5. Drag it from the Production Library and drop it on 0101.mpg.

6. Preview your work.

    You should see Jupiter getting all wobbly on you. I chose this as our first filter because there's nothing subtle about it. You *know* you've applied a filter. Let's grab another very unsubtle filter and continue.

Steps, Adding a Second Filter
1. Go back to the Production Library's Video Filters.

2. This time locate the folder named Special.

3. Find Bubble amongst the thumbnails.

4. Drag it out and drop it on our clip.

5. What's going to happen? Something wonderful!

    Preview your work. You should now be looking at something out of a Stanley Kubrick nightmare: weird space bubbles floating over a gooey Jupiter. But it gets better.

Steps, The Order Matters
1. Delete both filters. Do this by right-clicking the clip and selecting the Delete Attributes

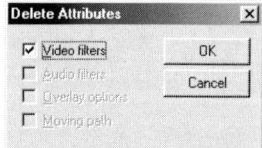

menu item. As you can tell by the disabled checkboxes, you can delete other things too. Since this clip only has filters, that's the only checkable item. Click OK.

2. Drag the Bubbles filter to the clip.

3. Drag the Water Flow filter to the clip.

4. Preview your work again.

   The nightmare is worse this time. By applying the filters in a different order, we get a very different effect.

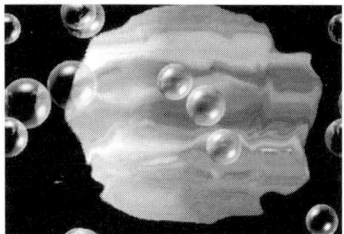 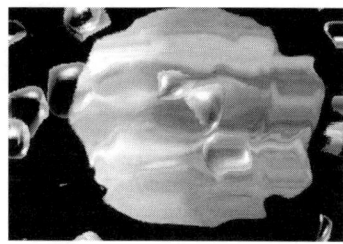

Water Flow then Bubbles   Bubbles then Water Flow

Now I never promised this would be an aesthetically pleasing exercise! Just an exercise. But we've learned three important things:

- You can make your video do weird stuff with a video filter.

- You can apply multiple video filters to a clip.

- You can change the effect by changing the order of the filters.

In the next exercise, we'll learn how to change the order of the filters without having to delete and re-add them. But I'm sure you already figured out there'd be a way to do that.

Effects Manager

As you add more and more effects to your clips, being able to easily edit (and synchronize!) them becomes important. That's where the Effects Manager comes in.

Objective
To see how the Effects Manager allows editing multiple effects easily.

Reference Project
projects\chapter07\filter1.dvp

Steps

1. Open the project. It's where we left off in the last exercise.

2. Select the 0101.mpg clip.

3. If the Effects Manager (or EM for short) isn't open, press Ctrl+8.

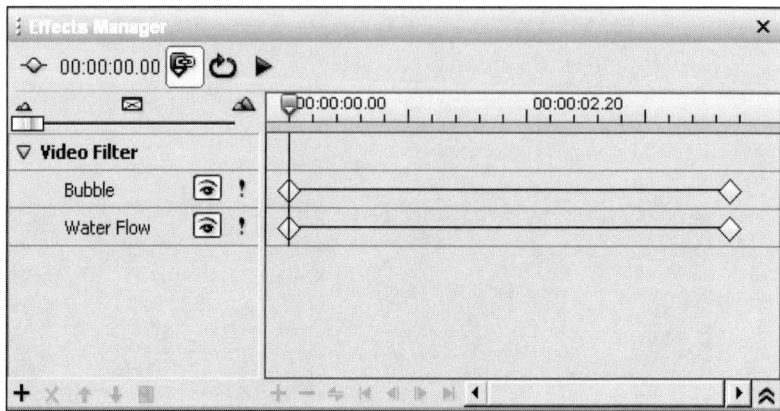

Here are the filters we applied to our clip. I just mentioned the ability to change the order of filters without having to delete and re-add them, so let's learn that first. Unfortunately you can't just click and drag to re-order them. Click on the Bubble filter, then note the button bar below the effects list.

The first four buttons let you add, remove, move up, or move down an effect. We'll get to the last button later. Right now, we just want to change the order.

Click the down arrow. The filter order should swap.

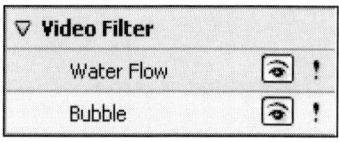

A note on the list order. Each new filter added appears at the bottom of the filter list. Since the first filters are processed first, this means the order is somewhat counter-intuitive to the timeline. On the timeline, clips on higher tracks appear in front of clips on lower tracks. In the filter list, filters lower on the list appear in front of filters higher up. Sorry.

A note on those buttons. The good news is, just like tracks, each filter has mute and solo buttons. Click an open eye to close it, and the filter will not be processed. Click the ! button and only that filter will be processed.

Steps, Editing Effects
1. Click the Bubble effect in the EM to select it.

2. Click on the first diamond just to the right.

This is a keyframe. When selected, keyframes turn red Selecting a keyframe will cause that big empty area on the EM fill up with a bunch of controls. The exact controls displayed depend on what kind of keyframe 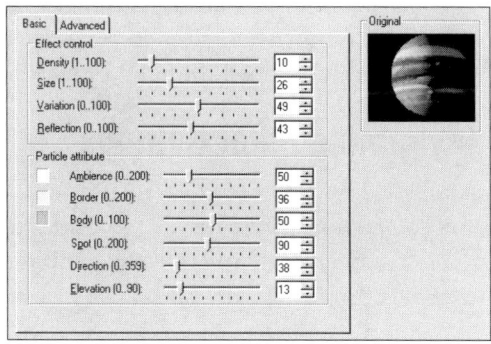 you're editing. As expected, Bubbles will have an entirely different set of controls than, say, Color Correction. So there's no telling what you'll see here.

If the entire control panel doesn't fit (as will be the case most of the time) the EM throws in scroll bars to help you out. If, on the other hand, you don't like scrolling around a little window to see all the controls, press that fifth button:

This opens up a normal, modal dialog box, with all controls in full view. This has two benefits: 1) you get to see everything at once, and 2) you get to see *everything*. By that I mean, sometimes the controls displayed in the EM are only a subset of what's actually available. The drawback is you've left the Effects Manager. This primarily means you can no longer easily synchronize events with external points (such as cues on the timeline). Also, you leave the nice, big keyframe manager behind.

Anyway, for what it's worth, I suggest looking at both while you're learning until you get a good feel for the difference.

3. Now click on the Water Flow effect's first keyframe.

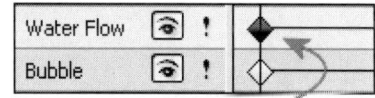

Observe that the EM has now changed. You now have access to the Water Flow effect control (it has only one, which is a good contrast to the Bubbles we saw above).

4. Change things.

   Yep. That's the last step of this exercise. Change things. Click on all four diamonds, and just start changing the values of various settings and see how the results are reflected by previewing.

   Remember the cartoon cat with the hammer? You're now setting the start and end keyframes. You're the senior animator stating how you want the start and end to look, then shuffling off all the grunt tweening work to Video Editor. Refer back to page 54 for a refresher.

Keyframing Filter Settings

Our first "roll your own" transition used a combination of transitions and color clips to create a new Fade-to-White transition. Now we're going to something similar, only combining transitions and video filters to create a Cross-blur transition.

Objective
Combine video filters and transitions to make your own custom transitions.

Reference Project
projects\chapter07\crossblur.dvp

Steps
1. Open the starter project.

2. Drag 0111.mpg to the timeline, but do not overlap the clips.

3. Using the scissors, slice one second from the end of 0101.mpg.

4. Slice one second from the beginning of 0111.mpg.

   There should now be two 0101 clips and two 0111 clips, like so:

5. In the Video Filters gallery locate the Focus folder.

6. Drop the Average filter on the smaller Jupiter clip.

   Note. When a clip has a video filter applied to it, Video Editor flags it with a small "F" icon:

7. Click on the first keyframe for the filter and set the cell size to 2.

Chapter 7 • Beyond Just Editing

8. Click on the last keyframe for the filter and set the cell size to 32.

9. Going back to the timeline, right-click the clip and select Copy.

10. Click on the smaller Saturn clip. Right-click it, and select Paste Attributes from the popup menu.

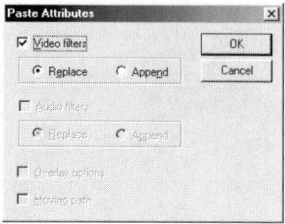

This is an extraordinarily handy feature, and you would do well to memorize it right now. Attributes can be pasted to any number of clips. Multi-select as many clips as possible and in a single paste operation, you can copy filters, overlays, and moving paths.

For our purposes, we have a single video filter. Just press OK.

11. Click on the Average filter in the Effects Manager.

12. Since we want to reverse what we just did, this is a great opportunity to click the reverse-keyframes button: ⇅. This takes the attributes of the first keyframe and swaps it with the last keyframe. And by golly, that's exactly what we need right now.

13. Lastly, add the transition. Drag the short Saturn clip so that it halfway overlaps the short Jupiter clip. Then drag the remaining Saturn clip to close the gap.

14. Preview your work.

Note 1. You might wonder why we didn't completely overlap the short clips. Well, to be able to pull off this particular effect, you really need the blur to begin *before* the transition. Otherwise, the crossfade transition masks most of the effect.

Note 2. You might also wonder why we cut the original two clips before applying the filters. Theoretically, with keyframes, you shouldn't have to do this. You could set one keyframe at the beginning, one in the middle, then one at the end, changing the intensity of the filter at each keyframe. This might conceptually look like this:

The trouble with this is not many filters have an "off" feature. For example, the lowest blur setting is 2. That would mean the clip would be somewhat blurry for the entire duration of the clip, and not just the last part, like we want. To get around this, we break it into two clips, and only apply the filter to the second one:

See? The first clip has no filter at all, and the second clip has an easy two-keyframe filter. This is also easier to work with from the timeline, since the part containing the clip is a physically separate object on the timeline. The only time this becomes difficult is when you want to change the point in time the affect occurs. Now, instead of moving one keyframe, you'll have to trim two clips.

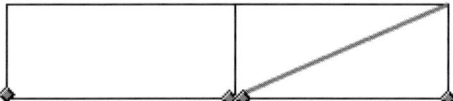

Multiple Keyframes

Let's take a quick minute to look at using more than two keyframes. By default, every video effect comes with two keyframes. You simply can't have fewer than one at the start and one at the end.

Objective
To see that clips can contain many keyframes.

Reference Project
projects\chapter07\filter2.dvp

Steps
1. Open the reference project.

And that's it. You've just personally witnessed the easiest exercise in the entire book. Of course, we're not quite finished yet. Open the project *and look at it too*. Click on either clip and look at the keyframe settings in the Effects Manager. The glass clip has a *lot* of keyframes:

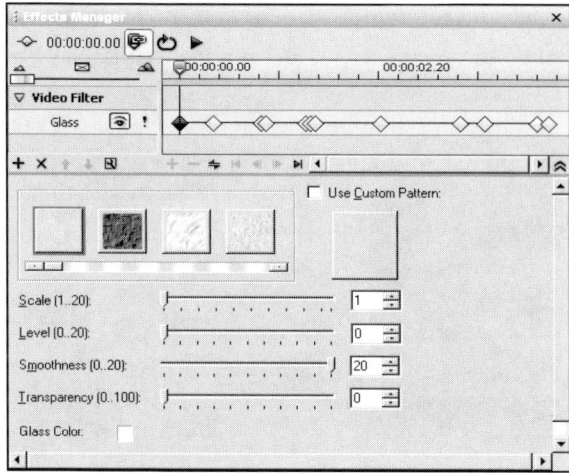

If you preview this, you'll see the effects sliders bouncing all over the place. It's a bit over the top, but there to show you what's possible.

A Note on Keyframe Attributes

Take a look at the "Glass Color" setting above. If you click through each keyframe you'll notice one where the color changes from white to blue. Like most keyframe attribute settings, this value can change over time. Compare this with the next clip, using the "Old Film" filter. This filter has a similar color control called Shift color. This setting, however, is global for the entire effect. It cannot be set per keyframe.

So how can you tell the difference between the two? You can't. It really comes down to trial and error, and your own experience. It's just helpful to keep in mind that not every keyframe attribute is actually associated with keyframes.

Undoing Changes in the Effects Manager

If you're like many users, you've been conditioned over the years to press Ctrl+Z to undo what you just did. You must resist this impulse while working with the Effects Manager. At this point the Undo applies to the last timeline action. If you just added an effect and are now editing it, "undo" means "delete the effect without any confirmation." Take care!

Picture in Picture

A single effect may be made up of many different tools. Conversely, a single tool can produce many different effects. The moving path is one of these tools, and many of its uses run counter to its "moving" name. Picture in picture is one such effect. It's a prime example of a moving path that doesn't move.

A Quick Intro to Moving Paths

There are five fundamental types of moving paths: 2D Basic, 2D Advanced, 3D, Cylinder, and Sphere. The two pictures here show the Preview Window and Effects Manager when an Advanced 2D Basic Moving Path has been applied to a clip. There's one **very** important thing you

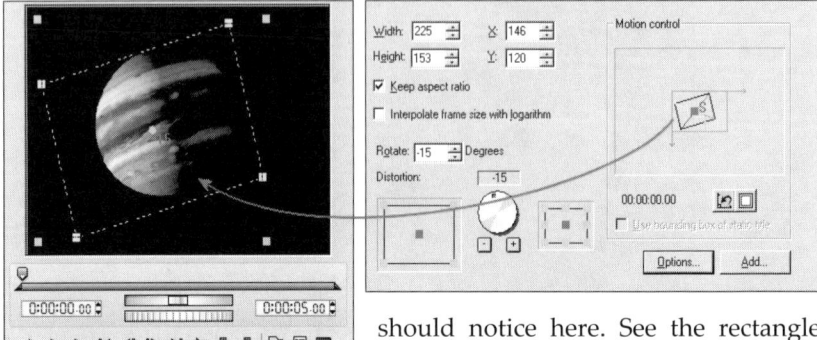

should notice here. See the rectangle and those dots on the Preview Window? Those aren't just for show. Those are *alive*. You can reshape, reposition, and resize moving paths *directly on the Preview Window*. I've drawn an arrow between the EM and PW to show how the two windows stay in sync. Make an edit on either one and it will be reflected in the other.

Just as with video filters, moving paths are controlled by keyframes. At the very least, you set the start and end positions, and Video Editor tweens the remaining frames. Therefore, what actually makes a moving path *move* are changes in values between keyframes. Consequently, if the values between keyframes don't change, then there's no movement. And that's not a bad thing, because that's exactly what we'll capitalize on to create standard picture in picture effects.

Objectives

- To finally display two full video clips in the project at the same time: our first real layering exercise.

- To learn how to create "static" moving paths to generate picture in picture (PiP) effects the hard way.

Reference Projects
projects\chapter07\start.dvp
projects\chapter07\pip.dvp

Steps
1. Open the starter project.

Chapter 7 • Beyond Just Editing   179

2. Insert a new timeline *below* Video1.

   Betcha didn't think you could do that, huh? Click on the Add / Delete tracks toolbar button.

   Select the option to Add Tracks (the default) "before first track" (also the default). Multiple tracks can be inserted at once, but we just need one for now.

3. From the Project Tray, drag clip 0102.mpg to the new Video1 track. Place it directly under 0101.mpg.

4. Scrub the timeline as a sanity check. You'll only see the big Jupiter image. That's the one we're going to "pipify." [Yes, I just made up another word.]

5. Back in the Production Library, drag the default 2D Basic Moving path to the 0101.mpg clip.

6. Click on the first keyframe in the Effects Manager to display:

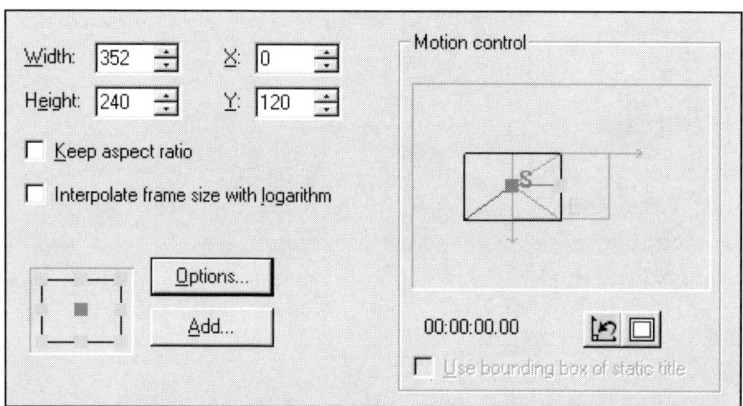

7. Check the Keep aspect ratio box.

8. Change: Width=160, X=250, Y=170.

9. Right-click the first keyframe.

10. From the popup, select Copy and Paste to All.

    In our case, "all" only includes the single, end keyframe. But this certainly is the quickest way to make all keyframes the same. And when all moving path keyframes are the same, there's no movement.

11. Preview your work.

Not bad, huh? Some of you may even be wondering why I called this the hard way. After all, it wasn't *that* much of a chore. There is, however, an easier way.

If you take a closer look at the Moving Path gallery in the Production Library, you'll see a folder called "Picture in Picture." These are pre-defined static moving paths that will do those most of the above steps for you, in a single click-and-drag action.

So what was the point of going about it the long way? There are a few reasons, actually. First, if you just clicked and dragged, you wouldn't have learned anything. Second, as you can tell from the picture here, these pre-defined PiP paths are rather limited. There's inevitably going to be a time where you want something wholly new.

In this particular case, I wanted to create an effect that would work in the "title-safe" area of the frame, and not run all the way into a corner, like the pre-defined paths.

Split Screen

A split screen is similar to the picture-in-picture effect: you have two separate video sources displayed at the same time. However, the way you go about creating a split screen is different because you have more choices. Each method gives you a split screen, but each with a slightly different effect.

Objective
Create a split-screen effect using a Moving Path.

Reference Projects
projects\chapter07\start.dvp
projects\chapter07\split-screen.dvp

Steps
1. Open the starter project.

2. Drag 0112.mpg to track Video2.

3. Trim 0112.mpg to match 0101.mpg's length.

Chapter 7 • Beyond Just Editing

4. Drag any 2D Basic Moving Path object to 0112.mpg.

5. Select 0112.mpg and head up to the Effects Manager.

6. Click the first keyframe, right click, and Copy and Paste to All.

7. Go back to the timeline. While 0112.mpg is selected, press Ctrl+C.

8. Select clip 0101.mpg, right-click, and choose Paste Attributes.

9. Click OK.

10. Go back to the EM and edit 0101.mpg's new moving path.

11. Change the anchor point to the upper-left.

    Technically, this step isn't necessary for this exercise, but I want to draw attention to this control. The X, Y values entered for a moving path are always relative to one of these nine points.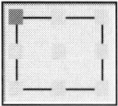

12. Now set X=176, Y=0 and copy this keyframe to the end keyframe.

13. Preview your work.

If you examine the final reference project, you'll notice several split screen methods. The exercise we just completed is the first one in the project. The rest are variations, all of which use moving paths, except the last one, which uses a static transition. There's even a cropping sample.

Also note: There are annotated color clips in a muted track identifying each. I use this technique from time to time to make notes to myself.

Mirror Image

Let's say you want to create a mirror image. You might expect there to be a filter for it. And if you look at the list of available filters, sure enough, there *is* a filter called Mirror. But this effect is hardly what you expected. It looks more like a "House of Mirrors" than a mirror image.

As it turns out, the video filter named "Flip" is what you want. This will allow you to create a mirror image, either horizontally, vertically, or both. But we're not going to use that here. After all, how will we learn anything if we're always taking the short cuts?

In order to create your own mirror you'll have to use a moving path—specifically, a 3D moving path. A property of these paths is that when the backside of a clip appears, it treats the clip as if it were painted on glass. Let's take a look.

Objective
Gain more insight into Moving Paths.

Reference Projects
projects\chapter07\start.dvp
projects\chapter07\mirror.dvp

Steps
1. Open the starter project.

2. From the 3D Moving Path folder, drag the basic 3D clip to the timeline. Drop it right on 0101.mpg.

3. Center the clip by setting the X value to ½ the width. In our case, that's 176 as pictured here.

4. Now, in the Rotate area of the dialog, set the Y rotation at 180°. This rotates the image a half circle around the Y-axis, thus generating a complete image reversal.

5. Copy these keyframe settings to the last keyframe.

6. Preview your work.

You should see a perfect mirror of your clip. Plus you learned a bit more about Moving Paths and their use.

Matchmoving

In its most general sense, matchmoving is about synchronizing the movements of objects from two different video sources. In modern filmmaking, matchmoving and camera tracking technology is typically used to synchronize live action and computer-generated shots. (Think of a live action running horse shot with a sweeping crane movement to be inserted into a computer-generated fantasy landscape.) This takes some skill to pull off. Naturally, there exists hardware and software (costing many hundreds of times more than MediaStudio Pro) to help get the job done.

Chapter 7 • Beyond Just Editing   183

But that doesn't mean you can't do a little of this on your own using Moving Paths. Since they give you the ability to place any image at any size at any place on a frame-by-frame basis, *theoretically* you can do anything. Of course, *theoretically* you can reproduce artistic masterpieces pixel-by-pixel with Microsoft Paint. Whether it's practical or not depends on the task and how much effort you're willing to expend.

This exercise is designed to give you a taste of using moving paths to match the movement of an object, and use that path information.

Objectives
- To get a feel for how moving paths can be used to match the movement of objects in different video sources.

- To learn how to use the generated path information to apply a video filter to part of a clip.

Reference Projects
projects\chapter07\start.dvp
projects\chapter07\matchmoving.dvp

Steps
1. Open the starter project and delete the reference clip.

2. Create a new timeline.

3. From the Project Tray, drag video clip 0104.mpg to track Video1 and image clip circle.bmp to track Video2.

4. Drag the end of circle.bmp to match the duration of 0104.mpg:

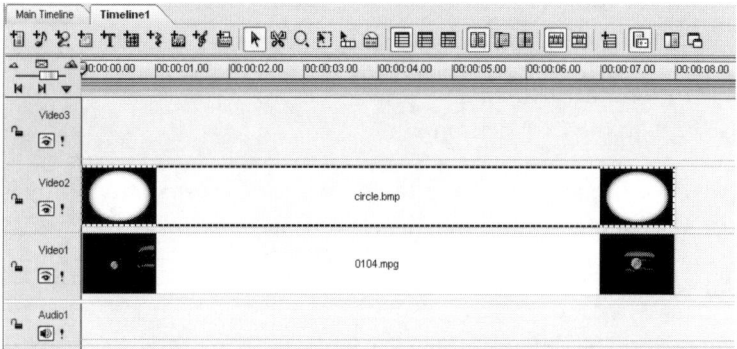

5. Apply a 2D Basic moving path to the image clip.

6. Click the first moving path keyframe in the Effects Manager.

7. Check the Keep aspect ratio checkbox.

8. Change the width to 40 pixels.

9. Drag it so that it completely covers the Voyager spacecraft.

10. Right click this keyframe and select Copy and Paste to All.

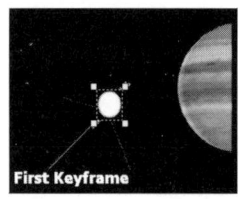

11. From the Preview Window, begin advancing frames. Voyager shoots to the left side of the screen, then stops and changes direction at frame 00:00:01.05. At this point, add a new keyframe.

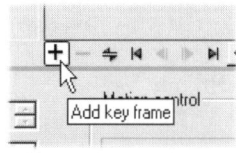

12. Drag the dot to Voyager's new spot.

13. Click on the last keyframe, 00:00:07.29.

14. Move the spot over Voyager again.

15. Resize the path to 60x60. This compensates for the fact that the spacecraft is now closer to the camera.

16. Preview your work.

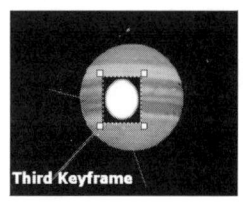

The tracking between the first two points needs help. There is some unanticipated acceleration which we'll have to account for. However, the motion is smooth between the second and third keyframes, and I think we can leave that the way it is.

Steps, Motion Refinement

1. Go back to the first keyframe.

2. Advance frame by frame until you see a clear separation of the spot and the spacecraft. For me, this was 00:00:00.12.

3. Add another keyframe.

4. Reposition the dot at the new keyframe.

5. Now advance to frame 00:00:00.25.

6. Add another keyframe and reposition dot again.

Chapter 7 • Beyond Just Editing

7. And even though I thought the second part of the path originally looked okay, I can now see it needs a bit of work. Advance to 00:00:01.20 and add yet another keyframe.

8. Ever so slightly, slide the dot to the right. It was dragging a bit.

9. Once again, preview your work.

It looks a lot better now. Still not a perfect match, but by now you should already get the idea of how this works. You're welcome to go back and try further refinements, but for the purposes of demonstration (and of our next task) this is suitable.

Steps, Doing Something Useful

1. Hide (or *mute*) track Video1.

2. Select File | Create | Video File...

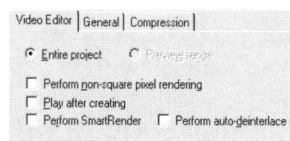

3. Create a file called videomatte.mpg in the chapter07 project folder. Click the Options button and set Video Editor options like so.

4. Under the General tab, for the Data track, select Video only, then click OK to close the dialog box.

5. Click Save to create the video file. After it finishes...

6. Go back to the Main Timeline.

7. Drag a fresh 0104.mpg clip to track Video1.

8. With the clip selected, press Ctrl+D. This is a shortcut to display video filters.

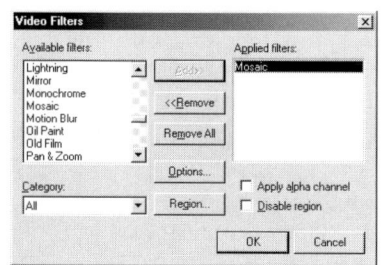

9. Under Available filters find Mosaic and click Add>>.

10. Click the Region button[5].

---

[5] Although Video Filters appear in the Effects Manager, there is no way to add a region without going through this legacy dialog box. It's another one of those minor differences, where the Effects Manager simply doesn't cover all the functionality. On the other hand, once the region has been defined, it does appear in the Effects Manager.

11. On the Mask drop-down list, select Video Matte.

12. Locate the videomatte.mpg file we just created.

13. For both keyframes set the threshold (gray level) to 2.

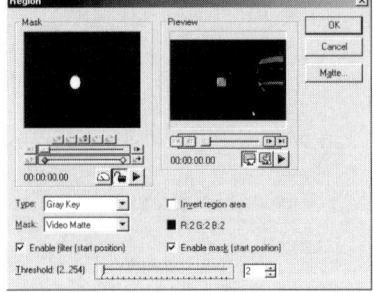

14. Click OK.

And for one last time, preview your hard work! You've just placed Voyager into the Spacecraft Witness Protection Program, his anonymity intact.

Until now, all of our video filter exercises have applied the filters to the entire frame. But as you've now seen, the region filter allows the effect to be applied to only a portion of the screen. After we tackle keying, we're going to do another exercise like this, but with something more complex than a circle.

Moving Path Mania

So far, we've only applied motion paths to one or two clips at a time, and only on a single timeline, at that. Video Editor provides 99 tracks and (nearly) infinitely nested timelines.

Objectives
- To not learn anything new, but have some fun.
- Okay, actually this is a demonstration of how nuts you can go with moving paths, multiple tracks, and nested virtual clips.

Reference Project
projects\chapter07\movingpathmania.dvp

Steps
1. Open the starter project.

2. Stand back in awe.

I don't really want to go into the steps I went through to create this mess. The important part is that *I didn't use any tools or techniques you don't already know about.*

This project is a mental exercise to help show how simple ideas and concepts can be ramped up into something very complex.

It also shows how much Video Editor's performance can slow down when lots of virtual clips and additional timelines are involved. So while you do have nearly unlimited potential, you probably don't have an unlimited power source to keep it all running. Suffice it to say that Instant Preview will not give anything close to satisfactory results, unless painting one frame every few seconds works for you. This twenty-second project took nearly six minutes to render on an Athlon 64 3200-based system with 1 GB of RAM.

Keying

This can be a difficult subject to understand. But once you get a good grasp of the basics and have tried it out yourself a few times, it sinks in pretty quickly. Even so, every new keying task can present new challenges. Just when you think you have it mastered, along comes something *else*, and you can feel like a novice all over again. Keying truly is a science unto itself.

Even if you've never heard of keying, you've seen it. Everywhere. You can barely go ten minutes watching TV without coming across it. Yes, it's the ubiquitous "blue screen effect" where the subjects are filmed in front of a blue screen and all the blue parts are later replaced with something else.

This is called *keying* because the process *keys in* on a color to do its thing.

This particular type of keying is called *chroma-key* due to the fact that you're keying in on a particular color. There are other types of keying as well. *Alpha-key* is where an alpha channel is used for keying. *Luma-key* is where luminance, or brightness levels, are used for keying. *Gray-key* uses the gray levels of an image to get the job done. These are a few of the more common types.

Video Editor supports ten different types of keying, but the two most common are blue screen and alpha-keying, so we'll start there.

Blue screening

The concept is simple. Start with two images. Imagine the first image being scanned pixel by pixel, from top to bottom, and the color of each pixel tested. If the color matches (or closely matches) the key color, the corresponding pixel from the second image replaces the pixel in the first image. This is easy to visualize with some letter-filled grids:

A	E	I	O
U	A	E	I
O	U	A	E
I	O	U	A

Image 1

\+

X	B	C	D
X	X	F	G
X	X	X	H
X	X	J	K

Image 2

\=

A	B	C	D
U	A	F	G
O	U	A	H
I	O	J	K

Composite

The yellow grid, Image 1, contains only vowels. The green grid, Image 2, contains only consonants. Our key "color" is X. When the keying process scans the second grid, every X is replaced with the corresponding cell from the first grid. The result is the composite grid you see on the right. Note you will not find a single X in the composite. The key color is always removed in the process. (At least that's the goal! It doesn't always work out that way.)

In the opening paragraph, I made a parenthetic note about "closely" matching colors. This is because *no* natural image will have a completely uniform keying color. The algorithm has to take into account varying colors. For example, you might say, "I'd like to key out X, but both W and Y are close enough, so treat those as you would the keying color:

A	E	I	O
U	A	E	I
O	U	A	E
I	O	U	A

Image 1

\+

W	B	C	D
W	X	F	G
X	X	Y	H
X	Y	J	K

Image 2

\=

A	B	C	D
U	A	F	G
O	U	A	H
I	O	J	K

Composite

Hopefully this helps get the basic idea across. The actual implementation in Video Editor is a bit more complex, but logically-speaking, the approach is the same.

One question asked by people new to this technique is, "Why blue?" (This is an especially good question in this day and age where blue screens are in the minority.) Blue was chosen because orthochromatic films were not sensitive to blue and it was possible to combine two negatives with the least work. This is a relic of the 1930s when the technique evolved. In modern practice, the color doesn't really matter (in theory). The only true requirement of the color is simply that it *not* appear anywhere else in the overlay image. (Picture the guy wearing the green tie in front of a green screen.) In order to satisfy this requirement very bright and unnatural colors are employed. There's less of a chance that these will appear in other parts of the image.

Alpha What?

Yes, yes—we have some new stuff to learn before going any further. We'll start with a short lesson in color. As you probably learned back in second grade, there are three primary colors: red, blue, and yellow. While this is true of finger paints, it doesn't help us in video, which uses something called an *additive* color process.

When dealing with light (which includes television and computer monitors) the three primary colors are red, blue, and *green*. All three colors combined create white. The complete absence of all three colors is black. Each pixel in an image is made up of some mixture of these three colors.

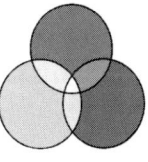

To see how they work together, let's first take them apart. Using our cloud picture from back on page 22, I've split it into its three component colors:

Red channel   Green channel   Blue channel

You may have noticed at this point that the red image doesn't look red at all. In fact, all three just look like the same black and white photo, only differentiated by brightness levels. This is because each channel only represents the *amount* of that color, not the color itself. This amount is stored as a number between 0 and 255.

Black is 0, the absence of any color. White is 255, the color in its strongest form. Every shade of gray in between represents the amount of that color that will contribute to the full image. Since we're looking at a picture of a bright blue sky, with very little red in it, the "red" picture looks darkest. The "blue" picture, by contrast, is very light, meaning *lots* of blue is present.

Okay, so what about that alpha thingy? Isn't that what we were talking about in the first place? Yes it is! You see, we're not limited to just storing visible color information in an image. Beyond the three plain color channels, there can be additional channels, which are called *alpha* channels.

The alpha channel is used to represent transparency information. So the same way the gray values of each red, green, and blue channel are combined to determine the final color of a pixel, the gray values of the alpha channel dictate its transparency.

Having 256 levels of transparency allows for much more natural looking overlays than could ever be achieved through a simple "on or off" transparency setting.

Alpha Channels in Action

Blue screening requires two sets of image data to achieve a composite effect: a background image and a foreground image. Alpha keying, on the other hand, makes use of three sets of image data:

- The background image
- The foreground image
- The foreground image's alpha channel

It's very important to think of the alpha channel as a third, independent image. If you grasp this concept right away, you'll be off to a better start than most (including me, way back when). Otherwise, you'll be left to figure out paradoxical statements like this on your own:

- A black pixel is not transparent therefore it allows the background image to show up in the composite image.
- A white pixel is transparent and therefore blocks out the background image.

Hmmm... doesn't make much sense at first glance. But the riddle is solved when you remember that the alpha channel's transparency applies to the color channels in the same image. So let's look at those statements again, with some extra words added:

- A black pixel is not transparent therefore it *blocks the RGB channels of its foreground image. With the foreground image blocked, this* allows the background image to show up in the composite image.
- A white pixel is transparent and therefore *allows the RGB channels of its foreground image to pass through. Displaying the foreground image effectively* blocks out the background image.

Enough words already! Let's just look at a real life demonstration. I have a 4-channel image of a space shuttle. The alpha channel has been created to match the outline of the shuttle, as shown here:

Chapter 7 • Beyond Just Editing 191

Three combined color channels   One alpha channel

Now let's take one more image, a nice picture of earth from orbit, to be our background. If we place the shuttle picture in front of our background image in an overlay track, Video Editor will automatically block out all black areas of the alpha channel and only let the white areas through. Our space shuttle will have been magically teleported from the runway back into orbit. Pretty cool, huh?

Background image   Composite

As far as *how* you actually accomplish all this, stay tuned. This is just some background info to get you used to the idea. We'll be doing some of this for real later on in the book. But I will touch on one more important point before moving forward.

Creating Alpha Channels

Okay, these alpha channels are great, but how do you go about creating them? Exactly where did that shuttle-shaped alpha channel come from? Well, I made them myself, and I used Paint Shop Pro. I created a selection, saved it to an alpha channel, and saved the overall file in the Targa file format. The shuttle selection was created by carefully tracing around the shuttle itself. Most graphics packages support this kind of functionality in one way or another, and you'll need to learn these techniques if you want to use them in your productions. In any case, MediaStudio Pro itself does not provide the means to create alpha channels. They'll have to be made with other software packages.

I won't lie to you either: it can be tricky. Depending on the subject matter, you could spend a good long while creating your own masks. Not to mention needing pretty good mouse skills. The shuttle above was relatively easy given it has lots of nice straight lines and easy angles. But I don't know if most people would want to tackle something like a lion's mane. If you need that kind of power, there are dedicated tools for the job.

> **Storing Alpha Channels**
> Although some file formats can store an unlimited number of channels per image, these are usually proprietary formats, and not usable within MediaStudio Pro. The reality is most standard file formats don't support any alpha channels, and of those that do, most only support one.

My recommendation is to start simple. You don't even have to try to make anything fancy like this. Start with geometric shapes. You can even begin with a simple "half and half" mask: letting half the scene through and blocking the other half. Give it a shot. It's kind of fun.

A Brief Keying Exercise

I hope this has cleared up keying. I've either made it brilliantly clear or have permanently confused you on the topic. Hopefully the former is true! Keying is still a very simple concept, only made complex in its implementation. The best way to get a full understanding is to try things out for yourself.

Objective
To learn how to apply a stock green-screen overlay to a clip.

Reference Projects
projects\chapter07\start.dvp
projects\chapter07\keying.dvp

Steps
1. Open the starter project.

2. Delete the default clip to clear the timeline.

3. From the Project Tray, drag 0121.mpg to track Video1.

4. Now drag 0131.mpg to track Video2, placing it directly on top of the first clip.

5. Head back to the Project Tray, but this time open the Audio folder. You'll find a clip called jet.wav. Drop it on track Audio1.

We've pretty much ignored audio up until now, so I thought this would be a good time to throw some in. It's especially fitting for this exercise, as we're already combining multiple clips into something new. At the end of the exercise, be sure to preview the project with and without the audio, just to see what a difference it makes.

6. Continuing, head back to the Production Library and find the Overlay gallery.

7. Open the folder called Blue Screen.

8. Click the Green Screen thumbnail.

9. Drag and drop it on the green clip.

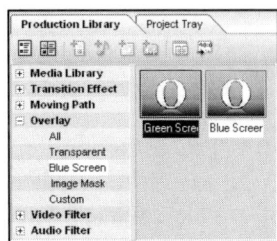

And that's it. Just think—all that talk for just a tiny bit of work in the end. As you might expect, though, real life isn't always that easy. The next exercise will demonstrate something a little more realistic.

A Longer Keying Exercise

In the last exercise, we were able to get away with very few steps because our computer-generated keying image was pixel perfect. Real life doesn't always work out that way.

Objective
To learn how to tweak green-screen settings.

Reference Projects
projects\chapter07\start.dvp
projects\chapter07\keying2.dvp

Steps
1. Open the starter project.

2. Delete the placeholder clip.

3. Go to the Image folder under the Media Bin in the Project Tray and drag background.jpg to track Video1.

4. Change its duration to 2-seconds.

5. Now drag clip 0141.mpg from the Project Tray to track Video2.

6. Press Ctrl+R to display the Overlay Options dialog box.

7. On the left-hand side if this box, there is a dropdown list called Type. Give it a quick click to see the different types of overlays available.

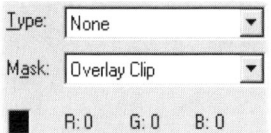

8. Choose the top one, Color Key.

9. Move the cursor to the top-left window. The cursor will change to an eyedropper.

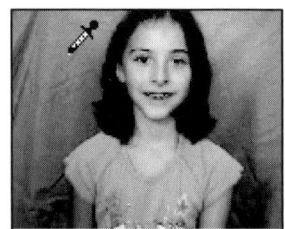

10. Click once, anywhere in the green. Look down at the color picker box and observe the R, G, and B values. I happened to pick 57, 131, 83. That's *mostly* green, but a far cry from *green* green: 0, 255, 0.

11. The right hand image is the overlay preview. Right now it should look like the Overlay Clip, but with a few pixels turned black. These are the pixels that match the color you just picked.

First big keying tip. Change the "Preview as" dropdown from Result to Mask. Working in Mask mode first is the best way to see what's *really* going on with your keying attempts.

Our overlay doesn't look like much at this point. This is due to the unevenness of the background color. If you look on the lower right, there's a Similarity slider. This tells the keyer how close a color has to come to the key color in order to be considered a match. Slide it around and watch the mask preview change.

Here are four different similarity settings. Yours will differ slightly.

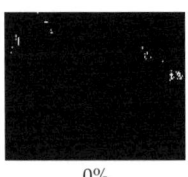   

   0%   5%   10%   15%

If you're getting to the point where you're close (say, between 10% and 15% as shown here) there are two cheat mechanisms:

- The first is the transparency setting. Depending on conditions, this may be enough to make the last problematic areas go away without adversely affecting the overall mask.

- Second is the softness setting. The softness slider allows ten different levels of softness to be applied to the edges. If I were to give them numbers, they would be:

   0 – No Softness
   1 – A *Lot* of Softness
   2 – An Extraordinary Amount of Softness
   3 – A Guinness Book of World Records Contender for Softness
   4 through 10 – Words Can't Describe It

In other words, you don't have a lot of control over this. Soft is either off or extremely on. I'm still puzzled to this day why these settings exist. I have yet to find a single instance where anything other than 0 or 1 returns acceptable results, and 1 only works in a very small handful of special situations. Try it out. You'll see what I mean.

So as you can see, we're probably not going to get very far with this particular approach. By the time we've eliminated the background, parts of the foreground are also getting keyed out. That's not good.

What went wrong? Three things:

- The poor background color.

- The video clip compression.

- The Color Key keying type. I have a feeling we're looking at the most ancient of keying algorithms, not well-suited to handling adverse keying conditions.

Now! Do you want the good news or the bad news first? Okay, bad news first: adverse keying conditions are more common than ideal keying conditions. The good news? We have other keying types at our disposal.

Let's ditch this and try again.

Steps, Part 2
1. Close the overlay dialog box and clear any overlay settings you may have left behind. (Right-click, and select Delete Attributes.)

2. Press Ctrl+R to get back into the overlay options.

3. Under Type, jump all the way to the bottom: Blue Screen. (I *really* wish this was at the top of the list. Really, really.)

4. Move up to the Overlay clip to get the eyedropper back.

5. This time, select a green *area*. If you click and drag the eyedropper in Blue Screen keying, it will take an average of the area for your keying color. This helps out a lot. Try to pick one of the lighter areas near the top of the frame.

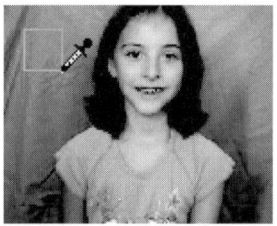

6. Switch the Overlay preview to Mask, as before.

7. Move the Similarity slider gradually to 100%:

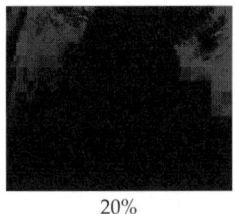  

    20%   60%   100%

Wow. What a difference an algorithm makes. Same poor background. Same blocky file. But that's a clean mask given the circumstances.

8. Change the preview mode from Mask to FG only then to Result. All three modes are helpful at different stages in keying.

9. Close the dialog box and preview your work.

It looks pretty good. You may be worrying a bit about the funny looking hand. This is a combination of two problems: interlacing and compression. But when I render the original file and play it back to TV, both of these problems go away. It's an important reminder: **keep formats consistent throughout the entire editing process**.

Creating a Garbage Matte

A garbage matte is used to entirely block out large, bad portions of a background. There are a few reasons you may have unusable (or, I should say, un*key*able) areas in the background color:

- The background doesn't cover the whole frame
- The edges of the background "fall off" too quickly.
- The background contains wrinkles or other imperfections.

Objectives
- To learn how to create and apply a garbage matte.
- To use color clips for something rather useful.

Reference Projects
projects\chapter07\keying2.dvp
projects\chapter07\keying-garbage.dvp

Steps
1. Open the keying2 reference project. We're going to pick things up where we left off in the last exercise.

2. Select clip 0141.mpg.

3. Right-click and select Replace With | Video File.

4. Locate 0142.mpg and click Open.

5. Preview and look closely at the corners.

In this second, longer shot, the camera was pulled back so that the background no longer covered the entire frame. In the upper corners, part of a piano keyboard is visible. In the lower left, the carpet is showing through. We need a garbage matte to fix this.

Steps, Part 2
1. Create a second timeline and call it "0142.mpg (gm)".

   This name is my own convention: clip name followed by "gm" in parentheses, for garbage matte.

2. Slide a new 0142.mpg clip to Video1.

3. Insert a color clip into track Video2. Make it RGB(50,120,80):

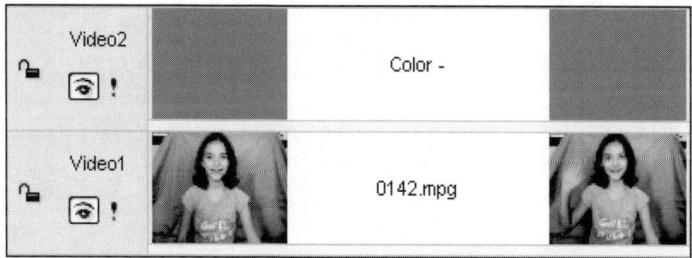

4. Apply a "2D Advanced" moving path to the clip.

5. Click on the first moving path keyframe in the Effects Manager.

6. Using the green border handles on the Preview Window, shrink the color clip to fit the center of the frame.

   Tip. Because the Preview Window does not have a "pasteboard" area, it can often be difficult to grab the corners. Try this instead: First drag the color clip so that one corner is in view. Then resize, using the green handles. Once resized, you can drag the clip back to the center. As shown here.

7. Grab the lower right *yellow* handle. When the cursor looks like ↘, drag it toward the center. Compare with this picture.

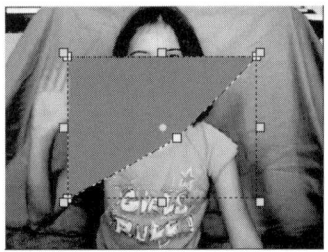

8. Now grab the upper right yellow handle, but this time move the cursor until it shows rotate: ↻

9. Rotate to the left slightly so that the long edge is roughly parallel to the missing background in the upper left.

10. Now drag the whole clip to the upper left, to cover the empty spot. If all has gone well, it should look like this shot here.

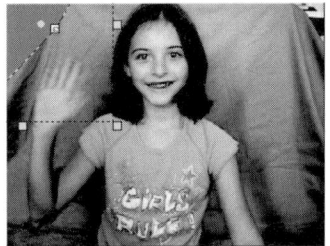

11. Copy this keyframe to the end keyframe, to keep it from moving.

12. Repeat this procedure (more or less!) to cover the spot in the upper right and the carpet in the lower left.

   Tip. Use the existing color clip as a starting point. From the timeline, make sure the color clip (and only the color clip) is selected. Holding the Ctrl key, drag it up to track Video3. This creates a copy of the clip. Do it one more time to create another copy in Video4:

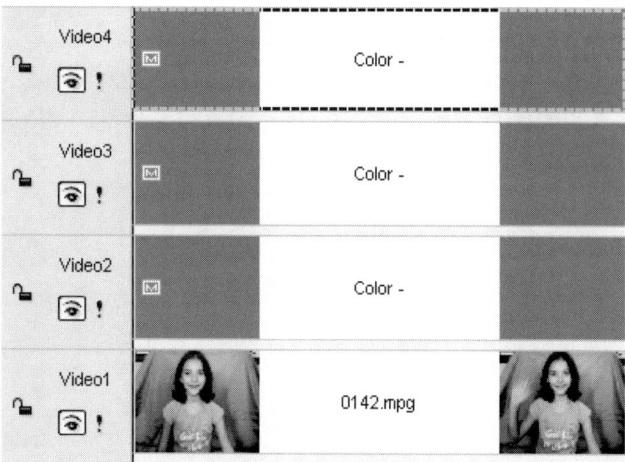

By selecting each color clip and going to the Effects Manager, you can move the first "color matte" around to cover the affected areas.

13. Add this timeline to the main timeline.

14. Select the original 0142.mpg clip and press Ctrl+C.

15. Select the new 0142.mpg (gm) virtual clip, right-click, and select Paste Attributes. (Might as well re-use all our Overlay hard work.)

16. Move the original clip out of the way and replace it with our new garbage matte virtual clip.

And that, as they say, is that. Preview your work. If you ask me, I think our trick worked like a charm. Here are few more notes on the topic before moving on.

- Since we used moving paths, obviously this means you can create moving garbage mattes. It takes a little more work. At the simplest, start and end positions might cover it. At the worst, you'll have to do some complex matchmoving with lots of keyframes to make it work.

- There is carpet showing behind the girl and over on the right, which we didn't bother covering. Due to the nature of the background image we used, you can hardly tell. This is a notable point: many aspects of keying—decisions made and shortcuts taken—depend greatly on the project you're working on. In some situations, you can get away with almost anything. Other situations require the utmost care for a perfect overlay.

Dealing with Common Keying Problems

The next most common problems with keying: bad contrast, bad lighting and soft edges. Sometimes you can work around these. And, well, sometimes you can't. As always, it depends on the situation.

Objective
To learn how to deal with adverse keying situations.

Reference Projects
projects\chapter07\keying2.dvp
projects\chapter07\keying-adverse.dvp

Steps
1. Open the keying2 reference project to begin.

2. Delete the clip in track Video2.

3. From the Project Tray, drag 0143.mpg to Video2.

4. Press **Ctrl+R** to create the overlay.

5. Select "Blue Screen" as the overlay type.

6. For the overlay color, use the eyedropper and grab a good rectangle from the upper left corner. I got RGB(44, 96, 43). You should immediately notice two problems:

   - The green level is pretty low: only 96.

   - The green-to-other-color ratio is also very low, only 2:1. This in and of itself isn't a problem because theoretically *any* color can be a keying color. But our little snowman has a green hat and scarf. Uh oh.

7. Switch the **Preview as** setting to Mask.

8. Slide Similarity to 100%. The mask will look like this. White is good: the background will show through. Black means it won't, so most of our Snowman is okay. But the hat and scarf look gray: they're too close to the background color.

As expected, the uneven shadows near the bottom of the frame are getting lost as well. You can tell from the mask they are nearly identical to the hat and scarf. Viewing the overlay result, it's not looking good. What to do, what to do!?

For starters, head up to the Advanced Control. It may look mysterious, but it's a very powerful feature. It won't be able to fix every keying problem, but you'll be able to work bits of magic you never thought possible. You can modify five attributes with this puppy: gamma, cutoff, threshold, min value, and max value. If these terms don't make any sense, don't

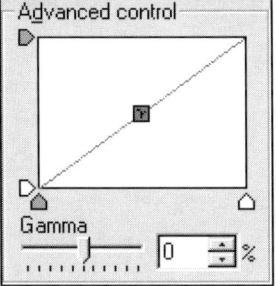

worry. There's no vocabulary test at the end of the chapter. It's more important to get a feel for exactly what they do.

9. Drag the **gamma** slider down to -88%. Changing the gamma percentage modifies the luminance levels of mid-tones, leaving blacks and whites untouched. Lowering this percentage lowers the darker levels, thus brightening the mask. Raise raises dark levels, darkening the mask. At -88%, all of the background is gone, along with all the hat and scarf.

10. Drag the gamma slider up to +100% for comparison. See how it this drastically affects the transparency, independent of the similarity slider?

11. With the gamma at +100%, click on the marker along the bottom left. This is the **cutoff** value. As the cutoff rises, gray values below this value automatically become transparent. For now, set it to 30%.

This is about as close as we're going to get. The hat is *mostly* opaque. We lost some of the scarf, and bits of the background, but it's close.

But you have to ask yourself: is it close enough? I would say no. So what else can we do? Not much. As already mentioned, you can play with the overall **transparency** and the **soft edge** setting. At best the soft edge covers up small areas. However this is almost always at the cost of creating a halo around your subject that is the same color as the background. This might be perfect in some situations, but for most it will be unacceptable.

No, about all you can do with an unusable background is re-shoot. Either use the same background (but improve the lighting and image quality) or change backgrounds. With Snowman, we'll have to deal with the green hat and scarf somehow. This would be a good time to switch to a blue background. Or red. Or orange. It doesn't matter as long as you meet the two requirements for your background: it's 1) uniform and 2) dissimilar. View the second reference project to see the overlay settings for two additional background colors.

Steps, Part 2

1. In the same project, drag 0144.mpg to track Video2.

2. This time, try keying out the background yourself. It's even more poorly lit than the last one, but that's not what I want to focus on for this exercise. I'll wait till you're done.

   All set? Good. How did it go? Compare yours to mine. I didn't do anything magical. I selected the upper-left area for my color and slid the similarity to 100.

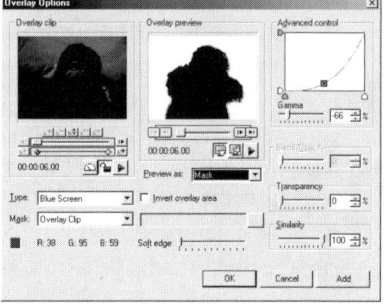

3. Preview your work. Notice anything? The keying itself isn't too bad, given the conditions. In a lot of ways, the Blue Screen algorithm can be very forgiving, and that's good news for rank amateur blue-screeners like me. There are two other issues. Winston here (yes, his name is Winston) is furry, and fur always presents challenges. First, it's hard to get a good clean key around fine details like this. Second, it can also be problematic for video encoding. On a highly compressed MPEG-1 image such as this, the blockiness is magnified.

   Examine Winston's left arm. The compression artifacts are very pronounced. Where this may have gone unnoticed to our eyes, it sticks out like a sore thumb to the keyer.

Compare this to the second picture which is the overlay generated from the original DV source. Keep in mind, DV is also compressed and will therefore always suffer from keying artifacts. But it's compressed in a completely different manner and, as you can see here, does better. Just another reason to always edit in your native format. Convert later!

Before wrapping up, take a look at the fifth and last keying sample in this file. In this one, Winston is well-lit, as is the background. There are certainly wrinkles in the backdrop (not to mention a good shadow of Winston in the lower right) but I left it like this to again demonstrate how forgiving the Blue Screen algorithm and advanced controls can be.

Due to the light changes, I used the **threshold** setting to help clean up the background. Due to the movement, I also set different start and end keyframes to give a clean key throughout the frame.

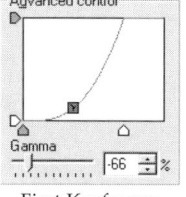 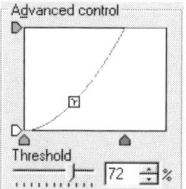 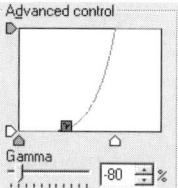 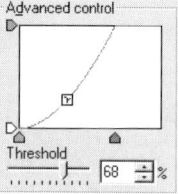

| First Keyframe: Gamma | First Keyframe: Threshold | Second Keyframe: Gamma | Second Keyframe: Threshold |

If you look closely, there is still a touch of green along the edges in places, and sometimes that just can't be helped, even under good conditions. If the work you're doing requires flawless keying, then you will most likely need to pour a lot more money into it. But for most mid-range applications, where you're not filming fuzzy monkeys, the tools work rather well and are relatively easy to use. In just a few steps we've been able to produce reasonable overlays with less than ideal conditions.

On the other hand, if you *do* need better keying results and you don't have buckets of money to spend on it, you can improve your key by shooting against a screen that closely matches the final background plate. For example, if you know you're going to use this yellowish image as your background, then shoot Winston against a similar screen. If the yellow bleeds through a bit, it will blend with the background naturally.

Matchmoving Revisited

Back on page 182 we used rudimentary matchmoving techniques to create a moving matte to apply a mosaic filter to a region of the clip. This exercise will be nearly identical in technique and purpose, but uses a complex shape and makes use of alpha channels instead.

Objective
Use an image matte and moving path for more complex matchmoving

Reference Projects
projects\chapter07\start.dvp
projects\chapter07\matchmove2.dvp

Steps
1. Open the starter project and delete the placeholder clip.

2. Create a new timeline.

3. Drag 0122.mpg to the timeline.

4. Switch to the Project Tray's image folder. Drop rover-mask.tga on the timeline in track Video2.

5. Stretch it to fit 0122.mpg.

6. Preview. Although rover-mask.tga looks like a pure-white image, it does have an alpha channel. Each pixel on the RGB channels is set at 255. But we're not using them. Just the alpha channel.

Chapter 7 • Beyond Just Editing 205

> **The Rover's Matte**
>
> If you're wondering where this alpha channel came from, I created it Paint Shop Pro. Since MediaStudio Pro has no facility for creating alpha channels, you *will* have to go elsewhere to do this yourself.
>
> I won't go into the details, because the specifics are different for different image editing software. Further, it's outside the scope of this book. In short: you'll need to work it out on your own. Start with your image editor's help file or manual. You may be able to find tutorials online.
>
> That said, I'll give you the bird's eye view. I noticed in this clip that the rover *pretty much* looked the same throughout, and decided I could get away with an image matte. It wouldn't match perfectly, but for the application I had in mind, I didn't need it to. In other words, for 10% of the work I could get 90% there. That seemed like a good trade-off.
>
> At no point is the entire rover visible. So I took one picture (using the Source Window's "Save image to" feature) at the beginning and one at the end, and stitched them into a whole.
>
> Once I had the entire rover image, I traced around it with a freehand selection tool, then saved the selection as an alpha channel.

7. As before, drag a 2D Basic moving path to the rover image clip.

8. Using the Effects Manager and the Preview Window, reposition the image clip so it covers the background rover.

   Note. Unlike last time, you *may* need to change the aspect ratio of the clip in order to make it fit. **Hint**. Align the solar panel disk first and worry about the rest later. **Tip**. You can move the clip around on the Preview Window with the arrow keys—much easier than mouse jockeying. **Another Tip!** If you hold the shift key down while moving the arrows, you can stretch the image. **Last Tip!** If the arrow keys don't seem to be working as advertised, make sure the Preview Window has focus!

   I ended up with both Width and Height set to 295. X=160, Y=45. Copy this keyframe to the end.

   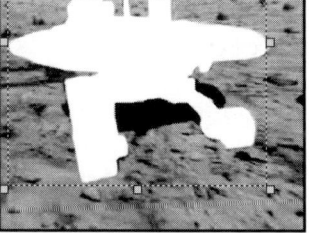

   For the first moving path keyframe, things should be looking quite a bit similar to the picture here.

9. Aside from some image shake, the camera position stays the same for the first part of the clip. At about 00:00:00.20, the camera begins to tilt up. Set a keyframe here.

10. Around 00:00:02.10, the tilt stops. Set another keyframe.

   At this point, I'm going to shut up and let you drive. The basic idea of resizing/repositioning the overlay at each keyframe to match whatever's going on in the background should be obvious. So I want you to put the book down, and try it on your own. When done, check the second reference project.

11. After your keyframes are set, hide the Video1 track and create a video file called videomatte2.mpg.

12. Return to the Main Timeline.

13. Place 0122.mpg in track Video1.

14. While it's selected, press Ctrl+D.

15. Find "Oil Paint" on the available filters list.

   Tip. When the list has input focus, you can press the "o" key to jump directly to entries beginning with that letter.

16. Add Oil Paint and click the Region button.

17. Load the videomatte2.mpg file, slide the threshold back down to 2, and this time invert the region area.

18. Compare your own settings to the dialog box shown here.

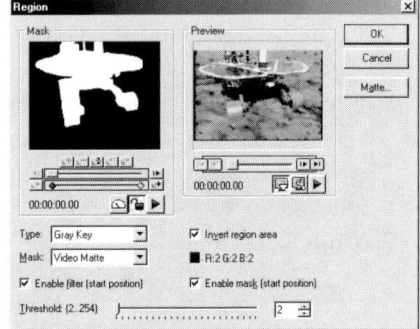

19. Click OK.

20. Click OK again.

Okay! Preview your work. We now have a crisp, in-focus rover running over a painted Martian backdrop. It looks pretty cool, doesn't it? I realize we're not done with this chapter yet, but we've covered a *lot* of ground so far. If you haven't already done so, go get something to drink and relax for a few moments. You deserve it. And while you're up, get me something too. Thanks.

Fade to Black, One Last Time

In Chapter 6, we looked at two different ways to create a fade-to-black technique. Now that we've learned how to do overlays, here's a third method.

If you're wondering which is best or which one I would recommend for a particular situation, it's a coin toss. Sometimes you may choose one over the other based on what else is on the timeline at that point. Sometimes it's just a personal preference. Each approach has its pros and cons.

Objective
To learn how to use overlays to fade a clip.

Reference Projects
projects\chapter07\start.dvp
projects\chapter07\fade-to-black.dvp

Steps
1. Open the starter project.

2. Select the clip and press **Ctrl+R** to display overlay options.

3. Add two keyframes, as shown here. The exact positions don't matter.

4. Move to the last keyframe.

5. Move the transparency slider to 100%.

   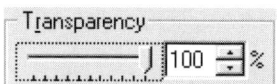

6. Move to the first keyframe.

7. Set transparency to 100% here too.

The clip now has two fades (both in and out) to black. Maybe. Since we've used transparency settings, it's really going to fade in or out of whatever is below it. In this case, the clip is in track Video1 and our default project background color is black. If this was in track Video2 and another clip was in Video1, the result would be like a crossfade between the clips. So you can see the specific "fade to back" approach you pick depends on the particular situation.

Soft Edge Split Screen

Just like the last exercise, it's time to revisit an earlier technique now that we've learned a bit more. The original split screen techniques were varied, but they all had one thing in common: sharp edged splits. In this exercise, we'll learn how to create a split with soft edges.

Objective
To learn how to use overlays and image mattes create a soft split screen.

Reference Projects
projects\chapter07\start.dvp
projects\chapter07\soft-split.dvp

Steps
1. Open the starter project.

2. From the Project Tray, drag 0121.mpg to track Video2. Trim to match.

3. Press **Ctrl+R** for Overlay options.

4. From the mask drop-down, choose **Image matte**.

5. When prompted, locate **halffade2v.tga** from the top level matte folder. (This folder is next to the projects folder on the CD or in your Getting Results installation location.) You should see this when done:

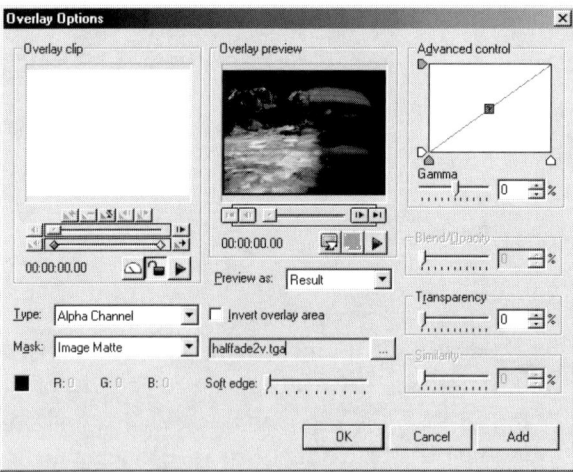

6. Click OK.

The only real trick is having the right image matte at your disposal. I've provided a number of them in this matte folder. Try them out!

Smart Compositor

In a nutshell, Smart Compositor is a way easily to add highly user-editable stock footage to your projects. There are only two steps to using Smart Compositor (or SC for short). The first: click a thumbnail. The second: customize it. And considering the second step is optional, you can see there really isn't a whole lot to this.

But, in just two easy steps, you can jump-start projects in a way you never could before with MediaStudio Pro. When word of SC first hit the streets and people began discussing it, many "pro" users scoffed at the idea of a tool that did all the editing for you. Many of the initial naysayers rallied around a common point: "If I wanted a drag-and-drop, already-been-done-for-you video editing tool, I would have purchased VideoStudio." It's an understandable initial reaction, but misses the point entirely:

- First of all, the addition of Smart Compositor didn't *replace* anything else in Video Editor. It's not as if Ulead ditched the entire timeline in favor of assembling prefabricated video snippets. If you don't want to use it, the rest of MediaStudio Pro is still at your disposal.

- Second of all, they aren't prefabricated video snippets anyway. It might look like a bunch of stock video ready for drag-and-drop, but each Smart Compositor "clip" is actually an entire DVP file, ready for insertion into your own projects. And, being nothing more than a Video Editor project means you can do anything you want to these things. No one's limiting anyone in any way.

You'll quickly find it's a pretty cool new tool, just begging for extensions. Let's take a look at it.

Objective
To get familiar with Smart Compositor: what it is, how it works, and what it can do for you.

Reference Project
none

Steps
1. Start a new project from scratch in a "full size" format.

2. Insert a Smart Compositor clip.

3. The first Step is to select a template. Thumbnails are grouped into categories, selectable from the menu at the top-left.

4. Select Documentary.

5. Select DO01_A.

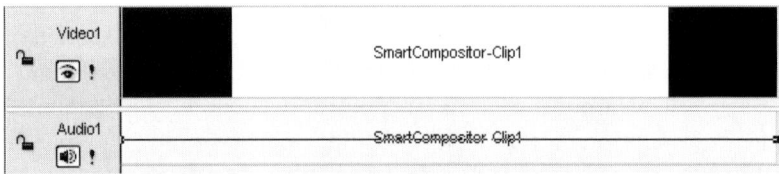

6. Click Insert.

I wanted to skip the customization step and jump right to the timeline to immediately demonstrate there isn't anything magical about SC clips. This is a Virtual Clip.

7. Double-click the clip to open it in a secondary timeline.

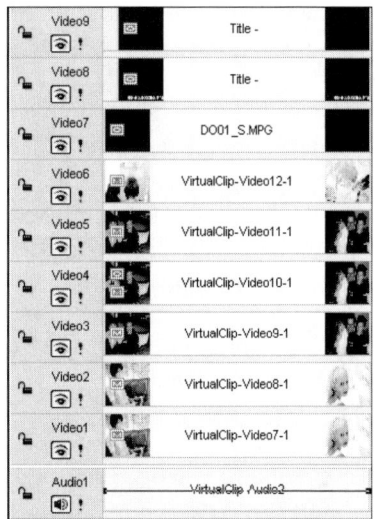

Zowie! Look at all that. Maybe I was wrong. That certainly *could* be magic.

But it isn't. They're just clips. Clips and overlays and moving paths and filters and all the parts and pieces we've already learned.

And don't you see that's the best part? At this level you can do *anything* you want to. Even better, let's say you saw something in the original and thought to yourself *how on earth did they do that?* You have the ability to drill down into the project as far as you need to go to understand it. This ability, more than anything else, removes any lingering illusions of magic.

For now, go back to the Main Timeline. We're going to give this another go.

Steps, Customizing

1. Click the Insert Smart Compositor clip again.

2. Select the same one, but this time click Next to customize.

   Before we actually change anything, I need to get a couple things off my chest. As much as I like SC, I have a few issues with the implementation of the customization step:

   - The window size is fixed. Further, none of the individual window parts are resizable.

   - The Project Tray is completely inaccessible. You *must* use clips from the Production Library, and frankly, I just don't do that any more.

   - There's no way to tell which clips are which at a glance. I really don't see how the name "Media Clip 0" helps anyone. Usability would take a gigantic leap if we had slightly larger tracks and thumbnails.

   - There's no way to keep the playhead at a specific position. When I examine how a particular clip is used in a template, I naturally move the playhead forward to see. In my subsequent confusion over what "Media Clip 3" means, I click on it, which automatically rewinds back to 00:00:00.00. Getting a feel for the template's organization becomes an aggravating exercise.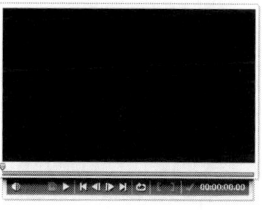

   - If one media clip uses an overlay clip, they're segregated into separate tree folders. Having more than one level of hierarchy would help.

   - The Reveal All menu command doesn't.

   - Only the current title displays while editing. Therefore, if you try to position two titles, it's complete guesswork.

   - Not all title features available in Video Editor are available within Smart Compositor.

The easy answer to all of these: just don't customize within Smart Compositor. All of these things can be edited easily enough within Video Editor. Which begs the question: why even have this at all? It seems like Smart Compositor's customization environment is a tiny, crippled Video Editor which doesn't look or work anything like Video Editor.

Here's the real answer. It's not *supposed* to be another Video Editor, and as soon as you try to force this idea upon it (like I did) you'll only be disappointed.

Here's the Smart Compositor secret: keep it simple. Pick your template, swap the clips, and get out of there. The quicker you are the happier you'll be.

3. Continuing, click Cancel [6].

4. Go to the Production Library's Media Library gallery and create a new folder called chapter7. (Right-click on Media Library, select Create.)

5. Import the video files.

6. Add the Smart Compositor clip again and get back to the customization screen.

7. Open the Media Source "folder" and click on Media Clip 0.

8. Drag 0101.mpg to the Storyboard and drop it on *top* of the existing clip. This is how you **replace** a clip.

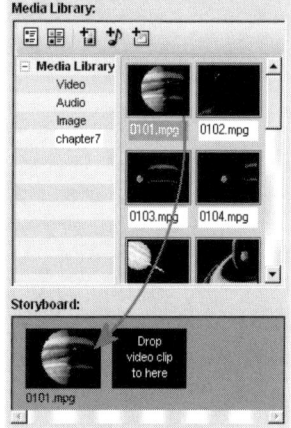

If you drop it next to the clip, it will be **appended** to the existing clip. New clips should match the length of the existing clip. If they are too long, they'll be truncated. If they are too short, the last frame will be repeated to fill the remaining time.

---

[6] You have to leave Smart Compositor to do these next steps. Although it allows you to import clips, it does *not* let you create folders, and I don't want to put all of the clips for this chapter into the default Production Library folders.

9. Replace the remaining clips as follows:

Media Clip 1	0101.mpg
Media Clip 2	0112.mpg
Media Clip 3	0112.mpg
Media Clip 4	0112.mpg
Media Clip 5	0102.mpg

10. Replace the title clips:

MediaStudio Pro	Voyager's Journey
"Tiny text"	A ten thousand day journey across the solar system...

    Additionally, increase the tiny text to 14 pt.

11. Leave the audio as-is and click Insert.

12. Drop it on the timeline to the right of the first (un-edited) Smart Compositor clip.

13. Unless you have a really fast computer, render out to a file and admire your compositing skills.

Further Smart Compositor Topics

Project Attributes
You'll notice the thumbnails don't say anything about whether they're intended for NTSC, PAL, DVD, VCD, or whatever. This is because the clips adapt to whatever project settings you may have. For the most part, it does a pretty good job.

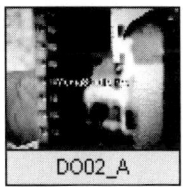

You'll notice, though, that I explicitly said to use a "full size" project setting for this exercise. This was solely due to the fact that title clips apparently do *not* adjust well. If you use this template on a small project (e.g., 352x240) you'll only see part of the main title and none of the smaller text. Everything else seems to adjust.

Creating Your Own
After customizing a clip or two, the most common reaction is, "I wish there was a way I could make my own!" If, by that, you mean creating a true, from-scratch template that shows up in Smart Compositor, you'll need the free *Smart Compositor Designer* tool from Ulead. You can find it at http://www.ulead.com/msp/free.htm.

The main reason for using the *Designer* tool is for sharing templates with others. However, if you just want to create quick, re-usable components, there's no reason you can't do all the work on the timeline and save it as a normal Video Editor project. The next time you need it, instead of clicking Insert from Smart Compositor click Insert Project File. In order to change clips, use the Replace command. See the exercise on page 252.

About the only issue you'll run into is replacing longer clips with shorter ones. Video Editor doesn't like that. But other than that, this is just as good as creating your own.

There have been rumors that Ulead will publish a tool for creating your own true Smart Compositor projects. This feature is just begging for it! After you've used it once or twice you just know there would be a great market for third party offerings. Hopefully it's just a matter of time before we see something like this.

The Endless Possibilities

For the newcomer, it's easy to think of Smart Compositor clips as being wholly distinct from the rest of Video Editor. After all, if you've never been able to create videos that look like this, you may begin to think it's just not possible. But as I've already said, there's no magic involved.

Always remember these two rules:

- Everything you see in Smart Compositor can be done with Video Editor alone.

- Not everything you see in Smart Compositor can be done with Video Editor alone.

How's that for a paradox? The reason it isn't a paradox comes down to one thing: there's a difference between content and editing.

From an editing point of view, everything you see in Smart Compositor is doable with the out-of-box tools. But from a content point of view, this isn't the case. Therefore, the cool opening you see in SC project DO02_A came from somewhere else. But, once turned into a simple video clip, you can edit to your heart's content.

8

Text and Titling

A look at the various ways of putting text on the screen using some common titling techniques and effects.

Why Titling?

Sooner or later you're probably going to have to put text somewhere in your video. While it's easy to click on the title clip tool and slap in some text, doing it in the most effective manner takes a little practice. Apart from that, the Title Clip is one interesting beast, so we'll be looking at the various pieces and parts of Video Editor's built-in titler.

But before we get started, we'll first talk about the most confounding aspect of video titling: the title safe area.

Title Safe Areas

Nearly everyone has made this mistake at one time or another in their careers. After spending hours getting the perfect title page created, the young editor sends it to a television set only to see something like this.

> *My Very First*
> *d Very Wonderf*
> *Title Page*

"What happened to *My Very First and Very Wonderful Title Page*?" he or she will exclaim aloud. "Everything looked just fine when I previewed it in Video Editor!"

The answer is due to something called *overscanning*. Back in the early days of television, it was impossible to manufacture a perfectly rectangular screen. In order to create a perfectly rectangular picture, however, manufacturers would mask off a portion of the display—cropping the picture to make it look nicer. Additionally, as picture tubes age, their scanning area changes, so overscanning also helps keep the picture the same size throughout the picture tube's life. Although display technologies have improved over the decades, overscanning is still used.

What this means to you, the video editor, is this: you must keep in mind that not everything you see on your computer screen can be seen on a television set. The exact area that can actually be seen on television, and that is available for your use, is called the "title safe area." The name says it all: this is the area in which it is safe to place titles.

To make matters worse, the actual size of this area is not constant. A good rule of thumb is 10%, but this can vary vertically, horizontally, or both. In general, the older the display unit is, the worse the problem. As picture tubes age, the cropping will change and skewing can worsen. In short, what looks fine on one television might look awful on the next.

Just to be perfectly safe, and to have your titles viewable on the widest range of equipment, I'd go with a 15% to 20% figure. This will not only ensure you stay within the title safe area, but also that you'll be safe from running titles right to the edge of the viewable screen. For a 640x480 screen, taking off 15% means you have a 544 by 408 pixel area in which to work. If you take off 20%, you'll have a 512 by 384 pixel work area. This may seem small, but unfortunately we'll be stuck with it for many years to come.

Title Animation

We covered the basic title clip in the last chapter. However, there's a lot more that can be done with titles than just display static text on the screen. We'll start with simple animation.

Objective
To learn how to apply animation effects to title clips.

Reference Projects
projects\chapter08\start.dvp
projects\chapter08\title-anim.dvp

Steps
1. Open the starter project. It has a basic title clip that says, of all things, "Basic Title Clip."

2. Double-click the clip to open the title clip editor.

3. Click the title once to select it.

This is important! You can't apply any type effects *if you don't select the title clip first*. I know it sounds silly to point out something this obvious, but it bites me from time to time.

4. Click the Animation tab.

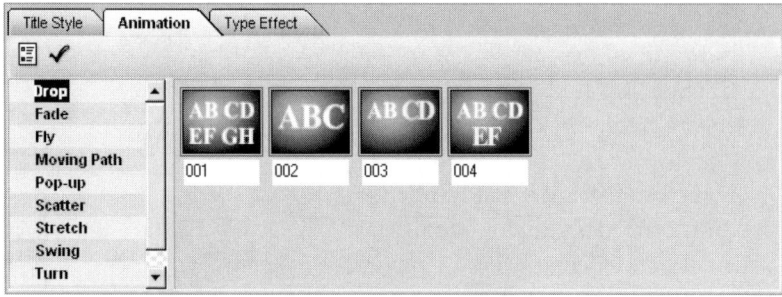

On the left is a list of the animation categories. On the right are the actual animations with very descriptive names. While this looks like a straightforward interface, it somehow still finds ways to trip me up, even after all this time. I'll touch on these as we go.

5. For now, click 001.

That's my first trip-up. Based on seven straight years of Production Library usage, I've been conditioned to drag stuff out and drop it on the thing I want to apply it to. Don't do that here. Select the text, click the effect, then back away slowly.

6. Click the Play button on the title clip's preview area. You'll see what the effect looks like right away. The background will be a rendering of the timeline at the current playhead position.

Next trip-up. The rendering you see isn't the *entire* timeline. It only considers tracks up to and including the current timeline. So if you have clips on Video1, Video2, and Video4, then place a title clip on Video 3, you won't see Video4 in the background. It's a bit disconcerting when you first run into this, so keep it in mind.

7. If you like what you see (you do) click OK and return to the timeline.

Steps, Customizing an Animation

1. Once again, double-click the title clip to open it.

2. Select the title.

3. Go to the animation tab.

4. Double-click the 001 drop animation icon.

This opens the customization dialog box, which is different for different animations.

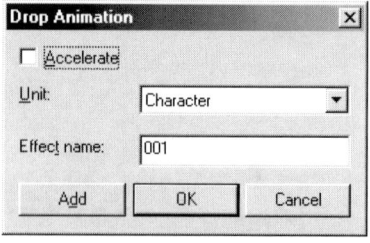

5. Change the unit to Character, as shown here. Click OK.

Something strange just happened, didn't it? The dialog box went away, and if you weren't paying attention you probably didn't see the selected animation switch from 001 to 002. The title clip editor seems *very* protective of its factory presets. Here's the list of rules, which you would do well to memorize:

- Factory presets may not be deleted.

- If you change the values of one preset to match another preset, it will automatically select the other one for you.

- If you change the values of a preset to something completely new and try to save it, it will complain that you can't do this because the presets are read-only. However it will create a new "user" preset for you. Ironically, the one it creates has the exact same name as the original, just in case you weren't already confused enough.

- If you do everything in that last bullet point, but also change the name of the factory preset, clicking OK changes the name of the preset *and* automatically re-selects the other matching preset. It just all seems very odd to me.

- If you change the name of a preset directly from the icon, do not hit enter to save the new name. That closes the whole dialog box.

6. Continuing, double-click 002 (since that's now been selected for us).

7. Check the Accelerate checkbox.

8. Click OK and Preview.

Removing an Animation

To remove an animation, open the title clip, select the title, go to the animation tab and do one of two things:

1) Uncheck the blue checkmark in the animation tab's title bar.

—or—

2) Click any gray area on the right.

Animating Two Titles at Once

Each title clip can contain multiple titles, each with their own independent settings, animations, and effects. We're going to create a title clip with two titles and fade them in and out at different times.

Objective
To learn how to independently apply affects to titles within a title clip and also learn how to set user-defined effect durations.

Reference Projects
projects\chapter08\start.dvp
projects\chapter08\title-anim2.dvp

Steps, First Animation
1. Open the starter project.

2. Open the title clip.

3. Select the title.

4. Click the "north east" arrow in the alignment compass.

5. Click the Animation tab.

6. Select the Fade folder.

7. For now, click the various fade animations and watch the blue bar on the title's preview window jump around:

This bar represents the range (in terms of percentage of clip duration) of the effect. The meaning varies slightly depending on which particular effect you're looking at. You'll see in a minute.

8. Double-click Fade animation 001.

9. Change the Fade style to Cross-fade.

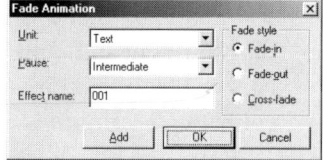

10. Change the Pause to User-defined.

11. Change the Effect name to Crossfade.

12. Click Add. Click OK.

13. Press Play to see the cross-fade in action.

14. Since pressing play deselects the clip, select it again and look at the blue bar:

For this effect, the blue bar shows the duration which the clip is at full intensity. It would have been *really, really* nice if they could have just used a standard keyframe controller. One of my biggest beefs with the MediaStudio Pro suite is lack of inner consistency.

But I digress. The black triangles can be dragged in either direction to change the duration of the fade in or fade out. Let's do that now.

15. Change it to look like this. The exact positions don't matter.

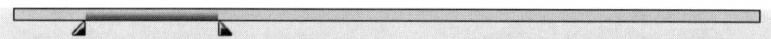

This will have the clip fade in very quickly, hold at full intensity for a short time (the blue part) then fade out slowly (the right gray part).

Steps, Second Animation

1. Double-click a blank area of the title preview to insert a new title.

2. Type "Second Title Clip" and click the southwest alignment.

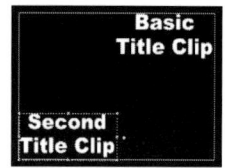

3. If you hit play, you'll see that by default new titles inherit the animation from the last title.

4. This time drag the blue bar like so:

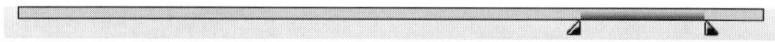

If you alternatively click the two titles in the preview area, you can watch this bar change. You'll also notice there are now *two* animation thumbnails named Crossfade. This is because the duration is part of the animation setting, and when you change any part of an animation's attributes it either: 1) re-selects an existing, matching animation, or 2) creates a new one for you with the same name. Click between the two titles and you'll see the two Crossfade thumbnails being selected in turn.

5. Click OK and preview.

6. Holding the Ctrl key, click and drag the title clip to create a copy.

7. Change the duration of the second clip to 5 seconds.

8. Preview again.

Now you can see that the blue bars are relative and not absolute durations. The effect is the same: quick fade in for one, slow fade-in for the other. But they last much longer.

This can be good and bad. Good, because the clips will automatically adjust themselves to duration changes. Bad, for the same reasons. If you had an animation synchronized to a timeline cue, changing the duration will throw off the synchronization.

(In practice, I would not implement title fades like this. I would use single-title title clips and normal clip fading tools, for this very reason: absolute control.)

Simple Scrolling Text

Scrolling (or rolling) text is standard. And, like a lot of things, there are more ways than one to accomplish this in Video Editor.

Objective
To learn several different ways to create rolling text.

Reference Projects
projects\chapter08\start.dvp
projects\chapter08\title-scroll.dvp

Steps, Method 1
1. Open the starter project.

2. Open the title clip.

3. Click the "Load file" icon on the left to load a text file into the titler.

4. Locate scroll.txt and open it.

The existing title will be deleted, replaced with a new title based on the text found in the file. When I did this, however, the text was black. So click on it, and then give it Title Style 001.

After doing that, here's what I got.

5. Increase the font size to 18.

6. Center the text.

7. Center align the title.

8. Now click the "Single title roll" button. It's the middle motion button.

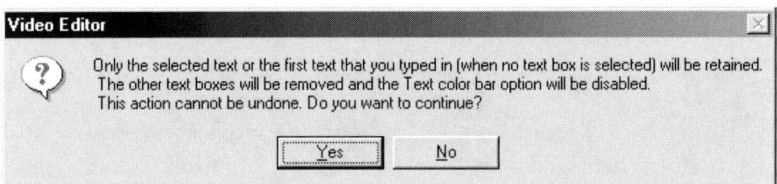

9. You'll get this warning.

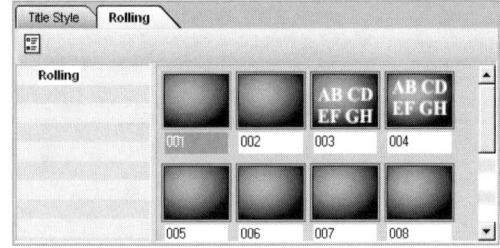

Certain text effects are mutually exclusive. The titler, as we've shown, can support multiple titles within a clip. However, when it comes to certain things, like this rolling motion, it will delete everything but the first (or currently selected) title. Just click Yes.

10. Press Play.

That's about as simple as it gets for scrolling. You have a few customization options, shown here. But to get even more control over scrolling, you can ditch this method and use animation effects.

Steps, Method 2

1. Click the "T" motion button. Video Editor may say you can't undo this action. If so, click yes. We're now back to "normal" mode.

2. Click on the title to select it.

3. Click the Animation tab.

4. Select the Fly animation group and click thumbnail 001.

5. Press Play.

By default, this method produces the same results. But it also offers more customization options. If you double click the 001 icon, you'll see these options.

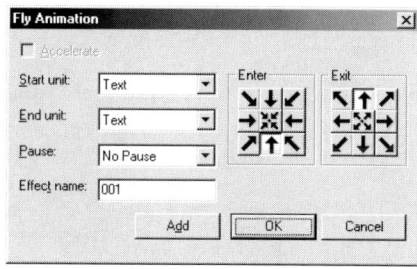

The Enter and Exit points on the right dictate the direction. This gives you 81 different paths for the text to take.

Like other animations, you can apply it to the entire text or a character at a time. Lastly, the Pause setting is available, allowing the text to roll in, stay for a given amount of time, then roll off.

Steps, Method 3

1. Pick it up from where we stopped.

2. Remove the animation. (Remember to click the title first, then uncheck the animation button.)

3. Center align the title in the frame and click OK.

4. Grab a 2D Basic Moving path, drop it on the title.

5. Now just set the start and end points on the path so they start and end off frame, like so:

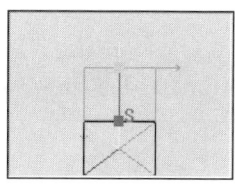   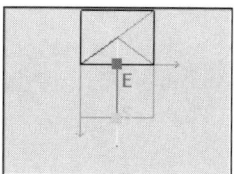

Path Start   Path End

6. Preview your work.

All three of these should look identical. You may find you prefer one over the others and use it all the time. Or you may find you switch between them based on the situation. It's up to you.

Steps, A Touch of Class

This effect is simple but really bumps things up to the next level. Instead of abruptly bringing the credits in and out of the frame, let's fade them in.

1. Ctrl+Drag the last title clip to make a copy.

2. Add a black color clip to track Video2 over this new title.

3. Change its duration to match the title.

4. Press Ctrl+R to bring up overlay options for the color clip.

5. For overlay type, select Alpha Channel. For Mask, choose Image Matte.

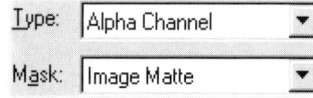

6. When prompted for the image matte, look for thirdfade.tga in the "mattes" folder.

   This folder is on the CD or in your local *Getting Results* installation location.

That's all there is to it. Click OK and take a look at the results.

It's not earth-shattering, but it is more elegant than the "straight up" method. *Note*: this approach only works when the color clip and the background match. It can't be used over a video background.

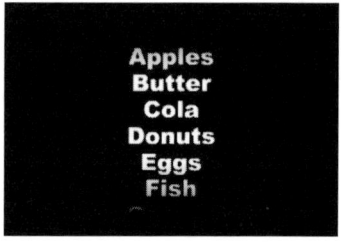

Open the second reference project to see how mine turned out.

Two Column End Credits

If your production calls for two column credits, you'll have to do a little bit extra work. There is no built-in feature that supports this, but it's not too hard to fake it.

Objective
To create synchronized, side-by-side columns of text.

Reference Projects
projects\chapter08\start.dvp
projects\chapter08\title-credits.dvp

Chapter 8 • Text and Titling 225

Steps, Left Side

1. Open the title clip in the starter project.

2. Click the "Load Text" button as before.

3. Load left.txt this time.

4. Apply the 001 style to the text.

5. Right-justify it.

6. Left-align it in the frame.

7. Click OK to return to the timeline.

8. Change the duration to 5 seconds.

Steps, Right Side

1. Ctrl+Drag the title to Video2 to create a copy. (Align 'em, too!)

2. Double-click the second title.

3. Load right.txt into this one.

4. Left-justify it.

5. Right-align it in the frame.

6. Click OK to return to the timeline.

7. Preview.

Hmmm... something doesn't look right. Oh wait. The two columns don't have the same amount of text in them. So when center-aligned within the frame, the tops and bottoms don't match up. Let's align the tops instead.

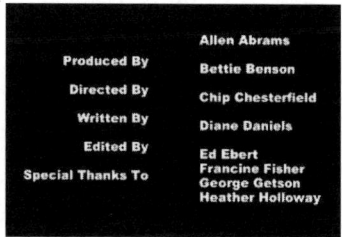

Steps, Realignment

1. Open each clip and click the appropriate top corner frame alignment button. This'll be north-west for left, and north-east for right.

2. Click the "roll" button for each clip in turn.

3. Preview.

4. Well, dag gummit! That ain't look right either.

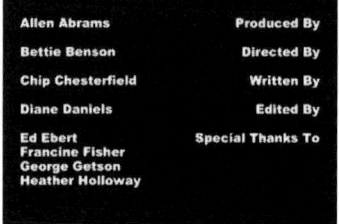

Unfortunately, when you go into the title clip's official "roll" mode, you lose all positioning information. Since the *left* text was right-justified, in roll mode it ends up on the right. Same with the *left*. Clearly this isn't the way we're going to get this done.

Steps, Re-realignment
1. Get out of roll mode, and back into normal mode.

2. Re-align the titles at NW and NE again.

3. This time, apply Fly animation 001 to each title.

4. Preview.

Ahhh! That's it. I didn't think we'd ever figure it out.

If you check out the second reference project, you'll find three copies of these end credits. In the second copy, I moved the columns closer together and colored the left text yellow. In the third copy, I stacked them on top of each other, instead of side-by-side. It could use a little extra space, but I wanted to use the files as-is. Be sure to take a look.

Text That Isn't

While you can do a lot of interesting things with the built-in titler, you really can't do just *anything*. To really get complete control over what you want your titles to look like, use graphics.

Objective
To learn how to use graphics and moving paths to create titles.

Reference Project
projects\chapter08\title-graphics.dvp

Steps
1. Open the reference project.

2. Double-click the first clip, credits1.tga to load it in the Source Window.

Chapter 8 • Text and Titling   227

3. As you can see, this is a single graphic (a very tall single graphic) that contains our "text." It's something you probably wouldn't want to try to reproduce in the titler. But using your favorite graphics program allows you to do all sorts of things. This just scratches the surface.

4. Go to the Effects Manager and examine the moving path. The frame size is 352x960, to fit the width of the project. This simple path (method 3 above) creates the rolling text.

5. Now select the next clip, credits2.tga.

6. Go to the Effects Manager and brace yourself.

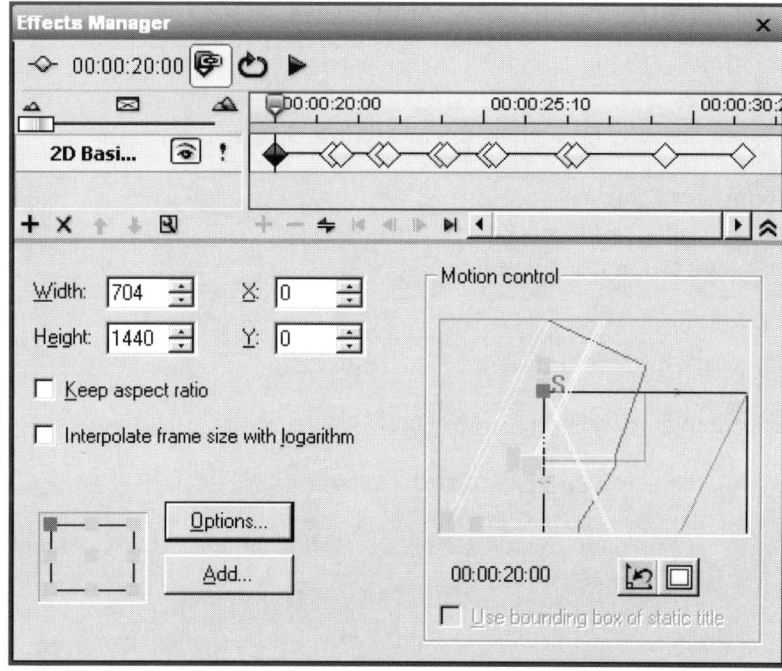

In this case, the width of the image is *not* set to the width of the project. This is because we're panning around the graphic like crazy. Thirteen keyframes complete this effect.

7. Now move to the third section (third cue on the timeline):

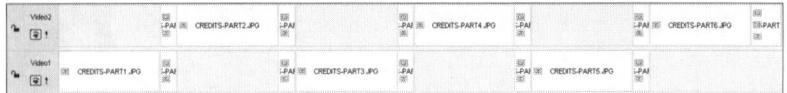

This borrows concepts from the first two, but is its own thing too. The long clips are simple moving paths. The short clips are also moving paths, but have a Motion Blur video filter applied to it. The short duration (10 frames) combined with the blur make the effect.

8. Preview the project to see these things in motion. If you want, add SmartSound auto music tracks to it and change the mood.

Applying Filters to Title Clips

Filters are a great way to dress up your title clips. While you're not restricted to any subset of video filters, you'll definitely find some are more useful than others (and some won't be very useful at all). Let's take a look at the in and outs of mixing video filters and titles.

Objective
To learn exactly how filters interact with Title Clips and alpha channels.

Reference Projects
projects\chapter08\start.dvp
projects\chapter08\title-filters.dvp

Steps
1. Open the starter project.

2. Change the title clip's duration to four seconds.

3. Click the clip and press **Ctrl+D**.

4. Near the top of the filter list is Animation Gradient. Select it, click the Add>> button, and click OK.

5. Scrub the timeline. You should see the colors change over time.

6. **Ctrl+Drag** the title to make a copy.

7. On the new title clip, add the Bubble filter.

8. Scrub again.

   I want you to take a good look at this because it demonstrates something fundamental about how title clips work. In order to help with this, try this short exercise:

Chapter 8 • Text and Titling 229

9. Create a pure white color clip. Place it after the title clips in Video1.

10. Select the second title clip and press Ctlr+C.

11. Click the color clip, right-click, and Paste Attributes.

12. Scrub the color clip.

    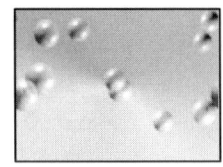

    Now, with this image in mind, go back and scrub the previous title clip.

    As you can see, the text acts like a small window into this filtered world. Every title clip comes with a built-in alpha channel. Title clips are in permanent "overlay" mode (as long as the background color is set to Transparent.) Essentially, this is what we have:

    Therefore, we have a problem—namely, we can only apply filters to the entire title *clip* and not just the *text* itself.

Steps, Illustrating the Problem
1. Ctrl+Drag the first title clip to just after the color clip.

2. Press Ctrl+D.

3. Remove the animation gradient filter.

4. Locate Gaussian Blur under the filter list.

5. Add it and click Options.

6. Set both the start and end levels to 5. That creates a pretty good blur without being completely unrecognizable.

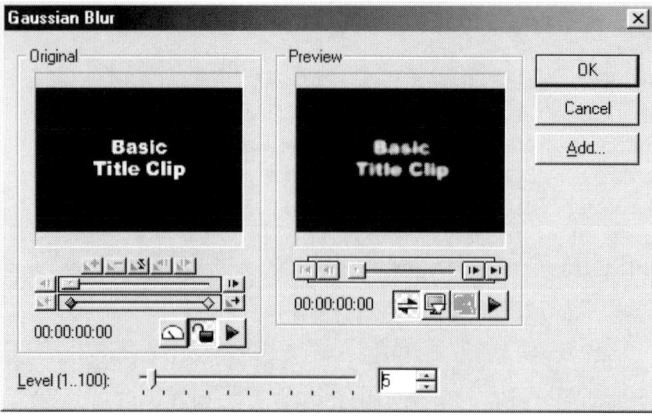

7. Click OK. Click OK.

8. Scrub the new clip.

Guess what? It isn't blurry. There's some blur going on in the frame itself, hence the slight color change. But the edges of the text are crisp as ever.

Steps, Fixing the Problem

1. Press Ctrl+D again.

2. Under the Applied Filters box is a checkbox called Apply alpha channel.

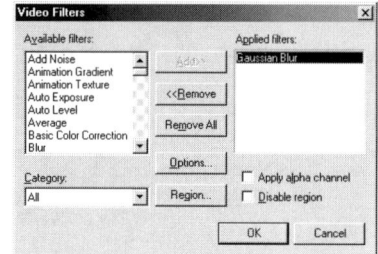

3. Check it! Hurry! Click OK.

4. Scrub the clip again.

Success! The text is now blurry!

But what magic occurred to cause this situation to suddenly right itself? Well, that little check box makes the video filter engine aware of the alpha channel in the clip. (This goes for any clip with alpha channels, not just title clips.)

Once it knows there's an alpha channel, it behaves differently. I don't know what's going on internally, but here's what it looks like to me: the alpha channel is merged with the RGB channels to create a flat image. Once flattened (for the sake of the video filter engine) the filters can now apply to all four channels as a single entity.

If this is still a bit difficult to visualize—and I realize it just might be—here is a quick summary with pictures.

Here is a Title Clip containing some of the most creative text I've ever written. The text is orange and has not been overlaid on any other clips. The background is the black color as specified as the default project background.

As shown, Title Clips come with a mask. For illustrative purposes, the white portions here make up the mask; the black portions are the areas that show through when using tools that support alpha channels.

The Zoom Motion filter creates an effect with a mask like this. Compare this carefully with the previous mask. Whereas before there were only dark areas for the text, now there are dark areas for the effect as well.

When we apply the Zoom Motion filter to the clip, this is the result. The text color is now varied as a result (just as our bubbles appeared through the text before). But all those cool rays we saw in the last picture can't be seen. This isn't what we want.

This is where the Apply alpha channel checkbox comes in. After checking this box, the image turns into this. The video filter engine now realizes it had some extra work to do, and does it.

This final image shows a clip behind the text. This demonstrates how this technique works for any overlay, not just text-on-black. Hopefully this all makes sense now!

Applying Filters to Graphical Text

As we've shown, it's often useful to bypass the titler and create titles using graphic files. If the graphic files do not contain an alpha channel, this presents additional problems when applying filters.

Objective
To learn how apply filters and overlays to title graphics.

Reference Projects
projects\chapter08\start.dvp
projects\chapter08\title-graphic-filtering.dvp

Steps
1. Open the reference project.

2. Insert image credits-part1.jpg on the timeline, next to the title clip.

3. Click it and press Ctrl+D.

4. Add the Gaussian Blur as we did back on page 229: setting the start and end levels to 5.

5. Back on the timeline, hit play.

Hooray, it's out of focus. Hmmm... well, that was easy. So what was the big problem? In a word: overlays. Check it out:

Steps, Part 2
1. Drag the image up to Video2.

2. Insert a new image in its place: trees.jpg.

3. Scrub the timeline. See? No overlay.

4. With the Frankenstein clip selected, press Ctrl+R.

5. Change the overlay type to Color Key.

6. Ensure the Color Key color is black: RGB(0,0,0).

7. Click OK and scrub again.

It's not *too* bad. Obviously, there's a thick black halo around the entire text, but considering the circumstances, I think I could live with it—for this particular situation.

You can soften the black halo using the overlay's soft edge setting. I have an example of this in the reference project.

If, on the other hand, you just can't live with it, then you have no choice but to go back and create an alpha channel for the text. That's really the best thing to do.

Typing Text

Used for decades in movies, the "typewriter" effect is a staple. This is where the text appears a character at a time, accompanied by typewriter sound effects. We have a couple different ways to simulate this.

Objective
To learn how to reveal letters one at a time using a variety of methods.

Reference Projects
projects\chapter08\start.dvp
projects\chapter08\title-typing.dvp

Steps
1. Open the starter project.

2. Open the title clip.

3. Change the text to look like this.

    I used 12 point Courier New. The monospaced fonts help suggest the typewriter. It just wouldn't look the same with a brush script. ☺

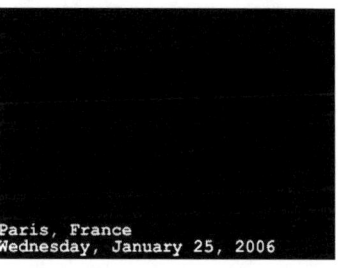

4. Click on the Animation tab.

5. Go to the Fade group and select 002.

6. Double-click to edit. Change the duration to "Short."

7. Click OK and let Video Editor create a copy for you.

8. Click OK again and change the title's duration to 5 seconds.

9. Preview your work.

It's not bad, but the letters are fading in too slowly. That's not how a typewriter works at all. First, let's punch it up with sound effects.

Steps, Part 2

1. Double click an audio track.

2. Locate typewriter.wav and put it in Audio1. Copy the clip and trim it so it fits the project length.

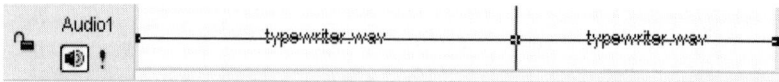

3. Preview again.

   Except for the typing sound extending past the typing, it suddenly seems a lot more realistic. It's amazing how the mind works. Still, though, I'd like to make the letters a bit snappier.

4. Open up the title clip and click the text.

5. Go to the animation tab. Change the duration from this:

   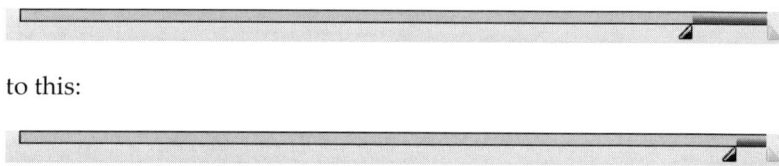

   to this:

6. Scrub the timeline to note when the last character appears. Shorten the second typewriter.wav clip so it ends at the same time.

7. Preview the whole thing.

This is actually pretty close. The typing sounds don't match up to the letters appearing. The letters appear uniformly. And yet it actually gets the same point across.

If you *really* needed the typing sounds and letters to appear closer together (or at least, non-uniformly) how do you think you'd go about it?

One (painstaking) way is illustrated in the project file. Look at the title clips underneath the color clips. The color clips have moving paths which move them in time with the typing sounds, revealing a letter at a time. I wouldn't recommend this approach. Just go with the easy-breezy way: the animation technique described above.

9 Slightly More Advanced Tricks

Create new techniques using already learned skills in an effort to answer common "How do I...?" questions.

Color Correction

No one takes perfect shots all the time. If your video suffers from poor coloring, for whatever reason, Video Editor provides correction tools. They come in two flavors: easy and ouch.

Objective
To learn how to use the Basic Color Correction video filter.

Reference Projects
projects\chapter09\start.dvp
projects\chapter09\color-correction.dvp

Steps, Create a Split Screen
Looking at color corrections helps if you can see the original and corrected versions side-by-side. So we're going to use a split-screen technique. (It's the same one used in Chapter 7's split screen reference project. You'll find it on the far right of that project's timeline.)

1. Open the reference project, start.

2. Delete the color clip.

3. Drop clip 0001.mpg on Video1.

4. Drop (or copy) the same clip on Video2.

5. Select the first clip and press **Ctrl+R** to display overlay settings.

6. Set keying type to Color Key.

7. Set the mask to an Image Matte and find half-mask.bmp.

8. Click OK.

9. Drag a 2D Basic Moving path to the clip.

10. Position the moving path so that the center "half" of the clip is on the left hand side of the frame.

11. Set the last keyframe equal to the first.

12. Copy the attributes from this clip to the clip on track Video2.

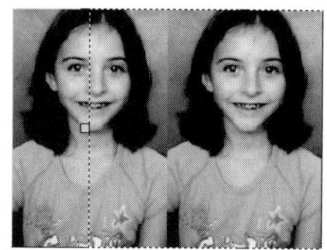

13. Adjust the moving path on the second clip so that its center half is on the right hand side of the frame.

14. Copy the starting keyframe to the end.

15. When complete, you'll have a perfect split screen with each half centered.

Steps, Basic Color Correction

1. From the Production Library, open the Video Filter gallery. Under the Darkroom setting find "Basic Color Correction."

2. Drag and drop it on the clip in track Video2.

3. That's all there is to it. Basic color correction is just that: a quick factory preset for enhancing the color for most normal situations. Preview the timeline and look at the side-by-side differences.

4. Now for manual correction. From the Effects Manager, click on the first keyframe of the filter, and change method to Manual:

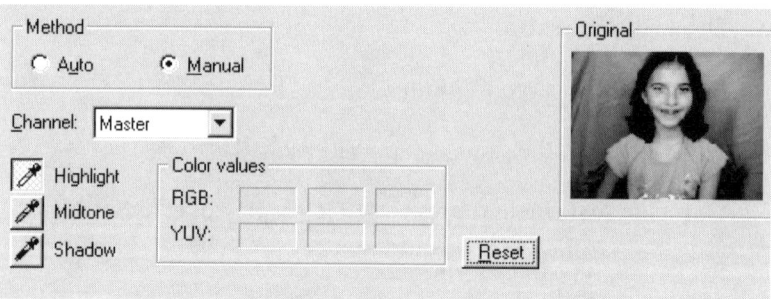

5. Leave the channel set to Master. The basic idea behind color correction is that you tell Video Editor what color values you want to target for highlights, midtones, and shadows.

    It's a science in and of itself, and I could probably spend a year perfecting an entire chapter on it. But whether you know what you're doing or not, it's a comfort knowing these tools are here.

    For now, let's give it some good old trial and error.

6. There are three eyedroppers. With the Highlight eyedropper selected, go over to the thumbnail and click a dark part of her hair.

    Yowsa! It turned nearly white, didn't it? You just told Video Editor that this dark color is a *highlight*. Which means that every color lighter than this *must be lighter than this*.

    Click around the image and see how just changing the highlight reference point alters the image.

7. Let's re-correct the highlight color. Click on the shiniest part of her forehead. We'll try that as an upper reference point.

8. Now select the Shadow eyedropper, and click on her forehead. Just like before, telling Video Editor that this bright color is dark, means that darker colors must be *really* dark.

    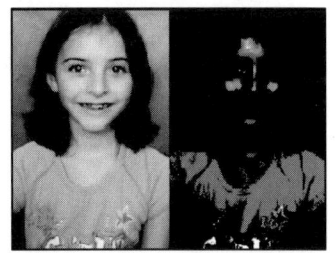

    Again, poke around with the eyedropper and get a feel for how this value changes the image.

9. Re-correct the shadow color. Click on a dark part of her hair.

10. Now let's get the mid-tones. Personally, I like my mid-tones to lean towards the lighter side. I feel (in general) it brightens up the picture better. Just like before, grab the eyedropper and click around. In the end, pick a spot on her shirt.

11. Check the reference project.

You'll see I've placed two sets of clips together. The automatic color correction vs. the manual color correction. (Here's an odd thing: I found the manual color correction rendered faster. Either that, or the basic color correction rendered *really* slowly.)

The big question regarding color correction is, "How do I know when it's right?" Well, that is a big question. Most people eyeball it. If it looks good, and is better than what you started with, you're only that much more ahead.

I would add, though, whenever possible view the results in your target medium. If this is destined for a television set, then see how the corrections look on a television set. Don't rely on the small RGB preview window.

Advanced Color Correction

The primary Color Correction filter is a monster. Just take a look.

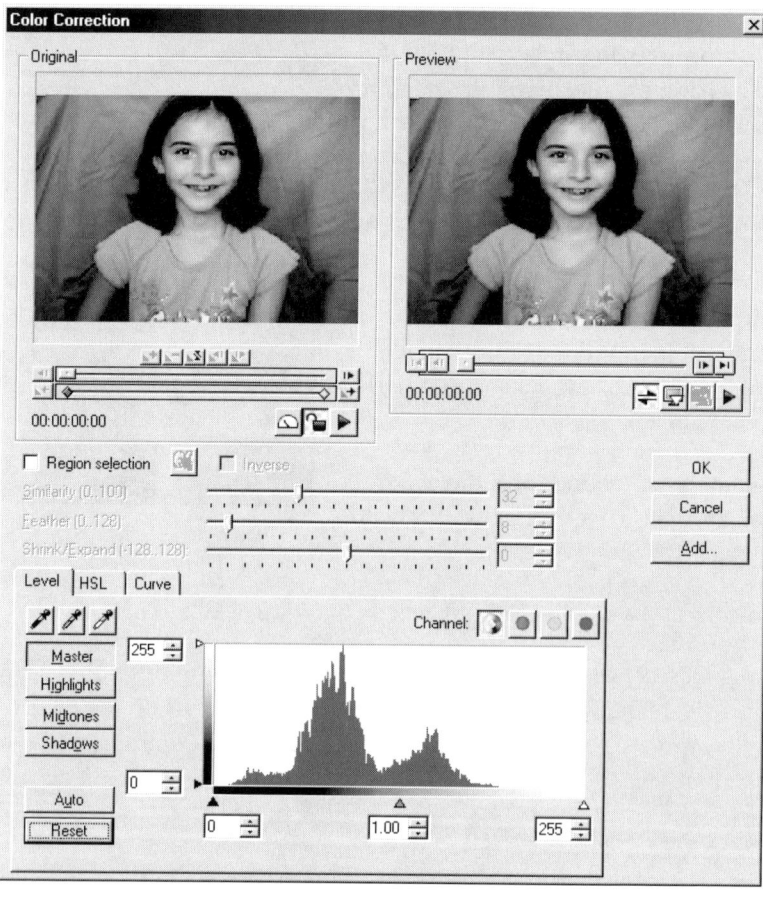

Chapter 9 • Slightly More Advanced Tricks

I'll be honest. This thing is not for the faint of heart. It's a powerful new tool that has made it into the top bullet points of MSP8 features. But (somewhat surprisingly) I've yet found the need to use it. I'm *very* glad they offered the Basic Color Correction filter, because—at least up until now—it has sufficed on every occasion. If I had to come into this thing every time I wanted to change highlights on a video filter, I'd probably have even less hair than I already have.

It's embarrassing, really. I'm a geek's geek at heart. Twiddling numbers, and levers, and sliders—heck, that's what it's all about, right? But I have yet to manage any real *correcting* with this filter. It's really easy to create some pretty interesting special effects. It's another story getting true color correction.

For those willing to venture into this, a few tips are offered:

1. Be gentle. You'll be more effective making very small, focused changes. Wild swings in correction values will create wild results. That much is guaranteed.

2. Try not to do too much at once and allow yourself *plenty* of time. Advanced color correction isn't something can be rushed. If you're short on time, use the basic color correction filter.

3. Start with the Curve tab. Move on to the Level and HSL tabs after you get a few good corrections under your belt.

Fading from Black & White to Color

This is actually an exceedingly easy effect, but I've seen the question asked often enough, so I thought I'd throw it in. In a nutshell, how do you change a clip from black and white to color (or vice versa)?

Objective
To learn to use the HSL filters to change the saturation of a clip over time.

Reference Projects
projects\chapter09\start.dvp
projects\chapter09\bwcolor.dvp

Steps
1. As usual, open the starter project.

2. Load clip 0002.mpg to track Video1. You can leave the color clip.

3. Click it and press **Ctrl+D**. (I still find this to be the fastest way to grab filters, if I know exactly which one I'm looking for.)

4. Find Hue & Saturation on the list. Add it and click OK.

5. On the first keyframe, set Hue and Saturation both to 0.

6. Copy that to the last keyframe.

7. From the Effects Manager, set two middle keyframes, like so: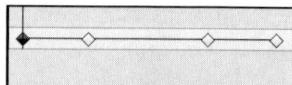

8. Now, on the first and second keyframes, set saturation to -100%.

9. Click Play.

Open the reference project to see this and other ways of doing this.

Old Film

This is another FAE ("frequently asked effect"). And since there's a built-in filter for it, it's also very easy to use. But use with caution. It can be very cliché if you're not careful.

Objective
To learn how to tweak the Old Film filter.

Reference Project
projects\chapter09\old-film.dvp

Steps
1. Open the reference project.

2. There are several sections, each with different tweaks of the Old Film filter settings. Examine each of them to see how the effect can be subtly tweaked.

3. Be sure to check out the last one: *really* old film. This clip has the Old Film filter applied to it twice. Betcha never thought to try that one!

The Lens Flare

Here's an interesting phenomenon. When a drummer plays, one of his or her aspirations is to become extraordinarily accurate. When a drum machine plays, the goal is to become *inaccurate* so it doesn't sound like a machine. Ironic that being "the best" is measured by how much you sound like what you're not.

It's the same with the lens flare. It's an optical aberration that no one would have ever set out to achieve on purpose. But now, because we see it everywhere, we want to take otherwise pristine footage and add optical aberrations to it to make it look more real.

Strange, isn't it?

Objective
Learn how to tweak the lens flare filter.

Reference Project
projects\chapter09\lens-flare.dvp

Steps
1. Like the last project, there are no steps. Instead, open the reference project and look at the three different ways I've used the filter.

2. The first two use factory settings. One, with the 35mm prime lens type, the other with the 50-300mm zoom lens. The third sub-project uses this latter lens, but customizes the settings. It also does a small (3 frame) crossfade so it doesn't abruptly disappear behind Saturn.

3. Click away on all these settings. The best way to learn this is by getting in there and doing stuff!

All right. Those last three exercises were pretty easy. I thought it was about time we had a break. But now it's time to start digging in again.

A Stitch in Time

In Chapter 6 we learned how to slow down or speed up video. We even learned to vary the slow up/down over time. There is, however, one more way to change the speed of the clip: the Step Time filter. Quite unlike the other speed changes, the Step Time filter does not change the overall duration of the clip.

Objective
To learn how the Step Time filter works.

Reference Projects
projects\chapter09\start.dvp
projects\chapter09\step-time-shortcut.dvp
projects\chapter09\step-time.dvp

Steps

1. Open the starter project. Delete the color clip.

2. Drop leader.mpg on the timeline in track Video1.

3. Drop leader.mpg on the timeline in track Video2.

4. Using the technique in the Color Correction exercise on page 235, create a split-screen of these two clips.

    OR just open the step-time-shortcut.dvp reference project if you're not in the mood and just want to skip to the good stuff!

5. Click the clip in Video2 and press **Ctrl+D**.

6. Press **Alt+V** to move focus to the filter box.

7. Type "Step Time" followed by **Alt+A**.

8. Hit OK. (How about that? You just added a filter without using the mouse!)

9. Go to the Effects Manager and look at the first filter setting:

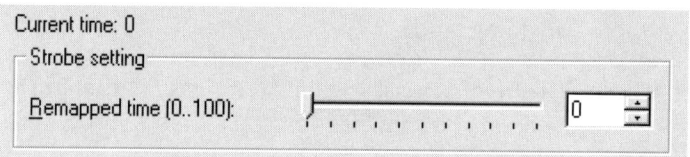

This is the core concept of this filter: time remapping. Unlike the clip's Speed setting, this filter does not alter the clip duration. Instead, it divides the clip into 100 parts and you tell it which part gets played at which point in time.

Seeing it in action is the best way to grasp this:

10. Leave the start keyframe at **Remapped time** 0.

11. Move to the end keyframe. The **Current time** display will change to 100, meaning you're 100% of the way through the clip. Change the end keyframe to **Remapped time** 50. This means, "At 100% of the way through the clip, only go 50% of the way through the clip."

12. Preview your work.

The clock on the right is now running at half speed, since we told it to only go halfway in the given amount of time. So far, this is identical to using a speed setting of 50% and trimming the clip back to its original length. Now it's time to get funky with time:

Steps, Part 2
1. Head back to the Step Time keyframes.

2. Set a new keyframe near the center of the project and change its value to 100.

   This means, halfway through the project, it will have played 100% of the clip. Double time.

3. Now go to the end keyframe and enter 50.

   This means that by the end of the project, it will have played to 50% of the clip. This seeming paradox has only one solution: it must go backwards to get there. In fact, setting the first keyframe to 100 and the last to 0 means the entire clip will play in reverse.

4. Preview your work.

As you can tell, messing with these settings can create some bizarre effects. While there is a bit of overlap with clip Speed functionality, there's quite a bit more of a "funky" factor to this filter.

The main purpose of this exercise, however, isn't about altering time. It's to highlight the fact that there are a *lot* of filters out there. After nearly a decade I still haven't tried them all. It's more or less on an "as needed" basis. I would recommend not doing what I did. Dig in there and learn what your tool can do. Then when the "as needed" time comes, you'll be more than ready for it.

Freeze Frame with a Frame

This is a fun little effect that doesn't take a whole lot of extra work. We're going to take the "camera flash" project on page 164 just a bit further.

Objective
To demonstrate the application of a bordered, moving path to a still.

Reference Projects
projects\chapter09\start.dvp
projects\chapter09\freeze-picture-frame.dvp

Steps, Create the Flash

1. Open the starter project.

2. Drop clip 0004.mpg on the timeline next to the color clip.

3. Trim the clip. Set the mark-in point at 8 seconds and the mark-out point at 12 seconds.

4. Slide it over the color clip to create a fade-up from black.

5. Place 0004-freeze.jpg at the end of the clip.

6. Create a 9-frame white color clip. (You can adjust this duration later to suit your "flash" tastes. I prefer the slow fade of a light bulb.)

7. Place it in track Video2 near the junction of the two clips, like so:

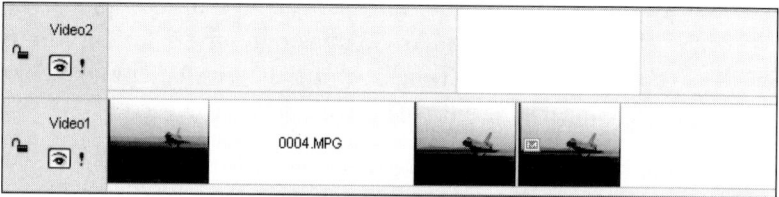

Place three frames to the left of the cut and six frames to the right.

8. Drag it straight down to create the flash effect:

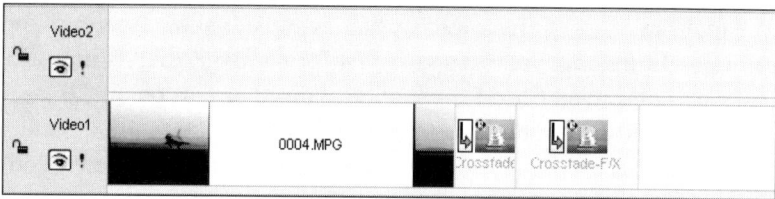

Steps, Create the Photo

1. Apply a 2D Advanced Moving Path to the still.

2. Set the start keyframe to:

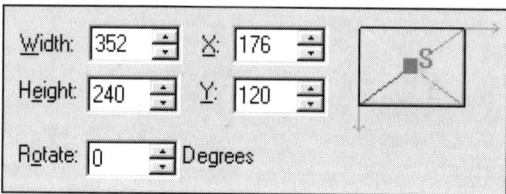

Chapter 9 • Slightly More Advanced Tricks

3. Set the end keyframe to:

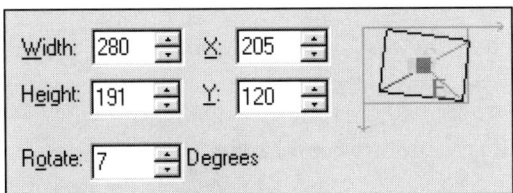

4. Click on the Options button and create a size 5 white border:

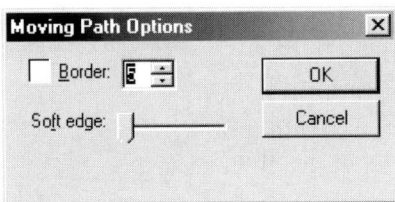

5. Once the moving path is set, the effect is done. Preview.

Add a Title
Open the reference project. You'll see (for fun) I've added a title to track Video2 as the photograph is pulling away.

Extra Credit
Make a minor change to this project. Use the same moving path on the still, but make it so the text appears directly on the photograph, not as an overlay.

The Next Level Freeze Frame

I like this effect due to its overall potential. I'll admit my implementation here is a bit lame, but it illustrates the technique. I know you can do better. The idea is that everything freezes, but the frozen parts stay in motion. It's similar to the moving photograph in the last exercise, but rather than moving the entire frame, it moves parts of the frame through the use of alpha channels.

Objective
To use image files with alpha channels to freeze a portion of an image.

Reference Projects
projects\chapter09\freeze-picture-frame.dvp
projects\chapter09\freeze-frame-plus.dvp

Steps

1. We'll save time by starting with the last project.

2. Delete the image clip, the white color clip, and the title clip (if you added one or are using my copy).

3. Where the previous image used to be, add the image file 0004-cleanplate.jpg.

    This is the same image as 0004-freeze.jpg but with the shuttle removed. I used an image editor to copy portions of the surrounding area to create a new "shuttleless" image.

4. In track Video2, directly above this clip, add 0004-freeze.tga. The Targa version has one thing the JPEG version doesn't. You guessed it: an alpha channel. I added this by hand.

5. Select the Targa file and press Ctrl+R to verify the overlay options. By default, Video Editor detects files with alpha channels and automatically turns on the overlay. Preview the mask while you're here.

6. Slap a 2D Basic moving path on this clip. The one I've chosen holds the freeze for about one second, then enlarges the image. You're free to try this or do something completely different. The end result isn't what's important.

7. For extra fun, I applied an Animation Gradient to the clean clip. I picked that spirally looking thing and gave it a good twist. I would highly recom-

    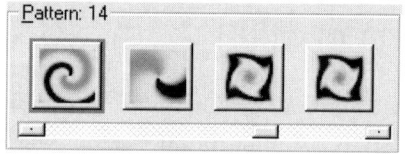

    mend trying other filters and see if something jumps out at you. Monochrome, Duotone, Lightning or Bubbles. It doesn't matter. Just have fun with it and learn. See what it sparks.

8. Now preview your work.

With imaginative use of alpha channels, funky paths, and oddball filters, you can really achieve some visually entertaining results with this "freeze" technique. Of course, like everything in life, moderation is the key. Whatever level of "funky" you decide upon just make sure it's commensurate with the overall project.

Chapter 9 • Slightly More Advanced Tricks 247

Apply Video Filters to Keyed Clips

There's a certain order to the effects pipeline, and it has a flaw in it. If you apply both a video filter and an overlay to a clip, the video filter comes first. Normally, this isn't a big deal: until it comes to blue screening. Most filters are going to destroy your blue screen in one way or another. So by the time the image gets to the overlay, you've most likely lost your key color.

Hopefully someday we'll get the overlay to happen first *and most importantly* have the matte information exposed to the filter. That will autogenerate a region for the filter, and everything will work as expected.

Until that day, you have to use this workaround. It's somewhat of a pain, but not too bad once you get used to it. It does, however, require an intermediate render.

Objectives
- To learn how to create a video matte.
- To define a region for a video filter.

Reference Projects
projects\chapter09\start.dvp
projects\chapter09\keying-with-filters.dvp

Steps, Demonstrate the Problem
1. Open the reference project and delete the color clip.

2. Place trees.jpg on Video1.

3. Place 0001.mpg on Video2.

4. Apply a blue screen overlay on the video clip to move this happy girl into the woods.

    The standard Green Screen overlay in the Production Library should work find for this, or you can try it manually.

    Since the sky looks dark and the trees look creepy, let's change the lighting on our subject to match the overall mood.

5. Apply the Light filter and use these settings:

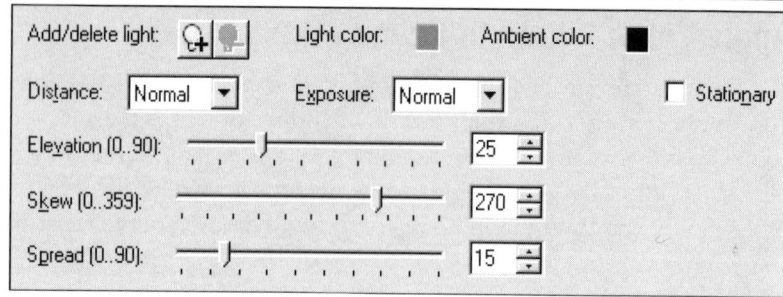

The Light color is RGB(68, 109, 140).

6. Now preview.

Well, we changed the lighting all right! But this killed the green in the process: the exact problem outlined in the intro. We need to create a video matte to exclude the green background from the filter processing. Ironically, this matte comes from the green background.

Steps, Fixing It

1. Create a new timeline.

2. Add a 3-second white color clip to Video1.

3. With the color clip selected, press Ctrl+R.

4. Select Blue screen for the overlay type.

5. Select Video Matte for the overlay mask.

6. Using your impressive keying skills, blank out the green background.

7. Click OK and scrub the timeline.

The color clip is white, hence our subject is white. The project background is black, so our new background is black.

Note. Although this exercise is primarily meant as a workaround for a different issue, *this* technique is very important. That is, within the context of gaining a better understanding of keying. This technique can stand on its own legs, and not simply as a workaround for a problem.

Chapter 9 • Slightly More Advanced Tricks   249

8. At this point we have to render the matte to a separate video file. This is one time where we can't use the timeline as a virtual clip. We need a real file. Select File | Create | Video File. Call it 0001-matte.mpg.

   For now, use the project settings, and create a VCD mpg. In real life, wherever possible, create intermediate renders as uncompressed videos. This avoids generation loss.

9. Back on the main timeline, click the 0001.mpg clip. Press Ctrl+D.

10. Click the Region button.

11. Change Mask to Video Matte and locate the new 0001-matte.mpg file.

12. Leave everything else as-is. Click OK. Click OK again.

13. Preview your work.

At last we have what we came for. The filter has not been applied to the green screen.

Caveat

If you're ever on a game show, and the host asks you, "In MediaStudio Pro, name one thing you can't do with a video matte for a filter region," you'll be in luck, because I'm giving you the answer: *you can't trim it*. The matte is what it is, and you cannot specify alternate mark in/out points.

Therefore, in order to avoid massive headaches, make sure the clip you're working on is physically trimmed as you need it—*before* using the technique we just described.

Consider these filmstrips:

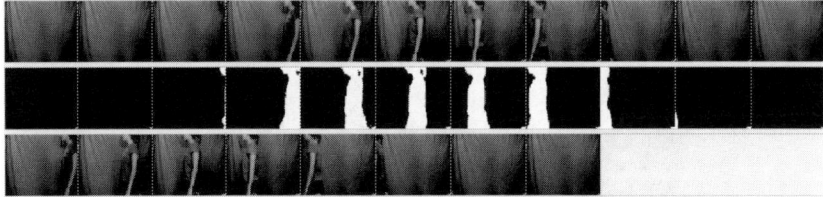

At the top is the original captured clip. The middle filmstrip represents the matte we created to allow us to apply a video filter and overlay at the same time. The bottom filmstrip is where we changed our mind, and trimmed the clip on the timeline. This is bad. As you can see, the clip and the matte are no longer in sync, and there's no way to sync them without re-creating the matte from scratch.

Not impossible, but for your own sanity, make sure everything's locked down first, so you only have to go through this once.

One Clip Transitions

Every once in a while you might find you'd like to apply a transition to a single clip. This is conceptually similar to applying a video filter to a clip. Except that the effect you want (such as a page turn) isn't a filter. Of course, you can't apply a transition to a single clip, so we'll have to cheat.

Objective
Objective

Reference Projects
projects\chapter09\start.dvp
projects\chapter09\one-clip-transition.dvp

Steps
1. Open the starter project and delete the color clip.

2. Drop any clip on Video1 for a backdrop. I chose 0004.mpg for no particular reason.

3. Create a new timeline.

4. Create two 3-second black color clips on Video1.

5. Create two 3-second title clips on Video2.

   I chose this bit of prize-winning literature for the text.

6. Compare your timeline one with this pic:

7. Now drag each title clip down on top of its corresponding color clip to create transitions:

Chapter 9 • Slightly More Advanced Tricks

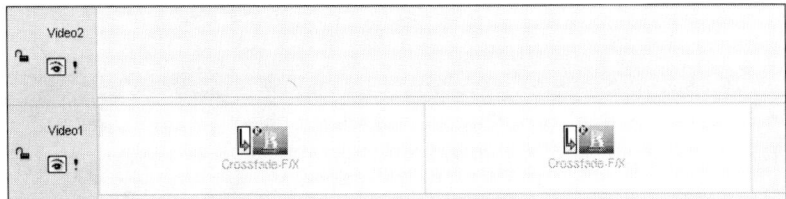

Since crossfades are exceptionally uninteresting in this context, let's change them to something a bit more remarkable.

8. Under the Slide transition gallery, grab the one named **Stripes**. Drag that to the first transition.

9. Under the F/X gallery, place Burn on the second transition.

10. Scrub Timeline1 to see the transition effects.

11. Add Timeline1 to the Main Timeline and place its virtual clip in track Video2.

12. Click it, and press **Ctrl+R** to create an overlay.

13. Set the overlay type to Color Key and the key color to black.

14. Preview your work.

While not perfect, it does a reasonable job of approximating the goal. If you find yourself in a pinch, go for it.

Three Clip Transitions

Transitions occur between two clips. We just faked out a single-clip transition. Now let's go the other direction with a triple play. As you might have already guessed, a virtual clip figures prominently.

Objective
Objective

Reference Projects
projects\chapter09\start.dvp
projects\chapter09\three-clip-transition.dvp

Steps
1. Open the starter project, discard the color clip.

2. Create a new timeline.

3. Drag clips 0002.mpg and 0003.mpg to Video1.

4. Replace the default transition with the Clock transition from the Sweep gallery. Do a quick scrub to confirm.

5. Add this timeline to the main timeline in track Video1.

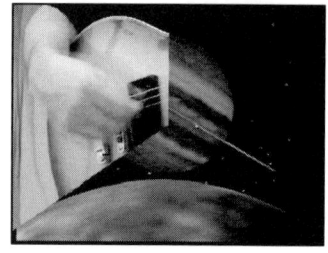

6. On the main timeline, add 0004.mpg to Video1, overlapping the virtual clip.

7. Use the Clock Sweep transition between these clips.

8. Preview and check your output with this image.

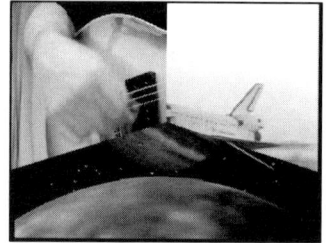

It's kind of cool, isn't it? And with no limit on the number of secondary timelines, you can nest transitions like this indefinitely.

Roll Your Own "Smart Compositor" Clips

One frequently asked question since MediaStudio Pro 8's release has been, "Can I make my own Smart Compositor clips?" While Ulead provides a separate tool for doing this, you may find you don't need it. And if you're like me (someone with a steadily declining supply of brain cells) you might not want to bother learning something you don't have to.

So before downloading *SC Designer*, ask yourself one question: *why?*

Do you want to create Smart Compositor clips to package up and sell, give away, or trade with others? Or do you just want to make them for your own personal use? Because if it's just for yourself, I've got good news. You don't need to make Smart Compositor clips.

There's nothing particularly magical about them. In essence, a Smart Compositor clip is a package containing a single DVP file and a set of media clips. There's a small wrapper around this package which makes them work in Smart Compositor, but when you get right down to brass tacks, it's a DVP file and media clips.

Obviously, using DVP files and media clips is what we've been doing for the last five chapters.

Chapter 9 • Slightly More Advanced Tricks

Objective
To learn how to create, save, and use reusable projects.

Reference Projects
projects\chapter09\start.dvp
projects\chapter09\reusable.dvp

Steps, Creating the Project
1. Open the starter project.

2. Shorten the color clip to 15 frames.

3. Create a new timeline.

4. In Timeline1, add 0015.uis to track Video2.

5. Create a blue screen overlay for the clip.

6. Create another timeline.

7. In Timeline2, drop in clips 0012.mpg, 0013.mpg, 0014.mpg, 0011.mpg, and doors.ucg into tracks Video1 through Video5 respectively.

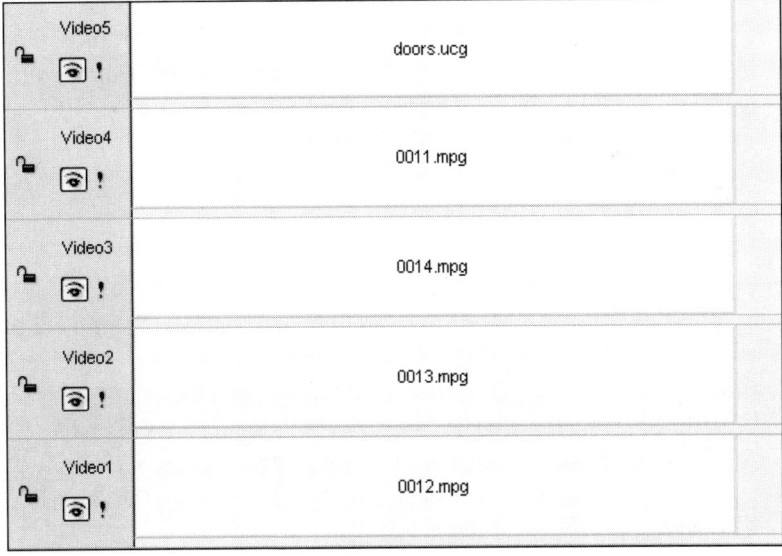

8. Apply basic moving paths to each video clip, placing them in the four corners of the frame.

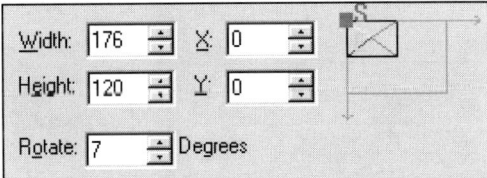

The top-left corner path is shown here. Note: these values assume you've selected the top-left control point for the box.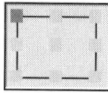

When complete, the four clips should appear in the frame like this. Due to the black backgrounds, the exact borders aren't readily visible, therefore go by the numbers for positioning.

9. The highest clip, doors.ucg, is a CG Infinity[7] file. Although it has an alpha channel, we don't want to use that for this exercise. For now, select the clip and press Ctrl+R.

10. Change the key type to Gray Key.

11. Click OK.

12. Scrub Timeline2 to see the results.

The CG Infinity file has boxes which change in size and color. As they go from black to white, they gradually become transparent due to the gray key. Eventually they reveal the entire picture below: which is a composite of four other images.

13. Add Timeline2 to Timeline1, just below the 0015.uis clip.

14. Scrub to see the space station spinning in front of our virtual clip.

15. Add Timeline1 to the Main Timeline. Have it overlap the color clip on track Video1.

16. Wrap up the project with three more items: 1) a white color clip to fade out the virtual clip; 2) a title clip on Video2; and 3) a Smart-Sound track. Here's what my project looks like. You can open the reference project reusable.dvp too.

---

[7] Available separately as part of Ulead Video Graphics Lab. It's a video vector drawing program which can be used to animate shapes and text. Video Editor has native support for its file type: UCG.

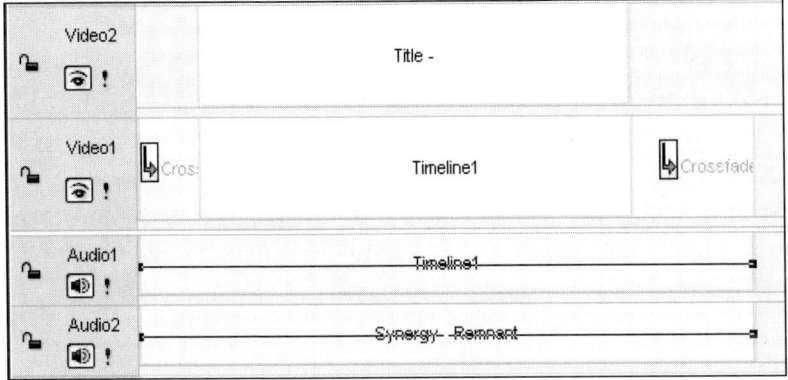

When done, just save it. It's not a Smart Compositor clip, but it's just as reusable and customizable.

Steps, Reusing the Project

1. Start a new, blank project.

2. Press F6 to display the program preferences.

3. Click the Edit tab.

4. At the bottom is an option which tells Video Editor how to treat an inserted project. The first option, "Part of cur- 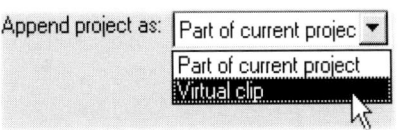 rent project" means the individual clips will be copied from the inserted project into the current project. The second option, "virtual clip" is a bit of a misnomer. True, it does insert the project as a single clip. However, unlike true virtual clips, you cannot open it into its component parts.

   For this exercise, set it to the first option: Part of current project.

5. Select Insert | Project File and locate reusable.dvp.

6. Once opened, drop it on the timeline. It will then look exactly the same as we left it: title clip, color clips, virtual clips.

7. Customization is now as easy as any other editing task:

   - For title clips, just click and edit as usual.

   - For virtual clips, double-click and open in a new timeline.

- For video and audio clips, right-click and select Replace With from the popup menu. This preserves any overlays, moving paths, transitions, or other attributes already applied to the clip.

- Delete existing clips or add new ones as needed.

At this point, when you're done: you're done. You've successfully created a reusable template and learned how to successfully reuse it. What more could you ask for?

Part III

INSTRUMENT RATING

Oh sure, anyone can fly around in clear skies and light winds. But when that storm brews up you're going to need advanced piloting skills.

Chapter 10 Tackling the Montage

Chapter 11 Two Real Life Editing Situations

Chapter 12 Examining Longer Projects

Chapter 13 DVD MovieFactory

10

Our First Projects: Tackling the Montage

Montages are a great way to pull together the skills we've learned in the context of a complete project.

Definition & Purpose

Now that we've had a chance to see what MediaStudio Pro is all about, it's time to roll up those proverbial sleeves and give it a go. The exercises in this chapter will be longer than anything we've done up to this point, but we'll take the "divide and conquer" approach to make our way through them unscathed.

I've chosen this format for our starter projects because the montage has a lot of bang for the buck. That is, you can get a very effective presentation with a relatively minimal amount of work.

So what is a montage? Just to make sure we're all talking about the same page, I'll use this definition. A montage is a collection of images shown in short succession used to convey a single idea or theme.

In other words, you pick a theme, capture clips related to the theme, and then stitch them together. In many ways, both music videos and movie trailers are different examples of montages. The montage may or may not tell a story, but it tends to be short, to the point, and visually interesting.

The Photo Montage

One of the easiest video projects is the photo montage. This is a simple transfer of stills (prints, negatives, or slides) to videotape, typically with music accompaniment. The photo montage has a very high "bang for the buck" ratio. There are two reasons for this. On the "bang" side, the photomontage is typically made up of photographs and music that really mean something to the client (even if the client is just you). So right there you have an emotional advantage before you've even launched Video Editor. On the "buck" side, you can put one together in less time than almost any other video production format. Once you've done a few, you can *almost* do them with your eyes closed!

Nearly all of them follow the same basic steps for assembly, as follows:

1. Digitizing
2. Retouching
3. Dropping
4. Finishing

The first two steps take place outside of the MediaStudio Pro context. The last two steps are done within Video Editor.

Digitizing

This is the act of creating a digital copy of your physical photographs. Much in the same way you capture video and audio for editing, you need to capture your photographs. This assumes, of course, that your photographs are not already in the digital realm. If you're using a digital camera, then there's nothing to digitize. But don't skip this step; you may need to use these other options from time to time!

Methods

There are a number of different ways to capture your photos. The easiest and most obvious is scanning. If you are dealing with prints, this is your best bet. Most low-end scanners do not come with transparency adapters. You will need a transparency adapter to scan slides or negatives.

If you don't have a scanner, (or a scanner isn't convenient) your next best choice is your camcorder. For small prints, you can place your photos on a well-lighted tabletop, and shoot straight down on the photos. For large prints, you can mount them vertically, and shoot them like a hanging portrait. For slides, you can get reasonably good results by simply projecting them on a screen or white wall and videotaping them. Once on videotape, either analog or DV, you can then capture them as you would any other video source. MediaStudio Pro even allows you to save still images during the Capture step.

No matter how you get your pictures into the computer, your final goal is to have a series of image files. If you're worried about recompression, and disk space isn't a problem, you can store them in an uncompressed format.

Scanning DPI Tips

The scanner manufacturers like to compete with each other on "dpi," or "dots per inch." The higher the dpi, the more data is captured, and the higher quality the image. You might be tempted to use your new scanner to grab photos at the highest quality settings, 300, 600, or even 1200 dpi or more. But this is overkill: you'd be scanning far more data than you'd ever be able to use in a video.

For example, let's say you have a 5 x 7 print that you scan at 600 dpi. 5 inches times 600 dots per inch equals 3,000 dots. 7 inches times 600 dots equals 4,200 dots. What's your frame size? Even full-screen NTSC DV is only 720 x 480—and you've just created an image at 3000 x 4200! Before your image ever makes it into your final movie, the software is just going to have to cram it back down to fit the 720 x 480 video frame size anyway. So don't waste time gathering more data than you'll need. It will take longer to scan up front and longer to render in the end.

The general rule of thumb is: the larger the photo, the fewer dots per inch you'll need. Because larger photos will have, by their very nature, more dots scanned.

You also have to take into account the picture orientation. Pictures wider than they are tall ("landscape" orientation) fit the television screen better. Pictures taller than they are wide ("portrait") follow a different dpi calculation rule.

Rather than measuring exact photo sizes and applying formulas to calculate the dpi, just use the following chart as a guideline.

Picture Size	DV quality	VCD quality
2x2	400 dpi	200 dpi
3½ x 3½	200 dpi	100 dpi
3x5 (L)	150 dpi	75 dpi
3x5 (P)	100 dpi	50 dpi
4x6 (L)	120 dpi	60 dpi

Picture Size	DV quality	VCD quality
4x6 (P)	80 dpi	40 dpi
5x7 (L)	120 dpi	50 dpi
5x7 (P)	50 dpi	35 dpi
8x10 (L)	72 dpi	35 dpi
8x10 (P)	48 dpi	24 dpi

As you can see, scanning very large photos for very small frame sizes doesn't require a whole lot of scanner resolution! If your particular picture size isn't in the table, then find the closest match and interpolate. It's not an exact science. Just remember to error on the side of a higher dpi. You can always shrink large images.

Scanning Caveats

Pan and Zoom. The dpi settings above assume you will only use the frame as-is. However, if you plan on moving around the image by panning and zooming, you'll definitely want to start with a larger image. That will give you room to move around.

Scan Safe Area. When you slide a picture to the upper right corner of the scanner bed, make sure you know your "scan safe" area. It could be that your scanner might not see image data all the way out to the edges of the bed. Scan a photo then compare the result to the original photo. Look for objects on the edge of the scan and see where the same objects appear on the original.

Title Safe Area. If you're ultimately planning to send your photos to the television, (via VCD, DVD, or good old videotape) remember the title safe area! It's not just for titles. The average family member typically is not a photographer by profession. Photos with large amounts of headroom or poorly centered subjects might only become worse when subjected to television's overscanning.

Original photo:

Even worse on TV:

If your subject is off-center and the background isn't an integral part of the photo, just scan a portion of the picture. Let's say you have a 5 x 7 photo, but the subject is only on the left hand side. Pretend it's 5 x 3½ and scan accordingly. *Be sure to readjust the dpi to reflect the size of your new scan area, not the size of the original photo.*

Original photo:

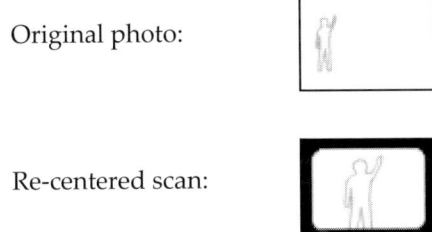

Re-centered scan:

Tips for Large Projects

If you're doing a big project, there are some shortcuts you can take to make the job easier. Scanning dozens or hundreds of pictures can be a time-intensive process. To make things go more quickly, sometimes you have to forget the rules.

Let's say you're doing a family photo history. You probably have pictures going back decades and they're all different sizes and orientations. How best to tackle that?

- If you plan to sequence the pictures after scanning, scan them in groups according to size. This will minimize the time you spend

- changing scanner settings. (Worst-case scenario: every other photo requiring different settings!)

- If most of the photographs are landscape oriented, but a few are portrait oriented, just capture them all in landscape orientation. You can rotate them later from within Video Editor. Again, that will save time fiddling with scanner settings.

- When you have many files, save the files with numeric names. Don't bother with aunt-tilly.jpg, uncle-dave.jpg, or at-the-beach.jpg. Photo projects require assembly line mentality. Just call them 001.jpg, 002.jpg, 003.jpg, and so on.

- If someone else has already numbered the photos, you're very likely to find oddball numbers (for example, "pictures 40-45 have to go between pictures 12 and 13.") Photo management can be a lot easier if you name the files 888-999.jpg where 888 is your number (sequential, no gaps) and 999 is the original number, kept for reference purposes.

- And speaking of photo management, keep all your files in the same directory. You may find you go back and retouch files after they're already on the timeline. If they're all in the same directory, you can take advantage of Smart Relink and save time.

- If this is a one-time, simple drag-and-drop project, don't bother putting them into the Production Library or Project Tray. It's best to just insert them directly to the timeline from the file system.

Retouching

The term retouching brings different images to different people's minds. I'm going to use it in its most broad sense: preparing the image for final use. This may or may not involve advanced retouching tasks, such as image enhancement, image replacement, or other time-consuming graphical chores. It will, at the very least, involve basic editing functions, like cropping and resizing.

Background

Your ultimate goal is to prepare the photo for inclusion in your video project. One of the most important considerations in this respect is your video project's frame size. By default, Video Editor will resize all clips to fit the project settings. That is, if your clip (be it image or video) is a different size than your project, Video Editor will stretch or distort the clip so that it matches the project frame size, kind of like this:

Chapter 10 • Tackling the Montage 267

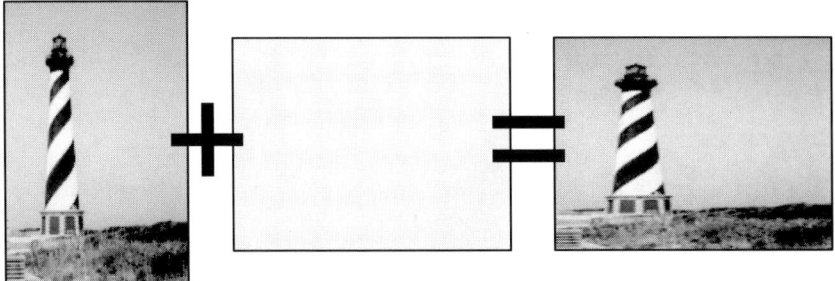

I'm betting that ten falls out of ten, this isn't what you want. You have two ways around this. The first method is to prep your photo to fit the project frame size before you even begin the editing process. The second method is to create a moving path for your photo with a size equal to the aspect ratio of your photo. These two methods are illustrated here:

Method 1. This is an example of the image pre-sized to fit the project's frame size. The black background color you see in this example is part of the physical image itself.

Pros. Total control over image editing. Quicker rendering. **Cons**. More prep time needed before you can actually begin editing.

Method 2. This is the image in its original aspect ratio placed in a moving path. The gray background color you see is provided by Video Editor and is completely customizable: even transparent when placed over other video sources.

Pros. Video Editor can do most of the work for you. Easy to overlay and better position control. **Cons**. More flexibility sometimes means more time tweaking—perhaps more than you intended. Longer rendering times.

We'll examine both methods in the following exercises. Be sure to examine the reference projects and take some time to observe the differences between the two.

Objective

To prep a non-standard image for the project and get familiar with your image editing software.

Notes

This first exercise is **optional** but it's good prep work for familiarizing yourself with your image-editing tool.

If you don't have a good image editing tool and don't feel like spending hundreds of dollars on one I would suggest PhotoImpact or Paint Shop Pro. You can get trial versions of both on the web.

- http://www.ulead.com
- http://www.corel.com

Reference Project

None

Steps

1. Start your image editing program.

2. Locate and open the image file in projects\chapter10\photomontage\0107.jpg. This is the first of eight scanned images for our montage.

   There are two problems with this image: the aspect ratio does not match the project and the image size is greater than our frame size.

3. First, we will need to resize the image. Most paint programs will have a "Keep Aspect Ratio" option for resizing. This means that if you enter a particular width, it will automatically calculate the height necessary to prevent any stretching of the image. Similarly, if you type in a particular height, it will automatically calculate the width to fit. If your image editor supports this feature, use it!

4. For the sake of example, we'll say our video project's frame size is 640x480. If you enter 640 for the image width, and you have checked off "Keep Aspect Ratio" you will immediately notice that the image height is far larger than 480. This happens with portrait-orientation. For these types of photos, instead first set the height to 480 and then the width will adjust accordingly.

5. Resize the photo. It should still look like the image above, but it will just be a different size than when you started. It should now be around 360x480. We still haven't solved the aspect ratio problem, but we're one step closer.

6. If your image editor has a "change canvas size" tool (some editors may call it "paper size") you can use that to fix the aspect ratio. This function will change the image's width and height without affecting any existing image data. In this example, that would mean expanding the canvas size to 640x480 and letting the existing image data fall in the center of the new size.

If you don't have this feature, you can simply create a brand new 640x480 image and copy/paste the existing image into the center of the new image. Either of these gets you to the same end.

Do one of these two things now.

7. When you're done, you'll hopefully see something like this picture. This image will drop on the timeline with no distortion. Further, an image pre-sized to match your project will render more quickly than an image that isn't.

Final Retouching Notes

When going from photographs to television, there are always things that don't make it through the translation well. The worst culprits are fine horizontal or vertical lines in the photograph. If your pictures are of people, these lines will primarily show up in clothes: striped shirts or pants. They can take on a shimmering effect. In order to combat this, you can use your image editor to slightly blur these lines so they aren't so sharp and distinct. A light feathered selection around the area and a "soft" filter or effect can do wonders without harming the overall image.

Also watch for red-eye. If you think it looks bad on photos, it looks even worse when it makes it to the television. Most image editors have red-eye removal tools. You'll do well to get familiar with them!

Lastly, you may be concerned about **non-square pixels**. In short you don't need to be. Video Editor transparently handles this for you. If your project has a 4:3 aspect ratio use 4:3 images and don't worry about the pixel square-ness.

Dropping & Finishing

Once your image files are ready, it's time to get them on the timeline. You can insert them one by one, using the Insert | Image File command, but this can be time-consuming. An easier way is to double-click a video track. By default, double-clicking inserts a video file. But you can go to the preferences dialog box and change the default to insert image files.

While this is a little easier, we can do much better. If you know you're going to work on a project with many image files, you will want to use the Project Tray to its fullest extent. Although we've just treated it as a place to store media clips, you can actually use it as an *editor* by using the Storyboard folder. We'll try both approaches in this chapter.

Types of Photo Montages

I like to look at photo montage projects in terms of how polished the final product turns out. To this end, I've made up four different "levels." If you do this for-profit, this is a good way to tier your services.

Level 1. This is the basic slide show. There is no music accompaniment and there are no transitions at all. It's simply one photo after another, for relatively uneventful viewing.

Level 2. This is the same as Level 1 but with music added. It gets somewhat more interesting, but there are still no transitions.

Level 3. Now we add transitions between the images. In addition to the photos, you can include title pages. It really feels like a finished product now. In fact, about 99% of the photomontage projects I do are at this level.

Level 4. This is everything in Level 3 but with every photo transition completely synchronized with the music. This is a very polished production, but also the most time-consuming.

Objective
Create a "Level 3" photo montage production. It will be set to music, contain one title page, and eight photos.

Reference Projects
projects\chapter10\photomontage\start.dvp
projects\chapter10\photomontage\method1.dvp

Steps
1. Open the starter project.

Chapter 10 • Tackling the Montage 271

Unlike the starter projects we've had up until now, this one has some audio in it. I preloaded (and pre-cued) the file for you, so we can concentrate on the photos. In Step 3 of the video montage project (starting on page 279) you'll learn how to cue audio files yourself.

If you can't see the cues, you need to make sure the cue bars are visible. Click View | Timeline Display Mode... and check the appropriate box.

2. Create a quick Title Clip, like the one shown here.

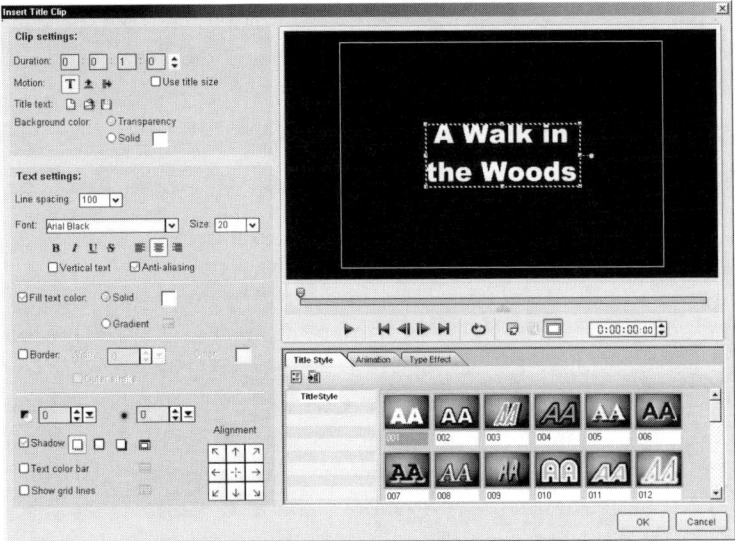

3. Drop it on the timeline in track Video1 next to the color clip.

4. Now slide it to the left, aligning the leftmost edges of the title clip and the audio clip.

5. Increase the title duration equal to the first two audio cues:

We're almost ready to drop our photos on the timeline, but we're missing one critical piece of information. Can you guess what it might be? It's the duration of each photo—what I call "frames per picture." Let's calculate that next.

6. You need to know two numbers for this:

   ✓ The time that must be filled
   ✓ The number of photos that need to be inserted.

   Since we already know we have eight files, all we need now is to find how much time is left. I find it convenient to drop a color clip on the timeline, slide it out to the last cue, and then see how long it is. Do that now. Your timeline should look somewhat like this:

7. Right-click that big color clip to find its duration.

   I get 00:00:23.03 for mine. In order to determine our frames-per-picture figure, first decide how many frames are in 23:03. Multiply 23 by the project fps setting (in our case 30) then add the frames. That gives us 693 (23 * 30 + 3). Divide this by 8, since we have eight photos, and our frames-per-picture number is 86.625. Since the number of frames has to be an integer, lop off the decimal place and call it 86. The reason you don't want to round up to 87 is because that would make your project go too long, and it's always best to come up a little short in the end.

   Our frame-per-picture count is close to three seconds, and that's okay. A comfortable pace is between 3-5 seconds per picture. If it's less than that, things are too fast. If it gets up to 8-10 seconds per picture, you're in danger of putting the audience to sleep.

8. Continuing, delete the temporary color clip.

9. Hit F6 to display Preferences and change the Default inserted clip duration to 86.

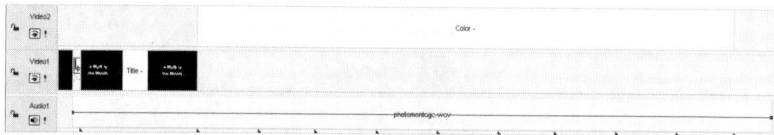

10. Switch over to the Project Tray. Under the Image folder in the Media Bin there are three folders: Retouched, Unretouched, and With Moving Path.

I placed these here as a visual reference, but not to use. You see, they were added with a 1-second duration, and we already know we want an 86-frame duration, so they won't quite work for us.

Of course, I could have added them with the correct duration, but then what would you have learned? ☺

11. With the Image folder selected, click the Import Image File button on the Project Tray's toolbar.

12. Select all the files with "r" in the name. *Tip*. Hold down the Ctrl key while clicking to select non-continuous files.

13. Click Open.

   If they didn't show up in the Image folder in the right order, right-click and sort by Item Name.

14. Select them all (click on 0100r.jpg, press the Shift key, then click on 0107r.jpg).

15. Drop on the timeline next to the title clip in track Video1.

16. Now drag the beginning of each photo over about a half second into the previous clip, creating transitions as you go, like so:

17. Place a black color clip (still 86 frames) at the end of the pictures, right-aligning its right side with the end of the music:

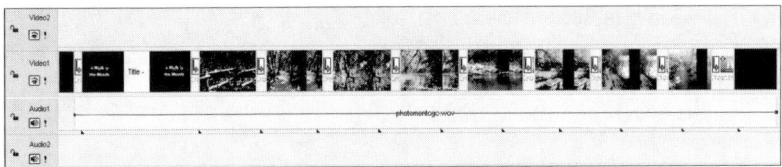

And that's about all there is to it. The only complex part of the project was pre-calculating the frame length for each photo. For a small number of photos (like this) even that isn't necessary. We could have dragged the clip durations around to fit. Or we can do it the easy way...

Dropping & Finishing the Easy Way

There's always more than one way to accomplish an objective. I mentioned earlier that you can use the Project Tray to help out. Yes, that's right, I made you trudge down the tedious path in the last exercise. But now let's let Video Editor do its thing. Same clips, different approach.

Objective
Re-create the previous production using the Project Tray's storyboard.

Reference Projects
projects\chapter10\photomontage\start2.dvp
projects\chapter10\photomontage\method1-approach2.dvp

Steps

1. Open the reference project start2.dvp.

    This project is the same as start.dvp except that the color clip has been removed and cues have been transferred from the audio clip to the timeline.

    There is no function which transfers cues like this. I simply clicked on the timeline at each audio cue and pressed F5.

2. Head over to the Project Tray | Media Bin | Image | Retouched folder. This time we *will* use these clips.

3. Select them all (even stub.jpg, which wasn't there before).

4. Right-click and select Copy to Storyboard.

5. Go to the Storyboard and drag stub.jpg up to the first position. (Drop it directly on 0100r.jpg and everything will move down accordingly.)

6. Click on the Add to Timeline button.

7. Wow, look at this thing. Let me 'splain. No, there is too much. Let me sum up.

    Most of the defaults are fine. We definitely want the clips to overlap. The default duration is meaningless when we synchronize to cues (which is what we're about to do). Uncheck the Pan & Zoom settings. Check Synchronize with cues.

8. Click OK.

9. If all went well, your timeline should look like this:

10. At this point, delete the stub clip.

    Hopefully you now see the need for it. We needed an empty track to pull this off right. We knew that a title clip at some point would need to be synched, but we couldn't put a title clip in the storyboard.

11. Add the 1-second color "leader" clip back in.

12. Re-do the title.

13. Put another color clip at the end to fade to black.

14. Preview your project (or check the second reference project).

    It's a good idea to compare both versions of the project: one without music synchronization and one with. The projects look virtually identical, but the results (to me, anyway) are like night and day. The simple act of synchronization truly takes the production to the next level.

    The Storyboard and Add to Timeline feature are a fantastic help. But before moving on to the next project, let's summarize the feature's good and bad points.

Storyboard Abilities

- You can arrange video and image clips in the order you intend for them to appear on the timeline before ever reaching the timeline.

- You can trim video clips when used in conjunction with the Source Window.

- You can move clips to the timeline with cuts-only or overlaps with customized transition effects.

- You can synchronize your transitions with cues, even repeating a series of cues throughout the timeline.

Storyboard Disabilities

- You cannot add audio clips, color clips, or title clips to the Storyboard. It only supports video and image files.

- You cannot synchronize to cues within clips: only cues on the timeline. This is unfortunate because nine times out of ten I'm trying to synchronize with the music. This forces the "cue transfer" I mentioned at the start of this exercise.

- You cannot synchronize with cues if there are already clips in the target track. This makes it difficult to create, say, a leader for your project, and then use the Add to Timeline tool.

Dropping & Finishing with Moving Paths

As mentioned at the beginning, there are two methods for maintaining the aspect ratio of your photos. Our first two exercises used the first method: pre-sizing photos to match the project frame size. This next exercise will use the second method: moving paths.

Objective
Create a montage applying moving paths to the image clips.

Reference Projects
projects\chapter10\photomontage\start2.dvp
projects\chapter10\photomontage\method2.dvp

Steps

1. Again, open the start2 project to begin.

2. This time, use the With Moving Paths clips under the Image bin.

   If you're wondering why these clips already have moving paths attached to them (and you should be) it happened when I imported them. At the bottom of the dialog box is an important checkbox, shown here. Keep that checked if you want moving paths automatically applied to each image, preserving the original aspect ratio. I'd like this to stay checked all the time, but what can you do?

   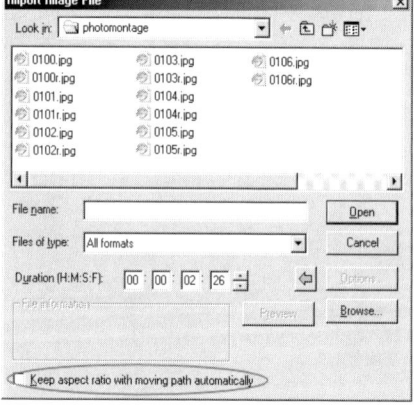

Chapter 10 • Tackling the Montage

3. Select everything in that folder and copy it to the Storyboard, like we did in the last exercise.

4. Put the stub.jpg clip at the front again.

5. Click Add to Timeline again. (Is this all sounding familiar?)

6. You guessed it: use the same Add to Timeline settings.

7. Click OK.

Once you put the title clip and fades back in, the output should be identical to the previous project. But with an added benefit: you didn't have to resize all your images before starting the project. These images essentially followed this path:

- From digital camera to disk.
- From disk to Project Tray with moving paths added.
- From Project Tray to Storyboard.
- From Storyboard to Timeline.

And to be honest, the middle two bullets can be a single bullet. You can import to the Storyboard directly, saving a step.

At this point, before going on to the next montage project, I would encourage you to try out the many different combinations of settings on the Add to Timeline dialog box.

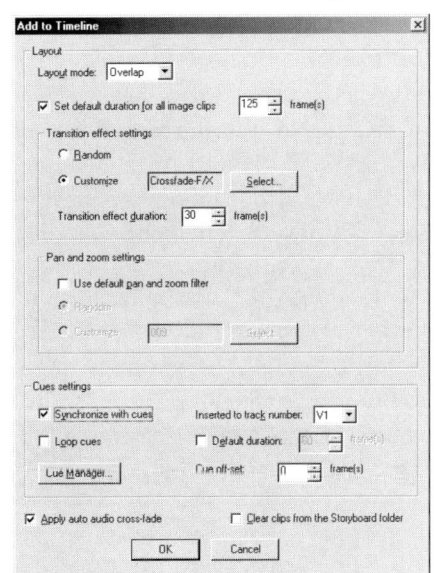

Just keep clearing the timeline and trying it over with different settings.

Try the Pan and zoom feature. Or don't overlap. Or don't synchronize, but set your own duration clip and transition durations.

The more you get to know this feature, the better off you'll be in an editing pinch. Luck favors the prepared!

The Video Montage

The goal of this project is to cover the Apollo 11 lunar mission in about two or three minutes. It's functionally similar to the photo montage: that is, a themed-set of related images set to music. But using video instead of stills adds another layer of complexity.

The five basic phases of creating a typical montage are: 1) capture video clips, 2) make your musical selection, 3) lay down the audio, 4) fit video to audio, 5) order a pizza.

Since the video and audio source files are provided on the CD, we can more or less skip the first two steps. Since pizza is *not* provided on the CD, you're on your own for that. I recommend pepperoni directly after completing a video montage project.

Step 1—Capture Video Clips

As mentioned, you already have the video clips. But it's very likely that for your next project, you'll be responsible for them yourself. So at some point you will have to capture your own video. Refer back to Chapter 3 for information on the Video Capture module.

Step 2—Make Your Musical Selection

Arguably more than the video clips themselves, the music sets the entire mood of your project. I very nearly made this Step 1, since it can very easily dictate the kinds of footage you want to shoot in the first place. Maybe we'll consider these two steps *tied for first place*.

Just like the video clips, I will dictate what music you use for this project. But when it comes time to do your own project, think about how the music changes everything about the video. As an exercise, just string some semi-random clips on the timeline, and put down two different music tracks. Watch the video with one, then with the other. Make some mental notes of how you felt about each one.

When doing your own projects, you'll have two likely music sources: an audio CD or an Auto Music clip. If you have a CD, you can use Audio Editor to digitally copy[8] (or *rip*) the music to disk. Audio Editor also lets you record from analog audio sources. To access Audio Editor's ripping feature, select Control | Record from CD or just press Ctrl+D.

---

[8] You do have permission to use your chosen music, right?

For this project, however, we'll use an Auto Music clip. We gained experience using external music in the photo montage project. Now we'll get experience using some "internal" music. It's pretty cool. Trust me.

Step 3—Lay down the Audio

In the past, I've called this step: *lock* down the audio. This was for two reasons: 1) the audio is the anchor and 2) this anchor isn't very pliable. But since we're using SmartSound QuickTracks for our music, we have a bit more flexibility. You still want to set the audio first. But later, if the video requires a bit more or less of a given track, you have the freedom to simply drag yourself a new music duration, and the audio re-arranges itself to fit.

In my mind's eye, I have a picture of how this project will be laid out, before I even start. I get this by looking at my captured clips and mentally projecting them forward into an assembled sequence. I see three primary parts: before take-off, take-off, and in space. I also see three different types of music to go with them.

Objective
Set up the music for the Apollo video montage.

Reference Projects
projects\chapter10\videomontage\start.dvp
projects\chapter10\videomontage\checkpoint1.dvp

Steps
1. Open the starter project.

2. Click the Insert Auto Music toolbar button.

All available libraries, music tracks and variations are displayed here. MediaStudio Pro ships with one library. As expected, you may purchase additional libraries. In fact, if you change the Scope drop down, you even get to preview selections from other libraries.

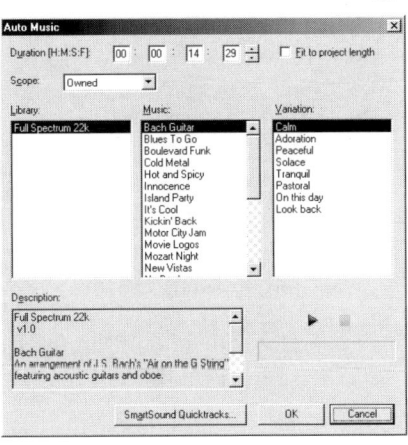

Each song comes with multiple variations. It's important to note that the list of variations varies depending on the specified duration of the track. For example, some variations fall off the radar at shorter samples. This is important to keep in mind if you pick a certain variation, then trim its length later on.

For this particular video, I just ran down the list, categorically dismissing music deemed inappropriate for this project, then narrowing down the remaining tracks, one at a time.

You're encouraged to take a quick break and try this out now, if you haven't already. I won't go anywhere.

3. Here's what I chose:

   Movie Logos : *Deep* (for the "pre launch", 15 seconds)
   Movie Logos : *Imminent 7* ("pre launch" and "launch", 30 seconds)
   Synergy : *Orbital* ("space" segment, 2 minutes)

   It was a complete coincidence that the names Imminent and Orbital worked out the way they did, given the subject matter. (Or maybe it isn't coincidence at all!)

   The next task is to cue the music. You have two choices:

   - Using instant play, use F5 to mark cues on the timeline.
   - Render the Auto Music tracks to an audio file, and cue that.

   There are pros and cons to each method, and the method you chose is based on both the project and your personal editing preferences. For this project, we'll use both.

   There are two reasons to cue:

   - To mark a regular rhythm or beat for synchronization.
   - To create "bookmarks" to remind you of important points.

   Again, we'll use both. Let's begin.

4. Move the timeline playhead back to start. (Press the Home key if the timeline has input focus.) From the Preview Window, make sure Instant Play is on. Press play.

5. Listen for the "booms" in the *Deep* piece. They're ominous so I'd like to mark their presence. Press F5 when you hear each one:

Chapter 10 • Tackling the Montage   281

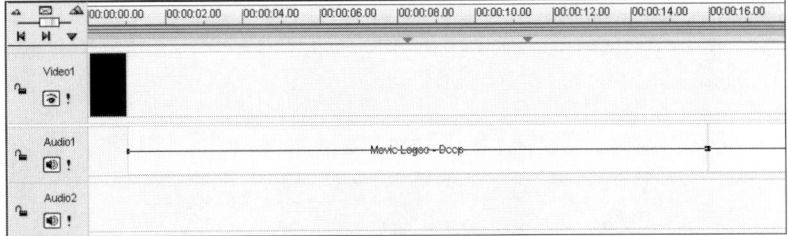

Using the Timeline Display Mode dialog box, you can enable waveform view. This gives you a visual reference of these "booms":

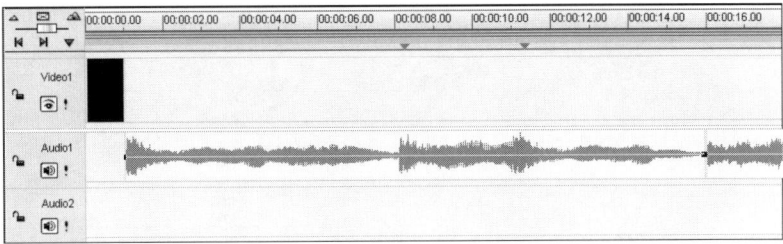

6. For the *Imminent* track, don't cue anything. There really isn't a strong rhythm to it plus I like the suspenseful feel to it.

7. For the *Orbital* track, we're going to render to an audio file, and cue that instead. This is for two reasons:

    ▪ We can't add cues to the timeline for it.
    ▪ We can't add cues to the audio clip either.

    Marking cues on the timeline would be a maintenance nightmare. At this point, we don't know if this is the final resting place of this piece. As soon as we move it even by a few frames, our cues are no longer in sync with the music. Since cues are not possible on the clip itself, we have to take matters into our own hands.

8. Create a preview range over the 2-minute *Orbital* track.

9. Select File | Create | Audio File...

10. Click the Options button and make sure Preview Range is checked.

11. Give it a file name (orbital.wav) and press Save.

Steps, Creating Cues
1. From Video Editor, select Switch | Audio Editor.

2. Open the wav file you just created. (Unfortunately, since the current working directory isn't shared between apps, you'll have to hunt it down yourself.)

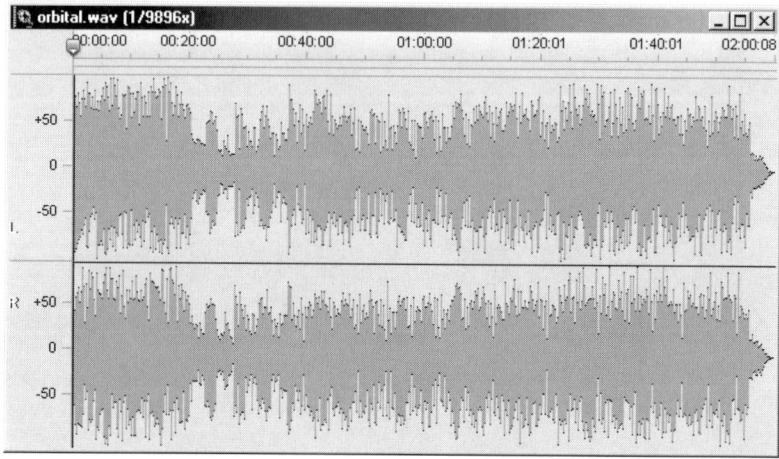

3. Here's how I cue. With one thumb on the space bar and the index finger of my other hand over F5, I begin. Space begins play. With eyes closed, I listen to the music and press F5 on the beats.

Which beats get cued depends on the music. Sometimes I mark every quarter note. Sometimes every other beat (if there's a more syncopated feel to the rhythm). Sometimes four notes on and four notes off. If there are sections where the beat falls off, I adjust accordingly.

For this, I'm using a combination: syncopated beats, only every other group of four, and leaving gaps for the rhythmic holes, like so:

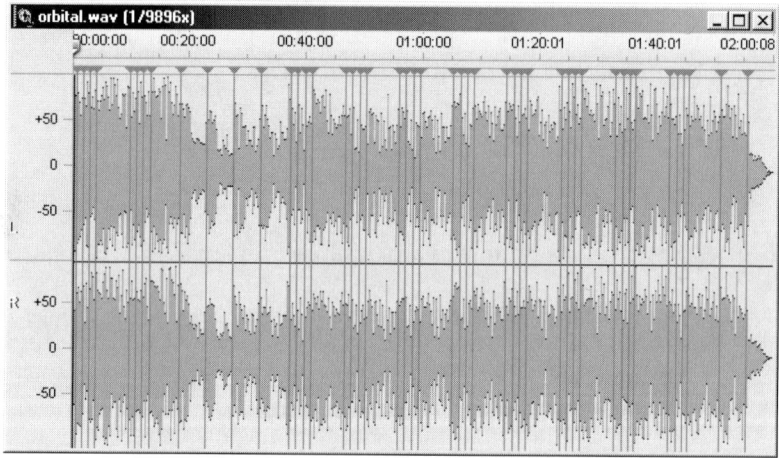

But I have to admit this is a very personal preference. Over the years, I've developed and grown accustomed to this. Everyone is different and what works for me may not work for you. However, if this is your first go at this, give this a try and see if it works for you.

4. Press Save.

5. Close Audio Editor and return to Video Editor.

6. Add the new cued audio file to track Audio2, under the original.

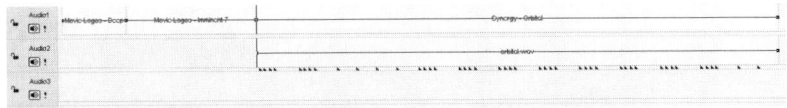

7. Check your work against the checkpoint1 reference project.

Summary for Step 3

- Insert Auto Music Selections at anticipated durations.

- Mark timeline cues.

- Convert SmartSound clip to file to create clip cues.

- Optionally compare results against checkpoint project.

Step 4—Fit Video to Audio

The overall goal of this video montage is to cover the Apollo 11 mission in two or three minutes. When placing the video clips, always keep in mind: *what is the best way to tell the story using the given material?* I've already mentally divided the project into pre-flight, take-off, and space portions. These segments, not coincidentally, are in chronological order. So before placing these things on the timeline, let's first get a storyboard thrown together.

Objective
Do a rough fit of the video to the audio.

Reference Projects
projects\chapter10\videomontage\checkpoint1.dvp
projects\chapter10\videomontage\checkpoint2.dvp

Steps
1. Start where we left off: checkpoint1.dvp.

2. Go to the Project Tray and double-click the window title bar to float it (if you don't already have it floating). Due to the larger number of clips, I want to see them all at once. Increase the thumbnail sizes if you wish. Right-click near the thumbnails and select Preferences.

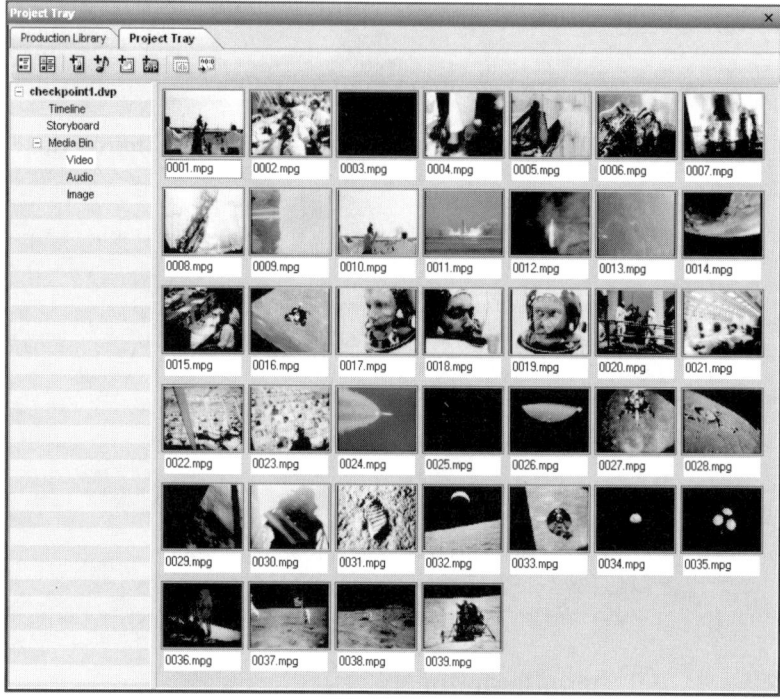

Don't be afraid to make this too big. For the next few minutes, this *is* our video editor.

3. The next step is to populate the storyboard. Do this in groups, in the chosen chronological order.

- Select[9] the astronaut clips: 0017, 0018, 0019 and 0020.mpg.

- Right-click and select Copy to Storyboard.

- Select the remaining "pre flight" clips: 0001, 0002, 0015, 0021, 0022, and 0023.mpg.

- And, again, right-click and Copy to Storyboard.

---

[9] Click normally on the first clip, then Ctrl+Click on the subsequent clips.

Chapter 10 • Tackling the Montage

- This time grab the launch sequence clips: 0003 through 0012.mpg and copy them to the Storyboard.

- Now the space clips: 0013, 0014, 0016, and 0024 through 0030.mpg.

- The moon clips: 0031 and 0036 through 0039.mpg.

- And finally the return clips: 0032 through 0035.mpg.

Now if my math is correct, all 39 clips should now be in the storyboard in rough chronological order:

4. Double-click the Project Tray window title to dock it.

5. For kicks, just dump all this to the timeline, as-is. Click the Add to Timeline button, make sure all clips overlap, use a 15-frame Crossfade transition, don't pan & zoom anything, and don't synchronize.

6. Drop it on track Video1 next to the color clip leader. Then click the "Fit in Window" button to see the entire project.

   The reason for this is to just get a feel for what we're up against. Projects will (almost) always have more raw material than will fit in the finished product. This is our initial assessment.

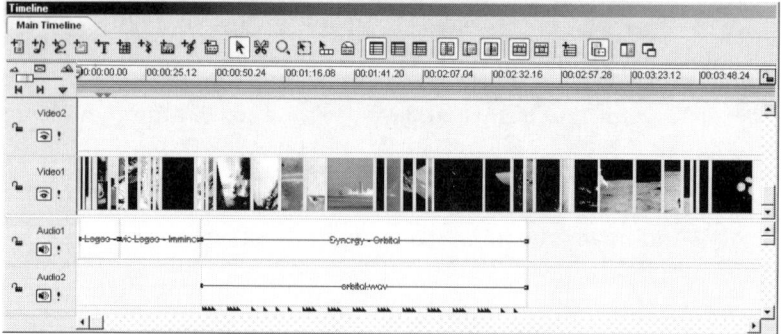

As you can see, in this form the project is over four minutes long. I really want it to stay at two to three minutes. So we have some serious cutting to do.

BUT... before we start cutting, watch this project. Seriously. I know it's nothing more than the clips strung together, but *technically* we just created a video montage. In fact, for kicks, mute the Audio2 track and drag the Synergy : Orbital music clip to the end.

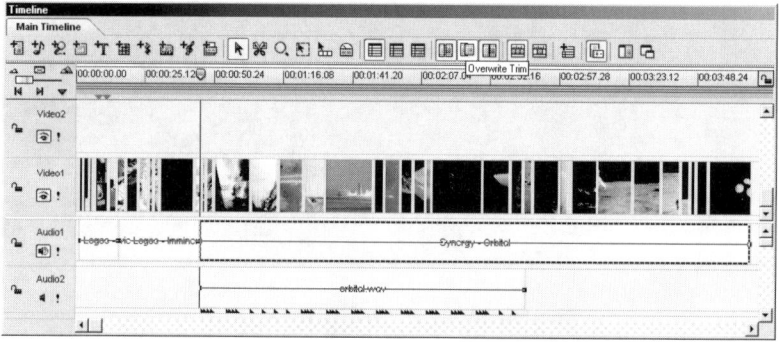

I'm calling this checkpoint2. Try it out.

Step 4—Fit Video to Audio Again

While there's only one "Step 4" in the process, it's quite natural to do it a number of times. I frequently liken the video editing process to working in clay. You start with an unshaped lump. Then you begin to work it into a crude shape of your final product. At each step you see things you didn't expect to see. Some of these things reinforce your original goal and some of these things cause you to change direction. The oddest part is that at every pass, you're technically "done." You can stop at any point and say, "This is my art."

Chapter 10 • Tackling the Montage

Now the dark side: since you're always done, you're *never* done. You'll find there's always one more pass, one more tweak, one more cut that will make it better. Only your experience, sanity, and looming deadlines will eventually tell you when to stop.

Objective
Run through the refinement passes to get our desired shape.

Reference Projects
projects\chapter10\videomontage\checkpoint2.dvp
projects\chapter10\videomontage\checkpoint3.dvp

Steps
1. Start where we left off: checkpoint2.dvp.

2. Review the project and make notes. Look at each segment and make notes (mental or written) about what you think of each section. Does it fit the music? Is it too long? Too short? Too quick? Too boring? Constantly ask yourself, "What would make this better?" Because guess what? It's within your power to make it better. You're not just a movie reviewer.

   Here are my notes.

   I like the way the "boom" music punctuates the astronaut images. It then occurred to me that this would look good in slow motion. It *also* occurred to me that we need a title page.

   This segue feels out of place. For one (not surprisingly) the music is off. For another, we get an outdoor shot before the man with binoculars turns and looks outside. Let's switch that.

   This scene adds nothing to the overall production. We have plenty of other pre-launch footage to get the point across.

   This is our first visual break with no real corresponding musical change. As I watched this, I started to feel the need for additional music. The two "Movie Logo" tracks act as one, so I no longer feel like we have three songs.

   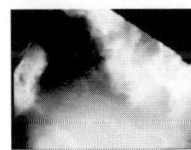

This is where my recent musical epiphany really hit me. Yep. We definitely need to treat the two movie logo tracks as one, leave *Orbital* where it is, and insert something in between.

At this point I'm feeling the whole launch sequence has gone on far too long. This definitely isn't a 4-minute project. We really need to start looking for clips to jettison.

Like this one. It just doesn't fit. I think we can get away with a single "earth view" and this isn't it.

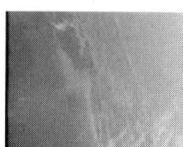

Whoa! Where did this come from? Looks like when we copied stuff to the storyboard, we got one out of order. But, it happens, so we deal with it.

Waaaaay too long, considering the clip that follows it is nearly identical. I like both though, so we may be able to cram them together.

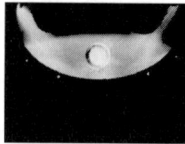

This is just begging for voiceover! As I watched this, the "one small step" speech was playing in my head. Let's put it in the video.

Again, this is feeling overlong. We want to get in, get to the point, and get out. It's a video montage, not a documentary.

Although chronologically, the video ends with the splashdown, the thought came to me that the footprint would make a poignant ending. Let's set this aside for the end.

We're at a fork in the road. Now that we have something to work with, do we start editing directly on the timeline,? Or do we trash the timeline, and go back to the storyboard? Since we're still operating at a high level, and it took zero work to get this far, let's go with #2.

Chapter 10 • Tackling the Montage 289

3. Click the Video1 track name. This automatically selects every clip on that track.

4. Press Delete. We have a clean slate!

5. Double-click the Project Tray window title to get our big view back.

6. Head back to the storyboard. Start by deleting the clips we know we don't want: 0024, 0015, 0022, 0013, and 0037.mpg. (Note, I didn't list all of them in my summary above.)

7. Now fix the chronological problems:

   - 0021 goes after 0020.
   - 0023 goes after 0021.
   - 0002 goes after 0023.
   - 0001 goes after 0002.
   - 0028 goes after 0026.
   - 0016 goes after 0028.
   - 0032 goes after 0036.
   - 0031 moves to the end.

   Here's our new storyboard:

We've cut clips, rearranged the order, but the trims are still wrong on the clips that are left. We'll take care of that on the timeline.

Steps, Pre Flight Segment

1. First things first: add the 1-second color clip leader back to Video1.

2. Insert a placeholder title clip after the leader. Change its duration to about 7 seconds. We want it to end close to (but not too close to) the first "boom" cue:

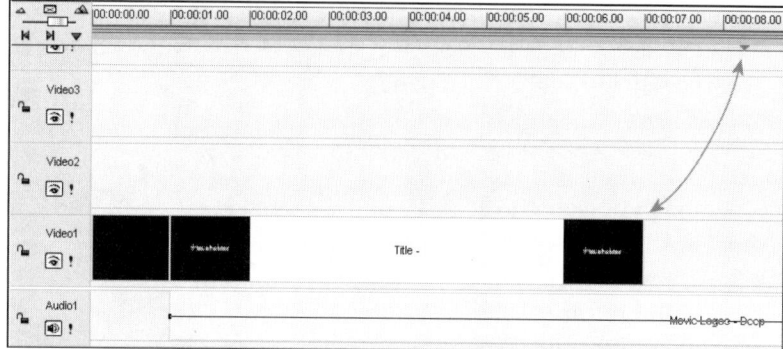

3. Instead of a sweeping "add everything to the timeline all at once" step, this time we'll take a more refined approach. Drag the four astronaut clips to the timeline first.

4. Slow the first three clips to 50%. Temporarily move them to alternate video tracks, to keep them from overlapping. At this point, they're way too long, but we'll fix that.

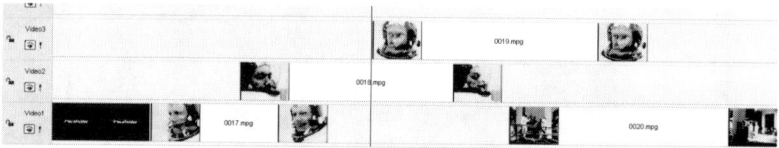

5. But first we need to fix the audio. It's obvious 15 seconds won't be long enough to cover this first segment. Press "R" once to switch from "no ripple" to "single track ripple editing." Drag the end of Movie Logos : Deep out to about 21 seconds.

Note. Every time you change the duration of a SmartSound clip, check it all over again. These "self-adapting" musical arrangements can make unexpected twists when to alter the time they need to fill. In our case, it changed our second "boom" cue. Adjust for that!

6. Turn off ripple editing and slide 0020.mpg to match the end of the music track.

7. Change the duration of each astronaut clip to just under 3 seconds.

8. Reposition them one right after another, like so:

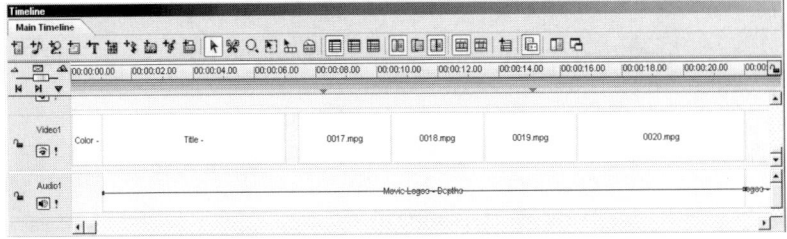

9. Now bring 0021, 0023, 0002, and 0001.mpg to the timeline. Let them overlap a little bit.

10. I'd like 0001.mpg to go a bit longer, so set its speed to 50% but cut its overall duration back to about 5 seconds:

11. New problem: *Imminent 7* is now too long. Cut its duration in half, to about 15 seconds. Our "pre flight" segment is done:

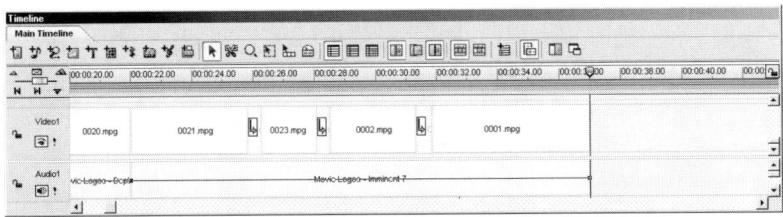

Steps, Liftoff Segment

This is where I felt we needed a musical change. After reviewing quite a few SmartSound Tracks, I settled on *The Limit* variation under *No Borders*.

1. Delete the existing *Orbital* music. (The SmartSound version, not the WAV file we created on our own.)

2. Click Insert Auto Music.

3. Find *No Borders* and its *The Limit* variation. Set the duration to 45 seconds and click OK. Place it on the timeline next to *Imminent 7*.

> If you're wondering where I'm getting the music durations from, they're just guesses. They're based on my own experiences, what I already know about this project, and how I think they'll work in the context of this project. I could be wrong. In fact, I was wrong about the first ones as we've already reset the durations on two of the clips. But that's what working in clay is all about. Push a little here, pull a little there: make it fit.

4. Select clips 0003 through 0012.mpg in the Project Tray.

5. Drag them to the timeline and drop them next to 0001.mpg.

   They're a bit longer than the 45 second music track we created, but they need to be trimmed and overlapped: both of which will drastically cut their collective duration.

6. Unexpected edit: I think the audio needs to overlap. I don't like the gap created between *Imminent 7* and *The Limit* when they're back-to-back. Make them overlap about 1 second.

   Note when overlapping audio, a tool tip displays showing you the duration of the overlap. (I wish video clips did this!)

   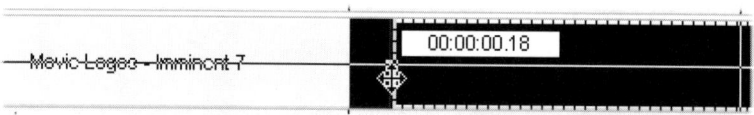

7. Now overlap 0001 and 0003 to mirror the audio overlap:

   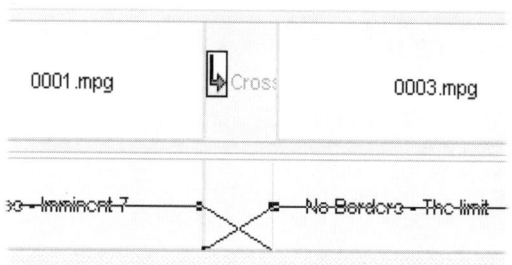

8. Drag 0004 to meet 0003, and delete 0005 which looks too much like 0006. Drag 0006 to meet 0004:

9. Now move 0007 over and trim it to just 3 seconds.

10. Bring 0008 into position and trim to about 6 seconds.

11. 0009's turn. Position and trim to about 5.5 seconds.

12. Drag 0010 over, cut it in half, and discard the *first* half.

13. Clip 0011 is way too long. Just use the last 5 seconds of it.

14. Clip 0012 is fine. Just make sure it's next to 0011.

15. Drag the clips so they all overlap a bit *except* for 0003/0004. There's an abruptness there I'd like to preserve.

Chapter 10 • Tackling the Montage

16. There's now a bit too much audio. Take two seconds from the *Limit* track, making it about 43 seconds.

At this point there should still be a little extra audio. That will be the amount we overlap with *Orbital*.

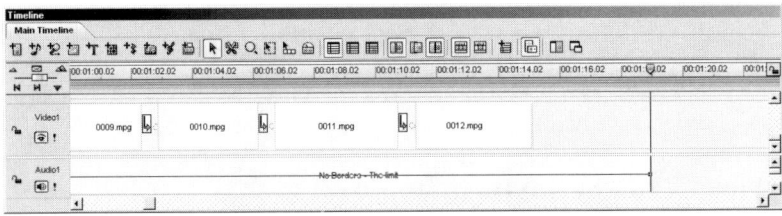

Steps, Space Segment
1. Find our long lost orbital.wav clip which we set aside on track Audio2.

2. Drag it up next to the *Limit* and overlap for the balance of its duration, like so:

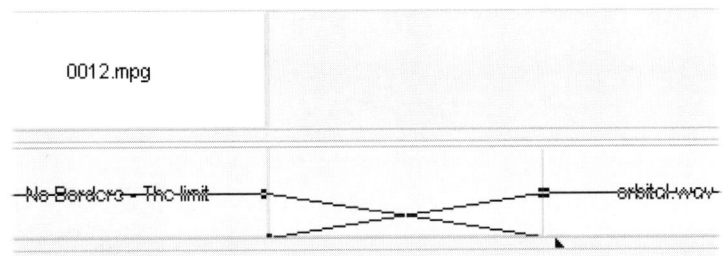

3. Go back to the Storyboard and drag the remaining clips to the timeline. This will be from 0014.mpg on up. Here's what my timeline looks like at this point:

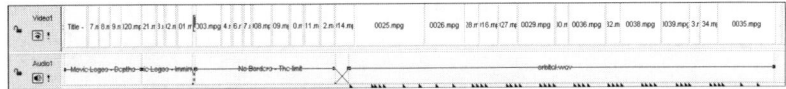

The video and audio durations are almost spot-on. *However* it runs out to nearly 3 minutes 15 seconds. Based on that first viewing, I'd like to get this down to about 2½ minutes. Shouldn't be a problem though, since we have lots of cutting to do.

4. Trim lengths and create transitions for the remaining clips in an attempt to get the project to the target length.

Those are all the instructions I'm giving. You possess the knowledge and the tools to do this. A meticulous "step by step" won't help.

I will give some tips, though:

- As mentioned, 0025.mpg is way too long. Start there.
- Single-track ripple editing will help as you do this.
- The orbit.wav file has cues. Synchronize your cuts to them!
- Since the music clip will go longer, just cut and fade early.

When you're finished, check against project checkpoint3.dvp. Your results will certainly be different than mine, but at a high level, they should be very similar.

Step 4—You're Not Done Yet!

Yes, it's time for our third round of Step 4. Sorry. While the checkpoint3 video looks like it's really starting to take shape, we still have a little ways to go before I'm willing to call it good.

Reference Projects
projects\chapter10\videomontage\checkpoint3.dvp
projects\chapter10\videomontage\checkpoint4.dvp

Steps, Opening
1. Start where we left off: checkpoint3.dvp. Same as last time: review the project and make notes.

We need a new title page, of course.

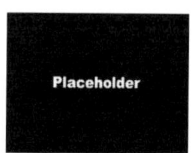

The synchronization in this short segment still feels (at best) unfinished and (at worst) clumsy. I want to work on it some more.

This needs a slow fade, not an abrupt end.

Ever heard a silent rocket? Me neither. We need to add some blast sound effects to this.

This also needs a fade—not to mention a minor re-tweaking of the music crossover. I was wrong about it before.

Oops. I left a gap between two clips. What to do! What to do!

Darn. Still don't have our voiceover.

Pace slows down here. Let's pick it up a bit.

Bad ending. No biscuit.

2. Let's clean up the title page. Double-click it to open the title editor.

3. Double-click the placeholder text.

4. Change it to "From the Earth to the Moon." (With my apologies to Tom Hanks. I don't think my two and a half minute project compares with a twelve hour mini-series.)

5. Change the line spacing from 100 to 80. It's under Text Settings on the left.

6. Click OK to save it.

7. From the Overlay gallery in the Production Library, look for the Transparent folder. Drag 100%-0%-100% to the title clip.

8. Drag this same overlay to each astronaut clip.

9. Drag the overlay named 0% to 100% to the 0020.mpg clip.

10. Double click an audio track and load countdown.wav on Audio2. Make sure the track isn't still muted from earlier.

11. This file has one cue, marking the point where the engines start. Align this cue to the beginning of clip 0003.mpg.

12. Make sure ripple editing is off. Then, using the scissors, cut the beginning of the countdown clip at the beginning of clip 0021.mpg. Optionally fade the clip in.

13. Load burn.wav at the end of countdown. Let them overlap.

14. Load burn2.wav at the end of burn. Again, let them overlap.

15. Fade out burn2.wav during clip 0012.mpg.

Steps, Fixing Up Outer Space

1. I like *where* clip 0012.mpg is so I don't want to move it. But I need *more* of it to create a crossfade to 0014.mpg. As is so often the case, we have two choices: slow it down or freeze it.

   I'm going to flip a coin. Heads, it's slow it down. Tails, freeze.

   Heads it is!

   Slow the clip down to 50% and change its duration to 7 seconds.

2. Scroll down to clip 0028.mpg. Change its speed to 75%. This will create a long crossfade, but leave it like that. Let's see how it turns out.

3. Somewhere near clip 0029, drop the eagle-has-landed.wav file in Audio2.

4. Align the left side of the clip to the left side of 0029. The start of the clip will be close to 0016.mpg. Trim the beginning of the audio to match the beginning of 0016. Then fade it in, like so:

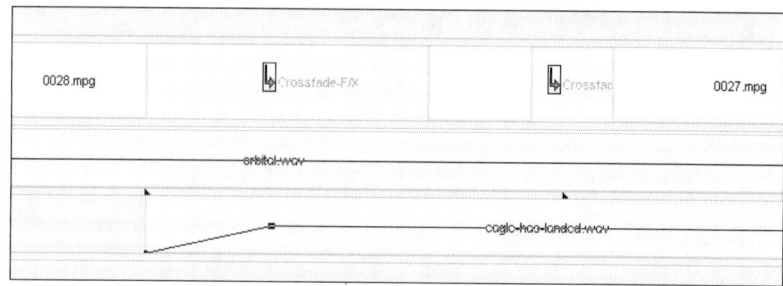

5. Now drop one-small-step.wav next to the previous file.

6. Change the default crossfade transition between 0029 and 0030 to a Fade to black (in the F/X transition folder).

7. Shorten 0039.mpg to 00:00:04.20.

8. Change the speed of 0033.mpg to 50%. Drag it to the left so it overlaps 0039.mpg. Should look like this:

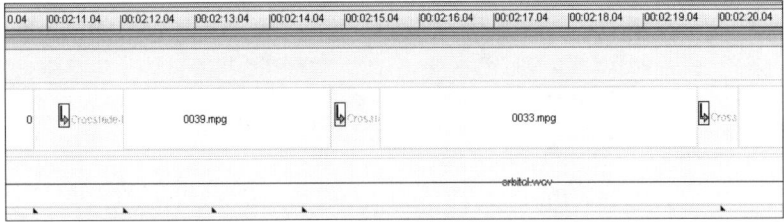

9. Change the speed of the final clip, 0031.mpg, to 25%. Trim the extra to match the end of the music.

   Since we've now cued the clips to the audio, we no longer need this wav file for our music. Think of it as scaffolding. We can get rid of it and replace it with the SmartSound clip. The music will still be in sync *plus* we get the benefit of having a perfect, pre-arranged ending created for us.

10. Check the length of orbital.wav.

11. Insert another Auto Music clip. Set its duration to 00:01:22.28, and choose, of course, the *Orbital* variation of the *Synergy* music.

12. Click OK and drop it in Audio3.

13. Delete orbital.wav (or, if you're paranoid, move it to a higher audio track and mute it.)

14. Move the new *Orbital* Auto Music clip up to its place in Audio1.

Render it out to a file and watch it. I don't know about you, but I think it turned out pretty well. In fact, after watching it a couple times, I think it's better than pretty well. You, of course, may have your own opinions and you're more than welcome to make your own changes. But for now, I'd say we're done! So let's not waste time getting to my favorite step…

Step 5—Order a Pizza

There are two reasons for the pizza. The first is you've worked hard and you deserve it. The second is: you'll need something to keep you occupied while the video renders. If you have a reasonably fast computer, you can render this particular video in about the time it takes to eat a slice. The slower the computer, the more pizza you will consume. So my advice is to make sure you have the slowest computer possible in order to maximize pizza intake.

Seriously, though. This is the step where we turn our project into a final video. This is where we render. If you've done this before and are comfortable with the process, you can probably safely skip ahead. For others interested in the details of rendering, read on.

During the rendering process Video Editor uses various settings to control exactly how the video is encoded. This is done on the Video Save Options dialog box—displayed by clicking the Options button on the Create Video File dialog box. The rendering details:

1. Select File | Create | Video File from the menu.

2. Find the location where you want the final video to be created.

3. Name the final video file in the "File name" field.

4. Select a file type of "MPEG Files."

5. Click Options. This displays the aforementioned Video Save Options dialog box. There are always at least two tabs on this dialog. Other file formats will have tabs that vary depending on file type. For MPEG files, there are these three:

   Video Editor Tab. On this tab you specify very broad settings for the rendering. You can choose whether to render the entire project or just the preview range. If no preview range is selected, this option is not available. A couple notes: you'll often want **SmartRender** enabled. This tells Video Editor to not render any frames it doesn't have to. That is, if it can find the rendered data it needs from the source material or from a previously-rendered preview file, it will just use that. Also, **keyframes** are not supported by all compression schemes. Lastly, the **cropping** button allows you to crop your frame, as you might expect. You can specify the cropping area by numbers or by the green boxes. When you render your video, the frame size of the finished video will be equal to the crop setting. Picture information outside this area will be lost. If you check the "Keep original size" box, then the cropped image will be re-sized back up to the original frame size.

Compression Tab. Even though this is the third tab, I've found it more helpful to visit it second. The reason: the settings on this tab dictate what you can and can't set on the General tab. If you fill out the tabs in order, you may find a setting you make on the General tab is subsequently wiped out when you make a change to a setting on the compression tab. The most important setting is right at the top: Media type. Most of the settings should be self-explanatory, such as VCD or DVD. The next settings are for Video Data Rate. If these are disabled, it's because your current Media type setting does not allow changes to data rate. That is, the data rate is built right into the Media type. Same with the audio settings. In general, leave the settings up to the software, unless you have good reason to do otherwise.

General Tab. The first option lets you choose which MPEG encoder to use. Right out of the box, you only have one choice: Ulead's MPEG.Now encoder. The next option tells Video Editor whether to render just the Video, just the Audio, or both. Most of the time you'll render Audio and Video together. Make sure your **Frame rate** is correct for your format. Select either 30 fps or 29.97 fps for NTSC and 25 fps for PAL. **Frame type** is one of Frame-based, Upper, or Lower, and should be pre-selected based on your other choices. For the **Frame size**, select the dimensions suitable for your compression.

Now, using this info, let's make the specific settings needed for our first full project rendering.

1. On the Video Editor tab, click "Entire Project." Check, "Perform SmartRender." Leave everything else as is.
2. On the Compression tab, select NTSC VCD as the Media type. This matches the source clips from the CD, which have all been pre-encoded to NTSC VCD. This sets the rest of the values on this tab.
3. On the General tab, select "Audio and Video" from the Data track drop-down list. Everything else will be set for you based on the selections you made on the Compression tab (which is exactly why I like using the tabs "out of order.")
4. Click OK. This closes the Video Save Options dialog box.
5. Click Save. This closes the dialog box, and begins rendering.

Formats Demystified

You've spent all this time perfecting your project and now you're ready to show it to the world. (But is the world ready for you?) Well, ready or not, you're going to have to figure out some way to get the video off of your computer and into a deliverable medium. I don't think your living room is big enough to have the world over for a viewing. And even if it was, there's no place for them to park.

Picking a Format

This requires knowing two things: 1) who your audience is and 2) what their viewing capabilities are. In other words, don't burn a DVD if you're sending it to your mom who doesn't own a DVD player. Simple enough!

Picking a Format

Wait a minute. Didn't we just pick our format? No, unfortunately, once you've picked your format, you then have to pick the format of your format. Although we use broad terms like "DVD" or "Windows Media" as if they were simple, singular things, the reality is quite the opposite. Most output formats contain a myriad of settings, letting you tweak to your heart's content (or till you're blue in the face).

Feeling Bewildered?

The format of your video is dictated by a combination of both where and how it's to be viewed. To illustrate this, take a look at this diagram:

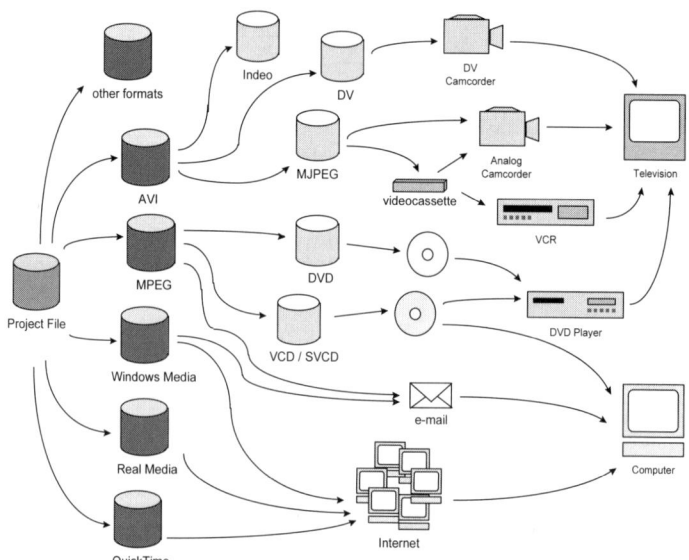

If you've ever felt bewildered by the terms, formats, and media, don't feel bad. As this picture shows, it really *is* a lot to think about. And it's constantly changing, so that beginners and seasoned professionals alike often have to struggle to keep up.

The diagram, too, is neither complete nor comprehensive. There's nothing stopping you from emailing a DV file (but please don't). There's nothing stopping you from playing a DVD on your computer. It's just meant to give a general idea of the possibilities.

In order to find the path to take, start at the end and work your way back. Do you want to watch your video on TV or on the computer? If it's TV then do you want to watch it with a VCR or with your DVD player? If it's your DVD player, then do you want a DVD, VCD, or S-VCD? See, if you work backwards, it's easier to find your way.

As promised, here's a quick run-down of the file formats. They are grouped into broad categories.

Container	AVI
Encoding	DV
Description	High-quality video compatible with all "DV" or "Digital Video" labeled equipment.
Suitable For	Sending the video back to your camcorder for recording on DV tape. Also for sending the signal through your camcorder to any external analog device supported by your camcorder.

Container	AVI
Encoding	*none*
Description	Uncompressed video. The highest quality video there is, and therefore makes **huge** files.
Suitable For	Intermediate renders, clean plates for artifact-free keying—anything where pure quality matters and disk space doesn't.

Container	AVI
Encoding	**Hardware Codecs (MJPEG)**
Description	Encoding suited for a specific type of computer hardware.
Suitable For	Creating video specifically for a given hardware video I/O card. Historically these are cards for capturing and playing back analog video streams.

Container	AVI
Encoding	**Software Codecs (Indeo®, DivX, XviD, etc.)**
Description	Encoding independent of computer hardware.
Suitable For	Intermediate renders, clean plates for artifact-free keying—anything where pure quality matters and disk space doesn't.

Container	MPEG
Encoding	**HD**
Description	High Definition
Suitable For	Devices capable of displaying and sustaining high definition video. Quality generally described as "ten times better" than the TV we've been watching our entire lives.

Container	MPEG
Encoding	**HDV**
Description	High Definition crammed onto the DV tape specification. While they're both considered "DV" this is only because they share the same tape transport. The encodings are very different.
Suitable For	Same applications as HD but with the benefits of the DV data rate and tape size.

Container	MPEG
Encoding	**DVD**
Description	High-quality MPEG-2 video. Can go direct to DVD without further encoding.
Suitable For	Creating your own DVDs, playable on most modern home DVD players.

Container	MPEG
Encoding	**VCD**
Description	Medium-quality CD video
Suitable For	Writing around 75 minutes of video to a recordable CD-R disc. Can be played on computers with VCD players or most modern home DVD sets.

Container	MPEG
Encoding	**SVCD**
Description	Better quality CD video
Suitable For	Same as VCD but only holds about 35 minutes.

Container	**WMV**
Encoding	**Streaming Windows Media Format**
Description	Medium-quality video.
Suitable For	Streaming video from a web site, as long as your clients are all running Windows. Possibly playable on non-Windows clients but no guarantees. Otherwise, very good for getting good quality out of small file sizes.

Container	**QuickTime**
Encoding	**Multiple...**
Description	Like "AVI" QuickTime is a container format, which can handle many different types of encodings: anything from uncompressed to MPEG-4. Originally developed by Apple Computer for the Macintosh, it now enjoys good cross-platform support.
Suitable For	Movie trailers. ☺

Container	**RealVideo**
Encoding	**Proprietary...**
Description	Proprietary streaming format by RealNetworks
Suitable For	Streaming video from a web site. Requires annoying client-side software to play. I never use it.

Still Feeling Bewildered?

I threw a lot of words at you and it's quite possible you still don't know what to do. First, go back a few pages and review. Second, here's my recommendation for the most common path.

- Capture in your native format.
- Edit in your native format.
- Convert, if necessary, to deliver.

For the very common "DV to DVD" route this means capturing and editing DV AVI files then letting the disc authoring tool encode to MPEG-2 for your disk. This encoding process may be very lengthy, but if end-to-end quality is the goal, this is the way to go.

Getting Video Out

Let's pause to see what we've done so far. We've created a couple montage projects. We've rendered a final video. We've learned about formats and various encodings. Now we're ready to get it off our personal computers and on to something else.

If the video is only going from one computer to another (via disk, download, email, or whatever) then you already know everything you need to know. For example, the file we rendered at our last checkpoint is just that: a file. It's no different from a spreadsheet or a word processing document. Except that it's probably a *lot* bigger. So if you do intend to email your videos, please check with the recipient first! (In general, this isn't a good way to distribute video files, broadband or not.)

If, on the other hand, the video is leaving the realm of computers, then there are other considerations. In general, this means heading back to tape or heading out to some sort of video disc.

Output to DV

Using the File | Export | DV Recording menu command, this function takes a DV video file (from the file system) and sends it to your camcorder for recording back to tape.

Once initiated, this dialog box displays. You can change where playback starts, or just click Next> to send the entire clip back to your camera. After that, you can start the actual recording process.

Output to Disc

In order to create a playable video disc, video files cannot simply be copied to disc. While the bulk of the disc is, of course, your video data, there are special encodings and wrappers which must be used to make it playable in an external device.

This is what "authoring" is all about: combining your video files (optionally) with a menu system and generating a playable disc. The two most common disc media are CD and DVD. Files in VCD or SVCD formats can pack a decent amount of okay-quality video onto normal, recordable CDs. But you know as well as I do, you *really* want to make your own DVDs. If you haven't done so already, well ... I'll just say it's pretty cool.

Exactly *how* you author is the topic of Chapter 13. For now, let's wrap up this chapter discussing one last output format.

Saving to VHS

This is not an explicit option on any Video Editor menu, but something you may need to do at some point. Although VHS will very soon join the honored ranks of eight-track tapes and pet rocks, it still has enough life in it that you'll find yourself needing to create videocassettes from time to time. One reason for this is homemade DVDs. While the DVD format in general has taken over the world, not all home DVD players will be able to play *your* DVDs. The discs used by DVD burners are made using a completely different physical medium than commercially available DVDs. (Which explains why your disc of *Shrek 2* is silver and the DVD you made of your kid's last birthday party is purple.) Due to the popularity of homemade discs (CD and DVD) most modern players have multiple lasers to read the different media. If the only thing your DVD player can do with your newly burned disc is display, "no disc loaded," then it's likely you need a new, more up-to-date player which can read and play multiple DVD formats.

Anyway, it's easy to walk to your own living room to see if your disk is playable. But what if you have to send someone a disc and you're not sure if they'll be able to read it? In that case, send the disc *and* a VHS tape. It's still the lowest common denominator out there for home video viewing. Until 100% of the DVD players out there support DVD-R discs, this will continue to be an issue.

So How Do I Do It? The process is actually very similar to capturing from analog, but just going the other way. There is, however, one exception, and it's a good one. When we captured from analog, the analog to digital converter wasn't a given. You either had to have this built into your camera, or buy a separate device or PCI card for your computer to handle it. Digital to analog conversion however is supported on just about every device. It's the exact reason why you can hook your camcorder up to your TV and watch it. The camera is generating an analog signal for your TV to understand.

Therefore, recording to VHS is virtually identical to just recording back to DV. Just follow these steps.

1. Make sure you have the A/V output of the camcorder attached to the inputs of a VCR. Most camcorders will use one of two types of cables for this. Either a standard video RCA video cable or a special cable,

fitted with standard RCA jacks on one end and a small 1/8" A/V jack for the camera on the other:

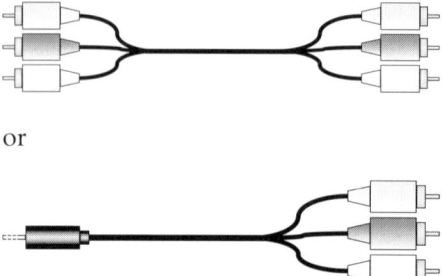

or

2. Put a blank tape in the VCR and ready it for recording.

3. Turn on your camcorder and set it to Play mode.

4. Click File | Export | DV Recording.

5. Locate your video file.

6. Click "Next" in the export Preview Window dialog box.

7. In the DV Recording – Record Window dialog box, click the preview button to send the video down the Firewire line, through your camera, and out to the VCR.

8. Begin recording the tape on the VCR.

9. When finished, press stop on the VCR.

Any Hints or Tips? Of course! Just one. If you know your project is destined for VHS, it's very helpful to have both a long leader and trailer at the end of your project. This gives you time between Steps 7 and 8 to get the tape rolling, and allows for clean, black signals to be recorded before and after your project.

What if I'm not using DV? If you're still editing in the analog realm, then getting your video back out to analog tape means creating your video using your hardware's native codec. If this is the case, you can very likely use a media player or Video Editor's Print to Tape feature. Playing videos in your hardware's codec means the video information is being sent to the card's output. With an analog video tape recorder connected to the card's output, the steps are analogous to steps 7, 8, and 9 above.

11

Two Real Life Editing Situations

Now let's look at two unrelated, yet useful, projects. One uses a script, the other uses multiple cameras.

Pulling It All Together

For those of you who have jumped immediately to this last chapter in order to find out what happens to Dumbledore, I regret to inform you, you have the wrong book. For those of you who have the right book, yet still jumped to the last chapter to discover the clever plot twist before anyone else, well, I only have more regrets. No plot twist.

But I do have something for you: longer and more involved projects. As expected, we continue to build upon everything learned up to this point, employing our new skills and knowledge to accomplish ... oh, never mind. Let's just get on with it.

The Scripted Project

This project will give us a good feel for what a real-life, planned video production is like. While you yourself may not be planning on writing scripts and launching major productions, what you learn here will still help you out in whatever it is you plan on doing with MediaStudio Pro.

In the last chapter, I mentioned how creating videos can be like working in clay. You begin with an unformed lump, and then you massage it to give it some initial form. As it takes shape, you continually push, pull, squeeze, and mold the clay until it gets closer and closer to your original vision.

If you were sculpting a human figure, you would not create the hand in perfect detail before you started anything else. You would want to build up the basic human form and add more detail with each reiteration. This approach works well for video production. We'll do it again here.

Definitions

The *storyboard* concept was introduced on page 96. And in the last chapter, we actually used the Project Tray's *Storyboard* to help us create a video. I should make a distinction between these two concepts. The *Storyboard* (with a capital 'S') specifically refers to the Storyboard gallery of the Project Tray—the tool that allows you to pre-arrange clips and move them to the timeline all at once. A *storyboard* (with a little 's') specifically refers to the standard industry concept. Ironically, we cannot use the Storyboard feature to create a storyboard.

Instead, we're going to use several tools, including the Video Editor timeline itself to create our storyboards. As you progress through this section, the reasons why should become clear.

Phases

This project will be broken into eight distinct phases. They are: Plan, Script, Drawings, Storyboards, Recording, Replacing, Refinement, and Final Cut. In the real world, the two Replacing and Refining phases may themselves be repeated a number of times. We'll do each of them once.

The Plan

We're going to create a quick "how to" video. I'd like it to be about two minutes, just to keep it manageable within the context of this book. Therefore our topic cannot be anything too complex. For example, let's not have a course on mastering the third movement of Beethoven's *Moonlight Sonata*. No, our topic is going to be "how to bake a batch of cookies."

I know, it sounds silly. But if you've ever watched a cooking show, you'll see there's a lot of opportunity here. It has all the elements we need and it will just fit the bill for our exercise at hand. The general plan will be to prepare and bake a batch of cookies, use text overlays for the ingredient list, voice-overs for the recipe and general instructions, and a little music to give it a mood. That will be more than enough to keep us busy!

The Script

Before starting, you'll need a script. This is the step where you turn your general plan into a firm set of instructions. The script is not going to be *exactly* what makes it into the final video, but it should be close. It gives us a foundation from which we can build our drawings and our storyboard. Let's use this:

Video	Audio
Intro: Fade in to title page	Soft/light background music fades in. Voice-over (VO): "Sarah's 2-Minute Recipes"
Fade to slow panning shot of finished cookies on a plate, with some basic decoration, etc.	Background (BG): Music fades, but continues… VO: Hot fresh cookies right out of the oven! There's nothing quite like them! Mmmm… This is a traditional recipe for chocolate chip cookies.
Close up (CU) of various ingredients, as they're being read. Overlay titles of ingredients, with their corresponding amounts in the recipe.	BG: music continues… VO: You'll need: Two and a quarter cups of flour. One teaspoon of baking soda, one tsp of salt, and two eggs. One cup of butter. ¾ cup of sugar. ¾ cup of brown sugar. One tsp vanilla and… Chocolate chips, of course.
CU of oven temperature being set.	VO: First, preheat oven to 375 degrees.
Various shots of mixing steps.	VO: Add baking soda and salt to the flour and mix. Add the sugar to the butter. Then add the brown sugar. And then the vanilla. Add eggs one at a time, mixing well each time. Gradually add the flour mixture. Stir in chocolate chips.
Show dough being placed on cookie sheet. Show first few cookies, then dissolve to the last few being done.	VO: Drop dough by spoonfuls onto an ungreased cookie sheet.
Open oven. Place sheet in oven. Cut to timer being set.	VO: Place in oven for nine to eleven minutes.
Cut away to clock counting down from 9:00 to 8:55 or so, then from 0:03 to END.	BG: Add a "beep" sound when the timer finishes.
Removing cookies from oven, followed by cooling, and moving to racks.	VO: When they're done, remove from oven and let cool for two minutes. After that, move to wire racks to cool completely.
Final shot…?	VO: Bon appetit!

I don't know about you, but I'm hungry now. Why don't we all take five minutes to get a quick snack, and then we'll pick it up from here when we get back. If you're dieting, just remember: if you break the cookies into pieces first, all the carbs fall out.

The Drawings

"Drawings? What do you mean by drawings? I don't know how to draw!" Perhaps not, but this is, nonetheless, a key step. But don't worry, it really doesn't require much in the way of artistic talent. The idea is to get your idea mapped concretely. It's all part of the overall visualization process. It gives you both a strong feel for the entire project and dictates what footage you will need to gather. This is key.

You can take a look at my two-page storyboard in the files storyboard1.jpg and storyboard2.jpg in the project folder. These are my rough sketches created from combining the script with the recipe. This *paper* storyboard shows what's will happen and in what order. It does not, however, impart a good feel for *how long* something will take. To do that, we have to use Video Editor.

The Video Storyboard

Video Editor is our tool of choice for our next storyboard. Now that our paper storyboard is finished, it's time to create the video storyboard. This is more sophisticated than the paper storyboard, in that we can impart a true sense of time to the sequence of drawings. As the video storyboard matures, it eventually serves as our animatic. From there, it's just a short leap to a fully finished video.

In addition to the two storyboard image files in the clips folder, there are a number of JPG images. Each of these is a 352x240 resolution image of each scene. All of them were taken from those two storyboard*.jpg files, except for image 012.jpg which is a combination of boards 9 and 12.

Objective
Begin molding our project using the storyboard drawings.

Reference Projects
projects\chapter11\cookies\start.dvp
projects\chapter11\cookies\phase1.dvp

Steps
1. Open the starter project.

Chapter 11 • Two Real Life Situations 311

2. Add a 1-second black color clip as a leader in track Video1.

3. From the Project Tray's Audio folder, drag music.wav to the timeline. Align it with the right end of the color clip.

4. From the Image folder, select 001.jpg through 014.jpg. Right-click and select Copy to Storyboard.

5. Switch to the Storyboard and click Add to Timeline.

6. Change Layout Mode to Sequential. Change image clip duration to 225. Don't set any pan/zoom or sync settings.

   225 frames!? Where did that come from? Well, the project is going to be about two minutes (or 120 seconds). There are sixteen distinct scenes based on the storyboard: 120 ÷ 16 = 7.5. From there, just convert seconds to frames. Since this is NTSC that's 7.5 × 30 = 225.

7. Click OK to add these images to the timeline.

8. Click Play on the Preview Window and take a look at the results.

   You can stop after the last image, since the audio goes on for a good while longer. I realize previewing might seem premature at this point, but I believe it's a good idea to preview projects in their entirety at every step. Things can jump out at you even at this early stage, so it never hurts to review your progress frequently.

   Time for some minor refinements.

9. Turn on ripple editing. Change the "title page" to 5.5 seconds.

10. Next up, the opening shot: 002.jpg. The length of this shot is about right, so don't change anything. How do I know it's the right length? The script! For this shot, the script calls for a voiceover of, "*Hot fresh cookies right out of the oven. There's nothing quite like them. Mmmm!*" While I watched this on the preview, I read this aloud, and it fit well.

11. Clip 003.jpg represents an ingredient page. I used a single drawing on the storyboard to represent a sample ingredient, but we'll need one per ingredient (seven in all) in the project.

    At three seconds per ingredient, let's change this placeholder to 21 seconds. To help get a feel for the timing, add seven placeholder title clips above 003.jpg. Title them: Flour, Soda/Salt/Eggs, Butter, Sugar, Brown Sugar, Vanilla, Choc Chips.

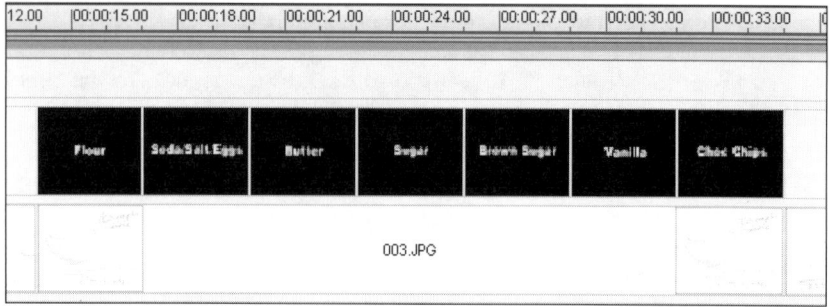

12. To continue, move on down the preview video reading the script out loud and see for yourself how things fit. Again, don't worry about exactness—there's far more tweaking ahead—this is just part of how we shape our clay.

For me, after doing this I realized both 007.jpg and 008.jpg needed to be in there twice.

After making second copies of 007.jpg and 008.jpg, I crossfaded the two 008.jpg clips. Then, down towards the right, I crossfaded 0011.jpg with 0011b.jpg, as a reminder for myself later.

If you're uncomfortable with this method, or just can't get the hang of it, just use the script and a stopwatch instead. Read aloud each part and time yourself. Then go back to the project and adjust the clips according to your timings. Also remember to allow for the visuals. It may take only two seconds to say a certain line in the script, but that may be eight seconds of screen time.

At this point, we're done with this phase of the project. We've created our video storyboard, and now have a firm point from which to build up the rest of the project.

Recording

Once your storyboard or animatic is complete, you're ready to get your source material. The details of recording, both video and audio, are outside of the scope of this chapter, so we won't go into much detail in this section on how to accomplish this.

For video, the key thing is that you know the composition and length of each scene you need to film. Keep a printout of the storyboard handy as you gather footage, to help keep you focused on the task. For audio, you'll have to arrange for audio recordings of the talent.

Once your footage and audio has been gathered (and you've eaten a couple of cookies) you'll need to get everything on hard disk. One extra step on the audio side is pre-cueing the file for editing. I've already done that in the narration.wav file.

When everything's been captured, you're ready to continue. If your fingers still have cookie crumbs on them, wash up first. You don't want that getting in your equipment.

Replacing

The real work lies in replacing all your temporary clips in the storyboard with real clips. There's a little bit more to it than a straight swap. For example, the actual lengths of the clips will change and we do not yet have our audio tracks complete. But the general idea is the same: replace all placeholders with the final video.

Objective
Begin molding our project using the storyboard drawings as a base.

Reference Projects
projects\chapter11\cookies\phase1.dvp
projects\chapter11\cookies\phase2.dvp

Approach
This particular project is far too complicated for a set of step-by-step instructions. After three days, you'd probably only find yourself at Step 427 and I don't think either one of us wants to go down that road. But fear not. Although the actual mouse-click count is high, the essential concepts are few. Let's continue. Begin with phase1.dvp, so that we're starting from the same point.

The clip replacement feature, which first used on page 197, gets a chance to show its usefulness again. The easiest way to access this function is by selecting a clip, right-clicking, and then selecting Replace With from the popup menu.

Before that, however, we need to split up that long 003.jpg clip. For phase1, we used this single clip to represent many clips. But if we're going to move forward, we need to work with the correct number of clips.

To do this: select the first title clip (to automatically reposition the playhead), click 003.jpg, then press the **U** key to slice it. Move on to the next title clip, and repeat until 003.jpg is cut to match the number of titles:

Once that's done, go down the timeline, and do the following replacements. *Tip.* Since you're going to execute the same command over and over, call up the Quick Command panel (from the Window menu). After you replace one file, the replace command shows up here, for quick one-click access.

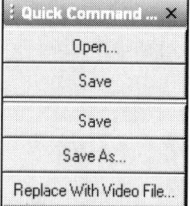

Replace	With	Notes
001.jpg	-	No file: replace with a title clip.
002.jpg	0030.mpg	
003.jpg (1)	0008.mpg	
003.jpg (2)	0007.mpg	
003.jpg (3)	0006.mpg	
003.jpg (4)	0005.mpg	Don't worry about the chocolate.
003.jpg (5)	0005.mpg	Yes, use 0005 again.
003.jpg (6)	0004.mpg	
003.jpg (7)	0005.mpg	And 0005 again.
003b.jpg	0003.mpg	Do not confuse with 0003x.mpg.
004.jpg	0009.mpg	
005.jpg	0010.mpg	
006.jpg	0013.mpg	
007.jpg (1)	0016.mpg	
007.jpg (2)	0017.mpg	
008.jpg (1)	0018.mpg	
008.jpg (2)	0019.mpg	
009.jpg	0020.mpg	
010.jpg	0021.mpg	
011.jpg	0022.mpg	
011b.jpg	0023.mpg	
012.jpg	0024.mpg	
013.jpg	0025.mpg	
014.jpg	-	No replacement yet.

If you've done this, you can check your work against the phase2.dvp project. If you're just reading along, you can open the phase2.dvp project just to see where we are. Bottom line: phase2 is identical to phase1, except we've replaced (nearly all) the storyboard clips with real clips.

Before continuing, run a timeline playback on the project and take a look. If you have a slower system, then render a preview first. Watch the video carefully. Even in this very early state, you will quickly start to form editing decisions.

So what did you think of the phase2 preview? The timeline has a few gaps. The in and out points are completely wrong on nearly every clip. There's no narration yet, just the background music. There's no ending to speak of at all. But what else do you see? I hope you see that you nearly have a complete video, content-wise. Don't dwell on all the things you have yet to do and instead appreciate what you've already done up to this point. We've come quite a way when you think about it. Now let's take it to the next level: refinement.

Refinement

We're far beyond the "lump on a pottery wheel" phase. We have something with form and substance. The next phase is refinement. Now we take the rough cut and sand down the edges. We will close those gaps, fix our trim points, add the narration, and create an ending.

Objective
Refine the rough cut.

Reference Projects
projects\chapter11\cookies\phase2.dvp
projects\chapter11\cookies\phase3.dvp

Approach, Video
This is where the high mouse-click count comes in. The refinement phase requires a lot of pushing, pulling, and tweaking of the timeline. We are definitely in the *art* realm more than *science* now. You need to draw on all the intuition and skills you have to really do this well. You can do it!

The first task is to go back through every clip and get the trim points figured out. Most of these were wrong on our first go around, which was not only by default, but by design. That's all we needed for the first pass.

For nearly all the "ingredient" clips, you'll want to trim the sections where the hands are in the way, as shown here.

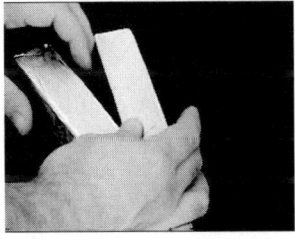

Go ahead and do that first, and see how our clip lengths end up. After that, work through the rest of the timeline.

Editing Notes:

- Disable ripple editing for the ingredient clips. Re-enable it after you've finished this "fixed" section.

- Clip 0005.mpg is used in three places. Make sure you get the correct section from 0005.mpg for each edit point on the timeline.

- The clips from 0003.mpg and down are all longer than the fixed 7.5 second length originally given to the placeholder images. Keep in mind that some of these clips (e.g., 0010.mpg) have more going on in them than meets the eye.

- It's sometimes helpful to move a clip to an open track to trim it.

- I added a cue in 0023.mpg at the point where the timer goes from 0:01 to *End*. We'll add a beep later on for this event.

Reference Projects
projects\chapter11\cookies\phase3.dvp
projects\chapter11\cookies\phase4.dvp

Approach, Audio
It's time to drop in the narration. This audio clip has more in it than we'll use. For example, it begins with two opening lines: *Sarah's two-minute recipes* and *Sarah's three-minute recipes*. When I started this, I had no idea how long the final video would be, but still thought the title sounded like a good one. I covered all my bases (well, at least two of them) by recording both.

When it comes to choosing one take over another, you, as the editor, must make the call. Sometimes the right take is obvious; sometimes it's a flip of the coin. No hard and fast rules about this one.

You'll notice that the audio file has been pre-cued as a convenience. Each cue corresponds to a particular segment of the narration. Since these segments are going to have to be moved around the timeline to match their corresponding scenes, it's easiest to take the scissors and slice them up at each cue point now. When you do cut, zoom in on the timeline to get frame-accurate cuts.

Hint. Cut just slightly to the left of each cue. If you cut right on them, the cue will not display. If this happens, press Ctrl+Z to undo, and give it another go. Try cutting using the U-key method: select the clip, move the playhead, and press **U**.

Chapter 11 • Two Real Life Situations

Before & After:

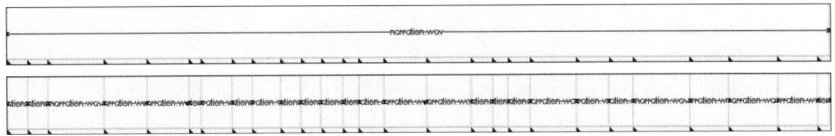

Getting back to the project, we need to make a trim pass on the audio, just like we did the video.

Tip. Press Shift+Spacebar in the Source Window to play the trimmed portion of the clip.

Tip. To insert a gap in the timeline (for example, to move all video clips down from a certain point) drop in a temporary color clip with ripple editing on. Slide the clip to another track and the other clips stay put. Delete the color clip.

Hint. Let the narration drive the length of the corresponding title clips. Once each narration clip is in place, add a half-second silence clip after it as a spacer. Then adjust the titles accordingly.

Before:

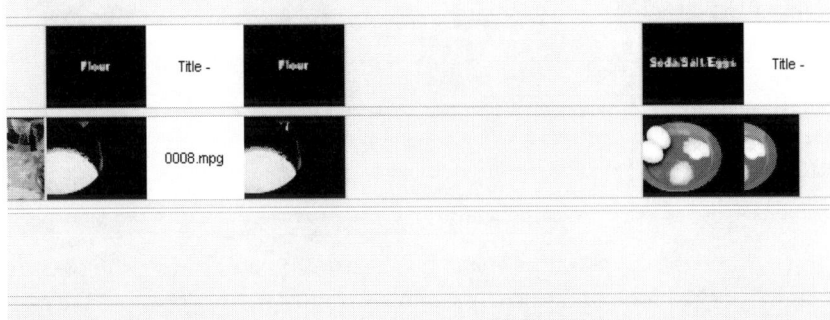

After:

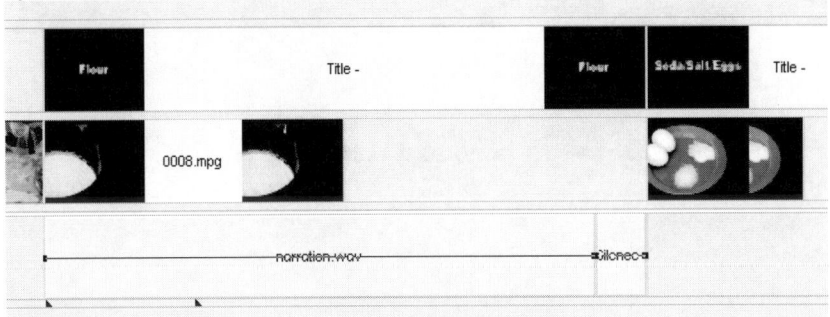

Editing Notes:

- I moved music.wav to Audio3, to keep the first two audio tracks open.

- I deleted the *2-minute recipe* sound bite.

- I deleted the first *This is a traditional...* take in favor of the second and united *You'll need* and *Two and a quarter...*

- I halved the speed of 0030.mpg to get both opening lines to fit.

- I trimmed many of the subsequent clips, since the ends of most bled into the beginnings of the following.

- I moved title and video clips, due to the audio changes.

After taking care of the title clip section, my timeline looked like this:

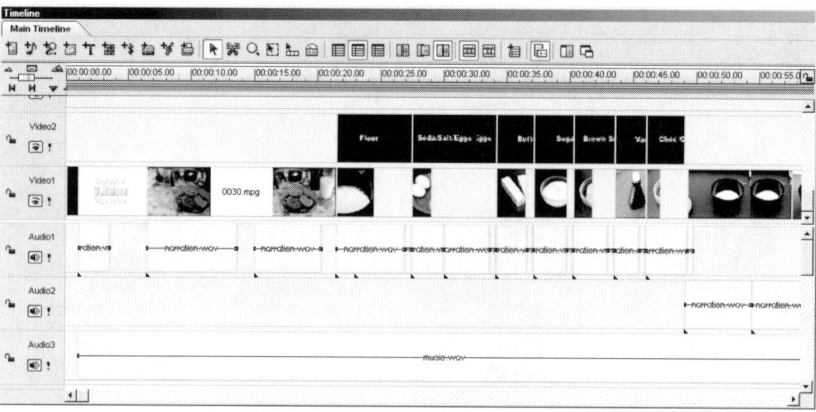

You can see the silence clips spacing the narration and setting the overall length for the video and title clips above. After that, I took care of the rest:

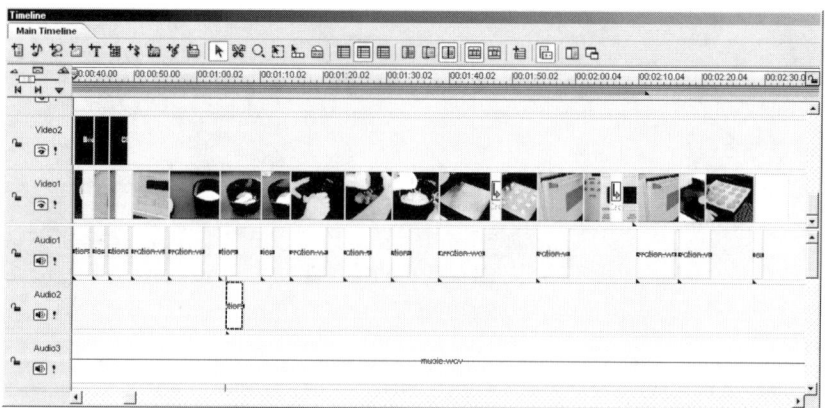

Chapter 11 • Two Real Life Situations

Oh no! Look at that audio left on Audio2. It's telling me to add the vanilla. But that's video clip 0011.mpg and we somehow missed getting it on the timeline during the storyboard phase. This is a good example of one of the benefits of building up a project in this fashion: you have plenty of passes through the project to catch alll you're mistaks.

To fix it, I'm going to turn on multi-track ripple, and drop in the missing 0011.mpg on track Video2 just before the eggs. Now we have this:

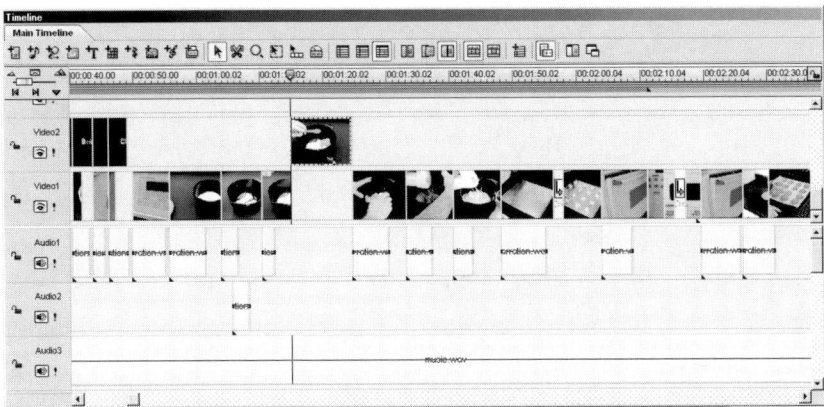

Slide it down into Video1 and move the stray narration into place. Turn off ripple editing. Open the phase4.dvp reference project to see what I've done and compare with your own edits.

> **Deep Thoughts**
>
> I realize I've pushed you out of the nest a bit on this one. But as the old saying goes, you learn to do by doing. This may have been a breeze, or you may have found it a pain. The problem is, editing techniques are very personal and what works for me may not work for you.
>
> I don't mind pushing and shoving clips around to get a job done. Another approach is to just start over with each phase. If you feel more hindered than helped by existing clips, then bulldoze the area and start fresh. Sometimes what's on the timeline isn't as important as what's in your head.
>
> Do what comes naturally.

Upon reviewing the output of phase4, I'm happy with the progress. It's starting to look like a real production. Time for another refinement pass.

Reference Projects
projects\chapter11\cookies\phase4.dvp
projects\chapter11\cookies\phase5.dvp

Approach

With the clips in place, this pass is rather straightforward. Here's what I did for further refinement:

- Faded the title in and out. (Used an overlay, but color clips and crossfades would have achieved the same effect.)

- Copied the fade to the opening video, 0030.mpg.

- Slid the first narration clip over so it starts after the 0030 fade-in.

- The ingredient clips are a disaster. They're way too short and really should be re-shot. However, let's say we don't have time. What to do? In this case, since they don't move anyway, you'll see I replaced them all with stills. Seemed like the best thing to do.

- Changed the title formats. I found it easier to change "Flour" then delete the others, using "Flour" as a starting point for each new one.

- Added fading between the ingredients. (Check out how I did it on track Video3. It's a bit unorthodox, but works great in certain situations! You can fade out a whole stack of tracks at once without having to use a virtual clip.)

- Closed up the gap between the chips and the oven temp setting.

- Added the beep.

- Replaced the end title with a second showing of 0030.mpg.

- Crossfaded between 0025.mpg and 0030.mpg.

- Trimmed and faded the music.

This is phase5.dvp. Check the reference project and examine the results. I like it ... *almost*. If you recall, I said the danger of this "clay" method is that you're never done. And if you're an insufferable perfectionist like me, you'll always find some excuse to give it "just one more pass."

This time, however, it really *is* just one more pass. I decided to make two changes to phase5.dvp, which you'll see in phase6.dvp.

- Added a logo over the entire ingredient sequence.

- Crossfaded all the clips. It just felt like it needed softening.

Multi-Camera Editing

When you have two or more cameras recording the same event, how do you bring the footage back to the studio and use Video Editor to do standard A/B roll editing? That's exactly the question we'll answer in this section. Editing with multi-camera footage has its own set of quirks about it, and if you're not careful, you can end up with a real mess.

It's likely that most of your multi-camera shooting will be of the "event" variety. An event can be anything from a wedding to a play to a sports match. You typically take two or more cameras out to the event, set up tripods, and shoot.

It might be that you've planned the whole thing out in advance and have total control over the entire production. It might be that you and two or three neighbors all went to the Friday night hockey game and taped it from different angles. No matter what your footage, the problem is the same: you want to create a single video switching between cameras.

Unlike traditional analog A/B roll edit bays, there's no way to roll both cameras at once and do your editing on the fly. That really isn't what they had in mind when desktop video was developing. Nonetheless, the technique can be applied to traditional timeline-based editing tools, and Video Editor is no exception.

Pre-Production & Production Planning

If you know you're going to do a multi-camera shoot beforehand, you can (and should) plan ahead to make post-production easier. For optimal results, it's best to use the same kind of camera for each angle, to minimize the inherent recording differences between cameras. Many factors go into the "look" of footage. Some factors are hardwired into the camera itself, such as a 1-chip unit versus a 3-chip unit. Others factors are based on certain camera settings, like white balance. If you can't use identical cameras, that's okay—but it is optimal.

Another important factor is synchronization. If you can't get the footage from all cameras in sync, you're going to have some real trouble editing. To begin, make sure all cameras are rolling, and then shoot a sync point. In movies, this is one of the functions of a clapper: to give both a visual and an aural synchroniza-  tion cue. Of course, you're not going to be able to take a clapper to every event you shoot, so some other means will be necessary. It's more important to establish a visual sync point than an aural sync point, for reasons we'll get to later. If you have a flash camera, or someone at the event takes a flash photo, that's a good thing to use. If you have nothing else, point the two cameras at each other and have one camera operator clap his hands in front of the lens: any "signal" that can be used to synchronize during editing.

If you have absolutely no pre-defined sync point at all, have no fear! You will still have plenty of opportunities to find some other sync point later. In fact, that's exactly what we're about to do in this exercise.

My last point is the **most important**: once you're taping, **don't stop**. And this goes for all cameras. Every time any camera stops, the synchronization between all cameras is lost. When it comes time to edit, you will have to constantly re-sync. This is a real pain. Trust me! Of course you can't avoid dead batteries and tape changes, but these are (hopefully) few and far between.

Capturing Considerations

Okay, you have your camera footage and now you're ready to get started. However, you have to capture it to disk first. With a long event like a sporting event or a play, you're probably going to have a *lot* of footage. A one-hour show shot on three cameras comes up to three full hours of raw footage. That's a lot of disk space, even in these days where large hard disks are commonplace. And even if you have enough disk space, you may still run into trouble with file size limitations. If your disks are formatted using FAT32 (hint: they shouldn't be) there is a 4 GB file size limit. MediaStudio Pro has a feature to help you around this limitation called "seamless capture." When a single capture hits the limit, it closes that file, opens another, and continues capturing. Your single capture session will generate multiple files in 4 GB chunks. That's about 19 minutes' worth of DV footage.

But I'd bet your disks are formatted with the NTFS file system. This does not have any practical limitations, and MediaStudio Pro has no reason to split single captures into multiple files.

> **Why Limit File Sizes Anyway?**
>
> It comes down to something called "addressing." The computer needs to be able to access any point in a file. It uses a numeric address to do so. When the first microcomputer file systems were developed, a 32-bit signed integer was used for this addressing, which meant a 2 GB upper limit. Video files, being no different from any other file on your computer, were subject to these same constraints.

> Keep in mind that these file systems were developed at a time when ten megabytes was considered a *lot* of storage. This is a time when the operating system came on 1.44 MB floppy disks. No one dreamed of disks being 2 GB let alone individual *files* being that large.
>
> In order to meet new demands, new file systems were invented. Microsoft developed NTFS, used in Windows NT, Windows 2000, and Windows XP. This file system is capable of supporting files as large as the disk itself. And it supports disks that are about 16 *billion* gigabytes. To give you an idea of how big this number is, you could create a video file containing 100,000 years of DV video.
>
> If you ever hit that limit, please let me know.

Capturing

The most important capturing requirement is the same as the most important filming requirement: **don't stop**. Capture as much as you can. If your event is longer than the amount of free disk space you have, break it into logical chunks. For example, let's say you have an hour-long wedding ceremony. You can capture the first twenty minutes of two cameras, then edit. When finished with the first part, repeat two more times for the second and third twenty-minute segments. It hopefully goes without saying, don't stop your capture in mid-sentence. Twenty minutes is just a guideline. If the vows happen right at 00:40:00.00, then adjust your segment accordingly, always working within your free disk space.

If your event is *really* long, then you probably want to break it up into segments even if you do have the disk space. I've never personally used a 2-hour clip before, but I can imagine it might get a bit unwieldy.

For this particular project, you get lucky again. The footage from all four cameras is on the CD. Oh, if real life was only so easy.

Edit Preparation

Before we really start rolling, we need to prep our clips. This first exercise focuses on synchronization and setting up the project for our quasi-A/B roll editing.

Objective
To learn how to synchronize multiple cameras.

Reference Project
projects\chapter11\multicamera\start.dvp
projects\chapter11\multicamera\prep.dvp

Steps

1. Open the starter project.

   For the first time, our project is not in NTSC VCD format. If you hit Alt+Enter to view the project settings, you'll find an unusual frame size listed. You'll see why in a moment.

2. From the Project Tray, find camera1.mpg and camera2.mpg. Drop them in tracks Video1 and Video2 respectively, adjacent to the color clip.

3. **Float the Preview Window**. Make sure Resize is checked and select the Full Size command. A quick scrub of the timeline should show:

   This is the 352x240 video clip stretched to 704x240.

4. Go to the Production Library and right-click on Moving Path.

5. Select Load... from the popup menu.

6. In the current project folder is a file called multi-camera-views.mvp. An MVP file is folder of customized moving paths exported from Video Editor. I created these paths to help save time with this project and to demonstrate how it's easy to share certain customizations between people.

   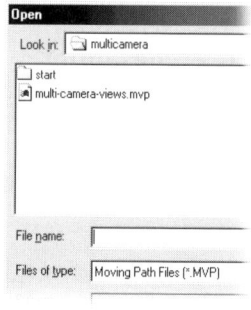

7. When completed, there will be a new folder in the Moving Path gallery called Multi Camera Views. Let's put them to good use!

8. From this new moving path folder, drag "2 Up Left" to camera1 and "2 Up Right" to camera2.mpg. A second quick scrub now shows this:

This is two 352x240 clips side by side in the 704x240 project. Now it's all starting to make sense! A double-wide project with a couple of moving paths gives us a full console view of this multi camera event.

All we have to do now is synchronize the clips.

9. Double-click camera1.mpg to load it in the Source Window.

The key is to find a common reference point in each source. For productions like this, I would begin rolling, point both cameras at each other, then do a quick wave across the lens: an obvious temporal marker. Of course, once we get to this scene our sync point is a good hour behind us. So we'll have to find something else.

10. Hit play and keep an eye out for anything "noticeable."

When I first did this, my attention was drawn to the dark-haired dancer in back. She was standing when no one else was: a good sign. About four seconds into the clip, I noticed her right heel hit the floor. Moving frame by frame, I locked in on 00:00:04.11.

Do the same and press F5 to cue it. Press the Apply button to make it stick.

11. Now load up camera2.mpg.

12. Hit play and look for this same event from this new point of view. I found it at (what looks like—it's hard to tell for sure) 00:00:03.11.

    Press F5 to cue and click Apply.

    Synchronizing the clips is now a simple matter of lining up the cues.

13. Slide camera2.mpg to the right until the cues align:

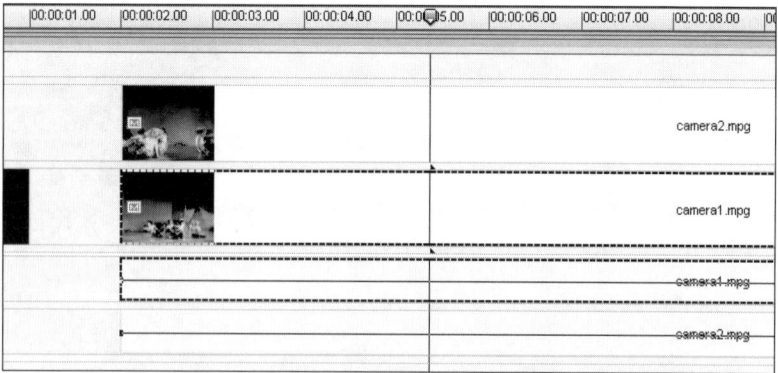

14. Now drag the left-hand edge of camera1 till it aligns with camera2.

    Do not move the clip! Grabbing the middle of the clip and dragging it anywhere else breaks the synchronization. You are only allowed to change the in (or out) points by dragging the start (or end) of the clip.

The *only* time you can move a clip is when you move *all* the clips to maintain synchronization. Select both clips and move back to the left.

15. Holding down the Ctrl key, drag the audio portion of camera1.mpg down to track Audio3.

16. Right-click and select Split, then delete the video portion.

17. Mute tracks Audio1 and Audio2.

Since we're going to be slicing and dicing these two tracks, we don't want the audio jumping all over the place. So we'll mute the soon-to-be chopped up tracks and only use the uncut copy in Audio3.

Rollin' Rollin' Rollin'

Traditional A/B roll editing is typically done by watching both video streams simultaneously and making edit decisions on the fly, just as if you were doing a live switch. With this side-by-side, double-wide project, we can pretty much do just that.

Objective
To learn how to synchronize multiple cameras.

Reference Projects
projects\chapter11\multicamera\prep.dvp
projects\chapter11\multicamera\phase1.dvp *through* phase3.dvp

Steps
1. Open the prep project.

2. Go to the Preview Window and click play.

3. While playing, press F5 every time you decide to cut from one camera to the other.

4. When finished, cut the clips at each cue.

    Tip. To cut the clips quickly: lock track Audio3, press Ctrl+L to select all clips, press Page Down to move to the next cue, and press U to slice. Repeat the last three steps for the remainder of the timeline.

    Locking the audio track makes those clips immune to trimming. All remaining (unlocked) clips get cut when you press U.

And that's all there is to it. Well... at least that's all there is to the *mechanical* part of it. Any monkey can keep hitting F5 without respect to overall production value. Don't bother saving this attempt: we can probably do better.

So how do you decide when and what to cut? I edited multi-camera events for years, and after a while came up with this mental checklist:

- Cut out the obviously unusable stuff first. Make a quick pass through and eliminate footage you know you won't use: shaky video, poor lighting, wrong subjects, and so on. If it's not on the timeline, you won't waste time thinking about it.

- Cut **in** the obviously great stuff. If there are certain perfect shots you *know* are going to be in the final cut, then cut out everything on the other camera(s) at that point. Again, it's a timesaver.

- Mark cuts when things get boring. The whole point of a multi-camera edit is to keep things visually interesting. If one camera has gone on for minutes and minutes, you've lost the point. Make a quick pass through and look for shots that start to drag on. Whether it's a good shot or not, cut over. *Tip.* If appropriate, cut to the audience occasionally. What's particularly nice about this is you don't have to sync it with the other cameras. As long as it's visually congruous with the stage action, drop these in anywhere.

- Cut on music cues. If, as is the case here, there is musical accompaniment, try to cut on even measures.

- Flip a coin. If you've done everything else and can't choose between two equally good shots, take a chance. Try both. See which one trips your trigger and run with it.

At this point check out the phase1 reference project. You can see where I've made my edit decisions and decided to cut:

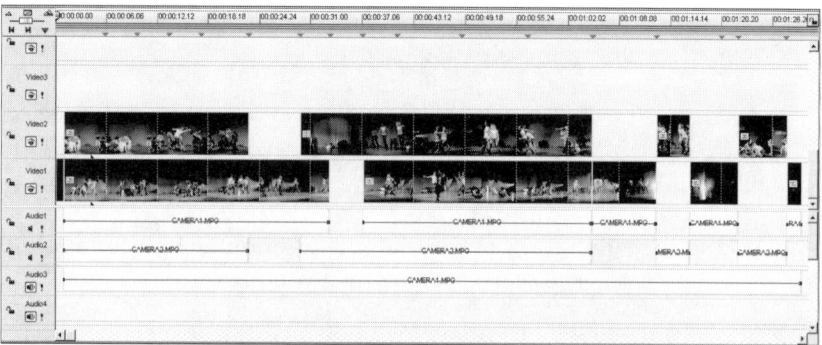

There were only two obvious bad parts towards the beginning. Towards the end, I favored the darker, spotlight scenes from camera1. The cuts on the right produce the familiar A/B roll "checkerboard" pattern.

Chapter 11 • Two Real Life Situations 329

Steps, Part 2

Unlike last time, we'll go through real step-by-step instructions on how to cut, switch and move clips around without de-synchronizing.

1. Begin with phase1.dvp.

2. Press Ctrl+G to display the Go To dialog box.

3. The first clip listed is the one we want. Click the Go To button, then click Close.

4. Click on the camera1 clip to select it then Ctrl+Click the camera2 clip.

5. Press **U** to cut both clips at once.

6. For openers, let's go with the long shot, camera1. Dispose of the leftmost portion of camera2.

Before:

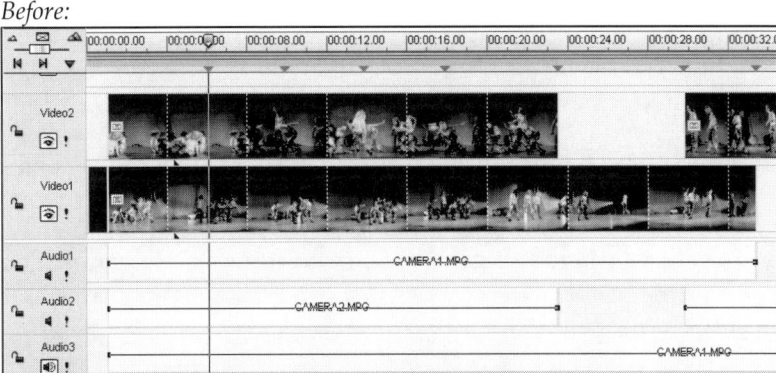

After:

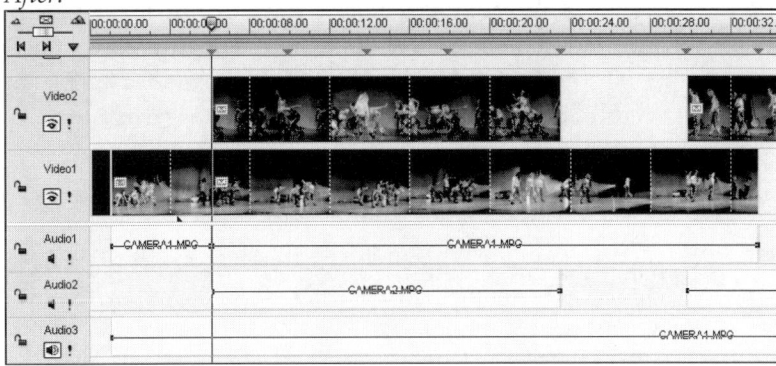

7. Now move to the next cue position.

8. Click-n-cut camera1 and camera2, as before.

9. Dispose of the left camera1 segment this time:

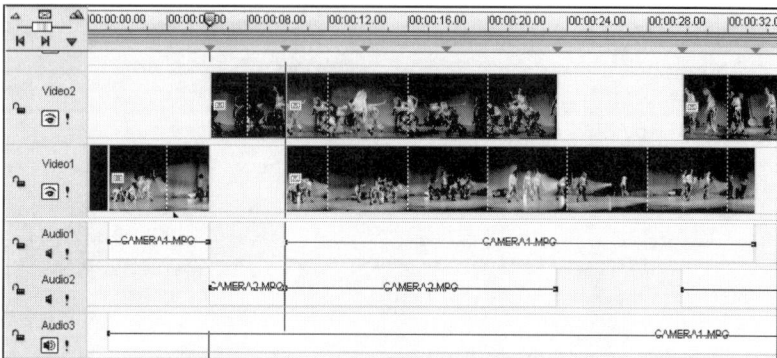

10. Now just repeat this process, walking down the rest of the timeline. There will be times you'll change your mind, at which point Ctrl+Z becomes your best friend. Like everything we've done to this point, it's a repeated refinement process.

Hint. You may find it easier to run through all the cuts first, then go back and remove the unwanted portions on a second pass. I do.

Check the phase2.dvp reference project to see my edits. Compare against your own work, if you're so inclined.

You'll see where I've gone back, changed my mind, and made new cuts (these will be the cuts that don't correspond to my original time-line cues).

Steps, Part 3

After reviewing the phase2 edits, I believe I would only make a couple of changes. First and foremost: get rid of the moving paths. Next, it needs a clean ending. Lastly, I think I'd like to throw in crossfades. Not so much because it needs it, but because it's one more thing to learn.

1. Begin where we left off with phase2. Open my copy, so we're staring from the same page.

2. First, change the project settings back:

    - Press Alt+Enter.

Chapter 11 • Two Real Life Situations   331

- Change Edit file format to MPEG files.
- Click the Edit button.
- Change Compression back to NTSC VCD.
- Everything else should fall into place.

3. Click OK twice. Then click OK again to dismiss the warning.

4. Next, we remove the moving paths. Press Ctrl+L to select all clips.

5. Right-click on any clip and select Delete attributes from the popup menu. Moving path will be checked by default. Click OK.

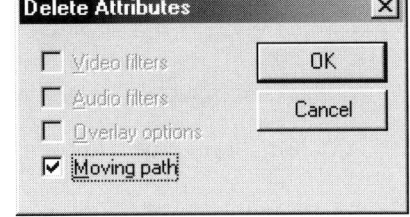

6. Fix the ending: go to the end of the timeline, pressing Ctrl+End.

7. The last clip is less than 2 seconds in duration. Drag its left side towards the left to lengthen it. Remember: *do not move the clip!* Only change the mark-in point. Pull it out to 5 seconds.

8. Grab the clip above it and pull it down to Video1 for a transition.

Before:
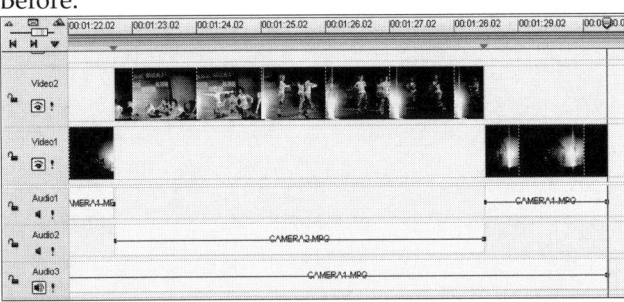

After:
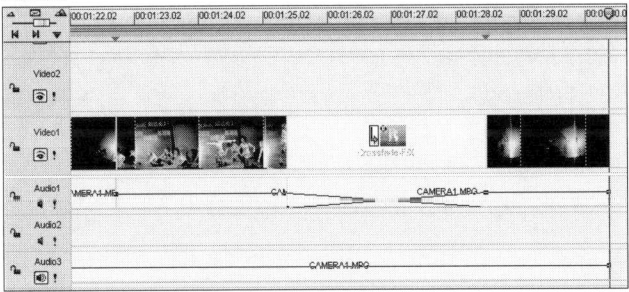

9. Add a keyframed overlay to the last clip to fade to black:

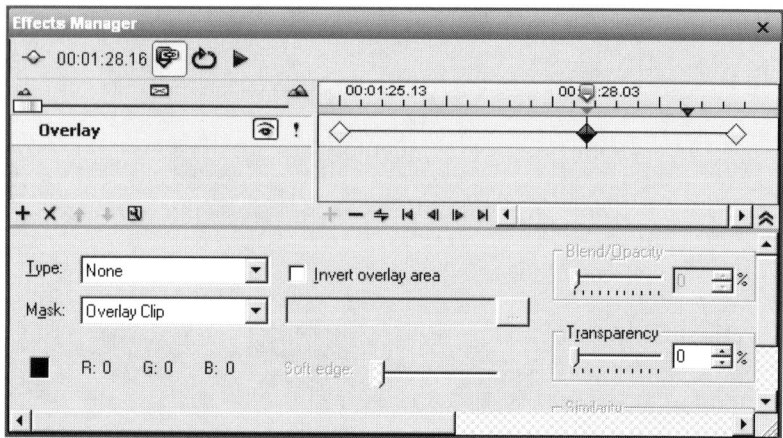

10. And don't forget the audio! Select the audio clip in track Audio3.

11. At the point of the above keyframe, 00:01:28.16, click on the audio clip near the rubber band. That's the line that runs down the center of the entire clip. Upon clicking, a small control point appears:

Taking the far-right control point, drag it down to the bottom of the clip. Congrats! That might be your first deliberate volume fade:

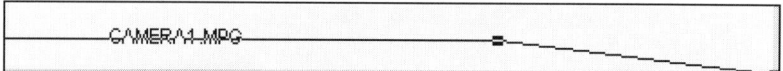

To be perfectly honest, I could call this done. With the exception of one crossfade at the end, this is pure cuts-only, multi-camera video. You can even leave the clips where they are.

But I want to put in the crossfades for tutorial purposes.

12. To create the crossfades take the clips on top and drag their ends out, left and right, respectively. Remember! *Don't move the clip!* ☺ After that, drag the right edge of the left clip on Video1 to the right and the left edge of the right clip on Video1 to the left. Then drag the top clip down a track. Got that? Me neither.

Let's save a thousand words and draw a picture.

Before:

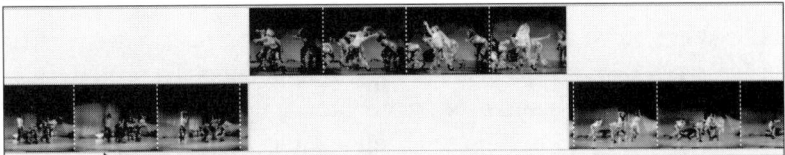

Widen the top clip:

Widen the lower two clips:

Drag camera2 to camera1 for the overlap:

13. Continue to the end of the project and we're done. Cross-check with reference project phase3.dvp.

For Further Study

For the sake of manageability, we just handled a two camera edit. However, there's no practical limit to the number of cameras you can edit this way. (Well, okay, the limit is 99, but if anyone needs to do a 100 camera edit, I'd *really* like to hear about it.)

Before the first phase of this project we did prep work: synching the two cameras and readying ourselves for the edits. If you look in the project directory there are prep projects for both 3- and 4-camera edits. There are even two versions of the 4-camera edit: one with the four cameras in a row and the other with a 2x2 matrix. Check them out!

Pause for Reflection

Now that you've worked through several long projects over the course of these last two chapters, this is a good time to look back on what we've learned. Although you've observed how longer projects are designed and assembled, it's important to keep in mind you've seen it *my* way.

If you recall on page 319, I said to do what comes naturally. It may be that my iterative, working-in-clay technique suits you to a tee. You may, on the other hand, find it the absolute worst way to work. What's important is that *you* discover what works best for you. I've provided a starting point. You take it from here.

Brian Ellis had some words to say on this which I feel compelled to share with you.

> *Your modus operandi is certainly very different from mine: I try to be less formal, adding one video clip at a time, analyzing it, deciding what to keep and edit and reject. I add the audio after the video, which I then adjust if needed. I always keep the original audio, clipping/fading it as appropriate. Any voice-over is recorded from a typed script on a different computer with each clip recorded separately from the others (of course, I have in my mind what will be said when doing the video, so that the video is at least as long as is needed, sometimes post-trimming).*

> *In other words, our techniques are diametrically opposed. I suppose the difference is similar to artists' techniques. I once took formal painting classes and I used to drive the professor mad because I never outlined a charcoal sketch on the canvas before daubing the oils. I knew what I wanted in my head, but she admitted the end results were as good as those who did a sketch. This stood me in good stead when I passed to water colours because there were no pencil marks on my paper.*

> *With video, I have the broad outlines in my head, not on paper, before opening Video Editor. I did learn from your exposé but I find it more exciting watching the project develop as I go along, rather than several reiterations which I found were beginning to pall on me by the middle of Phase 4.*

He makes the most important point. This isn't "paint by numbers." This is an art form. I'm just helping you learn the mechanics using my own preferred approach as a guide. Once you're comfortable with the mechanics, do what comes naturally!

12

Examining Longer Projects

Using two complex projects—a music video and a promo video—we'll give Video Editor a run for its money.

Where Do We Go From Here?

To round out this learning experience, we're going to take a look at two different projects. Both are more involved and more complex than anything we've done up to this point.

These projects exhibit many techniques we've learned throughout the book. While everything up till now has been showing the nitty-gritty, step-by-step, here's-how-you-do-this stuff, I find it equally important to step back and see them used in the context of a full-blown project. It moves us out of academia and firmly into the real world.

This, of course, dictates the need for a different learning angle.

Last chapter, you sometimes saw me replace "Steps" with an "Approach" instead. From here on out, that'll be the norm. The emphasis here is to demonstrate these techniques in action. We've already seen the details. Now's our chance to relax a bit, observe, learn, and not get bogged down on Steps 317 through 392.

As a learning aid, where relevant, the page numbers listed refer to the section in the book where the technique was introduced. For example, when you see (page. 170) it means to look at page 170 for the step-by-step exercise on it.

A Music Video

This project is a simple music video. The name of the song is "Nothing Without." It's a three and a half minute song, but for sanity purposes (yours and mine) I've cut it down to a minute and a half.

Philosophical Rambling

This is also where we begin to leave the world of video editing mechanics and enter the world of creativity. I have a few words to say about this, if you'll indulge me for a minute or two. Then it's back to business.

A Word on Creativity

Creativity is something we all have and yet most people tend to think quite the opposite. Being creative is not about becoming the next Warhol, Shostakovich, or Asimov. It's about you being *you*. Do not fall prey to the "But I've Never Done Anything Creative" line of thinking. You are crea-

tive every single day. This is evidenced by the fact that you speak at least one language. When was the last time you woke up in the morning, and were handed a script? Never. There are no scripts. There are no lines to memorize. You go about your entire day improvising and creating sentences and paragraphs that are brand new. From dawn to dusk, you flow through life without ever giving it a second thought. Yes, *that's* being creative and don't let anyone tell you otherwise.

The source of this creative power can be tapped for other endeavors, such as art, music, writing—or video editing, to name a few. I know you're probably thinking: *speaking in one's native language every day is easier than any of these artistic fields*. Well, that's absolutely true. So what's the difference? If you're creative in one area, why aren't you equally creative in all areas? It all boils down to one thing: *experience*. If you think of these artistic endeavors as being their own languages (and they are—but I could write another whole book on that) then it all becomes very clear. The only reason you might *think* you're not creative is only because you're not *fluent* in it.

To illustrate this, just look at this book. It can be argued that writing this book was a significant act of creativity on my part. But let's say I was forced to write it in Chinese. I don't think it would be a very good book, as the sum total of my Chinese amounts to *Kung Pao Chicken*. Does this mean I'm not creative? Not at all. I was simply required to perform creatively in a medium where I had no experience. And don't you see? That's the good news! It's something that can be fixed. All it takes is practice.

I'm not saying this is easy, but I am saying it's *doable*. You don't have to believe creativity is something you either *have* or *don't have*. It's not like the color of your eyes. It's something everyone has—you just have to find it, dust it off, and use it.

That last part is the most important part: *use it*. If I really wanted to write this book in Chinese, it wouldn't happen by my simply wishing it. I would have to spend time on it. I would have to practice. I would have to use it. The best way to learn a secondary language is through immersion. This means that to truly become fluent you must completely surround yourself with it all the time. It's no different for art. If you want to get really creative with video editing, you must do it all the time. Don't worry about creating a finished masterpiece at every single go. Create a lot of "nothing" along the way. Discard any pretension that you possess an immediate goal and just get familiar with the tools. Make mistakes. Trip and fall down. Produce really bad and ugly videos. You *will* come out stronger in the end. (Just don't show them to anyone!)

A Word of Confession
Writer's block. Even the most fluent wordsmiths in the world run into it. Knowing there's something there in your head but you *just can't get to it*—well, it's frustrating beyond words (pun intended).

When it came time to produce this video, I was at a complete loss. The outline I wrote for the book included this segment. I knew I wanted to do *something* but simply couldn't think of *anything*.

I spent days just staring at an empty timeline. Writer's block. *What am I going to do?* I asked myself over and over. Then I thought about my boundaries: a music video; female vocals; short; demonstrates book techniques. Hmmm. I immediately realized choosing the music was the key. As I scanned buy-out music libraries for songs with actual lyrics, my choices were extremely limited. This was a good thing! It didn't take long to narrow it down to this one song.

Once the song was chosen, I began to play it *repeatedly*. I would close my eyes and imagine things. As I listened to the lyrics, an idea popped in my head. The chorus goes, "It's nothing without you in my life. It means nothing without you." I saw a girl, alone and empty. And that's when the idea of looking through blank photographs came to me.

But I still needed a setting. Ironically enough, the answer came from Smart Compositor. The DI01_A clip had images in frames in what looked like a high-tech photo gallery.

A photo gallery. Hmmm. A photo gallery! Yeah, I can see that. The girl is in the photo gallery and the paintings in the gallery move. A great way to use moving paths in a creative manner. And she can go back and forth from being *in* the paintings or standing in front of them. And we can put "the band" in the  paintings too! After days and days of this creative dry spell, it suddenly started to rain.

A Lesson Learned

I didn't have to tell you about any of this. I could have saved some paper and ink and just jumped right into the process. But I truly believe that bringing this out in the open can only be helpful. We've all been there before and we'll all be there again. The way out is to *just do something*. Because "something" has a better chance of leading to something else than "nothing."

When people look at my videos and say, "I could never come up with anything like that." I have to respond, "That's right. You probably couldn't." And I would never be able to come up with whatever *they* do. Everyone is different. Give two different people the exact same topic and the exact same footage, you will get two completely different results.

Never look at someone else's work and give up because you think, "I could never do that." Never throw your saxophone in the river. Make your own music and don't look back.

Okay, thanks for listening. Now let's take a look at the "Nothing Without" music video.

Behind the Scenes

Before getting into the editing specifics of each scene, let's take a quick page to explain how we got where we are.

Project Structure

The project is divided into distinct scenes and nearly every scene is a virtual clip. Dividing the project into virtual clips made a lot of sense. This allowed me to create complex scenes on secondary timelines, then add simple moving paths and transitions to the virtual clips on the main timeline—just like regular clips! Whoda thunk? ☺

Chapter 12 • Examining Longer Projects

The scenes are numbered in order from 1 to 18. Scene 13 is missing not for any superstitious reasons, but because once filming began, it became irrelevant. I didn't rename the subsequent scenes. It would have been more work than it was worth. Scenes 16 and 17 somehow melded into one along the way as well.

Project Setup

Just like the cookie project, I began with a timeline-based storyboard. Using a combination of stills and test shots, I cued the music, laid out the entire project structure, and got exact times for each scene. I watched this animatic until I was comfortable with the pacing and structure, then drew up a shot list.

Computer Generated Sets

The shot list was used for both live and computer generated shots. I debated a bit about using CG sets, but in the end decided it was best. The main reason was to give lots of opportunities for matchmoving. The secondary reason was to give the video it's "look." I don't think it would have turned out quite the same in a real gallery.

Using trueSpace[10], I created a simple room, added lights, and rendered the animations. The lengths of each scene were pre-determined from the animatic. There was no guesswork involved.

Principal Photography

As with the computer generated shots, knowing the composition and duration of each scene made shooting relatively easy. I didn't have very good lighting, but after running some test shots on the green screen, it looked like the results would be "good enough" and I ran with it.

I could have gone through the expense and hassle of creating a perfect green screen environment, but that would have only proved what you already know. I figured doing something quick and on a shoestring would be much more realistic—and more helpful in the long run.

Final Note. To boost performance, turn off Auto Save before continuing.

---

[10] A mid-range 3D modeling and animation tool. Visit http://www.caligari.com.

Scene 1

The opening scene almost suggested itself. As I listened to the song and thought of the emptiness of the lyrics, this slow pull-back sprang to mind. Looking through the empty photographs seemed like the perfect introduction.

Approach

The matchmoving tasks begin right away. The foreground needed to be matched to the generated background via moving paths to make them mesh together well (p. 182).

Double click the virtual clip to open it in a new timeline. As you can see, this virtual clip contains yet another virtual clip: one using a garbage matte (p. 196). The garbage matte clip was overlaid on the background, and a moving path was applied to keep the subject aligned with the chair in a reasonable manner.

The second task involved applying a lighting filter to the subject. Since filters cannot be applied to clips with keying (p. 247) we had to create a black and white video matte to use as a region on the video filter.

The filter itself is applied to the virtual clip, after the blue screening and matchmoving have been completed.

Scene 2

The sole purpose of this scene is to reveal the blank photographs, since we're not exactly sure what the subject is looking at in the previous scene.

Why are they pink? Well, they're placeholders. At first I wanted to use completely black prints (with white borders) and then I wasn't so sure. I decided on a solid pink in case I wanted to key them out later. Well, that didn't work out either and by the time I changed my mind, I couldn't go back and re-shoot. So they're pink.

Approach

This is a straightforward keying job (p. 187). The foreground is placed over the computer-generated seat and floor, and that's about it. Click the Solo icon on Track 1 if you wish to see it. These two clips make up the virtual clip on the main timeline.

Scene 3

This is one of my favorite shots in the whole video, even if it's only one and a half seconds long (not counting the freeze frame).

Approach
This isn't a virtual clip. It's the raw footage with two of my favorite video filters combined: Duotone and DiffuseGlow. If you haven't tried out either of these filters, give them a shot. Especially the DiffuseGlow filter. For added fun, change their order, just to see how it changes the overall affect.

Scene 4

The fourth scene is similar in composition to the opening scene, but was easier to implement. Due to the fact that she's standing some distance from the background, no matchmoving was required. The two clips are used as-is.

Approach
This is the first scene where the audio and video is synchronized. She is singing to the pre-recorded track. The live footage was shot with the music playing in the background. She was actually singing during taping. When brought on the timeline, the two vocal tracks were synchronized, much in the same way we synchronized two camera clips during multi-camera editing (p. 321).

Important: the synchronization was done on the main timeline. Once the clip was locked in, only *then* was it moved to a secondary timeline for effects processing. Granted, the effects could have all been done on the main timeline, however virtual clips made it easy to add transitions.

Scene 5

Now things start to get interesting. Our singer is standing in front of two paintings, each of which contains one of the band members. There are few lessons to be learned here about keying, lighting, and creative video filters.

Approach
Double-click the virtual clip to open the scene05 timeline. Then double click scene05gm to look at the garbage matte. This was a *very* last minute

pickup shot. Against my better judgment I thought I'd try it hand-held. Note to self: stick to the tripod. But I skipped the reshoot because the whole point of this exercise is to learn.

It's also rotated 90° to the left. This isn't a mistake, I just liked the framing. Unlike the opening shot, where I changed the lighting in post, I wanted to see what would happen if I used a dark subject to begin with. I knew going in it would blend badly with the background, but it was an experiment, 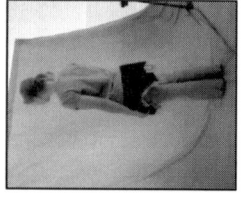 and it paid off. I think the lighting blends in well with the overall scene. Here are all four plates together, and how they appear in the final shot:

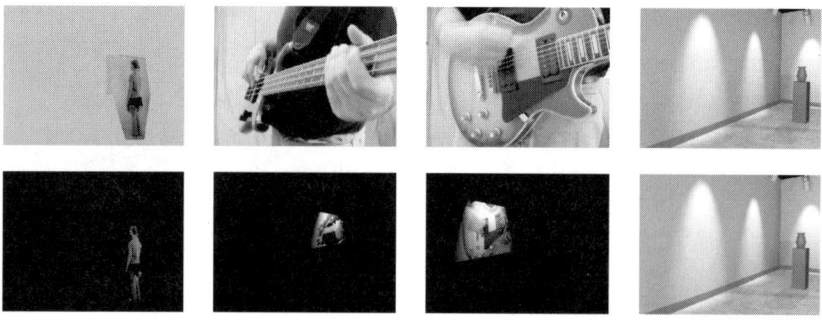

Let's now take a closer look at how those paintings get on the wall. There are two tricks: a moving path and a video filter.

A 3D Moving Path is used to skew the two video clips into looking like they're paintings hanging on a wall. Perspective is cranked up to 100, and the rest is tweaked to fit. The paintings do not move, so the start and end keyframes are identical:

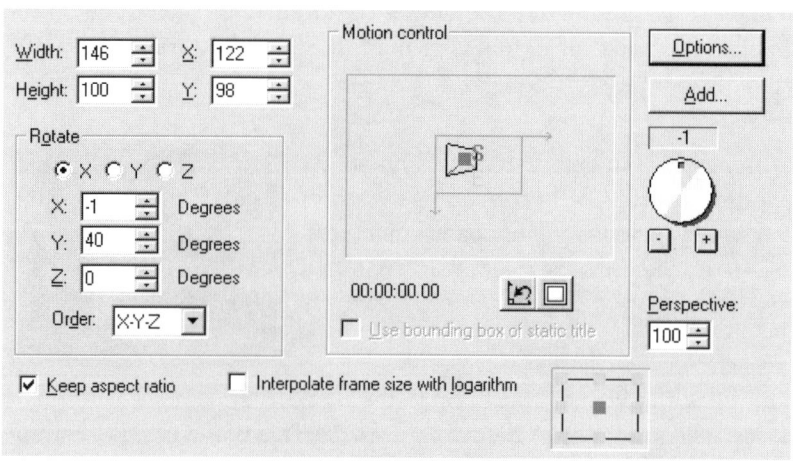

Chapter 12 • Examining Longer Projects

While that gets it on the wall, it doesn't blend in with the scene very well. Fortunately for our situation Video Editor comes with a Light filter.

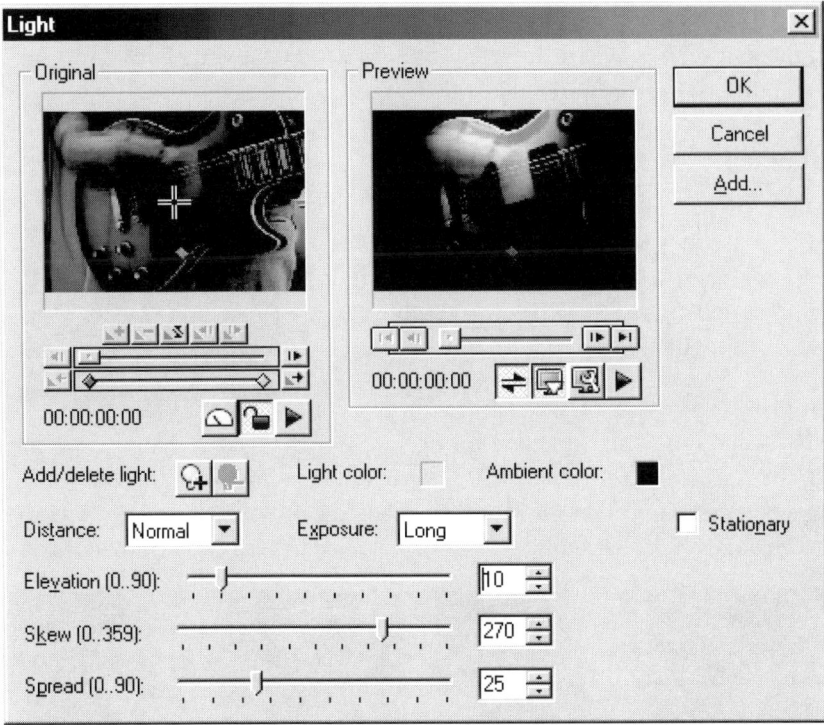

The Skew setting (set to 270) placed the light directly overhead (apparently 0° starts middle right and moves clockwise). After that, I simply tweaked the Elevation and Spread to approximate the spot lights on the background plate. The Ambient color (black) adds to the darkened room effect. The Light color was chosen to fit the overall yellowish tone.

After this timeline was placed as a virtual clip on the main timeline, a moving path was added to eliminate the static feel of the scene. Overall it worked out well. The hand-held shot didn't turn out to be much of a problem, given the size and context of that shot. (We're not so fortunate the next time.)

Scene 6

Just for a bit of variety, I did a close up of one of the paintings for this scene. I had a choice to change the background color of the guitarist clip, but decided against it. For some reason, I liked the way that tiny splash of green fit.

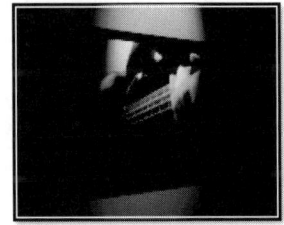

Had I wanted to get rid of the green, that just would have meant an extra virtual clip. (Which we will do anyway in the very next scene.)

Approach

Same as Scene 5, just a different angle. The 3D Moving Path and Light video filters were employed just the same.

Scene 7

Time for more fun with nested virtual clips! This is another scene I have a particular fondness for, if only because what I pictured in my head ended up in the project so easily. It's always nice when that happens.

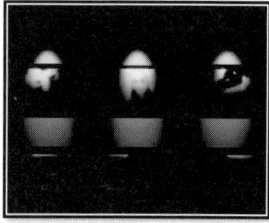

Approach

This scene has four clips: one for each painting (each a virtual clip) and the background (a normal clip). The virtual clips are used for keying out the green screen. This is in contrast to the previous scene where the green screen was left in. Now we get a chance to see both approaches.

Source   Mask   Foreground   Result

All I did was swap the green background for an orange one. (Not every keying exercise means putting your weatherman in front of a map.) I wanted a background which would be better suited to the subsequent recoloring about to take place.

That coloring uses my favorite Duotone + DiffuseGlow filter combo. Once those were in place, the same Light filter was also applied. Once colored, only the moving paths remained.

They're simply 2D Basic paths, just placed to make them look like they stick to their proper wall positions. Each position was tweaked to match the light cone from the Light filter to match the light cone on the background. That was my matchmoving reference point.

Here are the path illustrations. The top row shows the starting points of the left, center, and right clips. The bottom row shows the ending points:

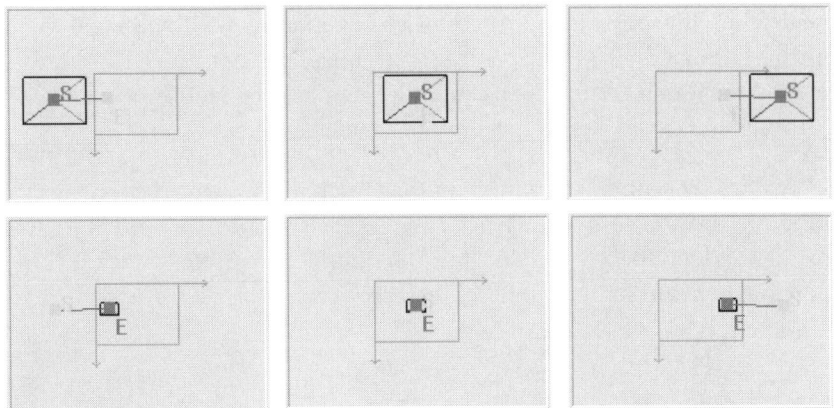

Scene 8

Another painting, but this time a new instrument. What *isn't* new is the implementation. Everything in this shot is what we've done for the other wall shots. The only change is to simulate a camera arcing around the painting, I used a 3D instead of a 2D path.

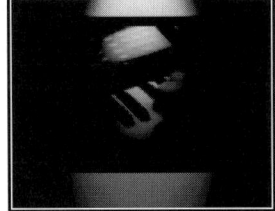

Scene 9

Here we have our subject wandering aimlessly about the gallery. She's clearly wondering if it was worth the $12 admission, with only a handful of paintings to look at. While this looks like every other scene we've done so far, there's a twist to this one.

Approach

This scene started out like any other one. We have the gallery. We have the moving path sticking the keyboard painting on the wall. And we have a keyed foreground subject passing by.

If it looks like it was grafted on as a last-minute thought, that's because it was. As I watched the scene without the girl, it was too bland. In an earlier idea, I had thought about putting many people in the gallery. I dropped that idea since I wasn't ready to take on that much work. But the idea of *one* person passing in front of the camera stuck, and when I had this more-or-less "empty" scene, I figured this would be the fit.

I also wanted to see how bad a background could get before it was unusable. My first attempt was successful: backlighting the screen created a near-white hotspot which turned into some kind of glowing magical orb in the final composite. Interesting, I suppose, but not what I wanted. I moved the lights around to the sides, hoping to get a mediocre color, and this time it worked. I got my barely keyable background.

Why am I so bent on showing you this? Well, it gives me a good excuse to show the softness setting in action. As mentioned on page 195, the softness effect doesn't have a "low" setting. To give you a visual comparison, here are settings 0, 1, 2, 3, and 10:

I wasn't happy at all with "0" and "1" is suddenly too much. There's no "0.5" to toy with. So, as it stands, I've set it at 1, and you can see the ghostly glow it gives your subject. I've only once found a situation where this is acceptable. If this were a real project I would definitely throw out this scene completely. (That is, if reshooting wasn't a viable option.)

Scene 10

Finally, an easy scene. This is a simple overlay on a background. The background has a moving path to give it some interest. In a test version of the project, I had the pull-back end up with the girl's face exactly over a painting of her face. When she disappeared, the painting stayed behind. Thinking back on it, it was kind of cool. I should have put it back in.

Scene 11

This scene is broken into two distinct parts. Both parts use the usual overlay settings, and in that respect this is no different from Scene 10. However, halfway through I cut the clip in two, and slow the second part down to half-speed. This *could* have been done with a variable speed setting and a keyframe. But I often

like to take the more obvious approaches. When you see *two* clips on the timeline, it's obvious that *something is different*. Keyframed effects aren't visible directly on the timeline. Two clips also helps when snapping across tracks, something you can't always do in the Effects Manager.

Scene 12

Ooo! Another cool scene. If at first glance this doesn't look different from what we've already done, then be sure to take a second glance. If you still don't see it, here's a hint: *look at this picture on the right.*

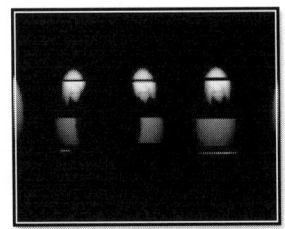

The vase on the stand is computer generated, just like the rest of the gallery. Yet the CG background *is* the background: meaning, everything else appears in front of it. Yet this vase passes *over* the three moving-path-based pictures. How does that work?

Approach

Easy. The vase is not part of the background. So it truly is in front of everything else. Open up the virtual clip and take a look:

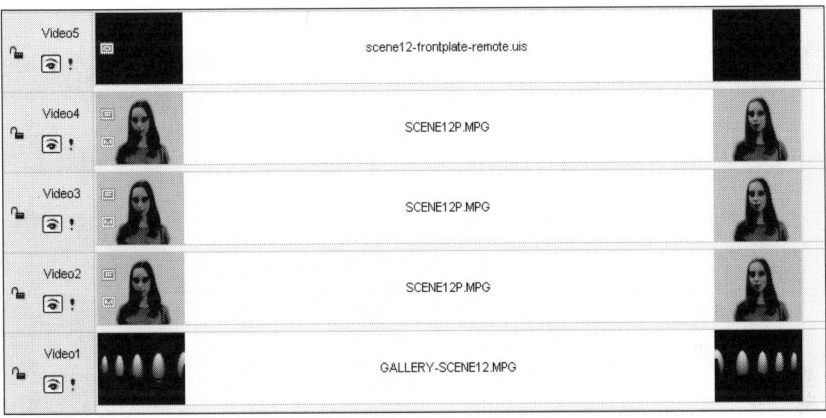

The top file has a UIS extension. This stands for Ulead Image Sequence. If you use any other software that outputs images sequences, then you'll definitely like UIS files.

An image sequence is just what it says: a sequence of images. Whereas video files hold all frames within a single file, an image sequence has a physical disk file for each frame.

The UIS format allows you to group these files together and treat them as a single clip on the timeline. For anyone using external animation tools (such as I've done with trueSpace for this project) this is a wonderful feature.

Although trueSpace can output AVI files, I chose to export an image sequence for a single reason: to preserve the alpha channel. Let's open up frame 100 and take a look.

Not exactly what you would call impressive: it's mostly black. But that's because this is a rendering of a vase on a stand in a dark room. [*Open this frame in an image editor and raise the gamma level to see what I mean. See? There really is a vase there!*] But this RGB image is unimportant. What's important is that I saved it as a Targa file with an alpha channel. If your image editor is capable of displaying alpha channels, open it up and you'll see this mask at the right.

So how does this help our project? Well, with an image sequence made of Targa files with alpha channels, we can show the dark, dark vase in the foreground and let the background show through. Right behind this clip are the portrait clips, and behind them we have our background.

One last thing. I used the soft edge feature on the overlay to make the vase look out of focus. That gives the scene some depth of field. (See? I told you I only found that feature useful once!)

Scene 14

This is similar to the second scene, but the camera is much higher this time. Again, this is primarily for visual variety.

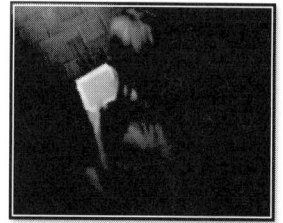

Approach

The foreground plate used a garbage matte, since the green background didn't cover everything. The lighting was poor, but inconsequential due to the light filter applied to the virtual clip after the fact. A moving path was also used to rotate the frame.

Scene 15

This is one of those unfortunate cases where the storyboard turned out better than the final shot. I had something much better than this in my head, certainly!

As it stands, it's not bad, though. I like the angle, but I wish we could see more of the painting in this shot.

Approach

Compositionally, this is very similar to Scene 5. In fact, it's a bit easier, since only three clips were involved: the gallery (back plate), the portrait on the wall (middle plate), and the girl (foreground plate).

The only twist in this scene is that I wanted to provide an example of using moving paths to implement a poor man's image stabilization. The girl is a hand-held shot and I intended to demonstrate what you can (and can't) do with moving paths as a corrective tool.

Open the garbage matte clip, look at pickup02.mpg, and examine the moving path and its keyframes.

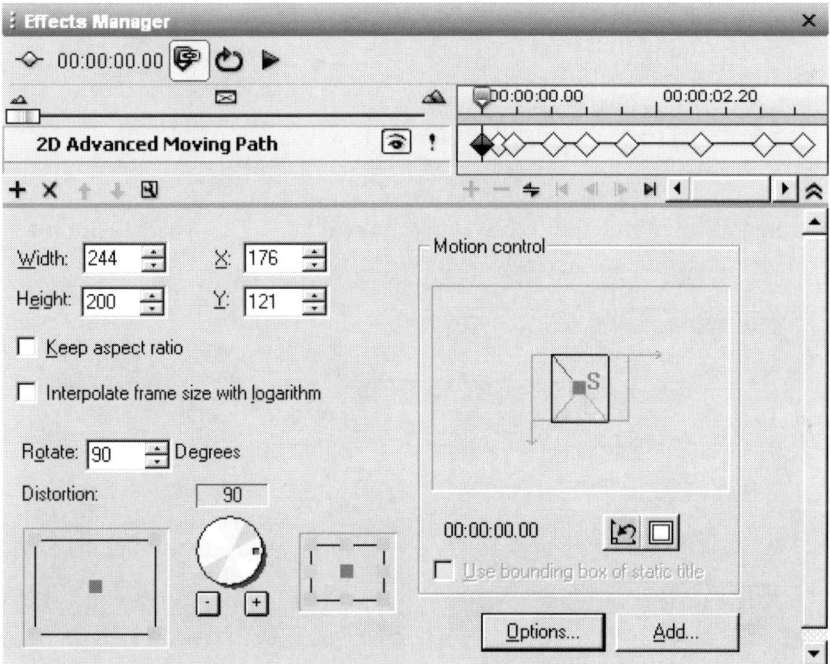

The general procedure is to set the start and end keyframes to keep the image locked in a given spot. How do I know what that spot is? Check out the color clips on tracks Video6 and Video7 of scene15gm. In the final render, these tracks are muted. Un-hide them and you'll see they show up as two small squares on the frame. I lined up the nose and toes and made the moving path adjustments to keep them in place. The result is passable. Not perfect by any means. I got it to "good enough."

Scene 17

Look ma! No virtual clips. Nope, it was time for another easy scene. Simple moving path with a green screen overlay in front of the gallery background.

My only regret on this shot is that it's somewhat boring. I would do it over again if I could.

Scene 18

Like Scene 11, this is another two-parter. The first part is the throw you see pictured here. The second is the freeze frame and fade.

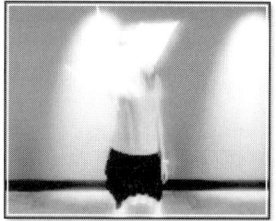

Approach

Like many of the other shots, this scene also uses a garbage matte. Unlike many of the other scenes, I didn't expect this one to need it.

Here's a tip. If you're using an external monitor on your camera during filming, don't forget about the overscan area! I did. Compare the monitor shot versus what was actually recorded:

After realizing my mistake, I left it in anyway, just to pass on this wisdom to you. The hard part is, I already knew this and I yet *still* forgot about it. Oh well, no biggie. That's what garbage mattes are for.

Once I got that taken care of, the rest was pretty straightforward. Open up the project and take a look at the filters and the freeze frame. No rocket science.

The Music

As mentioned, the music was originally about a three and a half minute cut, shortened to 1.5 minutes. Before wrapping up this walkthrough, let's take a quick look at how I did that.

I started by cueing the file, but only the parts I expected to use. After I listened to it for a few times, I knew what I wanted. The opening was good. The second verse could go. And there was a faux ending after the 2.5 minute point. That seemed like a good place to wrap it up.

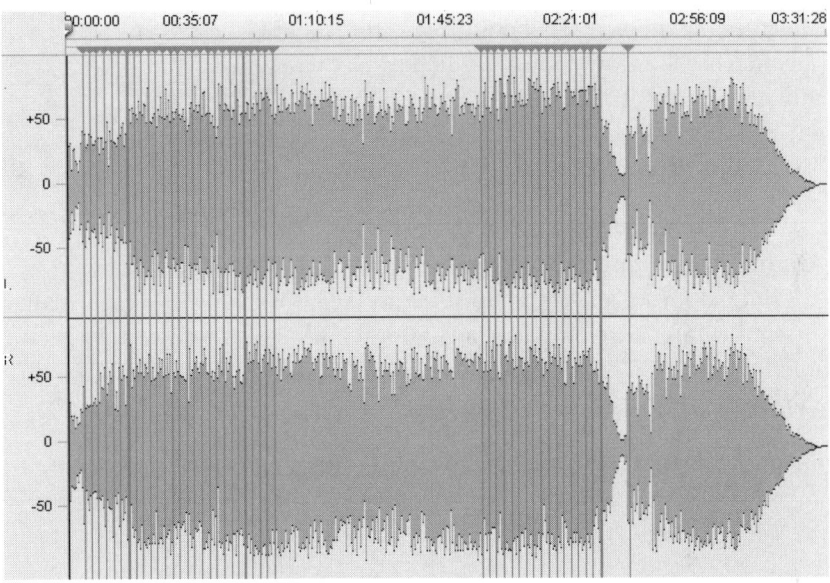

Once marked, I brought the file into Video Editor for re-arrangement. I also made an additional edit: the intro was twice as long as I needed it. I could cut it in half without damaging the overall piece. The idea is to cut on the cues, and then keep them aligned after the cut. This way you can (nearly always) seamlessly remove sections from songs:

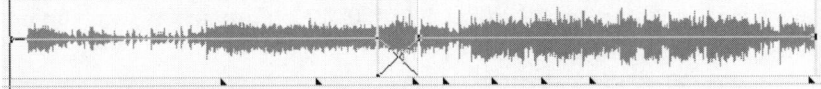

Sometimes a straight cut works, other times a small crossfade can help reduce or eliminate an abrupt change. I use both in this project. The crossfade shown here helps me cut the intro in half. The next one is a straight cut. Timed right, you can't even hear it.

Remember: with a clip selected, you can use the arrow keys to move it a frame at a time. Set a preview range to quickly review your results.

The Promotional Video

This pseudo promotional video is similar in purpose to the music video we just did: it's a good vehicle for looking into the details of how certain effects are accomplished. I only call it "pseudo" because it is, frankly, a bit pretentious. Anyone who knows me probably knows I don't take myself this seriously. That said, I do rather like the way it turned out anyway. And I think we can learn a bit more from it. So let's begin.

Opening Scene

I wanted to mimic the book cover for the opening scene. However, all I had was this still image and it looked quite uninteresting without any motion. That's when it struck me, this would be a good time to discuss how to give motion to motionless objects.

Approach, Opening Transition

A combination of effects were used to create motion. In no particular order, they are: moving paths, a keyframed filter, color clips, a cool transition, and animated titles. We've suddenly taken a very boring picture and really popped some life into it.

I really like the way this video starts off with a "pow!" The bright flash, the music, and the fade-into-scene really makes you sit up. Take a look at the settings for the first transition.

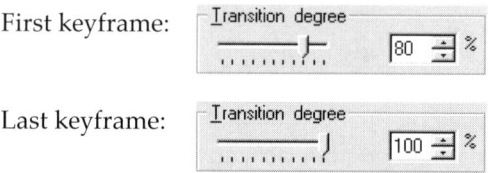

First keyframe: Transition degree 80 %

Last keyframe: Transition degree 100 %

I kicked off the video with this to make this point: there's no law that says transitions start at 0% and end at 100%. You can achieve very interesting effects playing outside the box.

Approach, the Virtual Clip

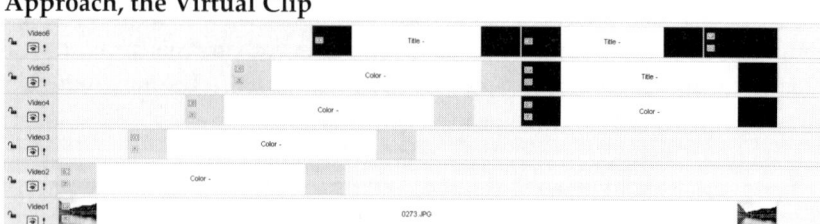

Upon opening the virtual clip, you'll see this mess of clips. On track Video1 is the still from the image sequence used at the end of the project. We generate motion with a *very* slow moving path and a keyframed lens flare (p. 240).

On tracks Video2 through Video5 are a series of color clips. These clips have had an advanced 2D moving path applied, reshaping them as shown. They've been timed to move across the screen and overlap a bit. A transparency has also been applied to them.

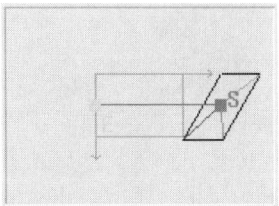

The main title is broken into three parts: the animated part, the fixed part, and the "video filtered" part:

While this may seem cumbersome (e.g., if you change the title you must change three different clips) I find it easier to work this way. Beyond that, however, is the need for quality. The water flow video filter doesn't have an "off" setting. Even setting it to 0 still creates some visible artifacts around the text edges. I decided to have a clean, filter-free clip, followed by the filtered clip.

Lastly, the line between the two text blocks is yet another color clip. A moving path squishes it down to "line size" and moves it into place.

Secondary Title Scene

When I produced my very first dance recital video (some ninety-eight years ago) I used an effect very similar to this. Namely, the zooming out text with a flashing white background. I didn't intend to copy this, it just sort of happened. At first, I was just going to leave it as a placeholder, and replace it with something

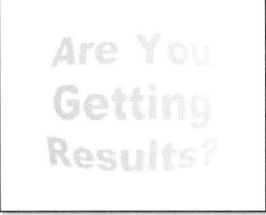

else later. However, it started to grow on me and so I left it.

Approach

Let's look at the title clips first. Each one is the same. It's a simple, straightforward font, with a Zoom animation applied to it (specifically, 001). Beyond that, are two video filters: Punch and Animation Gradient. The former gives it the obvious

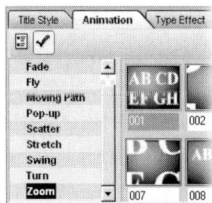

bulge during the zoom. The latter gives the text a small amount of depth. It's lighter on the right side than on the left. It's subtle, but if you know to look for it, you'll see it.

Track Video1 contains color clips. And guess what! Take a look at this. For years I've complained that I've never *not* had to click that "Pure Color" button. Well, what do you know. For once I actually used a 2-color clip. These have been placed at intervals matching the musical beat to make this section pulse.

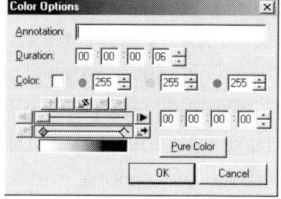

Key Concepts Scene

If anyone saw the demo video Ulead commissioned for MediaStudio Pro 7, you might notice I borrowed an idea or two from their production. I'll admit it. I liked it. However, a furor erupted on MUG when it was discussed whether or not MSP was capable of producing its own demo video. The answer was a resounding "yes and no," primarily due to that gray area where a video editor crosses into a special effects generator. I did like the 3D screenshots, though, so I reproduced that effect here.

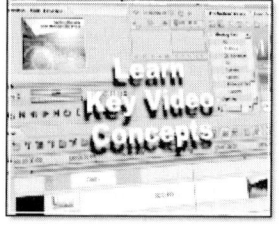

Approach

The obvious first step: get video screenshots. I've used several different tools in my day, but this time I settled on SnagIt. I was impressed with its ability to capture near full motion at its US$40 price point.

The next trick was to create the 3D motion. As you've already guessed, a 3D Motion Path was used. I came up with these final motions as a result of trial and error.

The screen capture itself has a filter applied: Blur. I wanted it out of focus for two reasons. First, I didn't want the background to compete with the text. The tiny amount of blur helps with this. Second, and most important, due to the VCD compression, there were horrible artifacts (aliasing and blockiness) with the very fine lines in the screen cap.

A tiny bit of blur smoothed these out and (ironically) made the end result *clearer* than it would have been without the blur. Try it yourself. Mute the blur and render to VCD format. Compare the results, both with and without the blur filter.

Lastly, the title clips. There are two physical clips for each title. The one on top is white and in clear focus. The one below is black and acts as a shadow. A blur video filter and transparency settings are used to give it this look.

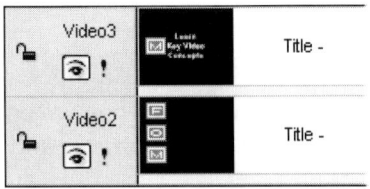

"Now wait a minute!" I hear you object. "Title clips can have shadows applied to them. Why use a separate clip?" The answer, in a word: animation. I actually move the two title clips along different paths. You'll notice the shadow doesn't move as fast as the main text. This is to create the illusion of vertical separation. It almost looks as if the text is rising from the background. We need two title clips for this. In a single clip, there's no way to apply one animation to the text and another to its shadow.

The 3D angle for both the text and the screen cap is the same. Once I finalized the motion for the screen cap, I copied the moving path attributes and pasted them to the title clips, before tweaking.

Essential Editing Skills Scene

This is quite similar to the previous scene. There are only a couple differences. First, we have *two* screen captures at work. The farthest one back is the screen cap from the previous scene, but trimmed at a different location (and zoomed into using a 2D Basic Moving Path.) The second difference: there's a color clip behind the second screen capture acting as a shadow. For kicks, I varied its background from black to brown over the source of the scene.

The title clips are essentially the same as before, but aren't in 3D for this scene. I hop back and forth between 2D and 3D just for visual interest.

Standard Functions Scene

Different scene, same approach as before. There are two screen caps. There are the same shadowed title clips. No new ground broke here: just continuing the motif set for this segment of the video.

Blue Screen Scene

This scene is most akin to the first "Key Concepts" scene. It uses one screen cap, the same 3D moving path approach, and the same two-in-one titles.

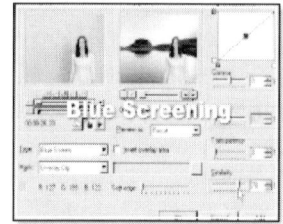

Again, no new ground.

Project Intro Scene

Here I used the same pulsing titles as the post-opening, secondary title scene, but with a twist. Using the technique in Chapter 8 on page 228, I've applied a filter to this title clip to give it a bit more flash than the first titles.

Approach

I won't rehash the details. Refer to the section in Chapter 8 for the specifics. But do open up the project, open the "Project Intro" virtual clip, and take a look. It's an odd approach, but effective.

Projects Scene

In this scene, a visual change in the project corresponds with the subject change. No more screen captures. Instead, some picture-in-picture fun. The titles are the only portion of this segment that visually tie it in with the rest of the project.

Approach, Virtual Clip

Open up the virtual clip.

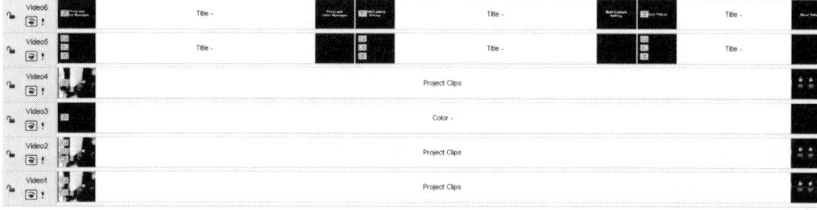

There are four visual clips in use: a virtual clip named Project Clips, and a simple color clip. They're stacked from Video1 to Video4, with moving paths applied to position them. The color clip on Video3 serves as a "shadow" beneath the clip in Video4. This visually offsets it from the other clips. Finally, overlays and filters are combined to "fade out" each clip, so that the farther back we go, the more subtle it gets.

The titles on Video5 and Video6 are the usual.

Approach, The Other Virtual Clip
Now look at the Project Clips virtual clip. There are four clips, one freeze frame, and one crossfade:

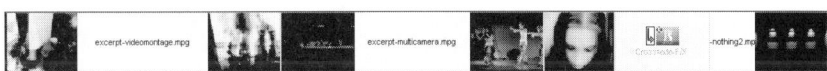

The first two clips are straight clips. No effects, no paths, no nuthin'. The last two clips look like this, if you pull them apart:

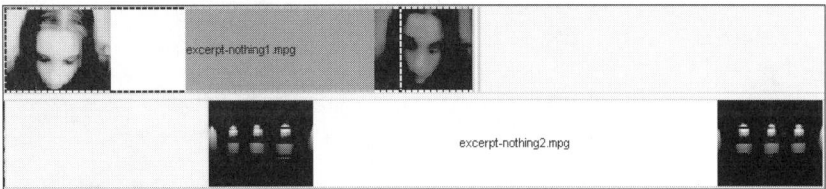

When overlapped, the freeze frame is nearly invisible. It begins *just* before the overlap area. It lasts for one second, cross-fading to a different part of the montage. Again, solely for visual interest. I wanted to put two good scenes together, not just use two adjacent scenes.

Flight Sequence

In the last project, the Music Video, we subtly used an image sequence for the foreground vase in Scene 12. Now we're using a blatant image sequence for the entire scene. The scenery was created in Terragen. Oddly enough, I completed *this* part of the project first.

Approach
I had already created the cover art for the book when I had this idea for the video: wouldn't it be cool if the cover "came alive." It would make a great ending sequence to use motion footage that stops *right* at the point where it matches the book cover.

I knew this would be tricky. The cut between the motion and the still would have to be pixel perfect in order to pull it off. Otherwise, it would just look lame. I had the advantage of being able to computer generate both the sequence and the still, but the sequence was rendered for video at 4:3 while the still was rendered at 6:9.

In the end, it took a lot of tweaking. Two things helped: 1) a soft overlay of the 4:3 image over the 6:9 image, which covered up minor pixilation differences; and 2) independently changing the width and height arguments on the moving path until the images meshed. (Viewing the results on a large Preview Window helped.) Once I got that, it was perfect.

The rest of this segment was made up of a simple lens flare (just as in the opening shot) and the title overlays.

Closing Scene

The zoom sequence turning into a book cover is definitely my favorite part of this project, and probably why I finished it before starting the rest of the project. This scene is conceptually simple: just a moving path with a title overlay. But there's more.

Approach
Open this virtual clip and you'll be hit with this.

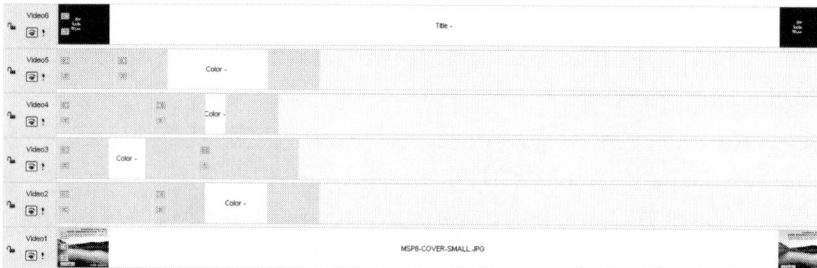

It's not as bad as it looks. The color clips are the ghostly boxes flying around. I'm actually not sure why I put these in there. I probably wanted something to complement the color clips used in the opening sequence. I worried afterwards that it might look like I was covering up the seams between the two shots through

misdirection, but by the time these come into place, the stitch has already been made. In the end I left them in for the obvious reason: demonstration purposes.

The book cover image in Video1 uses a moving path to put the book in motion, an overlay to fade it out, and a blur filter to help reduce compression artifacts. The moving path and overlay are timed to the audio.

The "On Sale Now" title has its own path, but is synchronized off the same cue as the book cover. I placed a cue on the timeline to help me synchronize the Effects Manager keyframes across clips. Compare these EM pictures for the title clip (top) and the image clip (bottom).

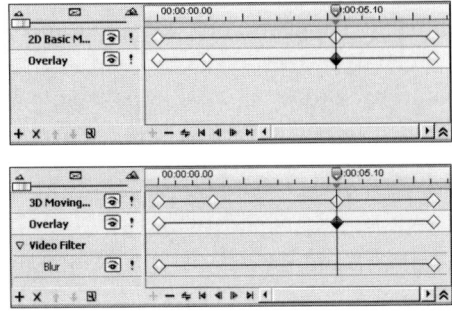

Closing Notes

Time for our project post mortem. Actually, we've already talked about the project enough, so I'd really just like to focus on the quirks of working with virtual clips and nested timelines.

Temporal Disorientation

If you've been opening and closing virtual clips right along with me, you may have noticed some peculiarities. First and foremost is the fact that the timeline's ruler, scale, view, and position applies to *all* timelines.

At first I thought this was a minor annoyance. But after several hundred hours of this, I'm going to personally reclassify it as a bug. Or at least a serious design omission. The main purpose of the secondary timelines is for insertion into other timelines as virtual clips. To illustrate my point, let's open up the "End Title" virtual clip.

Here it is on the main timeline:

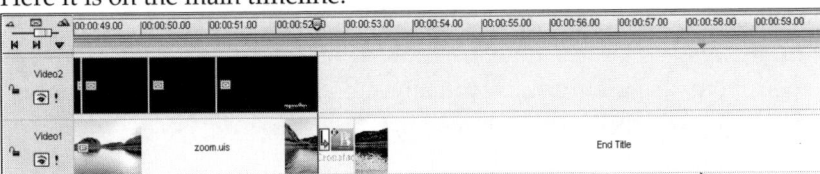

And here it is opened:

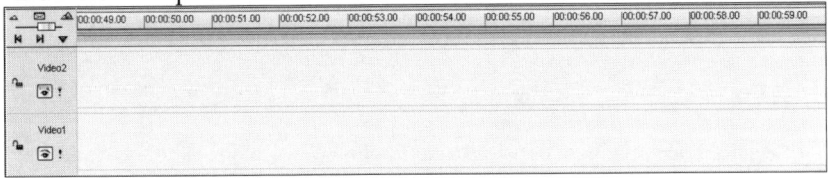

Hmmm... where is everything? Oh yeah, look at that. We're still looking at times 00:00:49.00 through 00:00:59.00. How is this helpful? Every virtual clip starts at time 00:00:00.00. Just because I *place* it at 50 seconds into a main project doesn't mean I want to *open* it at 50 seconds down the timeline. It's just wrong. But it doesn't end there. Obviously to work on it you'll have to scroll all the way back down to zero. But when you close it to go back to work on the main timeline, you're back at zero! Now you have to scroll all the way *back* to 50 second to get where you want to be.

For something that's supposed to enhance workflow performance, this is a serious deficiency. Maybe by the time you read this, you'll be on a service pack and they've fixed it. I can only hope so.

In a related issue, I'd like to be able to have independent timeline ruler units. If I'm working on the main timeline at a high level and the virtual clip's timeline at a detailed level, well, it's not so crazy that I'd want to look at the main timeline at 2-second resolution and the secondary timeline at 1/3-second resolution[11].

Performance

While we've done some pretty cool things with virtual clips, it comes with a hefty performance price. I'm really not sure what causes it, but once you start adding virtual clips and nested timelines, the time it takes to save a project grows enormously.

I really hope Ulead figures out a way to address this in a service pack. I'm willing to wait a few seconds to save a project. But I have some projects which take over *one minute* to save. And when you have Auto Save enabled at its default ten minute interval, this means it's possible that over 10% of your editing time will be spent with Video Editor locked up in save mode.

For these reasons, at this point in time, I have to recommend that you use virtual clips and nested timelines only when necessary. They're just to expensive to use gratuitously. It really shouldn't be that way, but unfortunately it's our reality at the moment.

---

[11] That said, you can toggle between two timeline units by pressing F9.

13

DVD MovieFactory

Now that we have several finished projects, let's make a DVD. It's time for a tour of the disc authoring tool.

Background

If you've never authored a disc before, the process may seem a bit mysterious. In all actuality, though, it's really quite easy. As long as you don't try to get too tricky with your menus, you can pretty much just click-click-click your way through the entire process. DVD MovieFactory has plenty of presets to keep you happy for quite a while.

Integrated Disc Authoring

The disc authoring tool is "integrated" in the sense that you can start it from within Video Editor. However, it's really a stand-alone program, and there's nothing stopping you from using it that way.

In your MediaStudio Pro 8 installation directory, there is a subfolder called "DVD Authoring". And within that folder is a program called DVDMF.exe. You can create your own shortcut to this program if you find yourself wanting to use DVDMF but don't always want to fire up Video Editor.

Just What Is Disc Authoring?

Authoring is the end-to-end process of disc creation, including the design and construction of menus, sub-menus, chapter points, background images, background audio, and all the other elements that make DVDs so darn cool.

DVD MovieFactory offers a tremendous amount of customization. You may never find the need to trade up to a more powerful authoring tool. I've been impressed with its capabilities.

Frequently Asked Questions

You may still have questions beyond just *What is Authoring?* Let's take a moment to ramp up on core concepts before hitting the exercises.

- *What can you put on a DVD?* Well, pretty much any video file you want, as long as it fits. If your source video isn't "DVD ready," that's okay, because the authoring tool will convert your sources to be compliant, although this can take quite some time.

- *Can I put more than one video or project on a disc?* Yes. You can add as many video and/or project files to your authoring project as you'd like. I've found no arbitrary limit to the maximum allowed—only the practical limit imposed by the capacity of the disc.

- *Can I create DVDs just like the movies I buy?* Well, in a word, no. The major limitation is that buttons can only have two functions: play a video, or play a chapter-menu. So something like a stand-alone "special features" menu isn't possible. There's no facility for adding alternate audio tracks or creating subtitles. But for most users at this level, these things simply aren't needed. Here's what you can do: create motion menus and motion buttons, use pre-defined templates or customize your own. Change the menu layouts. Customize your fonts. You can have multi-page chapter-selection menus. My guess is you'll probably use DVD MF for a quite while before you ever bump your head on the ceiling. When and if you do bump your head, look to Ulead's DVD Workshop.

- *Where's my authoring project stored?* DVD MovieFactory's project file has a DWZ extension. By default, it stores it far, far away from your projects, in a DVD MovieFactory folder stored under My Documents. However, using Save As, you can keep them anywhere.

- *Anything else I need?* You'll need a DVD±R burner and at least one blank DVD. If you have only a CD-R burner, you can do *most* of these things to create a VCD or SVCD disc. There are slight differences in the way menus are created and operated, however.

- *Is it as easy/hard as it looks?* Yes and no. The marketing materials will have you believe you can go from DV camcorder to DVD in a matter of minutes. This is true if your product is a one-minute clip and contains no editing at all. But many of us will customize, most of us will edit, and all of us will wait for encoding. But once you've gone through it a couple times, you'll know the steps and have a better feeling for what the whole process is like.

The Project

To get a feel for the entire authoring process, we're going to create a DVD using all the final, rendered videos from all the full-length book projects. Through this process we will demonstrate:

- How to add a first-play clip.
- How to customize menus.
- How to change the default templates.
- How to create chapter points.
- And lots more.

For full satisfaction, this project requires a DVD burner and a blank disc. If you don't have both of these, you can still do everything but the final burn. (It just won't be as much fun, that's all.)

> **How Times Change**
> In late 1997, Pioneer shipped the first DVD burner for just $16,995. Blank discs were $49.95 each. By the fall of 1999, you could pick up a burner for around $5,000, an astounding price breakthrough! Today, you can find them for as little as $40. If this trend continues, by this time next year they will pay you $10 to carry them out of the store.

Objective
Create a real DVD that you can play in a capable DVD player.

Reference Project
projects\chapter13\sample.dwz (see "readme" note in project directory)

Steps, Clip Selection
1. With Video Editor open, start DVD MovieFactory using the File | Export | DVD Authoring command.

2. You are prompted for a file.

    If you have more than one file to go on your disc, you can select multiple files here (as long as they're in the same directory). You can always add (or remove) files later.

3. For now, locate firstplay.mpg and click Open.

4. With firstplay selected, check Use first clip as introductory video.

5. Click Add Media.
Add media:

6. At this point, locate the main video project final renders for inclusion in our DVD:

- projects\chapter10\photomontage\rendered\photomontage.mpg
- projects\chapter10\videomontage\rendered\videomontage.mpg
- projects\chapter11\cookies\rendered\phase6.mpg
- projects\chapter11\multicamera\rendered\phase3.mpg
- projects\chapter12\nothing\rendered\nothing.mpg
- projects\chapter12\promo\rendered\promo.mpg

You'll have to add them one at a time, due to their separate locations. When complete, the project filmstrip will look like this:

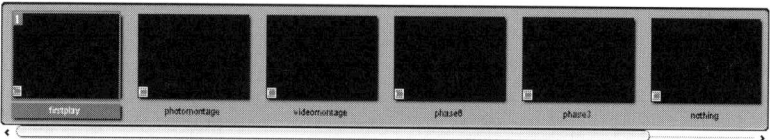

For this project, we're going to add chapters to two of our clips. We'll start with the video montage.

Steps, Chapter Creation

1. Click on the videomontage thumbnail and click Add/Edit Chapter.
2. Click Auto Add Chapter.

Auto Add Chapters

If you're anything like me, you might be confused at first between "Insert scenes as chapters" and "Auto scene detection." Then, once you figure *that* out you're left with the even *more* difficult task of trying to decipher when the Insert option gets enabled or not. Well, here's the scoop:

Insert scenes as chapters means that *scenes have been pre-defined for this clip.*

Auto scene detection means that *scenes have not been defined, but it will hunt for them.*

To pre-define clips, create DVD chapter point cues on the timeline. When you create the video, the chapter points are saved along with the file. For DV AVI files, they are stored in the file. For MPEG files, they are stored in a UPD file named after the video file. *If you delete the UPD file, you cannot use Insert Scenes.*

Without chapter points, DVD MovieFactory falls back on normal scene detection, analyzing frame-to-frame changes. This means guesswork though, and probably a lot of manual tweaking after-the-fact to get it the way you want.

3. With the dialog box as shown, click OK. At this point DVDMF will read the UPD file and generate the seven chapter points.

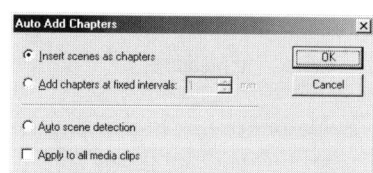

Chapter 13 • DVD MovieFactory 365

As you can see, the first two thumbnails are black. You'll find oftentimes that the first frame of a chapter isn't necessarily representative of the chapter's contents. Not to worry, they can be changed:

4. Click the first chapter's thumbnail. The big preview window will move to that frame.

5. Play until 00:00:04.00 then stop there.

6. Now right-click the thumbnail and select Change thumbnail. This automatically sets the thumbnail to whatever's currently displayed in the preview window.

7. Continue this process by selecting better thumbnail images for each chapter. Here's what I ended up with:

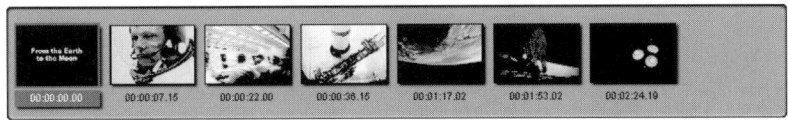

I left chapters 3 and 7 the way they were. The rest were chosen to better represent the spirit of the chapter.

8. At the top-right corner of the dialog box, change the currently selected clip to promo. This box lets you change chapter points for different clips without having to keep going back to the main timeline.

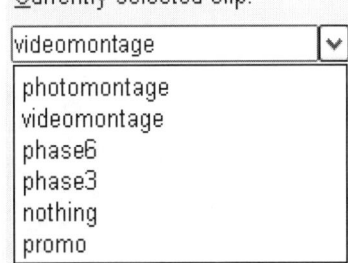

9. Click Auto Add Chapter again.

This time the Insert option is disabled. There is no UPD file[12]. You can use scene detection, but you know how that goes already. We'll learn more by creating chapter points manually. Click Cancel.

---

[12] Note that sometimes you'll get UPD files whether you explicitly placed DVD chapter point cues or not. In the absence of your own cues, Video Editor creates some for you.

10. Hit play and stop at around ten seconds. I'd like to create a chapter at the start of the black and white titles.

11. Move the frame position to 00:00:10.05.

    You can't, can you? This is because chapter points can only correspond with I-frames.

> **I-frames?**
>
> The MPEG algorithm achieves high compression ratios by storing no more data than it needs to. This means storing only the changes between frames and not the frames themselves. Obviously, at some point the entire frame needs to be recorded, otherwise "change" is meaningless. The I-frame (or, technically, the "Intra-picture") is this whole frame. It's Independent of other frames. For this reason, it's the only one suitable for chapter points.

12. Instead, move the frame position to 00:00:10.15 and click Add Chapter.

13. Move to 00:00:16.00 and add another chapter.

14. Create more chapters at 31.00, 34.15, and 45.15.

15. Leave the thumbnails as-is and click OK.

Steps, Menu Creation
1. Back on the main screen, click Next. You'll see the default template:

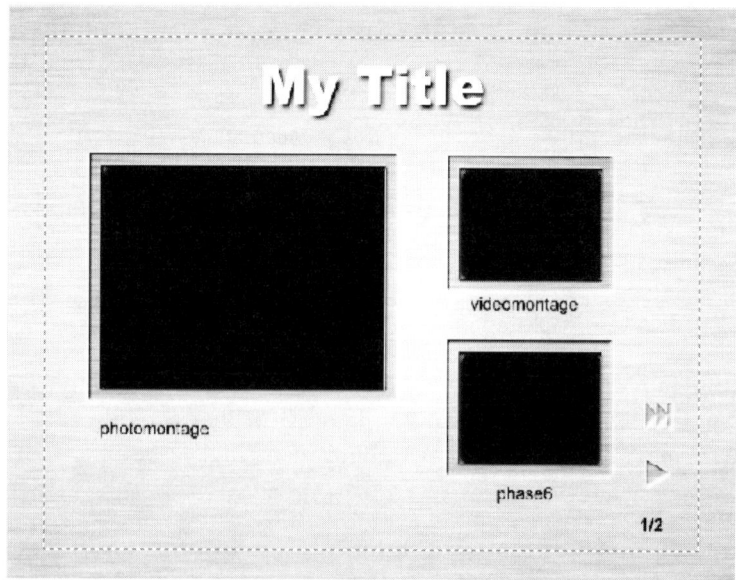

I'd rather find a layout where we can fit everything on a single page.

Chapter 13 • DVD MovieFactory   367

2. First, take a look at the templates:

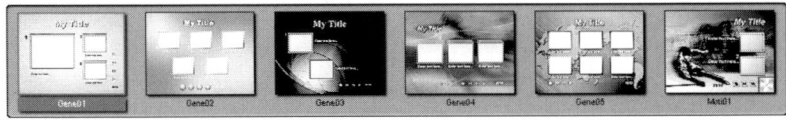

Each template has a set number of thumbnails on it. Don't worry, this is a function of the *layout* and not the *template*. Layouts and templates can be mixed and matched, therefore different numbers of thumbnails can be applied to each template.

And if you don't see anything at all that you like, you can pretty much build your own. By selecting your own backgrounds (image or motion), music, layout, and customizations, there's a huge number of combinations available.

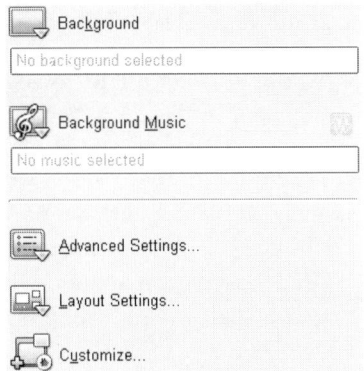

3. We won't go hog-wild on the customizations. For now, just select the blue one named Gen02.

4. There are a couple controls I want to make you aware of. Under the preview window is a drop-down called Currently displayed menu. Change that to videomontage.

Look! We're back to the brushed metal template. That's right, you can have different templates for each menu. We'll fix that soon.

Now check out these buttons: 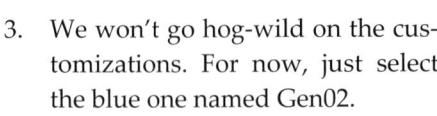. Click these to move between the various pages of a menu. (If all the items don't fit, DVDMF automatically creates as many pages as necessary to display all the thumbnails.) Additionally, you can change the background image on a per-page basis.

5. For now, just switch back to the Main Menu.

6. Click the Customize button.

7. Under Customize Template, choose Layout.

8. Scroll to the right to find La601.

This is the first layout with six thumbnails. The exact positions of the thumbnails can be changed later. But if you find one here you don't have to change later, then that's all the better.

9. Under Customize Template, choose Scene Frame.

10. Scroll and find F037. Click it and the preview will update to match.

11. Now click Add to Menu Template. This saves our customizations and adds it to the available list of templates for future sessions.

12. Click OK. The template now appears under Favorites.

13. Apply this template to all three menus.

14. Hmmm... the video montage has seven frames. I hate having six on one page and just one on the next.

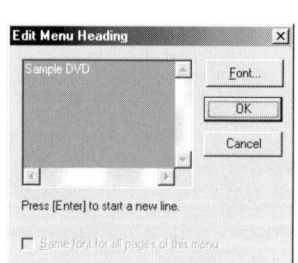

Click Customize again and change the layout to La801 just for this one page. That way none of our menus is forced to paginate.

Steps, Modifying Titles

The size, location, and typeface for each title can be changed. For this layout that means one title for the page and individual titles for each thumbnail.

Note. If you do not make any changes to the titles then *no* titles will display. If you make a change to any title, then *all* titles will display, even if you change the title back to what it was originally. I'm still wondering if this is by design or not. But it's worth mentioning.

1. Make sure the currently displayed menu is Main Menu.

2. Click **My Title** and move it to the top left.

3. Double click it to edit it.

4. Change the text to Sample DVD.

5. Leave the font as-is.

6. Click OK.

7. Move the round Play button to the right.

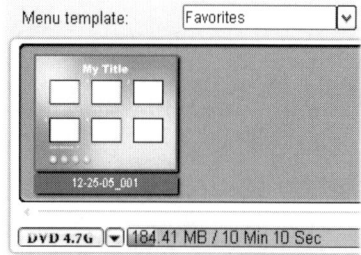

8. Double-click the thumbnail titles and change to something more appropriate than a file name:

   A Walk in the Woods
   From the Earth to the Moon
   Chocolate Chip Cookies
   Dance Routine
   Nothing Without (Music Video)
   Getting Results Promo Video

9. Deselect the Motion menu checkbox. I want to examine still menus before making them walk the walk.

10. Our thumbnails leave a bit to be desired as well. In order to change the thumbnail image, double click the thumbnail.

11. Go ahead and pick a different thumbnail for each project. That will look better than six black boxes.

    After changing the titles and thumbnails, here's what my Main Menu looks like:

12. Switch to menu videomontage.

13. Chapter menus have thumbnails preset, so we'll leave them as is. Instead, just change the titles. Here's mine:

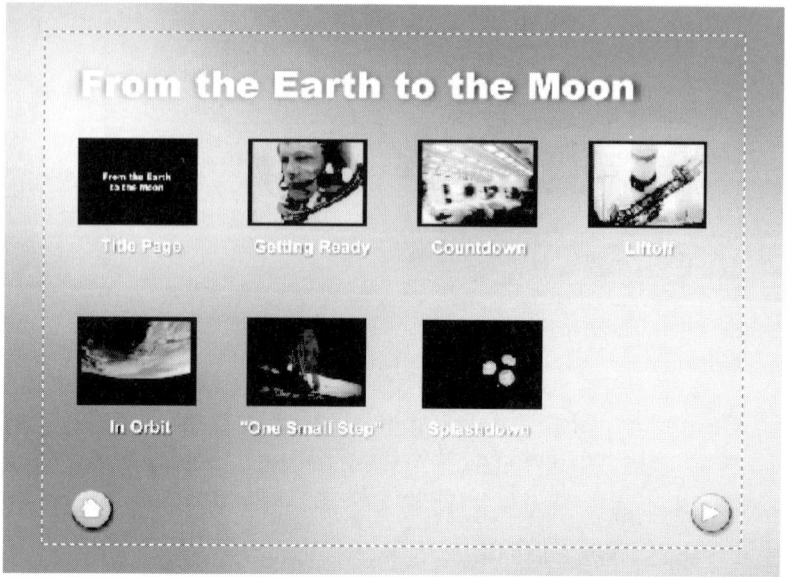

Tip. Double-clicking the "home" icon in the lower left switches the editor back to the Main Menu.

Another Tip. Don't forget to hit Ctrl+S from time to time. There is no auto save feature here and you don't want to lose your work.

14. Move to the Promo video menu and make changes. I've manually overridden the thumbnails and set new titles:

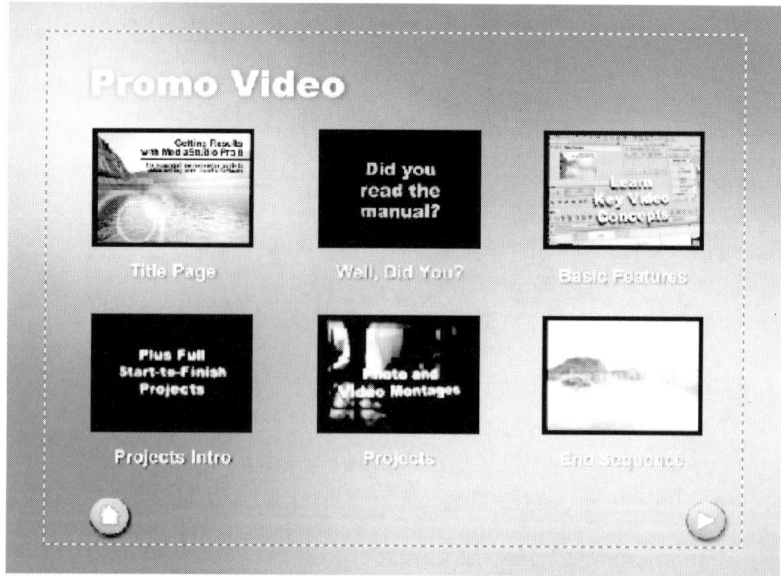

Chapter 13 • DVD MovieFactory

15. Go back to the Main Menu. Let's set a music background.

16. Click the Background Music button and choose the option for All Menus. This will let us set the music for all three menus in one fell swoop.

17. Go to the chapter12 Promo project folder and let's use the trailblazer.wav file. This music was written by Bjorn Lynne. I really like his stuff. Check it out at http://www.lynnemusic.com.

18. And that's it for the menus. We've hardly scratched the surface as far as full customization, but I think this gets you familiar enough with the basics and where you might take it on your own.

A Notes on Layout Customization
While customizing the layout is possible, it's not very fun. There are no automatic alignment tools (neither within nor across menus). There's no undo (other than "lose all changes"). In general, you're on your own. For the most part, I *don't* change the defaults unless I really have to.

Steps, Previewing
1. Click Next to move to the "virtual DVD player."

2. Clicking the Play button simulates inserting the disc into a DVD player. So click that.

   The "first play" video plays followed by the Main Menu.

3. For now, just try it out. A word of wisdom: although this interface allows you to select various screen elements with your mouse, keep in mind that home DVD players *do not have mice*. To really get a feel for how navigation will work, use your mouse to click buttons on the remote control only. This is a much more realistic way to test.

Steps, Revising
Rare is the time I get it right the first time through. If after watching your project through the DVD simulator you decide to change things, just click the back button.

1. The first thing I want to do is add motion menus. The menus are nice, but a bit boring. Fortunately, this is exceedingly easy. Just check the box next to Motion menu. Next to this option is a duration for the menu. They won't play forever, so you have to set a loop point. ☑ Motion menu   [20] sec

This value is up to you. With motion menus there are three things in motion: the menu background, the menu thumbnails, and the music. Not all will have the same loop points. At least, not by chance they won't. So it's up to you to decide.

Do what I do. Leave it at 20. See how it turns out. Fix it if necessary.

Tip. The motion setting is global. You can't have some menus with and some without. (Note that motion begins at the start of the clip.)

 2. Press Alt+J for Project Settings (yeah, I know—why be consistent?)

3. At the bottom are navigation controls.

   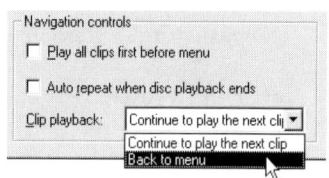

   The Clip playback setting is, to me, the most important. The top value acts as "Play All" meaning it won't stop playing until it makes its way through all clips. The bottom value gives you traditional DVD behavior: show the menu after each clip plays. That's what I set for this project.

   Personally, I've never used the other options. The first one is useful if you don't want to subject your viewers to the menu upon every single viewing. Put in the disc and it plays! What a miracle. I've only purchased one commercial DVD that did this ("Contact"). I wish they all did, especially the ones with seemingly 20-minute long intros. I wish there was a "don't show this again" checkbox!

4. That's all I wanted to change. Click Next to preview again.

Reviewing Previewing

The motion menus begin play at the specified thumbnail frame and loop at the 20-second mark. Change the loop sections by changing the initial thumbnail frame. The music abruptly ends when the loop is up, so if you really want to do this right, create a music cut specifically for the DVD.

But overall this looks pretty good. Let's make a disc. Click Next.

Burning

Click Burn. Really. There certainly are other options here, and you may want to change some of them from time to time. But so far I haven't. The presets are fine. I pop the disc in, it warns me about how long this will take. I nod my head, and some time later, I have a DVD.

That's about all there is to it!

The End

Although we have come to the end of the book, this is hopefully just the beginning for you. I hope this book has achieved its goals, and that you feel like you're armed with the information you need to move forward as a video editor. By now you should have shaken off any lingering feelings you might have had about being a novice. Additionally, you should feel proud of your accomplishments.

Although we've covered a lot of ground in these pages, there is still more to go. I've been doing this for years now, and I still learn new things all the time. The industry is constantly changing: the software we use and the hardware we run it on. The whole bigger-faster-cheaper trend shows no signs of slowing in the immediate future. Therefore we must be in a constant state of growth right along with it. The best way to do that is together.

If you're stuck on something, talk to other users: ask questions. Whether it's in person, on the phone, or on-line, nothing helps you through a problem like someone who's already been there. And then, later on, when *you're* the expert, you can pass on the favor to someone else.

My final words should be all too familiar by now: don't be afraid to experiment. I can't say it enough. You learn to do by doing. Books can help you get started, but you and only you have the power to keep moving ahead. Create good stuff. Create bad stuff. It doesn't matter, as long as you're creating. The important part is the practice. That's the key to true mastery.

Part IV

APPENDICES

Appendix A Getting Reoriented with MediaStudio Pro

Appendix B Better Shooting and Composition

Appendix C Text and Typography

Appendix D Tips and Things

Appendix E Troubleshooting

Glossary

Index

Getting Reoriented with MediaStudio Pro

If you're still in shock over the drastic changes that arrived with Version 8, then get a drink and read this.

What Happened Here!?

If you just opened up Video Editor 8 then this just might be the first thought which pops in your head. If you squint, it *kind* of looks like the Video Editor you've been using the last year or two (or ten). There's a Timeline. There's a Production Library. But there's something else. There's a *lot* something else.

And if you've been using MediaStudio Pro for as long as I have, it can be both disconcerting and frustrating to have to re-learn what you thought you already knew.

First, here's the good news. You *still* know a lot about MediaStudio Pro. While some of the changes are drastic, much of what we've grown to know and love about this software is still there. And now for the better news: you'll get used to this new way of thinking faster than you'd ever expect. In fact, you may be surprised at how hard it is to go back to the way you did things before. That's already happened to many people, including yours truly.

These are definitely changes for the better. Many of these features have been staples of the competition for a long time. We finally have an editor caught up with the times, if not gone a bit ahead of the times, particularly in the area of HD support.

Track Order

One of the first things you might notice is that the tracks are in the wrong order. The lower numbered tracks used to be on top and now they're on the bottom. What gives?

Well, this is the editing paradigm used by many other editors. Most people intuitively feel that if a video clip is *on top* of another clip then it will appear *in front* of that clip in the rendered video. So in a way, we're the ones who have had it backwards all along.

Take a look:

If you were to play this timeline, you would see the clip in track Video1 for one second, followed by the clip in Video2 for one second, followed by the clip in Video3 for the rest of the project.

I'll admit, this does take some getting used to. It's like the old trick where you have to connect the dots by looking at your hand in a mirror. But you'll be amazed how quickly your brain switches gears.

At one point during the beta, after using MSP8 for several straight weeks, I went back to Video Editor 7, and simply could not get the hang of it. I kept putting clips in Va trying to make them appear in front of Vb! It was very strange.

Transitions

You might next notice that the Va, Vb, and Fx tracks are gone. Gone? Gone! How do I make a transition between two tracks? You may try in frustration to drag a transition down to the clips only to be greeted with the "no can do" cursor:

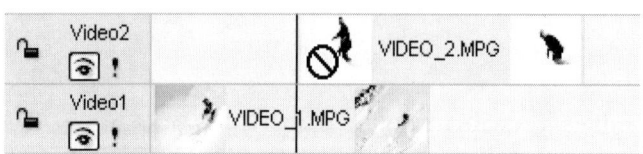

Appendix A • Getting Reoriented

What's an editor to do?

Transitions are no longer separate timeline objects. Instead, they magically spring into existence when two clips overlap. Using the above example, you can't drop a transition between VIDEO_1.MPG and VIDEO_2.MPG because there is no "between" between them. Instead, drag one clip straight down on the other. You'll now see this:

Hey look at that! A transition! And from out of nowhere! By default, Video Editor will use the Crossfade transition. You may change this default under preferences:

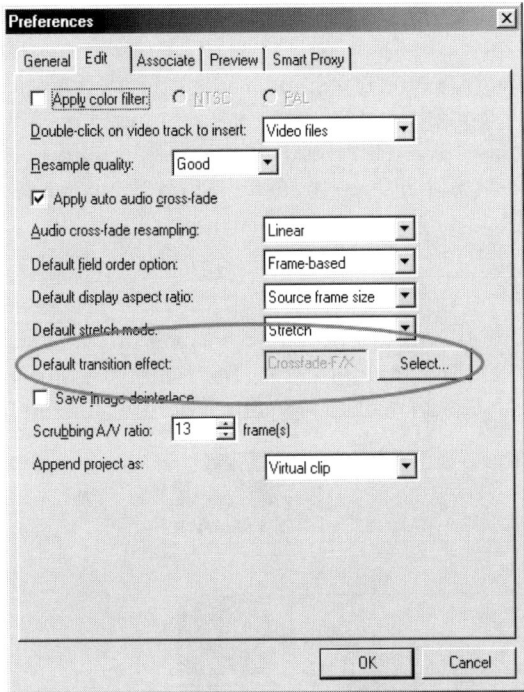

However, I highly recommend you leave it at Crossfade. If you go and change your default transition to, say, Accordion-3D, then please don't share your final projects with me. ☺ Crossfade is simple and elegant, second only to the straight cut for overall usefulness.

Side Effect #1

Having transitions behave like this gives you a huge leap in productivity and workflow efficiency. But it's not without its side effects. The first one I noticed was the simple fact that transition clips didn't exist any more. When editing, I invariably add the transition before I'm done with final trims, positions, and so on. Here's how it goes now:

1. Place clip1 on the timeline.
2. Place clip2 on the timeline so they overlap.
3. Get my transition working.
4. Realize clip2 isn't what I wanted and move it.
5. Damn! My perfected transition is *gone!*
6. Place clip3 on the timeline in place of clip2.
7. Do Step 3 all over again.

I miss being able to set the transition aside (or have it happily live free of any other clips) while I get my act together. I guess I need to wait and do the transitions last: live with the default crossfade until all the clips are set, then go back and finalize transitions, so I only have to do Step 3 once.

Side Effect #2

Since the transition effect is now just an overlap, what happens if the transition lasts as long as the clip? This is not uncommon, especially when doing a slow fade to black, as shown here in Version 7:

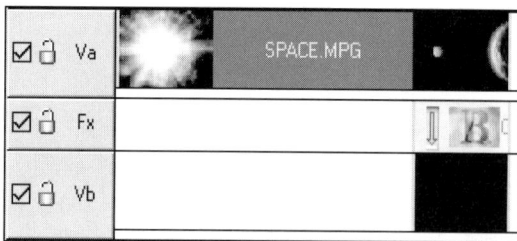

In Version 8 this bit of editing would look like this:

As you can see, the color clip disappears, being completely obscured by the transition. There's no way to tell if that's a color clip, a video clip, or what. Nor is there any good way to select it—at least at first glance.

Side Effect #1 of Side Effect #2

I'm sure Ulead quickly realized this case might arise. Therefore they added a popup menu at the transition to help you through this. Of course, like all popup menus, you don't know they're there until someone tells you or you just randomly try. So if you haven't randomly tried yet, then I'm going to tell you: right clicking is your friend.

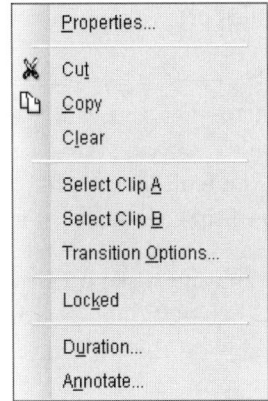

If you click on the transition then right-click, you'll see this menu. The three most important options are right there in the middle: Select Clip A, Select Clip B, and Transition Options.

Clip A is the clip on the Left. (It probably would have been nice to just say *Select Left Clip* but we'll take what we can get). Once you select either clip, focus moves to these clips, and you can now work with them: visible or not.

Don't be tempted to move the clip out of the way to work on it, because—as we've already stated—this vaporizes your transition. On the other hand, if you haven't done any customizations to the transition, then this is a non-issue. You may find it easier to quickly move a clip "out of the mix" to work on it, then move it back in. You don't *have* to do this, but you may find you want to anyway.

Side Effect #3

Since transitions are created by overlapping clips and you can overlap clips on any track... wow! That means you can have transitions anywhere! This isn't really a side effect, of course, but the actual purpose of single-track editing. The A/B roll editing paradigm was one of the things holding us back in the twentieth century. The benefits outweigh the nits.

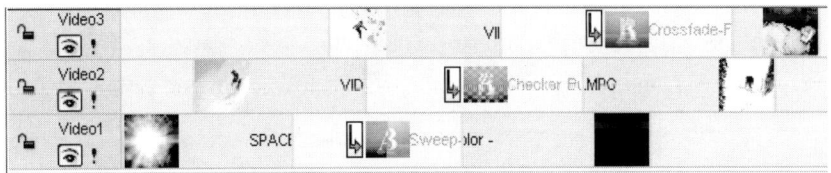

Multiple Timelines

Version 8.0 now supports more than one timeline. Before getting into them, it's important to understand this does **not** mean you can have multiple projects open. That is you cannot open project1.dvp on the main timeline and open project2.dvp on a second timeline. Video Editor still only supports "one project at a time" editing.

That said, you can *insert* other projects into any timeline. But this does just what it says: it inserts the project into the current project. It does not allow you operate on them as separate projects. This is not an MDI environment, like a word processor. Nor does Video Editor allow you to run multiple instances of itself. Maybe someday, but not this time.

What multiple timelines **do** allow for is what I like to think of as "drill down" editing. You are no longer forced to stack up piles and piles of clips on the timeline in order to make complex projects. Nor must you perform intermediate renders, bringing uncompressed results back on the timeline, just to continue editing.

You can create complex projects in intelligent layers, which improves both the ability to create and understand a complex project. Take a look:

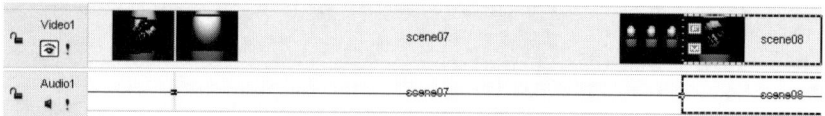

Note scene07. It looks like your average ordinary video clip. It's the only clip on the timeline at this point: tracks Video2 and above are all empty. However, if you double-click this clip, it opens up into a whole new timeline, called "scene07".

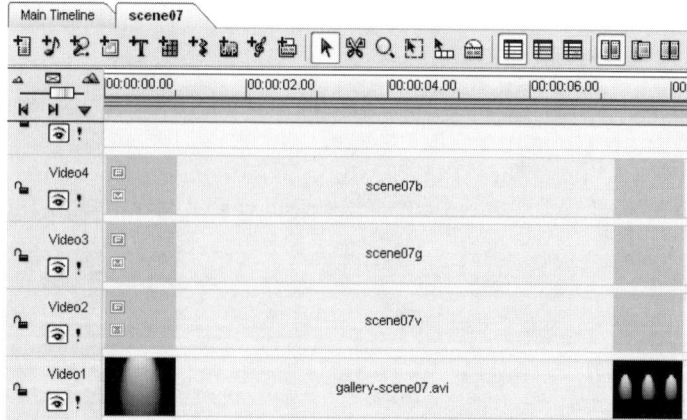

Here you can see that the original scene07 clip actually contained four other clips: scene07b, scene07g, scene07v, and gallery-scene07.avi. For fun, let's double click the top clip, scene07b:

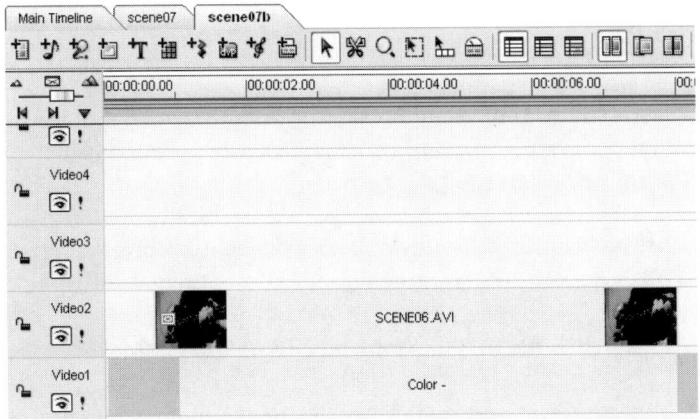

Wow. Look at that. It seems like scene07b itself was made up of two clips: scene06.avi overlaid on a color clip. That's pretty darn cool. If I were forced to accomplish this effect using only a single timeline, I would end up with one of two things: 1) a very complex, hard to understand timeline or 2) multiple projects with intermediate renders. Possibly even both.

So you can see how multiple timelines allow you to build complex things out of simple parts. Timeline scene07b is not hard to understand at all. It's just two clips with a simple blue screen overlay.

This is then added to timeline scene07 where a video filter is applied to it and a moving path added. This, along with the other clips is then added to the main timeline. So what is conceptually a single scene is, in fact, physically a single clip. Further, this clip itself can have overlays, filters, moving paths, and transitions with other clips. This is leaps and bounds beyond what we've been able to do before.

Virtual Clips

Rather than define a virtual clip, go back and re-read the previous section on Multiple Timelines. There! You've now seen virtual clips. Rather than trying to *explain* them it's easier to see them in action.

On our main timeline, the original scene07 clip is a Virtual Clip. In a nutshell, that means it's a clip made up of other clips. In practice, it is a clip created from another timeline. Although we examined these clips and timelines by drilling down from top to bottom, in reality they are created from the bottom up: each timeline being added to the previous until your final result resides on the Main Timeline.

I encourage you to try this. Start simple. Try this exercise:

1. Start a new project.

2. Right-click on the timeline tab row.

3. Click Create new timeline

4. In the new timeline, drag two video clips from the Production Library to Video1 and overlap them, creating a transition.

5. Right-click the timeline tab and click Add to Timeline | Main Timeline.

6. Video Editor will switch to the new timeline and put you in "drop" mode. Drop the virtual clip on the timeline.

Now do something with it. Add the Old Film filter. Put a moving path on it. Overlap it with another clip (virtual or otherwise) and see how it interacts.

When you're done, you can close the secondary timeline. It will warn you that the timeline will be deleted an that this action cannot be undone, but don't panic. Your virtual clip on the main timeline stays in place. If you want to edit the virtual clip again later, just double click and a new timeline will open for it.

One final note: you'll notice that virtual clips contain both audio and video tracks, even if the secondary timeline did not contain any audio. While you're free to split the audio track and delete it, it's recommended that you leave it as a placeholder.

Importing Old Projects

In general, you can open old projects with Version 8. However, there's no guarantee they will appear or behave identically. With so many fundamental changes, it's difficult to ensure 100% compatibility.

Just as with previous major version releases, it's recommended you finish in-process projects with the old version and start new projects with the new version. If you open a project from an older version, and it looks okay, you're certainly fine proceeding. You just have to treat it on a case-by-case basis.

What Happened to CG Infinity & Video Paint?

These two programs have been a part of the standard suite since Version 5's launch back in 1997. And if you've been around that long, you'll realize they haven't really changed a lot over the last eight years.

This time around, they've been dropped from the suite and are now sold separately as Video Graphics Lab. They've been re-skinned, so they do look like the rest of the suite. And they've been updated to support new file formats. But from a functional point of view, nothing has changed.

If you use CGI and VP, then keep your Version 7 copies around. You can use them quite happily right alongside Version 8. They'll even appear on the Switch menu. The file formats are the same and both can be dropped natively into Video Editor.

So What Else Is New?

This just scratches the surface. As you dig a bit, you'll find more new things await you. However they're just that: new things, and not changes to things you already know. This appendix was created to help you overcome the steepest part of the learning curve. Once you're comfortable with these essentials, the rest will follow.

Some of what lies ahead:

- The Effects Manager.
- Smart Compositor.
- Smart Proxy and HDV editing capabilities.
- WYSIWYG Title Clip editing.
- New color correction tools.
- And lots more!

There's No Going Back

As mentioned at the beginning of this appendix, once you get used to the way MediaStudio Pro 8 behaves, you may find it difficult going back to the old way of doing things. I *never* imagined that would be the case when I went through my own "re-orientation" phase. The changes were too radical. I would never get used to them. "Make sure you have an

MSP7 compatibility mode!" we shouted to Ulead. Thankfully, they didn't listen to us.

After just a couple of months of beta testing—as we found ourselves going back to Version 7 to cross-reference things—we now found ourselves disoriented with the product we'd been using for the last eight years. We found this extremely odd, yet very encouraging. It was reassuring to know that these "radical" changes had become second nature to us so quickly.

Sure, every once in a while I miss being able to leave a transition on a track all by itself. But it's a small price to pay for the big bag of features we got.

B

Better Shooting and Composition

Great videos begin with great images. In this appendix, learn pointers on getting the best footage possible.

Shooting Better Footage

Have you ever watched bad video? Of course, we've all *seen* it, but have you ever really *watched* it? Maybe it was your neighbor's vacation video. Or maybe it was the wedding your uncle shot. Or maybe—and most unfortunately—maybe it was something of your own.

Just what is it about bad video? What do you think of when you see it? How do you feel? Feelings can range anywhere from interminable boredom to downright anger, depending on what the video was for.

If you had to list just one characteristic of bad video that sets it apart from the good, it would come down to this: *you notice it*. Your attention is immediately turned away from the subject matter and to the execution instead. Every poorly lit scene, every bouncy camera movement, and every meandering shot—they accumulate to the point where your attention collapses under the weight. Eventually you have to turn it off and the odds that you'll ever watch it again are pretty slim.

> *"Ironically, an editor invests weeks or months of intensive work to achieve the impression that nothing has been done at all."*
> —Unknown

Your aspiration should be to spare your audiences from such an undeserved fate. Believe it or not, it doesn't take much to avoid the common trappings. With just a little planning and foreknowledge most can be easily overcome. There's a fine line between each good and bad shot.

Number One: Lighting

A well known tenet in the real estate business is that the three most important things about a property are location, location, and location.

In film and video, the three most important things are lighting, lighting, and lighting.

Lighting is, *hands down*, the single most important factor in video, film, or photography. Don't believe it? Go into a closet, close the door, and start shooting. It doesn't matter *what* your camera is pointed at—without proper lighting it just won't matter. Our "closet-cam" may just be an extreme example. But you can stand in what *to you* looks like a well-lit room but is completely wrong for your camera.

To demonstrate the importance of good lighting, try out this little experiment. Find a room in your home which gets a lot of sunlight. Shoot some video around the room on a bright, sunny day. Later that day, around twilight, shoot some more video of the same room. Then compare the two. It should almost look as if you used two different cameras. But the camera didn't change. The video tape didn't change. The room didn't change. Only the light changed. And that's all it takes to go from crisp & clear to gritty & grainy.

It's odd how in all the endless talk about quality people discuss file formats, optimal compression, re-rendering, data rates, and a myriad of other factors, but rarely do they talk about what it takes to start with great looking footage. I think most people assume you've already shot some great footage and now you don't want to ruin that in post-production. But great footage isn't something that just happens, you really have to go out of your way to get it.

So we'll take a look at various lighting situations, and how to best deal with them. Plus, we'll do it on a budget. Sure, you can have spectacular lighting if you want to spend thousands of dollars and fill up half your garage with equipment. But we'll be a bit more reasonable here! High-end lighting rigs are probably a bit out of the budget of the average user.

Not Enough Light

This is probably the most common situation. Let's say you're indoors, taping a birthday party. The room seems fine to you, yet when you play back the tape, it looks all dark and grainy. Let's take a look at some side-by-side examples. We'll start with a moderately lit room.

Appendix B • Shooting and Composition

How does it look to you? One of the first things you notice with under-lit footage is that it hardly has any color. Everything is grayish, flat, and drab. You'll also notice video noise: a grainy or buzzing effect which detracts from the overall picture.

Take 2. Here we've turned on all the lights, both natural and artificial. As you can tell, the overall grayness of the original image is gone, but it could still use some help. How? What more light is there? Well, you see there are two factors in lighting: 1) how much is present, and 2) how the camera sees it.

Take 3. This is the exact same lighting situation as Take 2, yet the colors are even richer and deeper. We couldn't change the amount of light present, but we did have control over how the camera sees it. In this last case all I've done is set the proper white balance.

White Balancing. If your camera supports manual white balancing, then all you will need is a good sized piece of white paper or card stock. Place it close enough to your camera so that all the camera sees is the paper. Then press the white balance button. This recalibrates the camera, and you'll have the best possible color settings for the given lighting situation.

Still not enough? What do you do if you've turned on every light, opened every window, properly white balanced the camera, and you still don't have enough light?

You still have a few more options:

- *Iris*. If your camera has a manual iris control, crank it open. (If you can't locate it, look for other terms such as **aperture, exposure, auto exposure, gain,** or **f-stop**.) If you do take over iris control, however, make sure you remember to set it back. You can potentially damage the camera by letting in extreme amounts of light.

- *Shutter Speed*. Remember that high shutter speeds don't allow the CCD to soak up a lot of light. Set this back to default levels (typically 1/60, or just "auto").

- *More Lights*! If all the existing lights aren't enough, bring more in. Go to the next room and grab a lamp or two. Torch lamps which bounce light off the ceiling are very good choices. If your camera has an on-board light or lighting attachment, you can use that too, but it tends to create a "spot" effect. This might be perfectly fine, or it might ruin the whole mood. Try it out and judge for yourself based on the situation. The upshot of it is: if you're shooting something important enough, it's worth taking a couple minutes to do your best.

If these tips don't help, well, you're probably just going to be stuck with a low light situation. They're not always avoidable, but at least you will have some tools at your disposal during editing to help make the best of a bad situation.

Too Much Light

When your scene is over-lit, you'll get a new set of problems. The video becomes washed out. As with the low-light situation, you lose colors. But instead of looking gray, everything will be white.

In this case, you'll want to try out everything we learned above, but just do the opposite. Obvious, but true.

- *Reduce Lighting*. If you can. Even if you're outdoors, it may be possible to find a shadier spot to shoot. If all of that is completely out of your control, such as an organized sports event, then you'll have to fall back on your camera to help out.

- *Iris*. If opening it lets more light in then obviously closing it will cut down on the amount of light. Double-check this setting.

- **Shutter Speed.** Try for a higher shutter speed to give the CCD less time to gather light. This will affect the overall look of the video, but go ahead and experiment.

- **Presets.** If your camera comes with special outdoor recording settings, then by all means give them a try. They might have already figured it out for you.

- **White Balance.** This one goes for all situations. Your scene might be washed out solely because the color calibration is off. Reset the white balance (as you should for every significant change in lighting) and then see how things look.

Uneven Light

This is the worst of both worlds. What happens when one part of the frame is too dark and another part is too light? This can be caused by many conditions but the most common cause is backlighting.

Although conceptually the camera functions much like the human eye does, this doesn't always hold true. A strong backlight against an under lit foreground normally spells doom for your image, as shown here. The camera is being bombarded with photons and self-adjusts to that level of light. Under-lit objects don't stand a chance.

Light the Subject. Bringing the subject's illumination up to the same level as the background will even out the image, and you'll end up with a really nice looking picture. Sounds great on paper, but to actually bring your indoor lighting up to outdoor levels, and to keep it evenly lit, just isn't feasible. You'd probably blind everybody too. More often than not, you'll have to fall back on the camera controls instead.

Open the Iris. Just like in low light situations, letting in more light will lighten up your subject. It will also brighten the background, but sometimes this isn't such a bad thing. Odds are the subject is your focal point, so washing out the background might just de-emphasize uninteresting parts of the frame.

Be Careful. There is such a thing as too much of a good thing. Where you cross that line is up to you. This amount of light might be just fine or it could ruin it the whole scene. Another **caveat**: is your camera position and angle stationary? If you're moving often, constantly changing the iris can become a nuisance. Plus, if you're changing it while recording, that's just that much more you'll have to edit out later.

Still not enough? If lighting the subject is out of the question and brightening the background just isn't going to cut it, then you're going to have to manually even out the scene. This may take some creative thinking. Try out these tips:

- *Block the Light.* If possible, move something between the bright backlit light source and the scene. If it's a window this could be as easy as closing the blinds or curtains. You may be able to temporarily hang a blanket to block the light source.

- *Move the Light.* As long as it's not a fixed wall, try moving the light source out of the way.

- *Move the Subjects.* If there's no way to block or move the light source, then move your subjects or the whole scene elsewhere.

- *Move the Camera.* If you can't change the light or the scene, then change your position. Move to a different part of the room. Change the camera angle. This could even be serendipitous—showing you a better spot to shoot from that you might not have thought of.

- *Check Camera Presets.* Again, has the manufacturer already thought of this? Look for presets designed to handle specialized uneven lighting situations. They may have already worked out a combination of settings that works for your situation. Give them a try.

- *Move the Clock.* If you have control over *when* the shooting takes place, then just wait for a better time. Sometimes just an hour can make all the difference in the world. You won't always be able to change the time of the party or the Christmas pageant. But you never know, sometimes it doesn't hurt to ask.

Appendix B • Shooting and Composition

- **Use Magic Fairy Dust.** Frankly, there just may not be anything you can do about a badly lit scene. You're always going to run into that situation where you can't turn off the sun, or have the wedding ceremony move twenty paces to the right, or hang upside down from the ceiling for that optimal camera angle.

If that's the case then hopefully this one bad scene doesn't make up 90% of your final production. Surrounding a bad scene with a lot of good stuff can help de-emphasize it, and it won't look like you're completely incompetent!

There may be some editing tricks that will help you out, but that will be completely on a case by case basis. You'll have to rely on your own experience and intelligence to take care of it. And if you don't have enough of either of those, you'll always have your own common sense! It can do wonders in a tight situation, given the chance.

> *"There is nobody so irritating as somebody with less intelligence and more sense than we have."*
> — Don Herold

Number Two: Composition

Now that your frame is properly lit, the next most important thing is how you arrange the subject matter. I can't put my finger on it, but subject matter perfectly aligned in the middle of the frame just doesn't look right. Perhaps it's because real life isn't perfectly balanced. However, when the subject matter is properly offset, a new kind of balance is brought to the frame. Not one of symmetry, but of the overall interrelation of the objects, be they foreground or background.

This brings us to one of the oldest tenets in frame composition: the *Rule of Thirds*. This involves dividing the frame into thirds: horizontally and vertically. By doing so, you create four imaginary lines with four intersecting points. These are your guidelines for aligning subject matter.

Portrait Framing

Let's start with the human face. Our eyes are naturally drawn to each other. They're the focal point of the whole face: one of the first things we see and the last things we remember. Getting the eyes in the right spot is paramount. Still, I can't tell how many times I've seen pictures with the eyes smack dab in the middle.

How does it look to you? Does it look okay, or does something seem out of place? To me, it always looks like the subject is falling down out of the frame. What we have here is too much *headroom*: the space between the top of the subject's head and the top of the frame. We don't want that...

Take 2. This suddenly feels far more natural. The headroom has been closed and we feel like we're looking directly across at her eyes. Further, the neck and shoulders are all right where we expect them to be. And all we've done is aligned her eyes along that top-third line.

Take 3. This creates a wonderful interaction between foreground and background, although it's still not what I would consider a final shot. You see, there's a waterfall behind her and I think it really needs to be in the frame.

Take 4. As the saying goes, "one step forward, two steps back." True, we *did* reveal the waterfall. And her eyes are still properly aligned along the top-right focal point. Yet we've messed up the *look space* (or *nose space*)—the area between the subject and the facing edge of the frame. This throws the image off balance again.

Appendix B • Shooting and Composition

Take 5. There we go! That's what we were looking for all along. Go back to the very first picture and compare the two. Look at each step in between. Be conscious of your own thoughts as you look at the composition of each frame. I've made the strong implication that each successive frame is *better* than the previous. This is, of course, highly subjective.

Break the Rules! Always remember, there's an exception to every rule[13]. I mean, if *every* frame were composed with strict rules, we'd never have any fun. The bottom line is this: think about each shot. Whether you consciously decide to follow established rules or consciously decide to break them, at least you've thought it out.

Action Framing

When the subject matter is in motion, it's very tempting to follow it around with the camera no matter where it moves. While this might be a good way to keep the frame filled with the subject matter, it also quite misses the entire point of an action shot. Think about how you might watch a dancer on stage. You don't fix your eyes on the dancer and move your head around to match her movement. No, you watch the stage as a whole and let the performer move about freely within those bounds. You should film in the very same manner.

Take a look at these three zoom levels:

Wide   Mid   Tight

---

[13] Except this one.

The wide shot will capture everything, but will also be quite uninteresting. Since the frame rarely *moves*, your audience's attention span won't last very long[14].

The tight shot is good in small doses to help break up the monotony. But, as just discussed, it does not do a good job of capturing motion. What you will end up with is a fixed subject against a moving background, when what you're trying to achieve is the exact opposite.

So that leaves us with the mid shot. The idea is to use your frame to create a small virtual stage. It should have enough space for the subject to move around in without being so far back that you can't see any detail. So if someone's dancing in a circle, frame the circle and let the subject move around. This does take a bit of foreknowledge about the 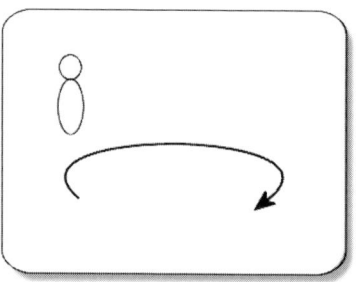 action, but after a while you learn to anticipate. Subjects rarely teleport between spots on the stage.

We introduced the concepts of "headroom" and "look space" above. You have the same concepts here. In particular, your "look space" becomes your action space. You don't want the subject to go flying out of the frame. If the subject is facing and or moving to the right, try to keep them in the left half of the 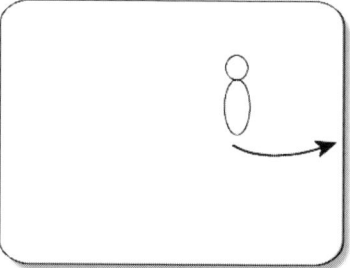 frame, and vice versa. That will leave you plenty of action space and better able to deal with unexpected turns in direction.

Although I've used dancing as an example, these techniques apply to sports, plays, and any other type of "action" event.

Nature Framing
I have some good news! Everything you've learned about composition up until now still applies. The rule of thirds, balance, headroom—they all apply. The only difference is your subjects aren't human.

---

[14] Their snoring and drooling really ruins the evening. Trust me on this one.

Here's a great example to start off with. We have a small waterfall in the woods with some very interesting surroundings. The waterfall is aligned on the left third-line. The entire right third is taken up with trees and earth. The top third has some trees going off into the distance while the bottom third is all water. It's perfect.

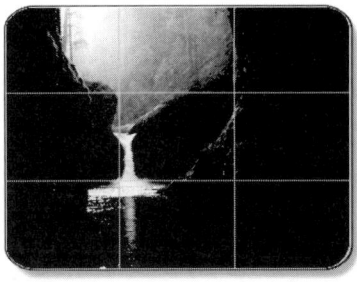

Another good example. The balance, the motion, the overall composition—it's all exactly what we like to see. You might notice there's no look space in this frame, but that's okay. The bird's entire body is taking up the frame. Plus, we don't really feel the same psychological need for look space when the subject is an animal. At least that's my take on it.

Framing the sky is all about getting as much sky into the frame as possible. Doing so helps capture that wide-open feeling. You really get the full sense of something *big* looking at this shot. Compare it to the next shot where the sky and earth are 50/50.

When the sky takes up less of the frame, you feel more closed in. This isn't wrong, if that's what you're going after. As always, rules were made to be broken. Just break them on purpose, not by chance.

Interference in Your Frame

This is about being aware of the entire frame all at times. You may have your subject perfectly lighted and perfectly framed but forget to see the forest for the trees. There have been many occasions where I thought I had the perfect shot looking through the viewfinder. Only later, while reviewing it, I find all sorts of interesting things that I didn't see—*even though I was looking right at them*. Some common mistakes are:

- **Watch the Background.** Are there people moving about? Is there a busy street? Will baby's first steps be recorded with George Carlin waxing poetic on the TV nearby? Your brain can easily tune these out in real life. The camera can't. And when you play them back, they stand out in such a way that your brain can't tune them out. The larger your viewfinder (or monitor) during shooting, the more things like this you'll catch.

- **Watch for Things Touching the Subject.** I don't mean objects physically in contact with the subject, but objects that come in visual contact with the subject, as framed. Your subject may be fifty feet away from that telephone pole, but based on where you're standing, it might be poking right up out of her head.  Somewhat amusing, perhaps, but probably not what you want. (Unless, of course, you're doing the old "holding up the Leaning Tower of Pisa" routine.)

- **Watch for Spare Body Parts.** If there are several people in the scene, you might find stray elbows or have half of a face in the frame. Once again, easy to overlook at the time, but distracting while watching later on.

- **Watch for Nothing.** Does your subject fill most of the frame? Or is most of the frame filled with "nothing?" If it's mostly nothing, then your subject can get lost in all the nothingness, and that can be yet another kind of distraction. Make sure that the thing you want your audience to see occupies the majority of the frame.

- **Watch for the Date & Time.** Oh, there's nothing so brutally amateurish and distracting as having the date and time fill up a significant portion of your screen. With DV, this isn't a problem, since this information is invisibly burned into every frame you shoot. But for analog shooting, make sure this isn't on. If you want the date and time recorded (and you should as it's great for historical purposes) then shoot a few seconds with it on. Stop shooting. Turn it off. Continue. It's a good habit to get into.

Depth of Field

Up until this point, we've been completely preoccupied with composition from a two-dimensional point of view. That is, arranging our subject matter top-to-bottom and right-to-left within the frame. But we have a third dimension to be concerned with. It's called depth.

The depth of field is the zone in front of the camera where objects are in focus. As objects move out of the depth of field, they become blurry. Optically speaking, there's only one point in perfectly sharp focus. But visually, there's a whole range where things are "close enough" and still look okay.

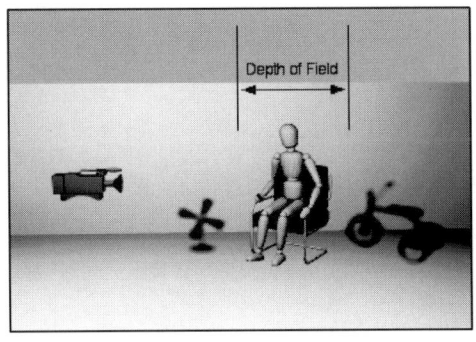

This range is not fixed and you can control its size with your camera's iris. To help get an idea of how this works, think of a pinhole camera—like what school kids use to view eclipses. When the pinhole is small, you get a very small, sharp spot of light. When it's large, the light spot is larger and fuzzier. Aperture affects focus.

The wider the iris, the more light you let it, and the depth of field is narrower. Of course, if your iris is wide open, it's most likely because you're in a low-light situation, and focusing consequently becomes more difficult. (Have you ever watched your camera's auto-focus frantically trying to find something in the dark? It has trouble with this too!) Not enough light means a wide aperture; a wide aperture means no depth of field; and no depth of field means very difficult to focus.

Conversely, when the iris is closed, the depth of field is greater, but you have less light to work with. But just like before, your iris is probably closed due to it being a very bright situation and therefore you may be shooting very well lit scenes.

So what's the point of all this? Well, you can get some dramatic effects by changing the depth of field. What is—or isn't—in focus changes the whole feel of the scene.

Test card

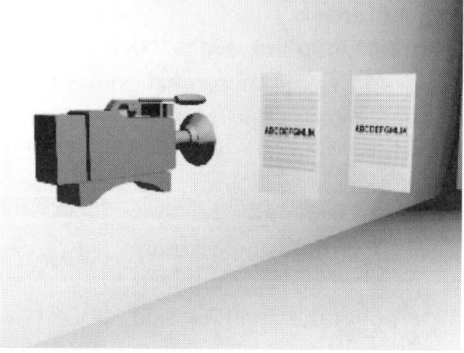
Depth of field test setup

To demonstrate this, I created the above setup. First, I printed out two test cards—just some bold letters and horizontal lines to give the camera something to look at. Next, I took one card and placed it about two feet from the camera, offset to the left. The other was about another two feet beyond that, offset to the right. I then recorded two different images. They turned out like this:

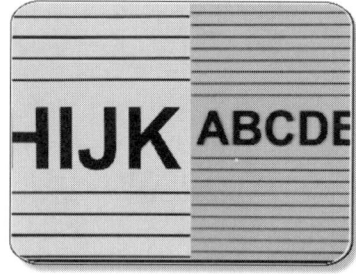
Wider depth of field

Narrower depth of field

The first image demonstrates a wider depth of field. The near card is in focus while the far card is somewhat out of focus (and darker too since it's farther from the light source—did you notice?). Compare that to the image on the right, where the depth of field is narrower. I did not touch the focus control on the camera, yet the focus has changed. This was done by opening the iris, and narrowing the depth of field, thus causing the more distant object to fall out of focus. With a wider iris, the shutter speed had to be increased to compensate for the extra light.

The next two images show this effect using a more realistic example. The image on the left was taken with the camera's default settings. Meaning normal iris, shutter, and exposure settings. The image on the right is in has a narrower depth of field. This causes the guitarist's hands (the closest and furthest things from the focal point) to become blurry. The center point remains in focus.

Wider depth of field   Narrower depth of field

Now if all this seems a bit complicated, you can check your camera for a "Portrait" setting. If it's there, it will set the aperture and exposure for you. Keep in mind though, you'll still have to play around with object positions and the zoom. Try it!

Number Three: Camera Position

There are actually two halves to frame composition. In the last section we talked primarily about where to place the subject matter. This section is about where to place the camera itself.

Camera Height and Angle

What is it about home video that makes it look like "home" video? Yes, we've already talked about lighting and frame composition. But even with perfect lighting conditions (let's say, outdoors on a sunny day) and even with the perfect amount of headroom, something still looks amateurish about it. Can you put your finger on it?

Well, I gave away the answer in the section heading. It's the camera height. I would easily bet that 75% or more of all home videos are shot from the same height. And a majority of them probably use the same angle: pointing right down at the kids. The explanation is obvious: you pick up the camera, you bring it up to your face to look through the viewfinder, and you record.

In 1993, Sharp introduced the ViewCam, the first consumer camcorder without a viewfinder. Instead, you had a four-inch LCD monitor right on the back of the camera. The idea is that this would free the world from the tyranny of the viewfinder: shooting from any height or angle was now possible. No more excuses!

Now, more than a decade later, the "large" LCD viewfinder is nearly ubiquitous. The implementation may be different—it's commonly a side-mounted flip-out screen. Further, it no longer replaces the viewfinder, but supplements it. Yet people still feel the need to bring the camera right up to their head. Great shots are missed every day.

Get Down. Take a look at this frame. This is the standard home movie camera height and angle. It's very obvious that a parent is holding the camera right at face level.

While there's nothing outright *wrong* with this, we can do better.

Compare it to the second frame. By bringing the camera down to waist level, you're now at the perfect height and angle to shoot this kind of subject matter. *What changed*? And I mean that from a psychological point of view. The answer is the key concept behind this entire section: **you're no longer an onlooker but a participant**. By standing

there and pointing the camera down, you're no better than a security camera recording facts. When you put yourself in the scene, it becomes emotional. Now you're *involved*. And that changes everything.

Get Up. You can go the other way too. It may be that in order to get "into" a scene you have to get out of it. Let's say you're in a crowded auditorium or stadium. In this case, you don't want your frame filled with the backs of people's heads. To get above the crowds, get the camera above them. If you're worried about getting in other's way, move to an aisle or to the side of the room, if it doesn't drastically change the shot you're trying to get. It also depends if you're trying to shoot for a half a minute or a half an hour.

Relocate the Camera. By repositioning the camera, you can also bring objects into the frame that otherwise wouldn't have been there. This technique can also help set the proper mood or feeling. For example, if you're outside taking some shots of your cat stalking around the backyard, bring the camera down and back it into a bush slightly. Let the leaves come around the edges of the frame a bit to give a little jungle feel.

Appendix B • Shooting and Composition 403

You'll end up with something much better than "here's my cat from security cam view." If you're at the beach, try moving behind reeds to frame your shot of the water. If you're at a softball game, get a couple shots of the game from the dugout to make it more visually interesting.

Samples. Take a look at the following shots that demonstrate these techniques and more. Study the side-by-side examples and try to internalize what makes one shot better than another[15]. The goal is to spark your own thought processes later when the time comes. *Note*. Keep in mind that each side-by-side shot was taken from nearly the exact same position. Only height, angle, and zoom levels change.

Each shot contains houses, but the one on the right de-emphasizes them in favor of the real subject: the sky. They still provide context.

The right pic is good in its own right, but zoom in on otherwise good scenes and see if you can find shots-within-shots, such as the picture at the left.

Just like *parent cam*, pet owners also tend to shoot at human eye level. On the right, we've dropped right down into the grass, with individual blades visible.

---

[15] I can't say it enough: "better" isn't absolute. I'm calling the pictures on the right hand side *better* only from a traditional frame composition point of view. There could be times and situations where the pictures on the left are better. Like everything in life, it all depends.

Although still taken from eye-level, the shot on the left is better than the one above. But becoming a part of the scene can make all the difference in the world.

This is an example of how *posing* doesn't look very natural. While you *do* want to be a part of your subject matter, you *don't* want the camera to get the attention.

Make sure your subject isn't lost in the frame. We can barely see our tree-climber on the left. A tight shot on the hands really lets you know what's going on.

The tree in the foreground on the left is good for framing, but we haven't captured the action very well. On the right we have our climber looking out of the frame at her goal.

You've probably guessed by now that camera work is an art unto itself. This book is about editing, so I can only scratch the surface on this topic. If you find after a while that filming is more your cup of tea, then by all means focus on the craft.

Stabilization Methods

I don't think there's anything more distracting than shaky camera work. Watching a video with the camera flying all over can actually start to hurt after a while. Remember, a steady shot is a happy shot. There are a few things you can do to either minimize or eliminate the shakes.

Image Stabilization. We already discussed this, but we didn't get into the details. This is good for helping to eliminate small hand movements, or to compensate for slight changes in motion, such as shooting from a moving car. But it's not a miracle worker. If you're really moving around, then your shot is going to move around right along with you.

Tripod. Nothing beats a tripod. Period. Set it up, put the camera on it, and that's it. It's not going anywhere. If you don't have one (or if you don't have a *good* one) it might be worth your while to invest in a better model. One key feature to look for is a detachable (or "quick release") shoe. Your average run-of-the-mill tripod has a post and screw on top to fasten the camera down. However, screwing and unscrewing this can be a real pain. The detachable shoe is a small piece that comes off the tripod and attaches to the camera instead. What you end up with is essen-tially a camera that can just pop right on or off your tripod. No screwing around necessary! The actual shape, size, and release mechanism differs by brand, but they all perform the same function.

In addition to keeping the camera steady, it can also help keep the camera level. In fact, some of the higher end tripods actually come with bubble levels built in, so you can tell if you're square or not. However, don't become over-dependent on this. Sometimes a good eyeball is better. I've had perfectly leveled tripods give me a slightly off-kilter shot. Adding an extra inch to that off leg fixed it, even though the bubble was telling me I was off.

The tripod is not without its downsides. Good ones are big and heavy and you're not exactly going to be able to move around quickly with them. Tripods are mostly for "set it and forget it" operations. Even smaller ones aren't the kind of thing you want to drag around Disney World just to get steady shots. For that, there's the monopod.

Monopod. As you might guess from the name, the monopod is very much like a tripod, only with two legs missing. The name itself comes from the Greek words *mono* meaning, "what good is a tripod" and *pod* meaning, "that only has one leg?"

The monopod is really a best-of-both-worlds solution. You get the flexibility of hand held shots without the burden of dragging a full tripod around. It's lightweight, the leg telescopes quickly, and it's perfect for when you want an "instant stand." Pop it open, slap the camera on it, grab your steady shot, and you're done. It folds up in a flash and you're on your way to your next scene.

Caveat. For both tripods and monopods, you have to watch the depth of the screw. Most modern DV camcorders are *small*. The tape mechanism is really darn close to the case, and the mounting screw hole can be dangerously close to delicate internals.

I guess that's the price of progress. Check your camcorder's documentation for this information, or simply take a close look at how your camera is set up before you tighten up a mount too hard.

Monitoring Recordings

As nice as the little flip-out LCD screens are, it's no contest when you put it up against a real television. In order to *really* see what's going on, nothing beats hooking up an external monitor. That doesn't mean you have to drag your 36" television out to videotape the school play. Small monitors designed just for this purpose are available. I recommend a nine or ten inch monitor for this.

(Anything bigger and you *are* dragging the TV out to the event.)

Why bother with this? The benefits are enormous. Simply separating the shooting from the monitoring means you're not tied to the camera as much. This allows you to raise the camera above your head where you otherwise might not—due to the viewfinder being too far away. LCD screens are atrocious for trying to attain good focus. With a crisp television screen to look at, this is real WYSIWYG (what you see is what you get). The ability to tightly focus, accurately check white balance, and monitor color, all add up to one thing: keeping total control over your video.

Number Four: Camera Movement

Since this is a motion medium, finding a good spot for the camera is only the beginning. You can add even greater dimension to your footage by moving the camera while shooting. Each camera movement has a name. They are:

Pan. Swivel the camera about its vertical axis.

Tilt. Swivel the camera about its horizontal axis.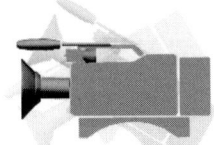

Pedestal. Raise or lower the camera vertically.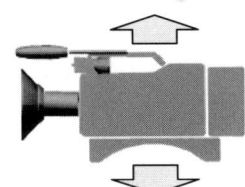

Truck. Move camera to the right or left.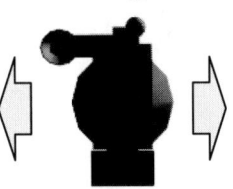

Dolly. Move the camera forward or backward.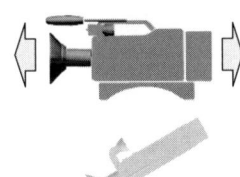

Arc. Move camera around an object.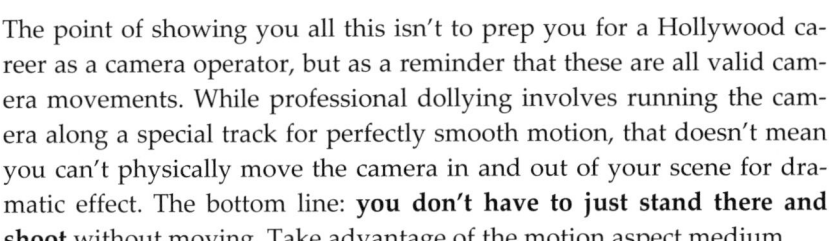

The point of showing you all this isn't to prep you for a Hollywood career as a camera operator, but as a reminder that these are all valid camera movements. While professional dollying involves running the camera along a special track for perfectly smooth motion, that doesn't mean you can't physically move the camera in and out of your scene for dramatic effect. The bottom line: **you don't have to just stand there and shoot** without moving. Take advantage of the motion aspect medium.

Pan and **tilt** are givens. You almost certainly do that right now when you tape with your camcorder. But try a **pedestal** for a shot: start in a squat position then slowly stand up. Don't change the angle of the camera, but raise it, level to the ground, while recording. If the kids are playing soccer, you can **truck** the camera down the sideline. Again, don't change the angle: stay perpendicular to the field: but advance while shooting, keeping the action properly framed. And the **arc** is a beautiful camera movement. The trick is to stay slow and stay steady. Walk around your subject, keeping it more or less centered, and you'll end up with a "stationary" subject against a background in motion.

A Final Word

In computer programming, the old saying went, "Garbage in, garbage out." Simply stated, that meant if you fed invalid data into a system, invalid data is what would come out. The same thing holds true for us. No matter how good the tools are, if you don't start with the good stuff, you can't end up with the good stuff.

C

Text and Typography

This appendix is a primer for learning the fine art of titling. We cover both typography and design elements.

Terminology

We'll start with a few typographical terms you should become familiar with. This list is by no means comprehensive, but serves as a good primer. We'll refer to these terms from time to time throughout the book.

Ascenders & Descenders. An *ascender* is any part of a letter that rises above the *x-height*. A *descender* is any part of a letter that falls below the *baseline*.

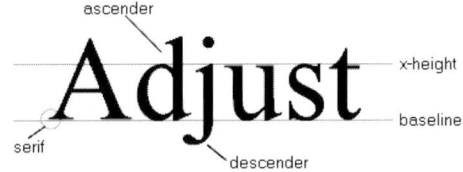

Baseline. This is the imaginary line upon which all text appears to rest.

Character. A *character* is the smallest unit of written language. The term actually refers to an abstract concept rather than a physical or graphical representation. Therefore **a** and **a**, although they look different, still represent the same character. Compare with the term *glyph*, which is the actual physical representation of the character. In this case **a** and **a** are two different glyphs.

Font. The term *font* has fallen into misuse with the advent of desktop publishing. If you ask someone, "What are Times New Roman and Arial?" most will respond, "Why they're fonts, of course." However, they are not fonts. They are *typefaces*. A font is a particular instance of a typeface at a certain point size, weight, and orientation. Therefore, *Times New Roman* is a typeface while *Times New Roman, eleven point, bold* is a font.

Glyph. This is the physical shape of a character.

409

Kerning. This is the adjustment of the spacing between pairs of characters to improve their overall look. For example, some letters, due to their shapes, don't naturally fit well with other letters without some additional adjustment. Common kerning pairs typically contain letters with exaggerated points or angles, or with holes, as follows: A, T, V, W, Y. Often, lower case letters can be moved closer to these letters to make the pair look more balanced.

Look at the examples at the right. In the first example, the **W** and the **a** have not been kerned. The vertical bar shows that there is a significant gap between the two letters making the **W** look much further away from the **a** than it could be. Compare this with the second example where the **W** and the **a** have been properly kerned. In this example, the vertical bar shows that some of the **W** extends over the top of the **a** and vice versa: the leftmost portion of the **a** extends underneath the **W**. Kerning is an important part of maintaining the balance and flow of your text.

Wash

Wash

Leading. This is the vertical space between lines of text. This word always looks to me like it should be pronounced "leeding" but it's actually "ledding". It comes from the word *lead*, which was a commonly used metal used in typesetting: a strip of lead was used to separate rows of type, hence the term.

Monospaced. A typeface is monospaced when every glyph in the character set is the same width. Courier is a good example. Note the two rows of letters here. Compare this to *proportional* spacing below.

```
iiiiiiiiii
oooooooooo
```

Point. A point is a unit of measurement commonly considered 1/72nd of an inch, although the actual value is about 1/72.27 of an inch. This value was set back in 1886 by the United States Typefounders Association. However, desktop publishing has standardized on the 1/72 value and this standard is more or less finding its way back into traditional printing. This means a 72-point letter is exactly one inch tall. For video editing, this points-per-inch figure is essentially meaningless. If I use a 72-point font in my video, it's certainly not going to be one inch tall on every television screen or computer monitor. Still, the *point* gives us a common unit of reference for type sizes.

Proportional. A typeface is proportional when every glyph is only as wide as it needs to be. In other words, the actual width of the glyph is proportional to the width of the character being represented.

Serif. Serifs are the decorative finishing strokes off the main brush stroke of a line. In the previous "Adjust" example, a circle has been placed around one of the serifs of the **A**. (In fact, every letter in that sample contains serifs.) The **S** to the right has serifs at either end of the stroke.

Sans Serif. The word *sans* is French for "without." Therefore, *sans serif* literally means "without serifs." A good example of a sans serif typeface is Arial. Examine the two letters on the right to see the differences between serif and sans serif.

Typeface. A typeface is the general design, style, and overall look given to a set of glyphs. The terms *font* and *typeface* are often (and mistakenly) interchanged in the "desktop" world.

x-height. This is a standard letter reference height, as measured by the lowercase **x**.

As mentioned, this is just a partial list. If this subject interests you, there are many good books available on the subject to help you with further study. In particular, *The New Typography: A Handbook for Modern Designers* by Jan Tschichold is generally recognized as the definitive treatise on the subject.

Quick Typographical & Titling Tips

Before tackling the elements of design, we should go over a few tips when it comes to working with type. I've compiled this list from mistakes I see on a fairly regular basis.

Proper Quotes

Since all our titles, by definition, are going to be done at a computer, you need to be aware of the differences in quotation characters. Way back in the early days of computers, there was a need for only two types of quotes: the single quote (or apostrophe) and the double quote. Early engineers had no need for anything like desktop publishing, and therefore our standard character set only allows for these two quotes within the first 128 characters of the standard ASCII character set.

The proper alternative to these "straight quotes" are publisher's quotes, and should be used whenever possible. Not only are they traditionally correct, they give your work a much more polished look. Some software will automatically convert straight quotes to publisher's quotes for you, and some won't. Be aware, though, even the software that does cannot always be trusted to do it correctly in all cases. Let's look at some examples.

At the right here, is a short sentence without proper quotes. This

> Then they'll say, "That's perfect!"

sentence simply uses the default apostrophe and double-quote characters. While this is fine and perfectly legible, it's not all it could be when design is taken into account. We can do better.

Now examine the same sentence using proper quotes. Note

> Then they'll say, "That's perfect!"

how these quotes curve in the right directions, improving the overall appearance of the sentence. You'll also note that the opening and closing double quotes are actually two different characters. This is very different from straight quotes, which do not come in pairs.

The Apostrophe Problem

The various algorithms that software applications will implement to change straight quotes to publisher's quotes are good for most situations. However they typically fail on an unpaired leading apostrophe character. This is the situation where you have an "implicit" contraction.

This is best illustrated with a few examples. At the right is the famous opening to *A Visit from Saint Nicholas*

> It was the night before Christmas
> can be contracted to
> 'Twas the night before Christmas

by Clement C. Moore. The word "Twas" is a contraction of "It was." For common contractions, such as ***do not*** becoming ***don't***, most software will correctly substitute the correct quote. But I have yet to see any word processor correctly substitute the proper quote in the case where the unpaired apostrophe leads the word, as in *'Twas*. The example above is wrong.

The correct apostrophe is seen here. It is now

> 'Twas the night before Christmas

oriented the same way as you see in the word ***don't***. Although *'Twas* is not a very modern phrase, a more common occurrence of leading unpaired apostrophes happens when you drop the century from a year. The proper way to display 1999 as two digits is actually **'99**. This is one I see used incorrectly all the time. I guess this is a lost art, but I will stand by tradition.

So, if your software does not provide substitutions (or it does, but they are incorrect) how do you type them in? No standard keyboard has publisher's quotes. The answer, in a Windows environment, is to use the Alt key codes. You can enter any character into any document by holding down the Alt key while typing four digits on the numeric keypad. The digits you type will represent the ASCII code representing your desired character. For example:

Character	Glyph	Number
Opening apostrophe	'	0145
Closing apostrophe	'	0146
Opening quotes	"	0147
Closing quotes	"	0148

Therefore, if you need an opening apostrophe, hold down the Alt key, then press 0, then 1, then 4, then 5 on the numeric keypad. Finally, lift the Alt key and you'll see your character. Note that you *must* use the numeric keypad. The top row of numbers on the main keyboard will not work. It's also critical to have Num Lock on. For a full list of character codes, see the tables starting on page 422.

Periods

How many of you learned to type on a real typewriter? Remember those things? I sure do. I especially remember grumbling in class when I was twelve years old: something along the lines of, "I *hate* this. When am I ever going to need to type in my life?" I didn't know at the time the answer would be, "Oh, only about twelve hours of every day." Come to think of it, I'm *glad* I didn't know that back then!

For those of us who learned to type on typewriters, we learned many "typewriter" rules. As you know by now, however, *typing* and *publishing* are not the same thing. Yet I see many "typewriter" rules carried over into amateur publishing and titling work. The most popular error is typing two spaces after the end of a sentence. The reason for this rule was due to the inherent nature of the typing mechanism: fixed-width glyphs. It didn't matter if you typed a capital **O** or a lowercase **i**, they were the exact same width. In order to visually separate one sentence from another—sentences created with equal-width glyphs—you had to insert an extra space between sentences, like so:

```
Now is the time for all good men to come to the
aid of their country.  I think every American
over thirty years old remembers typing this gem.
But that's not the point.  See the two spaces
after every sentence?  This was the old rule.
```

However, with publishing (or titling) you are not simply stringing together sentences. You are designing pages (or screens). Further, you are likely using proportional typefaces more often than not. Because of this page-centric approach to layout, the space between sentences is rarely equal, having been spread out to accommodate the overall page. Just take a close look at any paragraph in this chapter. See how the space between sentences varies? Typewriter rules do not apply.

Color Limitations

Another thing we'll be stuck with for a while is a limited color palette. When color was first introduced into the NTSC broadcast signal, it was done so at a cost: quality. The goal was to somehow introduce color into the signal without rendering current black-and-white technology obsolete. Engineers succeeded, but only to the degree that the image quality and color control both suffered. Just go into any electronics store and stare at a wall of televisions all playing the same program. It's striking how different each image looks. Granted, you are looking at many different manufactures of tubes and electronic components, but a good portion of the differences comes from the signal: NTSC. (Don't worry PAL users you aren't immune. Just because I say "NTSC" doesn't mean you can skip to the next section!)

It's sad, too. We spend all this time, money, and resources to create incredible images, only to dump them to tape and see our efforts wasted. You can buy better videotape, you can buy better recording equipment and cables, you can do anything you want, but in the end, you're stuck with bright shiny graphics being recorded on half-century-old technology. This is just a fact of life.

Color Boundaries

Here's a problem that packs a one-two punch. First, NTSC simply cannot deal well with the boundaries between certain colors. Second, neither can many video compression algorithms. The problem typically arises from high contrast areas: white on black, red and green. For the NTSC side, you'll get bleeding. For the compression problem, you'll get mottling—a natural compression artifact.

I've included two pictures here to show the mottling effect you'll see at a high-contrast color boundary. At the top is the original, uncompressed image. Below that is the compressed result. The compression artifacts—the mottling, noise, or bleeding you see at the boundary—are unavoidable. However, it's not an insurmountable problem. Although you cannot eliminate it completely, there are ways you can help minimize the effect. And these methods are especially important for text. We'll explore solutions and workarounds to these and other problems as we go. This has just been an introduction to get you familiar with some of the issues you may encounter during your editing career.

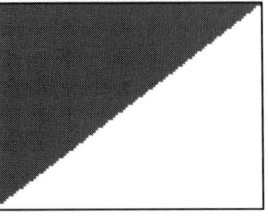

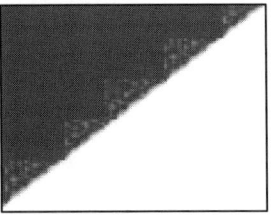

Elements of Design

Your goal as a title creator is to deliver a message. It does not matter if the message is informational, or meant to persuade, humor, or to entice any specific emotion. The key is simple: *you're communicating*.

Inextricably interconnected with the communication is the presentation. It's not just what you say but how you say it. And how you say it should not be an afterthought. It's not as if the *what* and the *how* are two separate entities. They should be thought of as two sides of the same coin, both inseparable and dependent upon one other.

Each time you go through the process of creating a title, consider:

- What is your goal?

- How can you get there effectively?

- If you don't like it, how can you fix it?

This is true whether it's a single word or a dozen screens of text. The steps you go through may only take you a few seconds or you may spend days on it, depending on the complexity of your project. But in any case, you should still go through the same basic steps.

What Is Your Goal?

If your goal is to deliver a message, then how can you attain it? There are many options, but I like to go about it by establishing what I like to call *The Three A's*: determine your **A**udience, pick an **A**venue, and create an **A**tmosphere. In other words, *where am I going, how am I getting there,* and *what's the mood?*

Audience

Your audience is the most important factor. In some cases, maybe the audience is just you. Yet you alone still count as an audience, and that's no reason to change these methods. In most cases, however, the audience will be someone else and knowing him, her, or them is important. Are you transferring photographs to videotape for an anniversary party? Are you assembling a training film? Are you creating a television commercial for a community theater? Hopefully your audience will be obvious at the beginning of a project, but there are times when it's either *not obvious,* or it *changes.* There can be times when the perfect title page has to be completely scrapped because of a change in audience. For example, maybe the photo project that was going to be shown at the bachelor party is suddenly going to be shown at the wedding rehearsal. A change in your audience can change your entire approach!

Avenue

Your avenue is how you get there. These are the tools you use and the ultimate medium used to display your message. In our case, the tools we use are our computers and our software. The software, specifically, is MediaStudio Pro, since this is our common denominator. The possible media for display will differ. Some content will never leave the computer. Some will end up on videotape. I've even used video editing tools to create printouts of video and graphics, so output is not always limited to an electronic display.

Atmosphere

Your atmosphere is the mood you create or the tone you set for the project. This is tied very closely to both your intended audience and your intended message. How do you want the audience to feel about the message? How do you want them to react? Are you trying to elicit an emotional response? Don't think that just because you're simply creating the ending credits to your latest production, that there won't be a desired emotional response from the audience. And by "emotional," I don't necessarily mean bringing your audience to tears simply by the way you scrolled "Produced by Me" up the screen. Perhaps your desired response is laughter, in which case you want to create a humorous atmosphere. There are many moods and many ways to work with those moods.

How Can You Get There Effectively?

The few next sections cover the major components of your titles: fonts, color, layout, and content. This is just an introductory level examination. I purposely avoid lengthy details about how to correct the mistakes shown here. My goal at this point is to create awareness.

Using Fonts Effectively

Nothing can make or break a message as much as the fonts used. Careful selection of typefaces and fonts is necessary because this is an area where it's very easy to lose control. Software makes it easy to select and apply fonts to text, but I have yet to see any software program ask, "Are you sure you want to use these two typefaces together on the same page?" Since there are far more font combinations that don't work together than those that do, when left completely up to chance, odds are you'll get a combination that won't work well. So let's not leave it up to chance!

• Charlie's First Rule of Fonts: **Less Is More**. When at all possible, try to limit yourself to just one or two typefaces while using only a very small number of fonts within that typeface. Take a look to the right. As far as a title page goes, this leaves a bit to be desired. The initial impression of a page is very important. This is the instant when your audience sees the page and grasps it, almost subconsciously. When you look at this example, what do you see? First of all, you see a lot of words. And what's worse, you see a lot of words using a lot of different fonts. So why is this a problem? The simple answer is clarity. Too much "design" on one page is visually distracting and will cause your message to be lost. And if your message is lost, then what was the point in the first place? Granted, you can still read this playbill, but it's unnecessarily difficult, especially when trying to grasp it quickly.

• Charlie's Second Rule of Fonts: **Make Them Legible**. This has nothing to do with color, contrast, scroll speed, or any of other factors that affect the overall look of your titles. This has everything to do with the faces themselves. With the huge number of typefaces available, there are a surprisingly large number of them that are difficult to read. Don't make your audience waste time trying to decipher a tricky font.

It should be obvious when you first glance at a typeface whether it might work or not, but when in doubt, try getting a second opinion. Sometimes just asking someone else can help you out in ways you wouldn't have thought of. "What do you think of this?" "Can you read it?" "What does it say to you?" Listen to the other person and gain insight about your design. Don't let your ego get in the way. Accept constructive criticism. If you have difficulty with constructive criticism, then I suggest this: get your second opinion from you: *your future self*. If you're unsure of your design, leave it for a day then come back later—after you've forgotten about it for a while. Then make note of your new "initial" impression. Sometimes a good night's sleep is all it takes.

* Charlie's Third Rule of Fonts: **WYSINAWYG.** Note the extra "NA" in this familiar phrase, meaning: what you see is *not always* what you get. There are actually very few instances where your font designs look equally nice in both the design medium and the display medium. The worst-case scenario is the transfer from an RGB monitor to videotape. Fonts that look good on your computer can look terrible on your friend's VCR. See the clean and crisp *Title Page* here? That's our original; what we designed.

The next image is the actual output after rendering. You can see how we begin to lose detail. And when displayed on a television monitor (especially when movement such as scrolling is involved) the text can take on a shimmering effect. Since this is related to our color boundaries problem, this is something we're just stuck with for now. Since the new rule is WYSINAWYG, the only way to compensate for this is to constantly preview your work in the final destination medium. If you're working on a title destined for tape, then near the beginning of your project render a test and print it to tape. Look carefully at the results. If things still look reasonably well, continue. If not, make adjustments. Then, as the project progresses (specifically, as you make major design changes) continue to check your work. What we're trying to avoid is what's known as *The Surprise*. Surprises are bad. Keep checking your work as you go, and you'll never run into the embarrassment of showing a someone a tape and being forced to fall back on, "Um, this looked really good on *my* computer."

Appendix C • Text and Typography

- Charlie's Fourth Rule of Fonts: **Always Use the Proper Case**. Most typefaces contain both upper and lowercase letters. Using the correct case for your lettering is very important mainly because improper use can make you look bad. The worst offense in this category is the all-caps error. Some typefaces were designed for all-caps, and some were not. Let me repeat that. Some typefaces were designed for all-caps, and some were not! Do not confuse them. In other words, *PLEASE, PLEASE DO NOT DO THIS*. See what I mean? This is just plain wrong. *If you must use a script, at the very least, please use the proper case*. Wasn't that a little better?

So there you have my four rules. And like all rules, they can be bent or broken. The ultimate goal is to get to the point where you internalize these guidelines, get lots of practice, and know when to follow them and when to break them.

Using Color Effectively

The choice of color can make or break your work as easily as the font selection. One problem area for color choice is *contrast*. Without the proper contrast, words might as well be invisible. For example, using all-white lettering on a very light background.

And like having too many fonts, having too many colors can also be a turn-off. Have you ever seen a web page where every other word and every other cell in a table was a different color? The first thing I think of when I see this is: *amateur*. It's hard to say that without sounding condescending, but the fact remains: overuse of color is a telltale sign that the designer has no grasp of the concept. Color is a wonderful tool for conveying a message. Color can also be your worst enemy.

Often times you will find your text isn't a simple color-on-color decision. It's one thing to create black text on a white background. It's another to overlay text on an image or video source. The next biggest color hurdle is proper blending with your background. When overlaying text on video, it's important to be conscious of how the text interacts with the background. It's all too easy to let your message get lost in its surroundings. Take a look at the example here. To be honest, I went a bit out of my way to pick a typeface and color scheme that did not go well together at all. (If you can read, "The next stop on our tour" in this image, you've got better eyes than I do.) But it does illustrate how a poor choice of colors can make your text fade away into oblivion.

By contrast, examine this next version of the title. This one uses a bolder font, and includes a drop shadow to help offset the text from the background. However, the color of our text hasn't changed, and it is still too close to the colors found in the background. This may be an improvement over our first attempt, but we can try to do better. A good place to start is by finding a color that is complimentary to the background. That should help make the text stand out.

Colors are formed in one of two ways: via the subtractive or additive process. The subtractive process is the one we all learned as schoolchildren. When white light hits a blue surface, we see blue because the surface absorbed all the colors in the spectrum *except* blue. That is, all the other colors were *subtracted* from the white light. According to the subtractive process, we mixed paints to learn, for instance, how blue and yellow make green. The three primary colors are red, blue, and yellow. They can be combined in pairs to create the secondary colors, purple, green, and orange. Split-complimentary colors are the colors found opposite each other when arranged in a circle. Red is across from green, blue is across from orange, and yellow is across from purple.

For us, the video editors, the additive process is important. This is how light—not pigment—is combined to form colors. Our computer monitors and television screens emit light. The three primary colors of the additive process are red, green, and blue. Their complimentaries are cyan, magenta, and yellow, respectively. When you need the highest possible contrast, put two compliments together. Just keep in mind the problems with high-contrast areas we discussed earlier.

I tried using two different complimentary colors for our current problem, and I won't waste any ink here showing you the results. It simply wasn't enough. Sometimes it takes more than color to get you out of a situation like this. We'll examine the alternatives later on.

Using Layout and Content Effectively

Last, and certainly not least, are layout and content. I group these two together because they are truly one in the same. Arguing the importance of layout versus content is like trying to decide whether your heart or brain is more important. It's impossible. They are both equally important, each serving a critical function in a symbiotic relationship. Neither will survive long without the other.

To jump-start your conscious awareness of the dual-importance of layout and content, just look around. Watch television. Get in the car and drive around looking at signs. Read a magazine. Find a newspaper. Go out to the mailbox and read some junk mail. It's everywhere, and a good ninety-five percent of the population doesn't see it. In fact, that's the hallmark of a perfect melding of layout and content: *you don't see it*. Consider for example this road sign. What's wrong with this combination of layout and content? Absolutely nothing. The layout is simple and straightforward, just like the message. How different it would be if instead you saw something like this other sign. Doesn't quite have the same impact, does it? In fact,

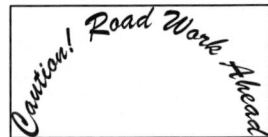

it looks rather silly—almost as if it were a joke. This is a contrived example, but one that will help you realize that content and presentation are equally important.

If You Don't Like It, How Can You Fix It?

This will invariably be the last step of any project—titling or otherwise. I remember reading many years ago a humorous page entitled, "The Laws of Projects." One in particular has stuck with me all this time. It stated: *Projects progress quickly until they are ninety percent complete. Then they remain at ninety percent complete forever.* How true! Revisiting the clay analogy, you start with a shapeless lump then begin to mold. You progress from zero detail, increasing levels of intricacy as you go. During your progress, you will find things you like and things you don't like. But therein lies the danger. You can possibly remain at ninety percent complete forever. There will always be *just one more thing* you can do to a project. But never forget the law of diminishing returns. At some point continued effort expended on a project will not significantly alter the final outcome. As an extreme example, you could spend an hour deciding whether a font looks better at 36 points versus 38 points. In the end, that could probably be reckoned an hour wasted.

So Why Bother?

In spite of that last paragraph, I don't want to scare you away completely from that tweaking stage. As dangerous as an endless "fix it" cycle is, it is nonetheless a very important step in the process. The trick is finding that fine line between perfecting your work and *over*-perfecting it. You do not want to deliver sub-par performance. But you don't want to spend any longer on a project than you absolutely have to.

How To Fix It

The first step is identifying what's wrong. The old saying goes, "I don't know much about art, but I know what I like." While humorous, there's actually a pretty good philosophy behind that statement. After you've edited, rendered, and then watched your video, certain feelings will strike you, both positive and negative. You'll know what you like and what you don't like. What I like to do is to take notes while watching, even if it's a clip as short as a minute. I'll play the clip over and over and over, continually taking notes about it primarily writing down the things I need to fix. Once I'm satisfied with my notes, it's back to MediaStudio Pro (or whatever tool I'm working with) to take care of the problems.

Exactly *what* you do at this point depends on the problem. Most of my problems I find are either timing or rhythm related. I like to have a good synergy between the audio and video, something we should all strive for. I like to make my edit decisions based on tempo, rhythm, and musical changes. However, sometimes these cues, although mathematically correct, might not always be "right" when it comes to the final video. There might be an offbeat cymbal hit in the music, not on-cue, yet located where you'd like to make a visual change. I'll note that in my critique-pass of the video then tweak the clips on the timeline accordingly.

Other problems might involve transitions, overlays, titles, and so on. The potential problems are limitless—as are the potential solutions. But if you find something satisfactory, and you don't think it will take an inordinate amount of time to fix, then go for it. It might be tedious, but the end result is what's important. When you're all done, the final video is all you have, and you will quickly forget the blood, sweat, and tears that went into its production. Don't apologize to your audience. Show them what you can do!

Character Tables

The next few pages show the extended 8-bit ASCII character set. To use one of these extended glyphs, press and hold the Alt key while typing the 4-digit number out on the *numeric* keypad.

Extended ISO Latin 1 Characters in a Serif Font

0128	€	0160		0192	À	0224	à
0129	☐	0161	¡	0193	Á	0225	á
0130	‚	0162	¢	0194	Â	0226	â
0131	ƒ	0163	£	0195	Ã	0227	ã
0132	„	0164	¤	0196	Ä	0228	ä
0133	…	0165	¥	0197	Å	0229	å
0134	†	0166	¦	0198	Æ	0230	æ
0135	‡	0167	§	0199	Ç	0231	ç
0136	ˆ	0168	¨	0200	È	0232	è
0137	‰	0169	©	0201	É	0233	é
0138	Š	0170	ª	0202	Ê	0234	ê
0139	‹	0171	«	0203	Ë	0235	ë
0140	Œ	0172	¬	0204	Ì	0236	ì
0141	☐	0173	-	0205	Í	0237	í
0142	Ž	0174	®	0206	Î	0238	î
0143	☐	0175	¯	0207	Ï	0239	ï
0144	☐	0176	°	0208	Ð	0240	ð
0145	'	0177	±	0209	Ñ	0241	ñ
0146	'	0178	²	0210	Ò	0242	ò
0147	"	0179	³	0211	Ó	0243	ó
0148	"	0180	´	0212	Ô	0244	ô
0149	•	0181	µ	0213	Õ	0245	õ
0150	–	0182	¶	0214	Ö	0246	ö
0151	—	0183	·	0215	×	0247	÷
0152	˜	0184	¸	0216	Ø	0248	ø
0153	™	0185	¹	0217	Ù	0249	ù
0154	š	0186	º	0218	Ú	0250	ú
0155	›	0187	»	0219	Û	0251	û
0156	œ	0188	¼	0220	Ü	0252	ü
0157	☐	0189	½	0221	Ý	0253	ý
0158	ž	0190	¾	0222	Þ	0254	þ
0159	Ÿ	0191	¿	0223	ß	0255	ÿ

Extended ISO Latin 1 Characters in a Sans Serif Font

0128	€	0160		0192	À	0224	à
0129	☐	0161	¡	0193	Á	0225	á
0130	‚	0162	¢	0194	Â	0226	â
0131	ƒ	0163	£	0195	Ã	0227	ã
0132	„	0164	¤	0196	Ä	0228	ä
0133	…	0165	¥	0197	Å	0229	å
0134	†	0166	¦	0198	Æ	0230	æ
0135	‡	0167	§	0199	Ç	0231	ç
0136	ˆ	0168	¨	0200	È	0232	è
0137	‰	0169	©	0201	É	0233	é
0138	Š	0170	ª	0202	Ê	0234	ê
0139	‹	0171	«	0203	Ë	0235	ë
0140	Œ	0172	¬	0204	Ì	0236	ì
0141	☐	0173	-	0205	Í	0237	í
0142	Ž	0174	®	0206	Î	0238	î
0143	☐	0175	¯	0207	Ï	0239	ï
0144	☐	0176	°	0208	Ð	0240	ð
0145	'	0177	±	0209	Ñ	0241	ñ
0146	'	0178	²	0210	Ò	0242	ò
0147	"	0179	³	0211	Ó	0243	ó
0148	"	0180	´	0212	Ô	0244	ô
0149	•	0181	µ	0213	Õ	0245	õ
0150	–	0182	¶	0214	Ö	0246	ö
0151	—	0183	·	0215	×	0247	÷
0152	˜	0184	¸	0216	Ø	0248	ø
0153	™	0185	¹	0217	Ù	0249	ù
0154	š	0186	º	0218	Ú	0250	ú
0155	›	0187	»	0219	Û	0251	û
0156	œ	0188	¼	0220	Ü	0252	ü
0157	☐	0189	½	0221	Ý	0253	ý
0158	ž	0190	¾	0222	Þ	0254	þ
0159	Ÿ	0191	¿	0223	ß	0255	ÿ

Standard ISO Latin 1 Characters in a Dingbats Font

Code	Glyph	Code	Glyph	Code	Glyph	Code	Glyph
0000		0032		0064	✑	0096	♊
0001		0033	✎	0065	✌	0097	♋
0002		0034	✂	0066	✋	0098	♌
0003		0035	✄	0067	☛	0099	♍
0004		0036	✍	0068	☚	0100	♎
0005		0037	🔔	0069	☜	0101	♏
0006		0038	📖	0070	☞	0102	♐
0007		0039	🕯	0071	✊	0103	♑
0008		0040	☎	0072	✌	0104	♒
0009		0041	☏	0073	✋	0105	♓
0010		0042	✉	0074	☺	0106	er
0011		0043	📧	0075	😐	0107	&
0012		0044	📪	0076	☹	0108	●
0013		0045	📫	0077	💧	0109	○
0014		0046	📬	0078	☠	0110	■
0015		0047	📭	0079	⚐	0111	□
0016		0048	📁	0080	⚑	0112	❏
0017		0049	📂	0081	✈	0113	❐
0018		0050	📄	0082	☼	0114	❑
0019		0051	📃	0083	●	0115	◆
0020		0052	📰	0084	❄	0116	◆
0021		0053	🗒	0085	✝	0117	◆
0022		0054	⌛	0086	✞	0118	✣
0023		0055	🗄	0087	✠	0119	◆
0024		0056	🖱	0088	✡	0120	☒
0025		0057	🖲	0089	✡	0121	⌂
0026		0058	💻	0090	☾	0122	⌘
0027		0059	⌨	0091	☯	0123	✺
0028		0060	💾	0092	ॐ	0124	❀
0029		0061	🖥	0093	✤	0125	"
0030		0062	⊕	0094	♈	0126	"
0031		0063	✍	0095	♉	0127	⬚

Extended ISO Latin 1 Characters in a Dingbats Font

Code	Char	Code	Char	Code	Char	Code	Char
0128	⓪	0160		0192	🕐	0224	→
0129	①	0161	○	0193	🕐	0225	↑
0130	②	0162	●	0194	🕐	0226	↓
0131	③	0163	●	0195	↵	0227	↖
0132	④	0164	⊙	0196	↵	0228	↗
0133	⑤	0165	◎	0197	↶	0229	↙
0134	⑥	0166	○	0198	↷	0230	↘
0135	⑦	0167	▪	0199	↶	0231	←
0136	⑧	0168	□	0200	↷	0232	→
0137	⑨	0169	▲	0201	↯	0233	↑
0138	⑩	0170	✦	0202	↝	0234	↓
0139	❶	0171	★	0203	✂	0235	↖
0140	❶	0172	✲	0204	✄	0236	↗
0141	❷	0173	✳	0205	✁	0237	↙
0142	❸	0174	✴	0206	✃	0238	↘
0143	❹	0175	✵	0207	✄	0239	⇐
0144	❺	0176	✶	0208	✂	0240	⇒
0145	❻	0177	✢	0209	✃	0241	⇑
0146	❼	0178	✧	0210	✄	0242	⇓
0147	❽	0179	✤	0211	✁	0243	⇔
0148	❾	0180	✦	0212	✃	0244	⇕
0149	❿	0181	✪	0213	⊠	0245	↘
0150	☙	0182	☆	0214	⊠	0246	↙
0151	☙	0183	◐	0215	◀	0247	↗
0152	☙	0184	◑	0216	▶	0248	↖
0153	☙	0185	◐	0217	▲	0249	▫
0154	☙	0186	◑	0218	▼	0250	▫
0155	☙	0187	◐	0219	⊂	0251	✗
0156	☙	0188	◑	0220	⊃	0252	✓
0157	☙	0189	◐	0221	∩	0253	☒
0158	·	0190	◑	0222	∪	0254	☑
0159	•	0191	◐	0223	←	0255	⊞

D

Tips and Things

From the obvious to the obscure, here are a number of tips I've collected and have found worth sharing.

General Tips

1. Save your work! Video editing is very complex and frankly, you just never know when something's going to go wrong. Don't get three hours into a project only to have your system lock up *right before* you decided to save. The Auto Save feature can really help out.

2. Save your work! Don't just save one copy of each project. Save multiple copies. I have seen project files get corrupted *while saving*. If that's your *only* copy of the project file, then you're just going to have to start over. Add a number to each save.

   For example, if your project is named myvideo.dvp, then save it as myvideo1.dvp for a while, myvideo2.dvp a little later, and so on. In a way, this is what Auto Save can already do for you. However I like using both together, as described on page 105. This not only protects you from crashes, but gives you "super undo" capabilities.

3. Check the work you've saved! There are rare instances where Ctrl+S isn't giving you the peace of mind you think it is. If a project does not get saved to disk correctly, Video Editor will continue to function and you're none the wiser. Periodically close your project and re-open it just to make sure.

4. If you don't see the New dialog box when you start Video Editor (or even when you select File | New), press F6 and check the Display New dialog box option.

5. If you get tired of seeing the Options dialog box displayed every time you drop a transition on the timeline, press F6 and uncheck Display Options dialog box.

System Tips

1. If for whatever reason your disks are formatted with the FAT32 file system, you should really consider changing, unless you have a specific reason not to. As MediaStudio Pro can be used only with Windows 2000 and XP, NTFS should be your first choice. It is possible to seamlessly convert all your disk partitions to NTFS, which do not have the limitations of FAT. Consult your Windows help file for instructions how to do this.

2. For optimal performance, you should have a separate disk drive dedicated for video files. System drives are inherently messy and simply not well-suited for video work. See page 101 for more information.

   To get an idea of why performance matters more with video, imaging opening a word processing document or a spreadsheet. If it takes four or five seconds to load, you don't really notice, nor do you even care. One or two extra seconds isn't going to ruin the file. Now, imagine as you're printing a video stream to tape it takes an extra second to get a particular frame out. Ouch. That glitch is there permanently. You'll have to start over. Running 25 or more frames per second for minutes (or hours) on end without a glitch takes a lot of work. It's within your power to help this situation by segregating the video files from the system files.

3. During installation, Video Editor asks where you want Preview Files stored. If you weren't quite sure what it was asking (and who would, not knowing anything else about the product?) then you can change the setting on the Preview tab of the Video Editor Preferences dialog.

   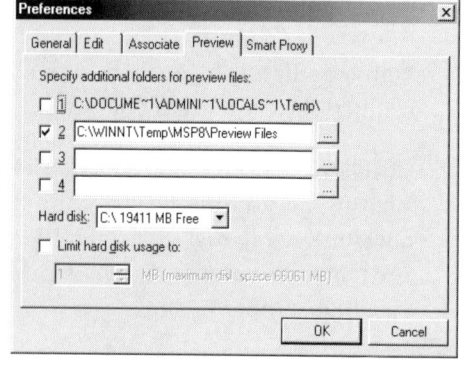

   These are the video and audio files rendered as a result of executing previews in Video Editor. If you keep them on your system drive, they'll be subject to fragmentation which can lead to poor performance within Video Editor. On the other hand, if you keep them on your video drive, then lots and lots of previews may degrade the performance of this drive. Ultimately, it's your call.

Editing Tips

1. The order of templates on the New dialog box can be changed by dragging. If there are one or two templates you use more often than others, why not bring them to the top. Of course, if you only use *one* template all the time, then the default *Previous Settings* is your ticket.

2. If you press the control key and drag a clip, an exact copy of the clip is created. The original clip stays where it was. This even works if multiple clips are selected—each will be duplicated.

3. If you have a preview range selected, you can fine-tweak it using the Edit | Preview Range command.

4. You can create a preview range automatically by right-clicking the bar above the timeline. The command "Set Preview Range" creates a range between the two nearest edit points.

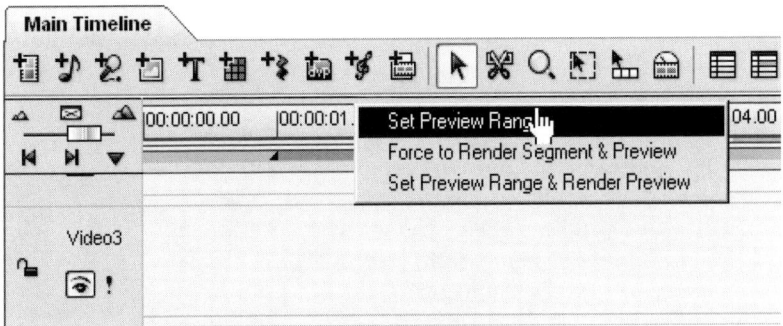

5. You can right-click keyframes to display a popup menu allowing you to delete, copy, or paste keyframes.

6. You can change audio levels directly on the timeline. A horizontal line runs down the center of each audio clip. This is the audio level. Clicking on this line creates a control point that can be moved up or down to increase or decrease the volume. To remove a control point, drag it down and off the audio clip.

7. Timeline cues can be named. You can quickly view the name of a clip by right-clicking on it. Right-click a second time to make the name go away.

8. To easily copy moving paths or other clip attributes from one clip to another, select the clip and press Ctrl+C. Then select the destination clip(s), right-click, and choose Paste Attributes from the pop-up.

9. Always add a leader to your projects. This doesn't have to be a full SMTPE countdown. A black color clip just a few seconds long is enough. When exporting back to tape (DV or analog) this buffer gives the recorder enough time to "roll up." This prevents the first part of your project from being cut off. Same thing goes for the back end of the tape. Let a few seconds of black roll at the end too.

10. To play only the trimmed portion of a clip in the Source Window, press the space bar.

11. Trimming a clip using the duration dialog box can *sometimes* be quicker than trying to set in and out points using the GUI. It gives you precise control regardless of your current timeline resolution.

12. If you have a video filter you want applied to every clip in the project, use Global Filters, set on the Project Settings dialog box.

13. Video Editor can create a project for you. From the Storyboard gallery in the Project Tray, load up your clips, arrange them, then click the Add to Timeline button.

14. If you've manually positioned a title clip within the frame, you can no longer use animation or text effects on it.

15. You can digitally transfer CD audio tracks directly to disk using the Record from CD function in Audio Editor. (A process known as *ripping*.) You can use Ctrl+D as a shortcut for this function.

16. If you're about to make an edit and it says, "This action cannot be undone" remember that *every* action can be undone if you save the project first. Save the project, do the action, and if you want to undo it, simply use File | Restore instead of Edit | Undo.

17. Delete extraneous clip or timeline cues, so they don't interfere with snapping while editing.

18. Tracks can be added or removed using the Add/Delete Tracks dialog box. Access this dialog box by clicking on the Add/Delete Tracks button on the timeline toolbar.

    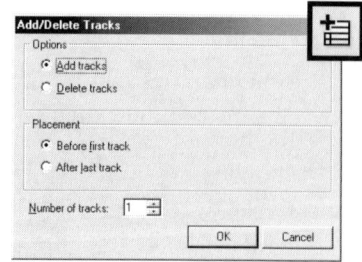

    More than one track can be added at a time. Tracks can also be added below track Video1 as well.

19. With ripple editing turned on, holding down the shift key while inserting a clip in the middle of another clip will split the target clip to make room for the new one.

20. In multi-camera editing, it's of paramount importance to not change the horizontal position of synchronized clips. In order to copy and trim a synchronized clip, do this: 1) **Ctrl+Click** and drag to make a copy in an empty track; 2) make sure the original clip and its copy are aligned; 3) use scissors to trim the copy. All remaining frames will still be synchronized with the original.

21. Star Wars-like scrolling credits can be simulated with moving paths. But you might find it easier to use an external tool. Movie Maker, which is bundled with Windows XP, can create this effect. Another good third-party tool is called LSText found at http://lsmaker.uw.hu.

22. In order to copy the Project Tray from one project to another, simply copy the associated *.veproj* file and rename it to match the destination. For example, let's say you have two projects: ProjectA.dvp and ProjectB.dvp, and you want to copy the Project Tray from A to B. Just copy ProjectA.veproj to ProjectB.veproj and open ProjectB.dvp. You may have to relink, depending on their relative locations, but it works.

23. Don't use virtual clips gratuitously. They are, of course, very effective devices, but they come at a performance cost.

Navigation & Keyboard Tips

1. When using a mouse with a scroll wheel, the wheel can be used for various navigation within Video Editor. On the timeline, you can scroll back and forth. In the Preview and Source Windows, it allows you to "play" your video a frame at a time.

    Unfortunately, the wheel motion isn't consistent between the two. For example, pushing the wheel forward moves forward on the timeline but backward in the Preview and Source Windows.

2. When moving long distances across the timeline, use the thumb of the horizontal scrollbar (the "thumb" is the little box in the scrollbar showing your current position). This is usually quicker than using the arrows, scroll wheel, or clicking outside of the thumb.

3. You can use the right and left arrow keys to move back and forth through the timeline. The J and L keys do the same.

4. If a clip is selected, the right and left arrow keys will move it on the timeline, a frame at a time.

5. The up and down arrow keys will move a selected clip between tracks.

6. The K key will play the timeline.

7. If a clip is selected, you can use the left and right arrow keys to reposition it one frame at a time.

8. If you have a lengthy project, and you need to move long distances, change your timescale resolution to something larger, 1-minute or more. This way each screenful of data covers more of the project.

9. The Ctrl+Home key sequence moves to the beginning of the timeline. (If it doesn't, it's because the timeline doesn't have focus.) Similarly, the Ctrl+End key sequence moves to the end of the timeline.

10. The Ctrl+PageUp and Ctrl+PageDown commands move you through the timeline stopping at every edit point.

11. If you've set a lot of cues and are having trouble finding a particular one, use the View | Cue Manager command.

12. You can go to any point in the timeline quickly using the Search | Go To command, or Ctrl+G for short.

13. You can find any clip quickly using the Search | Find Clip command, or Ctrl+F.

14. You can automatically display tool windows in Video Editor by pressing Ctrl+1, Ctrl+2, through Ctrl+8. Try it out!

15. You can press Ctrl+M while a clip is selected to display the moving path dialog box. If the clip does not have a moving path, then Ctrl+M does nothing. Similarly, you can use Ctrl+R for overlay options, Ctrl+A for audio filters, and Ctrl+D for video filters.

16. To quickly and temporarily select a new editing tool, press the **S** key for Scissors, the **Z** key for Zoom, the **T** key for time, the **E** key for track select, and the **F** key for audio crossfade. When you release the key, the tool will go back to the default clip-selection tool.

17. Pressing shift can modify some editing tool shortcuts. Shift+Z will zoom out of the timeline, Shift+E will select all tracks.

18. Pressing the **U** key will slice all currently selected clips at the playhead position. If no clips are selected, all clips will be cut.

19. With a clip selected, pressing the F7 key will launch an external program to edit the file. If the clip is a transition, then the Transition Options dialog box is displayed.

Selection Tips

1. You can select all clips in any track by clicking the track button.

2. You can select multiple adjacent clips by holding down the Shift key before selecting.

3. You can select non-adjacent clips by holding down the Ctrl key before clicking. You can also add clips to an existing selection in this manner.

4. You can select video and audio clips together using the Time selection tool, the Track selection tool, or the Select All command, Ctrl+L.

5. The Track selection tool allows you to select an entire track and even move the entire track all at once. This is similar to the full track select discussed in tip #1, but additionally has the ability to select across multiple tracks.

6. If you right-click on a clip while it isn't selected, you see attributes. If the clip is selected, you will get a pop-up menu containing just about every function applicable to that clip.

7. You can select multiple clips and then group them. Once grouped, you can move the collection of clips around as you would a single clip. You cannot, however, perform clip-related functions to the entire group. They must be ungrouped first.

8. In a file-selection dialog box, you can select all files by clicking the first file once, then while holding the shift key down, select all files in between. In a common Windows dialog, however, this frequently causes the last file to be placed at the front. You have two choices: with the control key down, click the first file twice (not a double click) and it will be placed in the selection range correctly.

9. In a file-selection dialog box, your other option is to press Ctrl+A to select all files. If you don't want all files, hold the control key down and click the ones you don't want to deselect them.

Miscellaneous Tips

1. There's a program preference labeled, Check Ulead's site at start every X day(s). It's a good idea to leave this on. Ulead doesn't abuse this nor do they shove things in your face all the time. If that were the case, I'd say stay away from it. But as it is, it's unobtrusive and can often display pertinent product information.

2. Edit with headphones.

3. If you're creating alpha channels in other programs and you keep getting confused as to which parts show through and which parts don't, just remember, "black blocks, white lights".

4. Keep disks running optimally by **defragmenting**. Right-click on "My Computer" and select "Manage." Under storage you'll see "Disk Defragmenter." Follow the prompts from this point on, beginning with Analyze. This is where Windows figures out how bad the spaghetti situation is. If it's bad, you then defragment.

5. When opening or saving files, you might see a small button with an arrow on it. If you click this, you'll see a list of all the recently used folders. This is a great feature if you navigate back and forth between several directories routinely. I wish this little widget was built into the standard Windows dialog boxes.

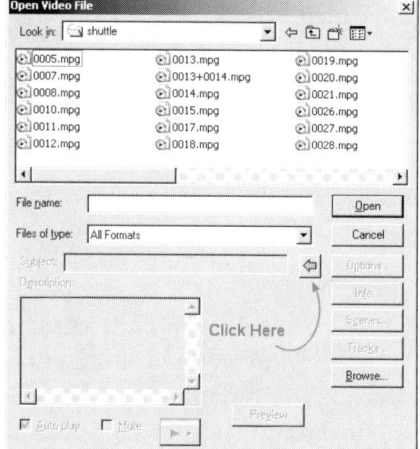

6. When physically numbering photos for a photo montage, be very careful that any numbers you put on the photograph do not damage the photograph. Also, if you use a dark marker, make sure the numbers do not show through on front.

7. If you get stuck on something for a while, just get up and walk away. I know it can be hard to do, but sometimes it can really help. Or just visit http://www.homestarrunner.com for a while.

8. If you've set up a project using certain settings: codec, number of overlay tracks, etc., you can save this as a project template. When

you start Video Editor, you can select this template from the New dialog box. You cannot save clips with a template.

9. Moving paths don't have to move. Set identical keyframes to stop a moving path from moving.

10. Transitions don't have to move either. You can set a transition to 50% at both the start and end points to get a "static" transition. This can be used for, say, a split-screen effect in conjunction with one of the Wipe transitions.

11. If you have special transition settings that you use over and over, click the Add button in the Transition Options dialog box. This will save the current settings to the Production Library, after which you can drag-and-drop these settings at any time.

    (Not only transition options: but moving paths, filter settings, and just about everything.)

12. Customized settings in the Production Library can be saved or loaded to or from disk. Right click on the appropriate *Custom* folder in the Production Library and click Save or Load. This is a good way to move settings from one computer to another or to share among friends.

13. Many drop-down lists accept values that do not appear on the list. For example, the frame rate drop-down lists contain standard values such as 30, 29.97, 25, 24, and so on. But there's nothing stopping you from typing 14 if you want.

14. Right click the instant play button for playback options.

15. Always check the Ulead site for program updates.

16. But don't download updates just because they're there. Video Editing is a very delicate equation. Always remember *if it ain't broke, don't fix it.*

17. Create a shortcut to DVD MovieFactory and you won't have to launch Video Editor just to do some disc authoring.

    By default, it's located in:

    c:\Program Files\Ulead Systems\Ulead MediaStudio Pro 8.0\
      DVD Authoring\DVDMF.exe

From Windows Explorer, right-click the file, and drag it to your desktop. Select "Create shortcut here" when prompted.

18. To squeeze every last pixel out of your screen, turn off the standard and panel toolbars. (Personally, I found I rarely used them, and enjoyed the extra space, however small.)

19. If you've started a project in a prior version of Video Editor, it's always best to finish it in that version. Projects in later versions cannot be opened in earlier versions, and if you run into a problem, you'll be stuck. A clean break between versions is best.

E

Troubleshooting

I'm quite certain that there are more things that can go wrong than I could ever write about in one appendix. I've tried to grab what I feel are the most common stumbling blocks and provide helpful solutions. But I'm counting on you to let me know if it's truly helpful or not. So, same thing goes here: you're encouraged to submit any problems or comments for a future edition.

Please use the feedback page at http://www.getting-results.com/feedback.

Capturing

Error message, "Either no video capture driver is installed in this system, or no device is connected."
If you have successfully captured video before, then there's a good chance a video capture driver is installed. Therefore, it's probably the second reason. If you have a DV camera using a Firewire cable, make sure the cable is securely plugged in on both ends. It doesn't take much for it to come loose, yet not fall out. Make sure the camera is powered on and is in Playback or VCR mode for capturing.

Why do I have to press OK to start capturing?
If you would like to begin capturing as soon as you press record, go to the video capture settings dialog box, click on the Advanced tab, and uncheck "Display message before capturing."

Capturing starts too soon. Can I delay capture?
Maybe. The "Display message before capturing" setting described above is only available when capturing from an analog video source through an MJPEG capture card, for example.

Do my captured images have to be BMP format?
No. You can change them to just about any image format on the Preferences dialog box, Capture tab.

Editing

SmartRender isn't working.
This is a broad area, but the most common problem, by far, is the fact that your project settings do not match the clips in your video. And even if your video clips already match, keep in mind that *any* changes to these clips means they will have to be re-rendered. By "changes" I mean: transitions, video filters, playback speed, title clips, and overlay clips. Carefully check that your file formats and project formats match: frame size, frame rate, compression, ... everything.

There are strange pixelly things in my video.
If your final, rendered video doesn't look quite right, try rendering the whole thing again, but this time without SmartRender. Make sure that box is unchecked when you create your video file.

There are out-of-place frames in my video.
It's possible you have confused preview files. Using the Preview Files Manager, delete them for your current project and re-render. Or try rendering with SmartRender turned off. Or both.

How can I save an image from the Preview or Source window?
From the Window menu, select Save Image To. You can send the image to the clipboard, to disk, or directly to the Production Library (referencing a disk file that Video Editor creates and names).

I've got a "buzzing look" in my video.
There are two main causes for a buzzing or vibrating look. The first is that field orders have been mixed. That is, some clips are upper field order, others are lower, and now they're mixed together in the same project. This will make the entire clip vibrate slightly but steadily.

If, on the other hand, only parts of the image are buzzing, it could be compression artifacts. Very straight or very fine lines are difficult for most compression algorithms to handle. For example, let's say you're doing a photo montage, and Uncle Stan's shirt has thin horizontal stripes. These might vibrate in the final image. To combat this, try softening the area in your image editor with a "soften," "blur," or "average" tool. It can do wonders without adversely affecting the quality.

I just created a Title clip, but the edges are cut off on my TV.
This is due to television overscanning. See page 215 for more information.

I've got noise at bottom of my frame.

This is a normal part of an analog video signal. It's not normally seen on television due to overscanning (again, see page 215 for more information). If you're planning on sending the image straight back out to TV, then you can safely ignore it. If your image is going to end up on a computer screen *or* if 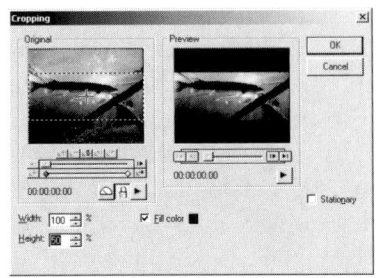 you are going to shrink the image so that it's edges are seen within the title safe area, then you should crop it.

You can do this with the Cropping video filter. Drag the filter to the clip in question and then go to the filter options. Set the width to 100% (since you do not want to crop the left or right sides). Set the height to a value just large enough to cover the noise. Be sure to make the end keyframe match the start keyframe, or your cropping will change over the duration of the clip.

Why are my files so big?

If you've rendered your one-minute project to a file, and find that the file is *huge*, make sure you didn't render uncompressed. First, check your project settings. Press Alt+Enter or use File | Project Properties...

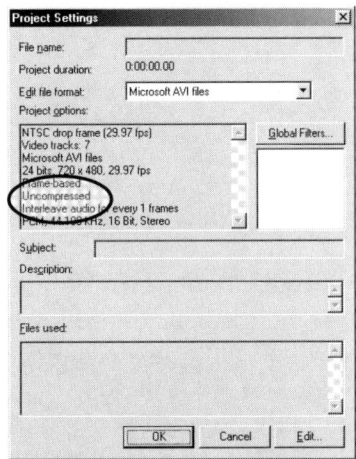

If your project settings look like this, you'll need to change them. Click the Edit button to display the Project Options dialog box. At that point, click the AVI tab, and set your compression correctly. (Anything but "None.")

So how big should your files be? Check out page 76 for a discussion.

The Preview Window isn't updating.

If you're doing something and expecting the Preview Window to update, but it's not, make sure you're actually looking at the Preview Window. Since the Preview and Source windows are frequently docked, you may be looking at the wrong window. It's happened to me.

What happened to everything in my Project Tray?
The thumbnails stored in file with a *veproj* extension. The file name is the same as the project name. If this file gets deleted, the Project Tray will appear empty. If this file gets corrupt or confused, the thumbnails appear as white boxes with Xs. I've not found a way to fix this, other than deleting the veproj file and starting over. Nor have I found any rhyme or reason as to why it happens at all.

I tried to undo a change in the Effects Manager and lost all my changes.
Changes made within the Effects Manager appear to be outside the normal undo system. Here's an example. Add a moving path to a clip. Change the start position. Change the end position. Now click Undo. I would *expect* the undo to apply to my changing the end position. However, it removes the moving path from the clip completely.

Now try this. Add a moving path to a clip. Press **Ctrl+M** to display the modal dialog box. Change the start and end positions. Click OK. Now click Undo. This time it undoes the changes we made in the dialog box. The path is restored to its state before we entered the dialog box.

Ouch. Be very careful with the undo function while using the Effects Manager. You may undo more than you bargained for. (Fortunately, Redo *will* undo the undo. So all is not lost.)

Video Editor freezes quite often, for thirty seconds at a time!
It's quite likely that Auto Save is turned on and saving every ten minutes or so. If you have a complex project (or even a not-so-complex project with several timelines) saving the project can take a while. And if Auto Save kicks in periodically, it will seem like random freezing. If this is the case, consider increasing the interval. If you like living on the edge, turn it off completely. Just remember, Auto Save is like a fire extinguisher: just because you've never needed it doesn't mean you'll *never* need it.

I saved captured clips to the Production Library and don't see them.
It's very likely they ended up at the top level of the Media Library. Don't click on the Video gallery: click one level up from there.

Do video filter regions support alpha channels?
Yes and no. You can use an image containing an alpha channel as an image matte for a video filter region. However, the pixel values in the alpha channel are either on or off. This is a bug. There's no workaround.

When I preview my work, I can't see any Video Filters.
Make sure "Apply video filters" is checked on the Video Editor tab of the Project Options dialog box. You can access this dialog box by first pressing Alt+Enter to display the Project Settings, then by clicking the Edit button.

I can't find *window name*! Help!
Every once in a while, perhaps due to a stray mouse click or some other issue, you may find a window has gone missing. The quickest thing to do is to recall a previously saved layout, such as Standard (1024x768). If after doing this, the window still isn't visible, then it probably went to a parallel universe.

The Effects Manager is missing all its controls!
It's probably just been all scrunched up due to resizing. Drag the window pane splitters out to re-expose the controls.

Audio

I'm trying to record narration but it's not working.
First, double-check to see whether it's not working at all, or if it *is* working, but recording sound very, very quietly. If you're system is properly configured, you should have no trouble recording. The trouble usually comes from using the wrong type of microphone. Most sound cards' microphone inputs are expecting "line level" signals, not "mic level" signals. Most microphones need to be amplified before they're usable. If you haven't yet purchased a microphone, look for one specifically designed for computer use.

Also, most computer mikes are "electret" which require a voltage to operate. A few sound cards, designed for professional use, don't provide this because they assume the user will be using a dynamic or condenser mike with the appropriate preamplifier.

I have the right microphone, but it's still pretty quiet.
Make sure you're speaking *very* close to the microphone. Also, you can boost your signal within Video Editor by changing the volume of the clip. In many cases, this works just fine. Just don't go overboard.

When I fade out my audio clip, it doesn't fade out at all.

It's possible that the music in your clip ends before the end of the clip, and that the fade out effect is being applied to silence, like so:

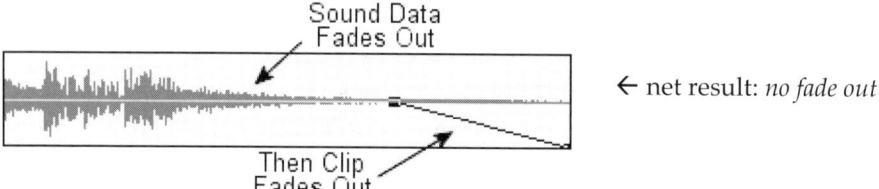

← net result: *no fade out*

If this is the case, trim your clip first. Make sure the end of the clip matches the end of the music, and things should work out.

I was videotaping outside and the wind is really loud!

Once recorded that way, there's not much you can do to recover. However, next time you can be more prepared. A screen will be needed to shield the microphone from excessive wind. This screen can be as small as a piece of foam that goes directly over the microphone to a large off-camera object deflecting the wind.

I've noticed my camera has 12 bit or 16 bit audio recording. Which should I use?

Most DV cameras default to 12 bit recording. It's a lower sound quality, but leaves two extra audio channels free for subsequent audio dubbing. The 16 bit mode records better than CD quality (48kHz to be exact) but does not allow audio dubbing.

Since you're now a PC-based video editor, it's unlikely you're going to be using your camera for editing: audio or otherwise. I would recommend going with the 16-bit audio, not just for higher performance, but for greater compatibility.

Disc Authoring

I can't add a chapter menu. I've checked the box, but I can't switch to it.

This is most likely because you have not set any chapter points. To fix this, go back to the first authoring step. While on this first screen click Add/Edit chapters. Once chapters have been added, on the next step you'll be able to select the menu from the Currently displayed menu drop down.

What if I can't turn off the thumbnail numbers?

If you see small numbers next to the thumbnails, but can't turn them off, your project is probably set up for VCD. For VCD disks, these numbers are required, since this format doesn't support the same kind of navigation you're used to with DVD.

Why is my audio out of sync with my video?
This is usually caused by a data rate problem. Be sure to use the templates and re-encode any time it asks you to, even if you think it shouldn't have to. Use 16-bit audio whenever possible. Also, using MP3 files as a source can be a problem. Try to use uncompressed audio.

Why won't my DVD play in my mom's DVD player?
Older DVD players will play *only* factory-pressed discs. Just because the data format itself is standard doesn't mean the materials are. Burnable discs use a completely different material to store their data. Home DVD players that aren't engineered to read these types of discs simply won't. The disc will spin for a while and the player will report "no disc."

The player will have to go out of its way to support formats other than DVD-Video. Virtually 100% of home DVD players play audio CDs. This isn't because DVD and CD discs are compatible, it's because they're literally building two machines in one. So it is with other optical disc formats. It's up to the manufacturer to decide which formats its players will support.

Fortunately with such home burning having such widespread popularity, the manufacturers were quick to jump on multi-format players. It's not uncommon to find a disc player for just $50 that plays DVD, CD audio, DVD-R, DVD+R, DVD-R/W, CD-R, CD-R/W, and so on. I'd say it's probably time your mom got a new player.

Also keep in mind that not all players will accept discs burnt in all formats. For example, very few NTSC DVD players will accept discs recorded in the European PAL format, although most PAL players will accept NTSC discs, albeit sometimes with degraded quality.

For anyone really interested in learning just about everything you'd ever want to know about DVD, I recommend Jim Taylor's *DVD Demystified*. It's the most in-depth book on DVD I've ever seen.

Miscellaneous Topics

Drop Frame vs. Non-Drop Frame
This is definitely in the Top Five Most Confusing Topics for beginners using NTSC. (The topic is irrelevant for PAL users.) Panic usually arises when someone is having trouble with SmartRender, and are worried that

their project properties say 30 fps and the output is 29.97 fps. The confusion is compounded by the fact that "dropping frames" is a bad thing. This is what happens when your system cannot keep up with the video, and it skips over frames in a desperate attempt to stay in time.

So if dropping frames is bad, why would someone specifically set their project settings to be "drop frame"!? The answer's easy: they're two completely different subjects. Time to set the record straight!

First Concept. When talking about drop or non-drop, we're discussing the *project* and not the video. Timecode is just a numbering system used to give unique addresses to individual frames. Standard SMTPE timecode uses hh:mm:ss:ff notation. The first frame is 00:00:00:00, the second frame is 00:00:00:01, and so on. When you've reached the total number of frames for one second, you bump up the second counter, and start counting frames over:

    00:00:00:27
    00:00:00:28
    00:00:00:29
    00:00:01:00
    00:00:01:01

Second Concept. The timeline's timecode is different from your video's timecode. The number of frames in your project is independent of how many frames are in your video clips. You could have a three-second video at one frame per second, giving you three frames total. If your project is 30 fps, it's going to create 90 frames irrespective of your clips.

Third Concept. With drop frame timecode, it's mightily important to note that no frames are actually *dropped*. If you're creating NTSC video, your video will be 29.97 frames per second. Period. That's just the way NTSC is, and nothing you can do in Video Editor can change that. It doesn't matter if your project is 30 fps, 24 fps, 15 fps, or 3.141592 fps.

However, 29.97 is kind of difficult for people to do the math in their heads. Thinking in terms of 30 fps is much easier, and no one cares too much about being off by 0.03 frames per second. The way drop-frame works is to count frames until that 0.03 frame difference adds up to a whole frame, then it skips over a number to compensate. This is to ensure that the timecode on the timeline accurately reflects the amount of real time that has elapsed. That is, if the timeline says 10 minutes, 0 frames, then your project is exactly 10 minutes long: no more, no less.

Non drop frame, on the other hand, just keeps counting frames as if it was 30 fps, but it isn't.

Take a look at this picture:

This is the timeline at 1-frame resolution for a project crossing the one-minute mark. You'll see frames for 59.26, 59.27, 59.28, 59.29, then 01:00.02. What happened to 01:00.00 and 01:00.01? They were dropped. But if you look at the video frames, no actual video frames were dropped. All we did was skip the numbering.

That's because at one minute, zero seconds, and two frames into the project, one minute, zero seconds, and two frames have elapsed. This is the cumulative effect of being off 0.03 frames every second. It's simply a correction that ensures the time on the timeline will be the same time as your wrist-watch.

Final Note. Look closely at the timecode in the above picture. Did you notice something? The separator between seconds and frames is a dot and not a colon. (00:01:00:02 vs. 00:01:00.02.) MediaStudio Pro uses this notation to indicate non-drop vs. drop-frame. Here's a helpful mnemonic: *a dropped dot is drop-frame code.*

You talk about "0001.mpg" but I don't see ".mpg" in my file name.
Windows distinguishes different file types by their extension: the letters following the final dot in the file name. For example, the file video.dvp has a file type of "dvp" or Video Editor Project File. If you do not see the file type, go to folder options click the View tab and uncheck the setting, "Hide file extensions for known file types."

I'm trying to use Smart Trim, but my clip doesn't show up on the list.
Let's say you have a long clip and you've cut it into several parts. You then want to save the individual parts as separate disk files. You go to File | Smart | Trim and you can't do anything. Why? I'm pretty sure this is a bug. It seems that if all the clips are still there, it doesn't see that any "trimming" has happened, and won't load it into the list. If you delete at least one of the sub clips, this will work.

In order to create a video with NTSC safe colors, I checked the appropriate color filter. I then added a graphic containing pure red. When I

rendered my video, the pure red came right through. Is the color filter not working?
Well, in a way—no, it's not working. This filter *only* works when using color pickers. So if you create a color clip, or pick a color for some text, or similar, the color filter will change it to a safe color. It seems a bit misleading to me. That is, you'd expect the filter to work no matter what. But it is what it is.

I've got some clips on the timeline that appear black. When I scrub, the Preview Window is black too. What's going on?
This is usually caused by a relink problem, often in conjunction with virtual clips. You have two courses of action:

1) On the timeline containing the problem clip (open up virtual clip(s) to get there, if necessary) explicitly use the Project | Smart | Smart Relink function. Or...

2) If that doesn't work, right-click each clip and use the Replace With function, replacing each clip with a copy of itself. I know, it sounds weird, but this has worked for me a couple times in the past.

Is there an easy way to relink image sequences?
Unfortunately, image sequences don't relink the way normal clips do in a project. In all reality, you have to re-create the image sequence from scratch. If you know, project files don't contain media clips—only "pointers" to media clips or references to file names. Image sequences are no different. The UIS file just points to the first frame of the sequence and the number of frames to expect. (For some odd reason, the UIS file also contains its own full file name, including the directory.)

Sometimes (and I haven't found the magic incantation yet) the UIS file will smart relink on its own, and you're all set. On the majority of occasions it doesn't, you'll have to re-create it.

Glossary

"I don't know what this word means!" We've all been there and we've all been frustrated or confused because of it. No one will disagree: the lack of a definition of a key term can hurt. You might feel inconvenienced. You might even feel dumb. But you should feel neither: it's a normal part of learning, an opportunity to expand yourself.

I've tried to compile a good list of terms. Of course, it's probably a given that the *one term* you're looking for is the *one term* that I didn't get in here. If so, let me know. I'll get you the answer as well as update the glossary for downloading.

A/A Roll. The process of editing a single video stream into a final mix.

A/B Roll. The process of editing two video streams into a single mix.

Action Space. In frame composition, an area kept open for the subject to move into.

AE. Abbreviation for Audio Editor.

Aliasing. The "jagged" or "stair-stepping" look that text or graphics show. It's a result of using vertical and horizontal pixels to represent non-vertical and non-horizontal information.

Alpha Channel. The name given to any channel beyond the three color channels of red, green, and blue, used for various effects, especially for transparencies.

Amplify. To increase the volume of an audio signal. When working in Audio Editor or with audio filters in Video Editor, amplification is one tool at your disposal for changing volume.

Animatic. A pre-production cut of a project, using a combination of rough audio, image, animation and video.

Anti-aliasing. A method used to smooth aliased text or graphics by blending the edges with the surrounding pixels.

Aperture. The component of a camera lens that determines how much light can get in. Synonymous with *iris*.

Arc. A camera movement technique whereby the camera rotates or arcs at a constant radius around the object being filmed or recorded.

Artifacts. Any unwanted side effects of a process. For example, when capturing video at a high compression ratio, the resulting video looks blocky. These "blocks" are known as artifacts of the compression algorithm.

Aspect Ratio. The ratio between the width of a screen and its height. The common television standard is 4:3, meaning there are four horizontal picture elements for every three vertically.

Authoring. The process of creating a disc, including menu creation, chapter point selection, graphics, and buttons.

AVI. Audio Video Interleave. File extension given to Microsoft Video for Windows files.

Batch Capture. A hands-off method of capturing, whereby the user makes a list of "in" and "out" points on the source tape, then the software does all the work after that.

BG. Abbreviation for "background."

Blue Screening. A keying method replacing a blue background with corresponding image data from a second source. See also *Keying*.

Bit Rate. See *data rate*.

Burning[1]. Image processing technique to make light portions of an image darker.

Burning[2]. The process of transferring data to and creating a recordable optical disc.

Capturing. The process of bringing real world information into the computer. Capturing video means transferring/converting video data from an external device to your file system. Capturing audio can involve the transfer of CD files or digitization of analog audio sources. Capturing

Glossary

images can mean grabbing stills from a video stream or scanning photographs.

CCD. Charged coupled device. The chip in your camcorder that converts light energy into an electronic signal.

CG. Character generator.

CGI[1]. Computer-generated imagery.

CGI[2]. Abbreviation for MediaStudio Pro's CG Infinity program. CG Infinity is part of the separate Video Graphics Lab program.

Chrominance. The color component of a video signal, controlling the levels of hue and saturation. Compare luminance.

Clip. The base object in the video timeline representing visual, aural, or other information.

Codec. A contraction of "compressor/decompressor." The software algorithm used to compress and encode video information.

Color Bars. A video test signal used to calibrate video devices for color correctness.

Color Clip. A clip made solely of color that can be used for backgrounds, fades, or other effects.

Color Depth. The number of bits used to represent a color. An n-bit color depth is capable of representing 2n colors. For example, 1-bit color depth gives you 21 colors, which is 2: black and white. Compare to 24 bit color depth giving you 224 colors, or 16,777,216 colors.

Color Space. The modeling system used to represent color. RGB (red, green, blue) is one color space. CMYK is another (cyan, magenta, yellow, black) typically used for print.

Component. Component video keeps the chroma and luma values of the video signal separate. The values do not interfere with each other, thus maintaining a higher video quality. An S-video cable is an example of this component separation.

Composite. Composite video combines the chroma and luma information into one signal. Standard RCA phono plugs are an example of this combination.

Compression. The method of reducing the amount of space a file needs. There are two basic types of compression: lossy and lossless. A lossy compression discards data in an irretrievable fashion. The JPEG and MJPEG compression algorithms are examples of lossy compression. A lossless compression scheme reduces data with the ability to completely recover it later. A zip file is an example of lossless compression.

Crossfade. The simultaneous fade out of one clip while another clip fades in. This is also known as a dissolve (not to be confused with Ulead's dissolve transition). Applies to both video and audio, but within Video Editor, crossfade is specifically a video transition.

CU. Abbreviation for "close up."

Cue. A method of marking a location within a clip or on the timeline to be used later as a "bookmark," alignment point, or other editing reminder.

Cut. The method of transitioning from one clip to another with no break or overlap. The single most common transition ever.

DAT. Digital audio tape.

Data Rate. The amount of video or audio data stored, played back, or transferred per second. Commonly expressed in kilobits per second, kilobytes per second, or megabytes per second.

Depth of Field. The area in front of a lens where objects appear in focus.

Device Control. The ability for software to control and external piece of hardware. For example, the Video Capture module being able to rewind, fast forward, and play a camcorder.

Dialog Box. A window used by a program when direct user input is necessary.

Digital. Any numeric representation of an electronic signal.

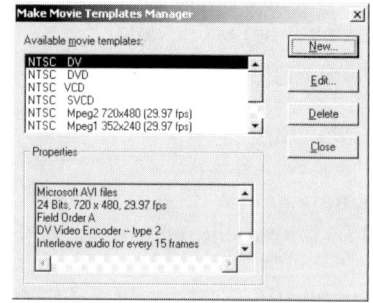

Digitize. The process of converting continuous analog input into a stream of numbers by sampling the signal amplitude at regular intervals and determining a corresponding discrete value for the sample.

Disc Image. A hard disk file which is a byte-for-byte representation of the file structure of a disc. Disc burning software operates most efficiently when burning from disc images. If you are planning on making multiple copies, burn to a disc image first.

DPI. Dots per inch. A unit of measure of print or screen resolution.

Drop-down list. An input control used to specify one value from a list of several choices. Some drop-down lists will only let you select from the pre-defined values. Other drop-down lists (called "combo-boxes") let you type in a custom value over and above what's in the pre-defined list.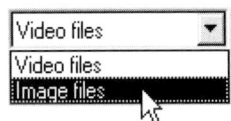

Drop Out. The visual artifacts caused by missing or corrupt sections of magnetic video tape.

DTV. Desktop Video. The method of using a personal computer to aid in the production of videos. Applies to both linear and non-linear systems.

Duration. The length of time it takes to play a video file or the amount of time a clip takes on the timeline. The longer the clip, the longer its duration.

DV. Digital Video. Technically, all non-linear editing is digital video, but the letters "DV" are reserved for video of a very specific compression and format. DV cameras record video information digitally from the start: never as an analog signal.

DV cable. Another name for a FireWire cable.

DVD. Digital video disc (or digital versatile disc).

DVE. Digital Video Effects.

DVP. File extension for a Video Editor project.

EDL. Edit Decision List.

Effects. Any process applied to a clip that alters the clip itself. Video filters, transitions, overlays, are just a few examples of effects.

Effects Manager. An all-in-one tool for accessing effects parameters and synchronizing keyframes for a clip.

EMI. Electromagnetic Interference.

Fade. A reduction over time in the intensity or volume of a clip.

Field. Half of a frame. In cathode ray tubes, each frame is painted in two passes: odd lines followed by even lines. The odd and even sets of scan lines are each called fields.

Filmstrip. A method of displaying a video file where individual frames are taken from the video stream and displayed end-to-end:

Filter. A method of passing a stream of data through an algorithm to produce an altered stream of data. In other words, the method used to apply special effects to audio or video information.

FireWire. A high-speed, two-way interface for transferring data. It wasn't specifically designed for video, but the video industry has been the largest adopter. Originally developed by Apple Computer. Also known as IEEE 1394.

Frame. The smallest logical unit of moving picture information. A rapid succession of frames displayed creates the illusion of motion.

Frame Rate. The number of frames per second in a video stream. If there are five full frames in one second of video, its frame rate is 5 fps.

Frame Size. The x-y dimensions of the frame, expressed in pixels. A typical full-sized frame has a frame size of 640x480. The actual values vary by hardware and target medium.

Freeze Frame. The method of "pausing" a frame in a video stream to create the illusion of a still picture, while, in fact, the video stream continues uninterrupted.

FX or F/X. Effects (Because the word sounds like the letters F and X.)

Gallery. Any folder in the Production Library or Project Tray that contains thumbnails. These thumbnails represent either various media files (video, image, audio) or MediaStudio Pro objects (filters, transitions).

GB. Gigabyte or 1,073,741,824 bytes. Sometimes 1,000,000,000 bytes.

Headroom. In composition, the area between the top of the subject's head and the top of the frame.

Horizontal Resolution. The measurable amount of video information contained in a horizontal scan line. Not to be confused with the number of vertical scan lines: 525 for NTSC and 625 for PAL. The horizontal resolution determines image quality.

IEEE-1394. See *FireWire*.

Image Sequence. A series of images stored as separate files, but when taken as an ordered unit, can be treated as a video stream. Files are typically named TEST0001, TEST0002, TEST0003, and so on. The file extension will vary by the image type.

Infinite Loop. See *Loops, infinite*.

Iris. See *aperture*.

IXA Files. A proprietary disc image format used by Ulead. See also *disc image*.

Jitter. Small, fast vibrations in an image caused by synchronization problems, such as mixed field ordering. Jitter is also used to describe fluctuations of a signal resulting in unstable output (audio or video).

JPEG. Joint Photographic Experts Group. Also the name given to the compression algorithm they developed.

KB. Kilobyte or 1,024 bytes.

Keyframe[1]. Some video compression schemes reduce data by only storing changes between one frame and the next, rather than storing two whole frames. Every now and then an entire frame must be stored, however, as a reference point. This frame is known as a keyframe.

Keyframe[2]. A point in a clip where certain attributes are set. Two such points can create two distinct states for the clip, such as a moving path where the clip begins with a frame size of 640x480 and ends with a frame size of 160x120. Or a color clip that begins red and ends blue. All the in-between frames are calculated by the software, a method known as tweening.

Keying. A method of successively replacing one pixel in an image with the corresponding pixel in another image, according to attributes defined by the type of keying. For example, color keying allows you to pick one color in the image and replace every occurrence of it with the corresponding pixel in a second image.

Leading. Typographical term. The vertical spacing between lines of text.

Linear Editing. This refers to traditional videotape-based editing. Since tape runs in a straight line from one end to the other, it's known as a linear format. You cannot get from one point to another without passing all points in between. Due to its linear nature, you cannot insert new material without affecting the existing material.

Longitudinal Time Code. A method of writing timecode on a video tape. It uses a linear audio track to store frame address information. It can be recorded before or after the video signal is recorded. Compare Vertical Interval Time Code.

Loops, infinite. See *Infinite Loop.*

LTC. Pronounced "lit-see". See *Longitudinal Time Code.*

Luminance. The brightness component of a video signal, the traditional "black and white" image, since only degrees of brightness are recorded, without respect to color.

Mask/Matte. An image used in conjunction with keying to help define or describe how pixels are replaced.

Matrix, The. Still a pretty cool movie.

MB. Megabyte, or 1,048,576 bytes. Sometimes 1,000,000 bytes.

***Menu*[1].** A small window displaying a list of options from which the user may select. Most applications have a menu bar across the top of the entire application. These menu items bring up pull-down menus. Right-clicking an object often brings up a pop-up menu.

***Menu*[2].** In disc authoring, a screen of choices or controls used to control playback navigation.

MJPEG. Motion JPEG.

Moving Path. A set of attributes for controlling the size and position of a clip through time. This can be used to move a video clip across the frame, to resize it or change attributes, or to create picture-in-picture effects.

MPEG. Acronym for Motion Pictures Experts Group. A specification and algorithm used for compressing moving images

MUG. The MediaStudio Pro Users Group. Look for more information at http://www.mugcentral.org

Glossary

NLE. Abbreviation for "non-linear editing."

Noise. Any undesired component of a signal not related to the original signal. Common video noise includes snow, static, drop-outs, ghosting, and so on.

Non-Destructive. A method of editing video that does not harm the original footage in any way.

Non-linear. This refers to computer-based, or hard-disk-based editing. Information is stored in a random access fashion across the disk. Since the data is in no particular order (i.e., it doesn't follow a straight line) this is known as non-linear.

Normalize. A method of boosting the volume of a clip to its maximum levels without clipping or distortion. It works best on waveforms without spikes but can also raise the noise level.

NTSC. National Television System Committee. A United States Federal Committee formed to standardize television. Also the name given to a method of encoding analog television signals used primarily in North America and Japan. NTSC can also stand for Never Twice the Same Color! Compare PAL.

Onion Skin. A method of displaying several frames simultaneously, allowing you to track motion in a single viewing. Each subsequent frame is displayed lighter, as if viewing through onion skin paper. Necessary for rotoscoping tasks.

Overlay. Combining different parts of two video sources into the same frame. This may be as simple as a "picture in picture" or as complex as masking off a certain color range of one image to display the corresponding parts of another image. (This is keying, just one type of overlay function.)

PAL. Phase Alternate Line. A method of encoding analog television signals used primarily in Europe, Australia and parts of Asia. Compare NTSC.

Pan[1]. In camera work panning is the rotation of the camera about its vertical axis.

Pan[1]. In audio editing panning is the act of moving the spatial position of a track from one channel to another. MediaStudio Pro has functions called "panning" however they are actually balance functions.

PCM. Pulse Code Modulation. A method of digitizing audio.

Pitch. In Audio Editor, the Pitch function allows you to raise or lower (that is) the audio without changing the duration. Theoretically, you could take a song in the key of C and raise it to D. In reality, you'll just make it sound weird.

Playhead. The blue arrow found on the Timeline or Effects Manager rulers, representing the current playback position.

Post-Production. All work done on a project after all footage has been gathered. This is the editing and assembly phase of a project—the part we editors are most concerned with.

Pre-Production. All work that goes into a project before any footage is shot. This can be anything from finalizing scripts to scouting locations to hiring talent to buying beer.

Preview Window. A window displaying a full preview of a clip or a project.

Production. The phase of a project where footage is gathered.

Production Library. A thumbnail-based media center for quick access to media files and program objects. See also *Gallery*.

Project. A collection of clips and their interrelationships. A project is stored on disk with a dvp file extension.

Project Template. A collection of project settings (which does not contain clips) that can be recalled and used when creating a new project.

Project Tray. A set of hierarchical folders within Video Editor used to store and organize links to various external media files. It can also used for creating a storyboard. It is similar to the Production Library, except that thumbnails are stored on a per-project basis.

QuickTime. Video compression scheme developed by Apple. QuickTime movies have a .mov file extension.

Relink. Your project files store "links" to files (video, audio, or image), and not the files themselves. In addition to the links, they also store a date/time stamp of the file. If you change a file outside of Video Editor, then return to Video Editor, it detects this change and asks if you want to relink the file, thus updating the information it stores with the clip.

Rendering. To put it simply, rendering is the process of taking one thing and creating something else from it. Architects can render a full drawing from a floor plan. You can render a word or phrase from one language into another. You can render lard from pork fat. In the video editing world, this is the process of taking your project and all the clips and attributes therein, and creating a single, final video.

Reverb. An audio effect used to simulate the echo effect of rooms.

RGB. Red, Green, Blue. The three primary colors on your monitor (an additive color process, not to be confused with Cyan, Magenta, and Yellow, the three primary colors in printing, a subtractive color process). RGB is also used as a function to describe the three relative levels of each color, as in RGB(0,0,0) meaning: no red, blue, or green (i.e., black).

Ripple Edit. A method of editing where changes to a clip in a track effect all subsequent clips on that track. For example, if you shorten a clip, the gap left behind is closed, and this change ripples down the timeline, moving all later clips over just enough to close the gap. It only works on one track at a time, however.

Rotoscoping. There are many definitions with subtle variations for this term. In its most basic sense, it's the frame-by-frame manipulation of a video sequence. Two examples: 1) the direct manipulation of a video, or 2) creation of a mask/matte. Rotoscoping is very powerful, yet very tedious.

Ruler. The timecode markings running along the top of the timeline.

Scissors. The tool used to cut one clip into two.

Scrubbing. A method of quickly previewing audio and/or video, typically by running a pointer across a timeline.

SECAM. Séquentiel Couleur à Mémoire. An alternate video signal encoding scheme, used primarily in France. Compare with NTSC and PAL.

SEG. Special Effects Generator. A hardware or software device for creating special effects.

Silence Clip. A special audio clip containing no audio data. Can be used as a placeholder or filler within an audio track.

SmartRender. A process where Video Editor renders only the portions of the project it needs to. If a section of the project is already compliant with the output settings (for whatever reason) it is not re-rendered.

SMTPE. Society of Motion Picture and Television Engineers. Commonly pronounced "simptee." This also refers to the timecode used to get frame-accurate editing in an analog environment. SMTPE timecode comes in two flavors: LTC and VITC.

Source Window. A control window allowing you to view, cue, or trim clips on the timeline. You can load clips from the timeline, Production Library, or from the file system directly into the Source Window.

Storyboarding. A method of production planning which uses an ordered set of rough sketches or drawings to visualize the final product.

S-video. See *Component*.

TBC. Time Base Corrector. A device used to "clean up" a video signal and correct time-based errors. After a signal has been recorded to video tape, slight variations in the encoding, due to various mechanical reasons, can introduce "time based" errors in the video. These will visually manifest themselves as waviness or sometimes noise. A TBC works by scanning the incoming signal, then outputting it at fixed, corrected intervals.

Thumbnail. A very small version of a large image used for quick visual reference and system efficiency. Typically used in groups.

Time code. Any numbering method used to uniquely address individual frames of a video.

Time Selection. A tool that allows you to select a range of time within Video Editor.

Timeline. The method of video editing whereby clips are sized proportional to their duration and placed chronologically with respect to each other. This is compared to a storyboard, where the clips do not indicate their durations.

Timescale. See *Ruler*.

Title-Safe. The area of a frame deemed "safe" for display on a wide range of televisions. Since televisions overscan much of the image is never seen, since it is outside of the display area. A title that runs from

Glossary

one side of the frame to the other, may not be completely visible if it ignores the title-safe area.

Titler. Any device used for creating overlaid text on video.

Titling. The act of creating and including text in a production.

Trimming. The method or action of discarding the unwanted beginning and/or ending of a clip.

True Color. 24-bit color, capable of representing more than 16.7 million colors, more than most human eyes can distinguish.

UCG. The file extension for a CG Infinity document.

UIS. Ulead Image Sequence. Also the file extension used for this file type. It's a short header file pointing to a sequence of image files. Can be treated as a single video clip within MediaStudio Pro applications.

Ulead. The Taiwan-based company specializing in graphics and imaging. The name is not meant to imply "you lead" as I've heard told many times before. The name Ulead is an anglicized rendering of the Chinese words yu and li (友 and 立), meaning "friend" and "build-up/establish" respectively. You can see the two words in their logo.

Uncompressed. Video, image, or other data in its purest (and hence, largest) form.

UVP. The file extension for a Video Paint document. Video Paint is part of the separate Video Graphics Lab program.

VC. Abbreviation for MediaStudio Pro's Video Capture program.

VCD. Abbreviation for Video CD, a specially-formatted compact disc containing video data in a specific MPEG1 format. Like DVD, supports menus (although not as versatile as DVD). SVCD is a higher quality version of VCD.

VE. Abbreviation for MediaStudio Pro's Video Editor program.

VHS. Video Home System. Still the most common consumer video format...but for how long?

VO. Abbreviation for "voice over."

Vectorscope. A specialized oscilloscope used to display the color information in a video signal and used to help calibrate equipment to correctly interpret color information.

Vertical Interval Time Code. A method of writing timecode on a video tape. It uses the space between frames (the vertical interrupt interval) to store frame address information. It must be recorded simultaneously with the video signal, and cannot be changed without destroying the video signal itself. Compare Longitudinal Time Code.

VITC. Pronounced "vit-see". See *Vertical Interval Time Code.*

WAV. The file extension for a Microsoft Wave File.

WYSIWYG. What You See Is What You Get. This term is used to describe the condition where the content during editing looks like the content's final form.

Y/C. Common abbreviations for Luminance/Chrominance, and used together like this.

YMMV. Your Mileage May Vary. Used when a specific example is given that may yield different results for you or apply differently to your exact situation.

Zoom Tool. A tool used to zoom in and out of the timeline by changing the timescale, or ruler unit.

Index

A

A/B
   field order 22
   roll editing 321
action space 396
additional timelines 142
aliasing 354, 447
alignment 124
alpha channels 187, 189, 205, 229
analog
   audio 278
   capturing 71
   output 301
   previewing 141
   sources 16
animatic 96, 310, 339
animation 54, 216
anti-aliasing 448
aperture 390, 399
arc 407
archiving 99
artifacts 77, 150, 415, 438
ascender 409
aspect ratio 267, 269, 276, 448
atmosphere 416
audience .... iv, 416
audio
   clips 20, 49, 276, 442
   editing functions 82
   effects 82
   format settings 80
   recording 23, 441
   troubleshooting 441
Audio Editor 80, 278

audio mixing 62, 154
authoring 304
auto music 279
auto save 104, 105, 360
auto write mode 63
auto-exposure 390
avenue 416

B

background color 161, 207
backups 99, 104
balance 82
baseline 409
batch capture 68, 73
bit rate 23
blue screening 187, 193, 247
bookmarks .... see cues
buttons
   clip selection 37
   scissors tool 37
   time selection 37
   time stretch 38
   track selection 38, 43
   zoom tool 37

C

calculating clip duration 272
calibrating video 68
camcorder
   connections 305
   control 73
   movement 406
   previewing 141

461

Sharp ViewCam 401
camera movement
    arc 407
    dolly 407
    pan 407
    pedestal 407
    tilt 407
    truck 407
camera position 401
capturing
    defined 20
    how to 71
    multi-camera 323
    seamless 322
CCD 390
chapters
    DVD 364, 442
chapters, DVD 363
character 409
chroma-key 187
clay analogy 286, 421
clip selection tool 37
clips 449
    definition of 49
    replacing 98, 313
    slicing 37, 122
    speed changes 147
codec 25
color
    boundaries 414
    calibration 68
    correction 235
    depth 22, 25
    limitations 414
    picker 161
    use of v
color bars 70
commands v
complexity bar 41
composition 393
compression 25, 75, 439, 450
Creative Cow 31
creativity 336
cropping 181, 298, 439
crossfade
    audio 37, 135
    video 46, 117

cue bars 42
cues 321
    audio 82, 316
    chapter points 43
    deleting 43
    management 43
    saving 80
cut 117

D

DAT 100
data rate 23, 443
deep thoughts 319
definitions
    audio clip 20
    capturing 20
    character 409
    color depth 22
    data rate 23
    digital 23
    DV 26
    fields 21
    frame rate 22
    frame size 22
    frames 21
    glossary 447
    overlaying 20
    project 20
    titling 20
    video clip 20
    virtual clip 20
depth of field 399
descender 409
digitizing 23, 24, 262
disc authoring 84, 304, 442
display modes
    video 47
    waveform 47
DivX 26
DMN Forums 31
dolly 407
dpi 263
drop-frame 443
dropping photos 270, 274

Index

DV
- capture 71
- compression 26
- defined 26
- exporting 304
- size 76
- timecode 398

DVD
- as backup media 100
- authoring 84, 304, 361
- compatability 443
- creating chapters 363, 364
- DVD Demystified 443
- DVD DiskRecorder 86
- DVD MovieFactory 84, 361

E

- editing modes 38
- effects
  - audio 82
  - freeze frame 150, 167
  - lens flare 240
  - mirror image 181
  - slow motion 147
  - split screen 180
  - transitions 116
  - video filters 169
- Effects Manager ...35, 54, 65, 171, 440
- elements of design 415
- even field 22
- exercises, overview .... v, 113
- export still image 51
- export to DV 304
- exposure 390
- external monitors 406

F

- fades 160, 162, 163
- fast motion 147
- field order 22
- fields 21, 452
- file formats 300

files
- locations 101
- management 98
- size comparisons 76
- size limitations 322
- trimming 129
- filter regions 185
- filters 169
- FireWire 71, 140, 306
- flip 181
- folder locations 101, 103
- fonts
  - bad example 417
  - definition of 409
  - rules of 417
- frame
  - composition 394
  - definition of 21, 452
  - dropping 443
  - freezing 150
  - rate 22, 299
  - size 22, 263
- f-stop 390

G

- gain 390
- gamma 201, 348
- garbage in, garbage out 408
- general timeline 39
- getting started 113
- glyph 409, 413
- gray-key 187
- green bar 42

H

- hard disks
  - as backup solution 100
  - separate for video 101, 102
  - sizes 322
  - types 100
- HDV 27, 76, 302
- headroom 394
- hide tracks 43

history of video editing 18
huge files 439

I

image sequences 253, 347
importing 53, 158, 273
Indeo 26, 76
installation 112
instant play 41, 51
intended audience iv

J

j-cut 156

K

kerning 410
keyboard shortcuts .. 36, 65, 431, 432
    audio editor zooming 83
    quote characters 413
    record audio 80
    select all clips 434
    slicing 122
    windows 65
keyframe controller 54
keying 187, 453

L

layouts, saving 35
l-cut 156
leading 410
lighting
    importance of 388
    not enough 388
lower field 22
luma-key 187
Lynne, Bjorn 371

M

magic fairy dust 393
management
    preview files 438
    projects 103
margin icons v
matchmoving 182, 204, 349
MediaStudio Pro
    capabilities 16
    limitations 18
menu commands v
microphones 441
mirror image 181
monitors
    external 406
    larger the better 398
    LCD 402
monopods 405
monospaced 410
montages
    photo 261
    video 278
montages defined 261
Moonlight Sonata 308
MPEG 76, 78, 113, 302
MUG 30
multi-camera editing 321
multiple timelines 142
multi-select 37
multi-trimming 125
music video 335
mute tracks 43

N

narration 313, 441
nested timelines 142
non-destructive editing 19
non-drop frame 443
non-linear editing 21, 455
non-square pixels 269
Nothing Without 335

Index 465

O

odd field 22
old film effect 240
online resources 30, 268
orange bar 42
overlaying
    defined 20
    keying 187
    text 419
overscan 215, 265, 438

P

Paint Shop Pro 191, 268
pan and zoom 264, 274
panning
    audio 82, 156
    camera movement 407
    images 264
pedestal 407
photo montage 261
PhotoImpact 268
picture in picture 177, 180
planning 87, 89, 321
playback options 141, 372, 435
playhead 38, 50
point 410
post-production 93
pre-production 89, 321
preview
    in real time 41
preview bar 42
preview files 438
preview files manager 103
preview range 42
Preview Window 50, 65
production 91, 321
Production Library 58, 65
project
    defined 20
    file 28, 103
    templates 97
Project Tray 34, 60, 113
proportional 411
proxy mode 17, 40

publisher's quotes 412
push away insert 138

Q

quick command panel 64
QuickTracks 279
quote characters 413
quotes
    common sense 393
    editing 387
    good plans 89
    intended destination 96

R

real time 29, 41
regions 185
relink 431, 446
relinking 113
rendering 29, 298, 438, 457
replace clips 98, 313
retouching 266
reusability 97, 252
reverse video 149
ripping 278, 430
ripple editing 38, 135
rule of thirds 393
ruler 41

S

sampling 23
sans serif 411
scan safe area 264
scanning 262
scissors tool 37, 122, 432
scroll lock 45
scrubbing 42, 457
seamless capture 322
selecting multiple clips 433
serif 411
shoe, tripod 405
shooting better footage 387
shortcuts 65, 431

shutter speed 390, 400
sidebars
    5MB disks 19
    file size limits 322
    principal photography 91
    SCSI disks 25
    transitions 120
slow motion 147
Smart Compositor 98, 209, 252
Smart Package 99, 104
SmartRender 42, 103, 298, 438, 458
SmartSound 279
SMTPE 444, 458
snapping 124
soft edge 201
soft edges 208
solo tracks 43
Source Window 52, 65
split by scene 128
split screen 180, 208
stabilization
    camera 404
    image 405
Star Wars text 431
status bar 45
storyboard 61, 96, 308, 310
straight quotes 412
summary timeline 39
Surround Sound 155
synchronized
    audio 443
    cues 61
    scrolling 224
    video 321, 341

T

templates 97, 158, 367
terms 20, 409, 447
three A's, the 416
thumbnail 47, 74, 85, 365
tilt 407
time selection tool 37
time stretch tool 38
timecode 41
timeline 36, 65

timeline display 47
timeline views
    general 39
    summary 39
timescale 41
tips
    editing 427, 429
    exporting to VHS 306
    lighting 388
    navigation 431
    photo montage 265
    scanning 263
    selection 433
    titling basics 411
    typographical 411
title safe 215, 265, 458
titling 20, 215
tools
    clip selection 37
    scissors 37, 122
    time selection 37
    time stretch 38
    track selection 38
    zoom 37
track selection tool 38
tracks
    about 43
    adding/deleting 40, 179
    Effects Manager 56
    missing 378
    precedence 46
    ripping audio 80
transitions 31, 116
trim window 64
trimming 121
    multi-trim 125
    options 131
tripods 405
troubleshooting 437
truck 407
trueSpace 339
Tschichold, Jan 411
tweening 55
typeface 411
typewriter effect 233
typewriter rules 413
typography 409

Index

U

UIS files 253, 347, 446
Ulead 459
Ulead color picker 161
uncompressed 76, 415, 459
UPD files 364
upper field 22
USB 72
usenet newsgroups 31
user groups 30

V

VCD 113
VCR 305
VHS 17, 71, 94, 305, 306
video attributes 21
video capture 67
video clip, defined 20
video filters 169
video montage 278
viewfinders 402
virtual clips 20, 142, 210

volume 62, 133

W

white balance 321, 389
wysinawyg 418
wysiwyg 140, 153, 406

X

x-height 411

Y

Yahoo! Groups 31
yellow dot 63

Z

zoom motion 231
zoom slider 45
zoom tool 37